BEYOND
LACAN

SUNY series in Psychoanalysis and Culture
Henry Sussman, *editor*

BEYOND LACAN

JAMES M. MELLARD

State University of New York Press

Published by
State University of New York Press, Albany

For information, address State University of New York Press,
194 Washington Avenue, Suite 305, Albany, NY 12210-2384

Production by Judith Block
Marketing by Michael Campochiaro

Library of Congress Cataloging-in-Publication Data

Mellard, James M.
    Beyond Lacan / James M. Mellard.
        p. cm. — (SUNY series in psychoanalysis and culture)
    Includes bibliographical references and index.
    ISBN-10: 0-7914-6903-4 (hardcover : alk. paper)
    ISBN-13: 978-0-7914-6903-3 (hardcover : alk. paper)
    ISBN-13: 978-0-7914-6904-0 (pbk : alk. paper)

    1. Psychology and literature. 2. Lacan, Jacques, 1901–
I. Title. II. Series.

PC56.P93M45 2006
801'.92—dc22
                                                                2005036229

10 9 8 7 6 5 4 3 2 1

In memory of
Connie Marshall Mellard Sr.
Alice J. Gilbert
James W. Gilbert
and
Charles McGraw

Contents

Illustrations

Acknowledgments

I want to express my gratitude for permission to reprint revised versions of previously published essays. Chapter 4, on Flannery O'Connor, appeared in *Prospects* 24 (1999): 625–43 and is reprinted with permission of Cambridge University Press. Chapter 5, on Susan Glaspell's "Jury of Her Peers," appeared in *Journal for the Psychoanalysis of Culture and Society* 3 (Fall 1998): 145–60 and is reprinted with permission of Ohio State University Press. Chapter 6, on F. Scott Fitzgerald's "Winter Dreams," appeared in *Arizona Quarterly* 58.4 (2002): 51–79 and is reprinted with permission. Chapter 7, on Josephine Hart's *Damage*, appeared in *PMLA* 113 (May 1998): 395–407 and is reprinted with permission of the Modern Language Association.

Introduction

In *Beyond Lacan*, I have several purposes. First, I want to show that Lacanian principles concerning subjectivity are readily—perhaps inevitably—manifested in fictional texts. In readings of several significant such texts, I want, second, not only to make those principles more accessible to readers but, third, also to demonstrate the validity—and power—of Lacanian theory to explain subjects and structures in them. Since readings of fictional texts illustrate Anglo-American assimilation of Lacanian theory, it is necessary, fourth, to explain how it emerged from Lacan's critique of Freud, how from Freud Lacan assimilated an understanding that the unconscious is textual—is indeed a textual unconscious—and how in reception of Lacanian theory critics frequently have defined an "early" and a "late" theory. At the same time, I want to show that in critical practice Lacanians have in effect constructed a "middle" Lacan conflating early and late. Finally, I want to show that although Lacanian theory remains important to psychoanalytic interpretation of literature and culture, a "beyond" of Lacan—Lacanian but also something else—seems now to be emerging in the massive elucidations of Lacan by Slavoj Žižek.

In part 1, "Toward Lacan," there are two chapters. In the first, "From Freud to Jacques Lacan and the Textual Unconscious," I show that there is an unfamiliar history in the emergence of Lacanian theory as it develops in relation to Freudian theory. Lacanian theory, as we all know, emerged from Freudian by way of Lacan's giving a particular twist to Freud's emphases. Whereas Freud understood from the beginning that language, in "the talking cure," was important to his enterprise, when he sought metaphorical *models* for his work, as is widely documented, he himself typically thought of it as "archeological." Lacan's innovation, in the 1950s, especially, was to foreground

1

language and give it pride of place through another metaphor, that of linguistics as metaphor, not linguistics as such. While Lacan supposed that he was merely returning to Freud by highlighting elements already visible in Freud's writings, his rereading nonetheless eventually generated a new theoretical edifice we came to call "Lacanian." But, *mutatis mutandis*, in a twist to Freudian theory that I believe is well founded, if, indeed, not in fact mandated, Lacanian theory, powerfully stressing language—Lacan's mantra is "The unconscious is structured like a language"—builds on an unacknowledged theoretical foundation in *textuality*. Albeit unacknowledged, it is visible not only in Freud but also in Jung's notion of a collective unconscious, as well as in other, recent and discursively powerful notions such as the political unconscious (of Fredric Jameson) and the optical unconscious (of Walter Benjamin and Rosalind Krauss). As for Lacanian textuality itself, I also show here that Lacan developed idea after idea through recourse to textualizing figures such as Schema L, Schema R, and Borromean knots, graphs of desire, an algorithm of signification, and formulas for sexuation, for metaphor and metonymy, for the four discourses, and more. In short, I suggest, no textuality, no Lacan. On a foundation in textuality, many have built a theory of interpretation, largely semiotic but not limited to semiotics per se, called "intertextuality." Intertextuality labels what any active interpreter knows, that when we *interpret*, we move, in a reciprocal way, back and forth, between codes—whether Freudian or Lacanian, Marxist or deconstructionist, feminist or multiculturalist, or whatever—and texts or interpretive objects (though any of these may be spoken, as in the therapeutic clinic, even these are necessarily rendered into texts if they are *interpreted*). Because it is in intertextuality, however, that we find our means for interpreting both literature and the unconscious, the concept of a 'textual unconscious' may eventually vanish, in a phenomenon that Jameson has called a "vanishing mediator."

In the second chapter, "Which Lacan?" I address debates about periods or phases of Lacanian theory. Though my approach may sometimes seem whimsical, the topic is quite serious, for one may not always understand, literally, which Lacan is the theorist invoked by a given critical interpreter. The dominant theory (one Žižek typically, disparagingly, calls the "current" or "standard" understanding) remains essentially an early theory, stressing, it is argued by some, the registers of Imaginary and Symbolic and essentially ignoring the Real. Until the 1950s, Lacan paid little mind to what he called only "the field of the real," not stressing it until he commenced the twenty-seven-year *séminaire* for which he is most famous—and controversial. More and more, in Lacanian discourse, there has come into play "a late Lacan," one that elevates the Real over the other registers. Nonetheless, *when* this Lacan begins is a much-debated question. The answer is, well, it depends. Some say 1953, the year the *séminaire* began, others say in 1959–1960 with Seminar 7's *Ethics of Psychoanalysis*, yet others say in 1964 with Seminar 11's *Four Fundamental Concepts of Psycho-analysis*. Then there are those who say in 1972–1973 with 20's *Encore*, or 1974–1975 with 22's *R.S.I.*, or even 1975–1976 with 23 on *Le sinthome*. You get the picture. Which Lacan and when emer-gent, let us say, are concepts essentially—and widely—contested. Regardless of one's answer to questions of which or when (and there are also Lacanians who postulate a series of three or more phases), the dominant view—which, not surprisingly, is that of Žižek and his cohorts—tends to be binary: whenever and on whatever grounds demarcations are located, there is most basically at least an early and a late Lacan. Occam's solution. Simplicity is better. But be forewarned, as I illustrate in a reading of one of Lacan's case studies toward the end of chapter 2, Lacan himself seems not even to know or, perhaps more to the point, at all to care whether one invokes early or late. So for Lacan is there just one?

Taking Lacan at his word, a word in fact never spoken, I take the view that while there is a late Lacan following an early, it is the early who, passé now, dominated Lacanian interpretation into the 1990s. But we must acknowledge also a paradoxical middle Lacan. There is a certain irony in how a middle Lacan emerged retroactively, after late Lacan. It emerged this way because it is a Lacan formed of our recep-tion—and conflation—of early theory and late. For historical reasons, largely based on availability of Lacan's texts, uses of Lacan into the early '90s belonged to early Lacan, where early stressed interactions between Imaginary and Symbolic in Oedipal constitutions of subjects vis à vis desire. Since then, critical uses have tended to employ either a de facto middle one of conflation or, increasingly nowadays, a late theory. This late one, stressing the Real, at the same time stresses threats of drive and *jouissance* to a stable subjectivity. Late Lacan is one, in its specific contours and emphases, propounded most success-fully by Žižek.

Since there is not much point, these days, in exhibiting early Lacanian readings (which, I might add, feature in my 1991 *Using Lacan, Reading Fiction*), in the five chapters of part 2, "Lacanian Exemplifications," I illustrate (in normal order) middle readings and late ones in analyses of several works of fiction. The two readings illus-trating a middle Lacan focus on Ralph Ellison's *Invisible Man* and Flannery O'Connor's *Wise Blood*. Both published in 1952, these two

novels were written at that historical moment when a notion of the
textual unconscious was finally being articulated within psychoanalytic, as in Lacan, and literary theory, as in New Criticism focusing on
the autonomous text. Ellison embraced it in his technique, but
O'Connor consciously feared psychoanalysis and yet unwittingly
expressed it. As I show in chapter 3, the very structure of Ellison's
novel illustrates a textual unconscious functioning in the novel to
access a subjectivity in its narrator. My analysis shows how an early
Lacanian theory of subjectification, operating through interactions of
Imaginary and Symbolic, may be augmented by a late notion of a Real
whose elements Ellison's narrator encounters not only in a maternal
presence expressing race but also in a place outside history where he
locates himself to write his book. Widely regarded as a story of initiation or coming of age, the novel is much taken up in the narrator's
constitution of an adult subjectivity. In its Lacanian contours, it necessarily devotes much of that constitution to Imaginary relations. In one
of these, the character Tod Clifton serves doubly in his relation to the
narrator. Clifton begins as a figure of Imaginary identification as ideal
ego, a relation characterized in mirror-stage terms marked by imita-
tion and aggression. But after Tod is murdered, the relation between
narrator and dead youth changes. Mourning transforms Tod into a
figure in the Symbolic, into a figure of authority, really a substitute for
the dead father of Symbolic Law. As that figure holding together the
narrator's subjectivity, he leaves the narrator bereft for a time after his
death. But through a process of mourning, a process Lacan discusses
in "Desire and the Interpretation of Desire in *Hamlet*," the narrator
regains his orientation within the Symbolic order and moves on to
take up his "father's" work, discovering for "his" people a proper
"brotherhood"—one apart from *The* Brotherhood. Since historical
reality does not yet provide a place from which to launch an appropriate revolution (one distinct from that projected by Ras the Destroyer),
the narrator goes underground, there to confront the two fathers concealed in the Law, the primordial (original) father of the Real, the one
of "the drip-drop" of bloody violence, and the oedipal father, the
Name-of-the-Father of Symbolic subject constitution. He has encountered forms of these earlier, on the one hand, in the legend of the
Founder (really an Imaginary Symbolic) and, on the other, in angry,
socioeconomically oppressed blacks whose existence as a sort of living
dead is symbolized by the "blood-froth sparkling their chins" and who
represent a Real from which may emanate a primordial father such as
Ras. Deciding that violence, the violent act, is not a proper answer for
himself or his race, he performs *his* act, the writing of his book, that

gives the best answer available to him in an America of the 1930s, 1940s, or 1950s.

In chapter 4, my interest lies as much in Flannery O'Connor's ambivalence toward the culture of psychoanalysis as in *Wise Blood*. In another reading in middle Lacan, I use fewer notions from the early theory, such as creation of subjectivity in interchanges between Imaginary and Symbolic, and more from late notions of drive, the Real, and *jouissance*. Drawing on details from the novel as well as from O'Connor's letters in *The Habit of Being*, especially those to "A" (now identified as Betty Hester), I discuss the complex relationship between her culture and her faith, between her attitude toward psychoanalysis— with its pronouncements on the dominance of sex and sexuality coming to her from a modernist *culture* of psychoanalysis—and her intense feelings about the place of her Christian faith in her life and art. While she vehemently rejects psychoanalytic interpretations of her texts, it is quite clear that as a modernist author she understood that her stature greatly benefitted from such readings of them. She vociferously rejected Freudian understandings of sex and sexuality, but, in ways that cry out for psychoanalytic interpretation, her fiction frequently exhibits these, not only in *Wise Blood* but also in such stories as "A Temple of the Holy Ghost" and "A Circle in the Fire." Many of these contradictions, within O'Connor as well as in her fiction, are expressed in what Lacan calls "*méconnaissance.*" It is a misrecognition of truths of the subject that *becomes* the subject's truth. It may involve any register— Imaginary, Symbolic, or Real—but especially features misrecognition of elements dangerous to subjectivity such as sexual *jouissance* and drive, the death drive, each associated with the Real. In O'Connor, powerful are the conflicts or contradictions regarding gender and sexuality, for they are expressed in interactions involving her own physical health (she suffered excruciatingly from and died of complications of lupus), her Christian faith, and her need to adhere to her modernist aesthetic in creating her fictions. Many such issues emerge from her intense, in part misrecognized, connection to her character, the *man* Hazel (Haze) Motes, for there we see how her sense of Christ's abandonment on the cross, her own physical trials from her disease, and her construction of a sainthood for Motes are all intricately intermingled, to say nothing of how complexly each of these plays into construction of O'Connor herself as "saint" by her devoted readers.

My three readings in late Lacan address Susan Glaspell's "Jury of Her Peers," F. Scott Fitzgerald's "Winter Dreams," and Josephine Hart's *Damage*. These readings move entirely into the realm of a late Lacanian paradigm. While I do not believe that a late theory produces better interpretations of texts than an early one produces, it is clear that, typically—with the caveat that one may always read against the grain—early and late produce ones fitting different genre expectations. Constructions of stories within an early, oedipal, framework are likely to produce comic stories, ones in which protagonists succeed in the business of becoming functional subjects. Such readings typically fit initiation stories, such as *Invisible Man*, stories of growing up, becoming a man, or—more and more in our time—becoming a woman. Constructions within a late paradigm typically give us readings that fall on the generic sides of the ironic and the tragic. By uncovering how drive, *jouissance*, a primordial father, or a maternal Thing all threaten to undermine subjects in their self-knowledge or entirely to engulf them, a reading for the Real may undercut any emplotment. Moreover, it seems the case that reading a typical oedipal story from the side of the Real inevitably becomes a reading against the grain, against ordinary fits between plot and paradigm. We may, in other words, use a late paradigm to identify ironic or tragic elements concealed beneath Imaginary or Symbolic resolutions or within any conventional oedipal subjectification.

In chapter 5, reading Glaspell's "Jury of Her Peers," I uncover the Real contradictions of Imaginary and Symbolic resolutions. Crossing Lacan's triad of registers, Imaginary, Symbolic, and Real, a late Lacanian reading examines Imaginary identifications, Symbolic inscriptions of law and subjects' relations to the Father, and then irruptions of the Real, in paradoxical coincidences of opposites and in appearances of the maternal Thing, das Ding. Glaspell's story, from the 1920s and based on a celebrated Iowa murder case at the turn of the century (which Glaspell covered as a reporter), was given a postfeminist resurrection in the 1980s. It was brought into the canon in part because it seems to offer a victory of female rebellion. It has been taken as a story of two women under—or "married to"—patriarchal law who rebel successfully against it. Ostensibly, they win out over obtuse patriarchal authority by concealing what, by detective work relying on women's "trifles," they understand as a wife's justifiable murder of an abusive husband. But a late Lacanian reading of the story suggests that, ultimately, their victory is only Pyrrhic. When the women decide to conceal from the law what they discover, they end up, paradoxically, supporting the very social and psychoanalytic structures that stabilize patriarchy itself. But what are women to do? Within traditional patriarchy, they—like the narrator in *Invisible Man*—are given only a forced choice: they may choose Lacan's *le père...ou pire*, the father...or worse, either the oedipal father (and comply with the Symbolic Law) or the primordial father of bloody violence, that is, the murdered husband as the Father himself, hidden *behind* the Law and supporting it. It is not much of a choice. If nothing else, the story—and a late Lacanian reading of it—suggests just how difficult it is for women to find any liberating choices at all.

In chapter 6, from within that late paradigm, I read against the grain of the standard oedipal story as it is represented in Fitzgerald's "Winter Dreams." A reading within that paradigm, like the analysis of "A Jury of Her Peers," uncovers an unexpected aspect of Fitzgerald's story. Widely anthologized and admired, the story is sometimes considered important largely for its anticipation of themes found in *The Great Gatsby*, arguably one of the greatest of American novels. But read from a late Lacanian perspective, the story turns out to be much more than a mere appendage to *Gatsby*. In its evocative language and psychoanalytic economy of characters (fathers, mothers, children), it not only reveals how the standard oedipal plot should go, but it also reveals the hidden underside of that plot, its relations to roles of the other, of women in their guises of lover and mother. Yes, the story reveals how a boy encounters his ego-ideal in a figure of the oedipal father, and, yes, the story reveals how the standard plot of boy-meets-girl displays desire's function in the role of the (beautiful) woman as the Symbolic Phallus, but, no, the story does not simply culminate in a comic ending in which boy-gets-girl and lives happily ever after. Why not? A late Lacanian reading shows that two fathers may be embodied in one person and thereby represent not only the oedipal father of the ego-ideal but also the father as punitive superego as well. The latter trumps the former and leaves boy-without-girl—at least that one girl too closely tied to narcissistic fantasy. Such a reading, asking us also to uncover the women's stories in "Winter Dreams," adds to Dexter Green's oedipal story that of Judy Jones as well and adds to the story of the two fathers, both embodied in Mr. Mortimer Jones, the story, however truncated, of Dexter's mother, a mother both Symbolic (in her support of his oedipal structuration) and Real (as an image of the maternal Thing's incestuous allure standing behind drive, *jouissance, objet a,* and narcissistic regression). Finally, such a reading of Fitzgerald's story suggests the complexity of the subject's story at all its levels, across each of the registers, Imaginary, Symbolic, and Real.

In chapter 7, I again interpret from within a late Lacanian paradigm, but here I do so by adding a current understanding that our postmodern age has brought us into a new epoch, one no longer dominated by an oedipal father within patriarchy so much as, in terms of Jacques-Alain Miller, *semblants* of the father, found almost anywhere, including, in terms of Juliet MacCannell, "the regime of the brother," where Imaginary brother-brother dyads displace the authority of the father. Whatever the terms, many now assume that, culturally, we are beyond—or outside—Oedipus. Symbolic authority, once placed in the father, seems now placed elsewhere, in *semblants* or Imaginary substitutes, and "father" necessarily becomes something else. In an analysis of Josephine Hart's *Damage*, a novel also adapted as a film of the same name featuring Jeremy Irons and Juliet Binoche, I again traverse the late Lacanian terrain not only of guises of the mother and the two fathers, but also of what Lacan calls "the two deaths," all to suggest that this novel constructs a new form of literary tragedy—one we may call "Lacanian"—that is constituted within an ethics, yes, but an ethics emanating from drive, on the side of narcissism, an ethics, that is, of *jouissance*. In *Damage*, there is a father who, as Žižek suggests of the bourgeois family nowadays, embodies both a father of ego-ideal—the Symbolic "dead" Father—and one representing the cruel superego—the primordial father of Freud's band of brothers, the father killed because he arrogates enjoyment, *jouissance*, to himself. A respected official high in British government, loved by family and friends, this double father, as ego-ideal, model of the Symbolic Father, falls in love with his son's fiancée and immediately uncovers in himself that other, primordial, father, a father from the Real whose unconscionable sexual predation causes the son's death. It is not the Freudian son killing the father, but the Real father, as it were, "killing" the son. For her part, the son's fiancée herself plays dual roles both as desire's traditional love object, one substituted for the subject's original object (the mother), and as femme fatale, at once a symptom of the man and that which, as paradoxical substitute for the father, gives him his consistency as a subject. In the interaction of the two illicit lovers, we uncover the power of drive—sexual drive-cum-death drive—and an ethics that motivates the novel's tragic denouement, one in which the father lives on, discredited, by choice socially isolated, and content to finish his life as one of the living dead, all in the service of his narcissistic enjoyment. It is not pretty. It is not *Oedipus* or *Hamlet*. But it is tragedy of a late Lacanian sort we may expect to find more frequently now that we have entered a new postoedipal universe.

In Beyond Lacan, there is only chapter 8, "Beyond Lacan: Slavoj Žižek, Things to Die for, and a Philosophy of Paradox." Coming to this chapter, readers will perhaps have noted that as I proceed from reading to reading—using, at the start, a middle theory of a conflation of early and late Lacan and, then, a more distinctly late Lacanian theory—it is plain that Žižek increasingly becomes a presence determining argument and vocabulary. By the time of my reading of Hart's *Damage*, "Lacan," early or middle or late, has virtually dropped out and in its place stands either Žižek's Lacan, or, more radically, simply Žižek. In my text, this displacement of Lacan by Žižek is symptomatic of what I take to be a significant paradigm shift: as Freud was displaced by Lacan, so now it appears that Lacan is being displaced by Žižek. Lacan was the beyond of Freud. Žižek may be the beyond of Lacan. This does not mean, however, that Lacanian theory disappears, any more than it meant that Freudian theory disappeared with the ascendency of Lacan. It is simply that Lacan gave us a different Freudian theory, and, now, Žižek appears to be giving us a different Freudo-Lacanian one. In Žižek, who has published more than twenty books in the last sixteen or so years, what seems a minor trait in Lacan—the use of mantric but ambiguous or paradoxical sayings—is in Žižek elevated (*sublated* might be Žižek's word) to a philosophy, a philosophy of paradox. As much as in Lacan, this philosophy is rooted in Hegel, the Hegelian dialectical procedure of analysis-cum-discourse, and perhaps the oddest thing apparent about Žižek, early on, is his paradoxical Hegelian materialism. For Žižek, the dialectic and its mode of analysis (reflection, contradictions, positing, negation, negation of negation, and the like) enable him to "discover" everywhere in Lacan (and in virtually any other topic) instances of paradox, contrariety, ambiguity. Everywhere are instances of deadlocks, impasses, contradictions that must be overcome or resolved, overcome, always, by paradox, by sublation, negation, negation of negation, chiasmic reversals of properties, resulting in other paradoxes, good paradoxes.

As there is an early Lacan and a late, so is there an early and late (or at least current) Žižek. But in the shift, late Žižek (that is, Žižek lately) typically trades one form of paradox (the logical, the liar's, paradox) for another (the mystical, perhaps). His recent work is much devoted to two sorts of discussion. Somewhat displacing early discussion of subjects of pop culture (film, especially, Hitchcock's films), one is of political and socioeconomic issues, issues that, for him, really are always one and the same thing. The second is Christianity, a topic that more and more displaces his pervasive treatments of German idealism. In his discussions of Christianity, he typically now trades "paradox" for "enigma" or "mystery," the enigma of Crucifixion and man-God, the mystery of the Trinity, thus trading paradoxes of one for paradoxes of another sort. In a career marked by a persistent oppositional stance (the sound of any Imaginary current or standard doxa being deflated is the hiss of Žižekian paradox), perhaps the oddest, most paradoxical feature of late Žižek is that his early, paradoxical, Hegelian materialism has given way to a self-described—equally paradoxical—stance as "Paulinian materialist." Gifted with perfect pitch for paradox, Žižek is extraordinarily interesting, and his work is rich in humor, topicality (anyone for Iraq?), and insights, but it is not quite apparent yet whether there is, or will be, a method, aside from ferreting out paradoxical patterns, that will emerge from that work. If Žižek is to transcend Lacan, he must produce an imitable methodology to go along with his philosophy. At some point, it is not enough to leave potential followers with nothing more than analysis of deadlocks and impasses in the works, theories, and ideologies of others. As several critics suggest, he needs a positive program of his own.

Part I

Toward Lacan

CHAPTER 1

From Freud to Jacques Lacan and the Textual Unconscious

[T]he unconscious is the condition for language [...] language is the condition for the unconscious.
                    —Jacques Lacan, "Preface byJacques Lacan," xiii

Everything can now be a text.
                    —Fredric Jameson, *Postmodernism*, 77

From Freud, that which takes us toward Jacques Lacan is an embedded concept of 'textuality.' Necessary for analysis, textuality, as an instance of a "vanishing mediator," may simply be assumed or safely disappear in analytic praxis. Concurrent with Lacanian psychoanalytic theory, textuality emerged as a pervasive ideological concept by the 1970s. Fredric Jameson defined it then as "a methodological hypothesis whereby the objects of study of the human sciences [...] are considered to constitute so many texts that we *decipher* and *interpret*, as distinguished from the older views of those objects as realities or existents or substances that we in one way or another attempt to *know*" ("Ideology of the Text" 18). As we trace a path from Freud through such adjectival notions of the unconscious as Jung's "collective," Walter Benjamin's "optical," and Jameson's own "political," we realize that from the start any *available* unconscious is a textual one. Lacan does not use the term *textual unconscious*. The term, if not the concept itself, seems to have originated in the work of a French critic—Jean Bellemin-Noël—indebted to Lacan. Bellemin-Noël says he used a term—*l'inconscient du texte* "the unconscious of the text"—as early as 1970, in a book to be titled *Vers l'inconscient du texte* ("Towards the Unconscious of the Text"). He claims that others such as André Green, Jeanne Bem, and Bernard Pingaud later used the term in essays published between 1973 and 1976 (see 191n2). By 1979, the year *Vers l'inconscient du texte* was published, American scholars

13

began to use the concept more or less emphatically. Since in his book Bellemin-Noel does not use the precise phrase *l'inconscient textuelle* "the textual unconscious" as such, it seems to have been Jerry Aline Flieger who first used it. In 1981 ("Trial and Error"), reviewing Bellemin-Noel's book, she converted *l'inconscient du texte* into the noun phrase *the textual unconscious*. In 1983, Robert Con Davis employed the concept of a 'textual unconscious' in "Lacan, Poe, and Narrative Repression" (989). In 1984, although more interested in the *literary* unconscious, Jonathan Culler not only used the noun phrase in a significant way but also theorized it more fully than any before him.

After Flieger, Davis, and Culler, as well as Michael Riffaterre, Shoshana Felman, Jameson, and others, the concept of the textual unconscious essentially becomes an unacknowledged legislator, a vanishing mediator, a term taken from Fredric Jameson ("The Vanishing Mediator") that Slavoj Žižek disseminates to Lacanians in *Tarrying with the Negative*. Textual unconscious is a concept intrinsic to the *intertextual* activity of interpretation of the unconscious and of literary texts, but once assumed (as in Freud) it may simply disappear and still do its work. By the late 1980s, explicit invocations of textual unconscious, while not rare, generally do in fact disappear, but the term still shows up often enough to suggest its mediatory primacy. Indeed, from psychoanalysis, it even invades psychology (see Steele); moreover, a number of literary studies—besides my own *Using Lacan, Reading Fiction*, including ones by Friedman, Downing, Rickard, and Tate—use it and draw directly upon its genealogy in Flieger, Jameson, Culler, Riffaterre, and others. Providing a thumbnail sketch of how the concept grounded different theorists and ideologies, Friedman also suggests how necessary but invisible is the concept:

> Adapting Kristeva's formulations of the text-as-psyche, critics such as Culler, Jameson, Shoshana Felman, and Michael Riffaterre [...] suggest that a text has an unconscious accessible to interpretation through a decoding of its linguistic traces and effects. For Culler and Felman, this textual unconscious is located in the interaction between reader and text, which they see as a scene of transference in which the reader "repeats" the complexes of the text. For Jameson and Riffaterre, the textual unconscious resides in the text, subject to the decoding of the reader, who occupies the authoritative position of the analyst. (164)

The very portability of the concept from one critical approach to another, in short, suggests its essential role as a mediator that effectively vanishes once analytic praxis begins.

1

> What is revealed here is [...] a textual unconscious in which the critic
> gets caught up.
>
> —Jonathan Culler, "Textual Self-Consciousness
> and the Textual Unconscious," 376

Since my interest necessarily foregrounds literary criticism, not clinical issues, Culler's essay provides a useful relay between the "literary" and the "textual." In his discussion of how the literary unconscious works, Culler invokes principles on which Julia Kristeva based her highly influential concept of 'intertextuality.' Since semiotics posits a subject of interpretation vis à vis an object of interpretation, it requires some form of relay or interface, either codes or structures, operating between the two. Kristeva started at the most fundamental ground of structure in using Roman Jakobson's premise that language operates along two axes, one of selection, one of combination (a premise underlying virtually all semiotic theory). Kristeva then argued that since any text is language based, every text in some critical sense must exhibit an intertextual relation to every other at least through the structural axes they share. That is, they relate through the fundamental semiotic structure of language. The concept of intertextuality provides Culler that interface between the literary and the textual unconscious because both conceptualizations depend upon Jakobson's grid—the axes of selection and combination—underlying language itself.

In a complex argument in which he takes a seemingly unpromising tack, Culler slides from one "unconscious" to the other. Focusing not on the textuality of the literary text as such, he addresses the transference between the analyst and the analysand. Describing transference, on the one hand, as a "drama of the analyst's involvement" with the patient and, on the other, as "the enactment of the reality of the unconscious" (371), he ends by reducing transference to a textual relation he in fact calls a "textual unconscious." But he finds this unconscious in the self-referentiality of the literary work, in how the text offers a way in which to read it. Culler says,

> I am arguing that what critics identify as moments of self-reference or self-consciousness in literary works may be the marks of a situation of transference. The critic who claims to stand outside the text and analyze it seems to fall into the text and to play out a role in its dramas. What is revealed in this

> transference is the *mise-en-acte de l'inconscient,* a textual
> unconscious, a structure of repetition: and it is the uncanni-
> ness of this repetition, continued in critical writing, that con-
> firms the appropriateness of speaking of this as a literary
> *unconscious.*

Nonetheless, Culler would argue that the importance of the fit between literature and the unconscious lies not in what it says of "the literary," but in what it says of the unconscious. Indeed, the "literariness" of the unconscious suggests it is the very nature of the textual itself that it shares with literature. Ultimately, says Culler, "What is revealed here is not the unconscious of the author but a textual unconscious in which the critic gets caught up" (376).

Although Freud no more than Lacan ever used 'textual uncon-scious,' clearly, the concept would have been understandable—and probably acceptable—to both. In "The Agency of the Letter in the Unconscious or Reason since Freud," Lacan essentially explains why this is so. The entire thrust of the essay is to lay out both why "the unconscious is structured like a language" and why the most appropri-ate way to analyze is based on linguistics, neither language nor linguis-tics taken literally but both taken metaphorically. Regarding Lacan's metaphorical "like a language," Bruce Fink, in *The Lacanian Subject,* has made a helpful suggestion. "Lacan did not assert that the uncon-scious is structured in exactly the same way as English, say, or some other ancient or modern language" (8). Rather, writes Fink, Lacan says "that language, as it operates at the unconscious level, obeys a kind of grammar, that is, a set of rules that governs the transformation and slippage that goes on therein" (8–9). Further, Fink points out, we may see this operation in how the unconscious "has a tendency to break words down into their smallest units—phonemes and letters—and recombine them as it sees fit" (9). It seems plain enough, then, that the repressed notion in this conceptualization of the unconscious is the tex-tual. It is the "text" of the unconscious of the analysand that, in analy-sis, in the "talking cure," becomes available for "linguistic" study.

In "The Agency of the Letter," perhaps the most systematically rig-orous defense of his linguistic approach Lacan ever offered his disciples (see Mellard, "Inventing"), he also makes certain claims about Freud's theory and practice that suggest why for Freud also the unconscious might well have been called "textual." In the essay, Lacan claims that whenever Freud spoke of the unconscious, he also, inevitably, spoke of "language." "Thus, in 'The Interpretation of Dreams,' every page deals with what I call the letter of the discourse, in its texture, its usage, its immanence in the matter in question. For it is with this work that the work of Freud begins to open the royal road to the unconscious." On this road to the unconscious, dreams are "read" quite literally as a rebus because of an "agency in the dream of that same literal (or phonematic) structure in which the signifier is articulated and analysed in discourse." Lacan takes the images of dreams as "signifiers" with which the analyst is to "spell out the 'proverb' presented by the rebus of the dream." Those signifiers are founded, Lacan argues, on the "principle" of a linguistic structure giving the analyst "the 'significance of the dream,' the *Traumdeutung*," the dream work (159). Thus, Lacan insists that linguistics has become necessary for him because Freud had already used a form of linguistic theory. "The unconscious," Lacan suggests, "is neither primordial nor instinctual." Rather, "what it knows about the elementary is no more than the elements of the signifier" (170). In that premise, he claims, Freud was there ahead of him in principle if not in expression. Consequently, given Lacan's premise, the unconscious is "like" a "language," and the ground upon which it operates is text or textuality. Indeed, Lacan recognized that, mutatis mutandis, the figural grounds of our thought change. What is more, if he had been a young psychoanalyst starting out in the 1970s instead of the 1930s, he would not in effect have said, "The unconscious is structured like a language and we must interpret it through the agencies of the letter." Rather, he would have said, simply, "The unconscious is a textual unconscious and we must interpret it as we would interpret any other text." By whatever name, ranging back to Freud's earliest enfigurations, the unconscious has always been textual.

2

[Tropes] are especially useful for understanding the operations by which the contents of experience which resist description in unambiguous prose representations can be prefiguratively grasped and prepared for conscious apprehension.

—Hayden V. White, *Metahistory*, 34

Psychoanalysis is constituted through figures of speech—tropes, that which Lacan might call "agencies of the letter." By way of a metaphor and extensions of it through metonymic associations, Freud brought about a revolution in the way we make meaning of our psychic life by transforming then-contemporary conceptualizations of the psyche. While he used many figures, he invented psychoanalysis through metaphors grounded in archeology. He developed his psychoanalytic theories at a time when both history and archeology were making great strides as intellectual disciplines. But while he loved history, he loved especially the thought of psychoanalysis as a kind of archeology (which also, of course, inevitably historicizes data) and even thought of himself as an archeologist of the psyche. It is the scholar, not Freud, who regards him as "the biologist of the mind" (Sulloway). Thus, in part because it was an almost inevitable figure of speech within his epoch and in part because Freud himself used it so frequently, the metaphor of archeology came to be identified with Freud's method. It is well known that Freud so loved the archeological metaphor that many, many instances of it are indexed in volume 24 of the *Standard Edition*. He coined it in the 1890s and used it throughout his career. It appeared as early as *Studies on Hysteria* (1893–95), "The Aetiology of Hysteria" (1896), *Fragment of an Analysis of a Case of Hysteria* (1905), and *Notes upon a Case of Obsessional Neurosis* (1909), and as late as *Civilization and Its Discontents* (1930), "Constructions in Analysis" (1937), and *Moses and Monotheism* (1939). As Lis Møller has shown in *The Freudian Reading*, the archeological is not just any figure; it is Freud's dominant metaphor for regarding the unconscious and constituting psychoanalysis.

But the value of the archeological trope to Freud and to us in understanding psychoanalysis is not merely its association with Freud's method. The trope's main value lies in the diegetic or explanatory extensions of the new discipline that archeological figures permit Freud. Typically appearing in metonymic associations permitted by the metaphoric ground, these extensions involve Freud's working out the implications of the originary metaphor. This process is essential to what structuralists and poststructuralists call "naturalization," the ways in which a new field becomes accepted as natural or ordinary. The metaphor, like any metaphor used in this cognitively constitutive way, served Freud well precisely in those moments when he needed to naturalize his method in a set of familiar terms. It not only both explained and justified his method, but it also defended him at those times he may have felt a weakness in it. "In face of the incompleteness of my analytic results," he writes in 1905, in *Fragment of an Analysis,*

> I had no choice but to follow the example of those discoverers whose good fortune it is to bring to the light of day after their long burial the priceless though mutilated relics of antiq-

uity. I have restored what is missing, taking the best models known to me from other analyses; but, *like the conscientious archaeologist*, I have not omitted to mention in each case where the authentic parts end and my constructions begin (*SE* 7:12; my emphasis).

Because Freud's explicit references like this one are thus quite numerous, and because there are as well so many other, less extended allusions to archeology, we begin to see that, indeed, the metaphors of archeology constitute for him, in Hayden White's terminology, a rather unconscious "tropology" (see *Metahistory*, for instance, and *Tropics of Discourse*). They represent a persistent way of thinking, speaking, explaining, and defending psychoanalysis. Indeed, as Møller says, archeology becomes the foundation for a "metalanguage of psychoanalysis, the language in which psychoanalysis represents itself as a depth psychology or a depth hermeneutics—an uncovering, a bringing to light, an unearthing, or an excavation of a hidden reality" (33–34).

As the metaphor of archeology constitutes the Freudian field, it also drives what White would call Freud's "diegetic" and "metonymic" extensions of it. According to White, metaphor constitutes by a naming, metonymy extends by dividing into parts, and metaphor and metonymy, together, function by the latter's converting an implicit "story" found in metaphor into an explicit narrativization of parts acting upon or in relation to other parts. As a metaphoric analogue, archeology provided the Freudian method two basic elements on which psychoanalytic discourse and understanding came to rely. One was a *topology*, the other was a narrative. From the metaphor's presumption of structural differences between surfaces and depths, Freud could construct a narrative based upon the movement from one to the other and back again. In their contribution toward the constitution and naturalization of the field and its methods, both topology and narrative perform functions essential to understanding and to the Freudian discourse.

Structural and topological features of the metaphor suggest at least two aspects of psychoanalysis. On the one hand, topologically, an implicit relation between a knowable surface and a mysterious, if not totally unknowable, depth represents the structural relation among the levels of Freud's topological spaces, whether the early one positioning conscious, preconscious, and unconscious or the later one positioning an id, ego, and superego. These topologies and the structural relations they entail permit one to claim, as Paul Ricoeur does, that "Freudianism is an explicit and thematized archaeology" (461). This claim suggests that whatever one does when positing Freudian reading, one has to posit levels of psychic functioning as much as the archeologist posits levels of cultural history. On the other hand, by its structural features, the metaphor of archeology suggests that psychoanalytic work is capable of moving from one level to another, from the known to the unknown, the conscious to the unconscious. In its physical way, archeology does precisely that in reclaiming buried levels of a culture's history and, by bringing them to the surface, permitting an understanding of their meanings. In recovering cultural artifacts from different levels or strata of an archeological site, artifacts that constitute a sort of iconic, physical history, archeology works with concrete objects that lead to representations of a history. Clearly, while psychoanalysis does not work with objects quite so material as archeology's, archeology makes both the data and the representations of psychoanalysis more easily comprehensible. As White suggests in *Tropics of Discourse*, understanding here moves from the familiar to the unfamiliar and back again, so that the comparison to the better known, though still rather new, discipline of archeology contributes immensely to our understanding of the yet newer discipline of psychoanalysis (4).

Where the first element the archeological metaphor brings to Freudian analysis is structural, enabling a dividing into parts by the spatial implications of the metaphor, the second element is narrative. Tropes imply stories. Constitutive metaphors invoke temporal and causal relations among parts or features the metaphor encompasses. The reason metaphor generates narrative is that "narrativity" seems a primal human heuristic, a fundamental way of encoding to make sense of the world. It is a virtual sine qua non of human cognition or perhaps even the condition of being human, a feature defining humanity we may add to the standard list of speech, laughter, and awareness of death. Whether or not it makes us human, within archeology and psychoanalysis, as various tropes enable or describe discourse and understanding, a move to narrative is, perhaps, inevitable because it is necessary to the very types of understanding of which these disciplines are capable. Neither archeology nor psychoanalysis makes merely bringing data to light the aim or end of their projects to achieve understanding. Neither discipline makes raw data (that is, the discrete unexplained metonymic objects) sufficient for an investigator. Investigators have to do something else. They have to construct a story, a narrative that organizes mental or physical objects (divided by metonymy into separate parts) into a sequence involving temporal succession and causal relations. As a constitutive metaphor of psychoanalysis, archeology brings narrative to a discipline that may not seem to need it. While all understanding may work by way of narrativization, narrativization certainly operates in some fields more overtly than in others. Clearly, it operates more overtly in archeology and history than in psychoanalysis. Thus, in bringing narrative to psychoanalysis, archeology focuses that point where history, archeology, and psychoanalysis converge. While, now, all three fields virtually compel practitioners to put their data into coherent narratives if their results are to bear meaning for their consumers, psychoanalysis does so *because* Freud's constitutive trope brought narrativity to Freudian praxis.

But practitioners may learn that narrative is a mixed blessing, for specific narratives in all three disciplines are subjected to questions of the same type. The major question bears on truth or referentiality: what is the referential relation of the narrative to "fact" or "truth"? In their links through narrative to history, both archeology and psychoanalysis invoke "others" critically important to notions of truth often taken for granted in the nineteenth century. For archeology, the metaphoric other is history, for archaeologists in the formative stages of the discipline saw themselves as simply practicing history by other means. The historian could merely assume what by his discourse the archeologist had to earn. Since truth and the specific narrative are so integrally related, nineteenth-century historians, for their part, generally assumed that the one yielded the other. In the nineteenth century, as White shows very fully in *Metahistory*, often in *Tropics of Discourse*, occasionally in both *The Content of the Form* and *Figural Realism*, truth and the narrative are construed as one, and what that "one" itself becomes *is* history. In the past two or three decades, however, any presumably secure connection between truth and narrative has been broken. And *history,* as White's work stresses, poses no fewer problems in regard to truth than had archeology itself in its formative stages. Nowadays, history connotes an origin, a signified, that to all but the naive realist is thought unavailable to the means—discourse—given to historian *and* archeologist alike for "recapturing" the past. In the nineteenth century, the golden age of historiography, history and historical meaning were thought simply a matter of *re*covering or *un*covering or *dis*covering something. In the twentieth century and after, particularly in our poststructuralist, postmodernist age, historical narrative, whether from a historian or an archeologist, is regarded as a construction, something that historians and archaeologists make, build, fabricate for themselves through language and the strategies of discourse.

While "fact" is important, the concept of 'truth' focuses another level of discourse. On the discursive or rhetorical levels of constitution and explanation found in classification and division, metaphor names a "field," and metonymy divides it up, but there is a "higher" level where synthesis occurs and draws together prior levels. The synthesis yields, it is always presumed, a sense that a discourse is adequate to handle the objects it inscribes. Truth, within a discursive field, is then the adequation of mimesis to explanation in a synthesized "whole." So long as we regard the Freudian discourse constituted by Freud's basic enfiguration as adequate to objects determined, tropologically, within its field, we can look upon psychoanalysis as a natural, ordinary, and, perforce, truthful or realistic domain. In all disciplines, as Thomas S. Kuhn famously argues in *The Structure of Scientific Revolutions*, once they are constituted within a discursive field that actually comes alive, a situation of normal or ordinary practice occurs within the standard paradigm. A standard paradigm operates precisely during that period when a synthesized whole, founded on its constitutive metaphor, is in praxis taken to be a representation of truth, fact, reality. But paradigms and practices and founding metaphors suffer vicissitudes. They fall on hard times. They come, almost inevitably, to seem inadequate. The moment we begin to suspect the unity, the adequation of the parts to the wholes, of practices to paradigms, as well as the arguments and stories predicated upon them, at that moment we cast a discipline into a period of crisis. Such a period of crisis may last for years or decades, or, if recovery never comes, a field may simply die out. But if recovery does come, it comes because there is a means of escape from crisis, and it is the same means used in the beginning in construction of the field. That means, of course, is tropological. If we save a field, we do so by discovering a new trope, a new founding or originary metaphor that will so *r*econstitute that field as once again to make discourse congruent with or adequate to objects it creates.

3

> [W]e only grasp the unconscious finally when it is explicated, in that
> part of it which is articulated by passing into words.
> —Jacques Lacan, *The Ethics of Psychoanalysis*, 32

While psychiatry and clinical psychology simply abandon the field of psychoanalysis, there have been many attempts to "save" the field Freud invented largely within his archeological metaphors. Some of these attempts can be found in adjectival modifications of the notion of the unconscious. The word *unconscious* has become almost as important for the modifiers attached to it as it is in itself, for nowadays adjectives modifying '*unconscious*' become more and more critical to the noun itself. The reality of the unconscious uncovered by Freud has been immensely important in our time, but the conceptual possibilities, without ever overshadowing Freud's foundational achievement, opened by it now seem equally important. Those possibilities are ones made visible in some of the modifiers we have come to associate with it. While the modifiers must always be subordinate to the basic Freudian noun, it is nonetheless the case that much of the history of developments in psychoanalysis and its related fields—including literary analysis—lies in those adjectives. These emerge, apparently, with Jung's *collective* unconscious and include others in no particular historical order such as *literary* unconscious, *optical* unconscious, and *political* unconscious. Indeed, several of these—namely 'collective' and 'political'—in fact represent major efforts, in instances perhaps of tail wagging dog, to alter or redefine Freud's basic concept. Jung's idea of the collective unconscious represents a serious effort to modify, and in Jung's view to save, Freud's original view of the unconscious. Though always in a process of modifying and elaborating his ideas, Freud conceived of the unconscious as existing in a system of levels or operating through separable functions. In the first topography, developed between roughly 1895 and 1915, Freud sees the perceptual system of the preconscious and consciousness as topographically separated from the unconscious. In the second topography, developed after 1920 and focusing more on functions than locations, he names the functions id, ego, and superego and claims the three encompass the entirety of consciousness and the unconscious. Whereas he makes the first topography descriptive and nominative, he makes the second functional and adjectival: that is, he himself uses '*unconscious*' as an adjective to identify types of functioning rather than as a noun identifying psychic places or topoi. In the second topography, Freud tended to anthropomorphize functions, speaking, for instance, of the superego as punitive or sadistic toward the ego. But as we shall see later in a discussion of Lacan's revision of Freud, these personifications do not constitute either the most important or the most epistemologically significant figures of speech available to Freud.

In articulating his concept of the 'collective unconscious,' Jung defines it as a place, a "region of the psyche." He distinguishes it from two other areas (presumably regions as well) he calls "consciousness" and the "personal unconscious." The personal unconscious, he says, is constituted by both ordinary forgetting, when content loses "intensity," and psychic repression, when consciousness is "withdrawn" from material, but it also includes "sense-impressions" that were never intense enough "to reach consciousness but have somehow entered the psyche"

(62). In any case, the personal unconscious is comprised of individual materials. "The collective unconscious, however, as the ancestral heritage of possibilities of representation, is not individual but common to all men, and perhaps even to all animals, and is the true basis of the individual psyche" (38). Arguing that this basic structure is transmitted genetically (60), Jung claims a biological or physiological basis for the collective unconscious. "This whole psychic organism," he says, "corresponds exactly to the body, which, though individually varied, is in all essential features the specifically human body which all men have." It is, shall we say, a matter of ontogeny recapitulating phylogeny. "In its development and structure," Jung avers, "it still preserves elements that connect it with the invertebrates and ultimately with the protozoa. Theoretically it should be possible to 'peel' the collective unconscious, layer by layer, until we come to the psychology of the worm, and even of the amoeba" (38). Whereas Freud represents the functions of the unconscious in terms of energy (as a kind of electrical system), Jung argues that where the personal unconscious functions through "complexes," the collective unconscious functions through "archetypes" that he calls "mythical traces" or "myth-motifs" (42). Among these archetypes, for example, are those representing the family as found in the holy family of Christian religions. "The deposit," says Jung, "of mankind's whole ancestral experience—so rich in emotional imagery— of father, mother, child, husband and wife, of the magic personality, of dangers to body and soul, has exalted this group of archetypes into the supreme regulating principles of religious and even of political life, in unconscious recognition of their tremendous psychic power" (43).

Archetypes function in the collective unconscious not through images but through the fantasies the primordial images generate. What is more, the archetypes are transformations—the "forms they assume"—of the instincts recognized by both Freud and Jung. The unconscious, "as the totality of all archetypes," says Jung, "is the deposit of all human experience right back to its remotest beginnings" (43). It is a "living system," however "invisible" it may be, that determines how individuals are constructed and live their lives. Thus, in the individual subject, the two regions of the psyche function in a symbiotic relationship. On the one hand, "The collective unconscious," Jung says, "contains the whole spiritual heritage of mankind's evolution, born anew in the brain structure of every individual. His [or her] conscious mind is an ephemeral phenomenon that accomplishes all provisional adaptations and orientations, for which reason one can best compare its function to orientation in space" (45). On the other hand, the unconscious is the source of the instinctual forces of the psyche and of the forms or categories that regulate them, namely the archetypes. All the most powerful ideas in history go back to archetypes. This is particularly true of religious ideas, but the central concepts of science, philosophy, and ethics are no exception to this rule. In their present form they are variants of archetypal ideas, created by consciously applying and adapting these ideas to reality. For it is the function of consciousness not only to recognize and assimilate the external world through the gateway of the senses, but to translate into visible reality the world within us. (45–46)

Thus, while Jung retains Freud's general idea of the unconscious, he modifies it significantly by positing a separate region in it that collects the deposits of the universal human experience.

Although not really a concept meant to save or replace the Freudian field, the concept of the 'optical unconscious,' originated in 1931 by Walter Benjamin in "A Small History of Photography," has been given new life by Rosalind E. Krauss. The concept has interesting consequences for any understanding of "the" unconscious in a postmodernist age. In *The Optical Unconscious* (1993), Krauss examines the unconscious subtending modernist art. Regarding modernism as an object structured as a discursive field, Krauss perceives that she can study the field of modernism not as a history but as a graph or table. "It struck me one day," she says, "that there was something to be gained from exploring [the] logic [of modernist art] as a topography rather than following the threads of it as a narrative," a logic focusing on what she calls "an ever more abstract and abstracting *opticality*" (my emphasis). She begins with an intuition that modernist painting is constructed upon a grid consonant with several other structures familiar to postmodernists: the Klein Group, the Greimasian square, the structuralist square, and Lacan's Schema L. The four terms of her modernist square are *ground* and *figure* across the top and *not ground* and *not figure* across the bottom. "I want this square," she says, "to represent a universe, a system of thinking in its entirety, a system that will be both bracketed by and generated from a fundamental pair of oppositions. This of course is the universe of visual perception, the one that is mapped by a distinction between figure and ground so basic that it is unimaginable, we could say, without the possibility of this distinction. The Gestalt psychologists have told us that: if no figure-detached-from-ground, then no vision" (13). Art prior to the modernists focused on the figure, but not so much at the expense of ground as in relative innocence of it. The modernists we might say foregrounded ground at the expense of figure. But if modernism shows that in premodern art there is an unconscious repression of ground, then its lesson must also be that in modernism there is a repressed or unconscious as well.

perspectival lattice
ground   figure................perception

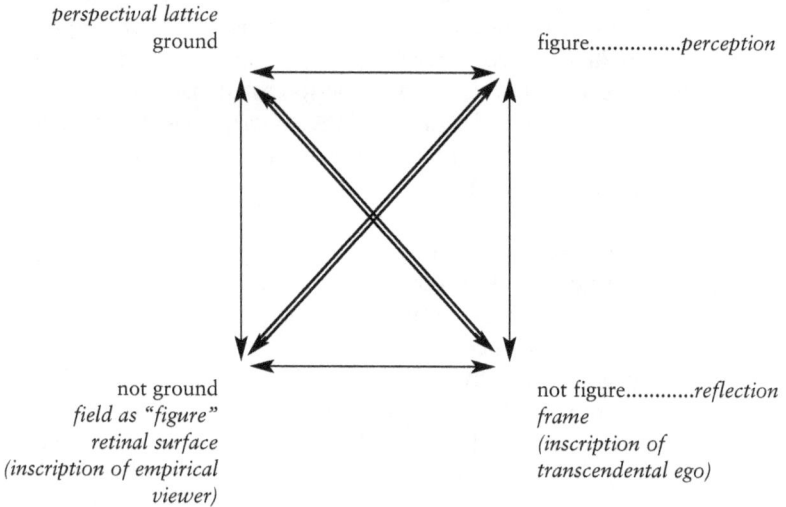

not ground   not figure............reflection
field as "figure"   frame
retinal surface   (inscription of
(inscription of empirical   transcendental ego)
viewer)

Fig. 1. Graph of the Optical Unconscious

In modernist art, as Krauss sees it, it is opticality—the presence of the components figure and ground making "pictures" and "vision" possible—that is the repressed. Her reasoning is complex. She begins her discussion of the optical unconscious *in medias res* with a description of the way the young John Ruskin viewed the world almost entirely as visual patterns. But Ruskin himself is not modernist. Rather, it is his way of viewing that—quite paradoxically—will eventually lead to modernism. The difference between modern and premodern, for Krauss, lies in the lessons of the grid she has constructed, the one rhyming with those several other grids, eventuating in Lacan's Schema L. Her schema—and Lacan's—leads her to perceive the dark or negative side of her square. Speaking of Lacan's schema as well as of her own, Krauss says, "Something dams up the transparency of the graph, cuts through its center, obscuring its relations one to the other." The ensuing darkness leads her to say what Ruskin cannot know. "Ruskin sees the pattern in the carpet," she writes, "in the sea, in the aspens. Sees their form, their 'picture.' What he does not see, cannot see, is how he has been made a captive of their picture." It is this area of darkness Krauss will name "the optical unconscious" or, rather, she will say "the darkness" is the area the optical unconscious possesses. "The optical unconscious will claim for itself this dimension of opacity, of repetition, of time. It will map onto the modernist logic only to cut across its grain, to undo it, to figure it otherwise" (24).

Thus Krauss, in her study of modernist painting, will look for this dark side, this photographic or mirroring negative of modernism's dominant ideology. Indeed, she will read the discursive field as a text and show that as a text mapped by those graphs it has an unconscious founded on the optical. "The problem of this book," she says, "will be to show that the depths are there, to show that the graph's transparency is only seeming: that it masks what is beneath it, or to use a stronger term, represses it" (24, 26). Still, Krauss does not expect to claim too much for the graph. As she says, the graph, like Lacan's Schema L, shows only that there is repression, that there is something outside the dominant system. It shows, she says, only "the repressive logic of the system, its genius at repression." It cannot show the content that is repressed. Because Krauss desires to reveal the repressed, the unconscious of modernist art, her study takes on a "political" aim. Thus she is especially eager to affiliate it with another whose aim is much more evidently political. "And so this book will be called *The Optical Unconscious*," she says. "Does the title rhyme with *The Political Unconscious*? It's a rhyme that's intended; it's a rhyme set into place by a graph's idiotic simplicity and its extravagant cunning" (26).

While Jung's notion of the collective unconscious remains the most familiar modification, its influence peaked in the 1960s with the rise and demise of archetypal criticism. In the last decade or so, as Krauss's invocation of Fredric Jameson suggests, the most influential *adjectival* modification of the basic concept of the Freudian unconscious has been Jameson's 'political unconscious.' Noting ideological changes, as his "Ideology of the Text" indicates on textuality itself, Jameson has often been ahead of the curve. In effect, joining the ideology of textuality to the unconscious, the concept of the political unconscious has gained widespread acceptance because the epistemological presumptions of the age itself—that which Michel Foucault, in a word, calls the "*épistème*"—clearly has taken a turn toward both the textual and the political. Jung's concept was especially useful to intellectuals at a time when the new knowledge from folklore, mythology, comparative religion, and cultural anthropology competed with psychoanalysis as means to explain human thought and conduct. The collective unconscious combined the fields of new knowledge by making the archetypes illuminated by those related social sciences an actual functioning part of the unconscious, by, indeed, making it the part that most determines the features of individual subjectivity and culture itself. These days, the authority given the notion of the political unconscious comes no doubt from its likewise combining two presumably competing modes of explanation of subjectivity and culture. One of these, of course, is the psychoanalytic, the other the social and, especially, economic mode of explanation found in Marx. For Jameson, the Marxist explanation—broadly construed as "political"—is the master modality.

The Political Unconscious, Jameson argues, will demonstrate that political interpretation of literary—and, perforce, other—texts must take priority over all other modes of explanation. "It conceives of the political perspective," he says of his book, "not as some supplementary method, not as an optional auxiliary to other interpretive methods current today—the psychoanalytic or the myth-critical, the stylistic, the ethical, the structural—but rather as the absolute horizon of all reading and all interpretation." By this claim, Jameson assumes that only Marxism offers a way to explain social or historical phenomena and the construction of the individual subject. His argument is distinctly contrary to a dominant theme of postmodernism, its opposition to master narratives. Instead, Jameson claims that these "matters can recover their original urgency for us only if they are retold within the unity of a single great collective story; only if, in however disguised and symbolic a form, they are seen as sharing a single fundamental theme" (17). That theme is, "for Marxism, the collective struggle to wrest a realm of Freedom from a realm of Necessity; only if they are grasped as vital episodes in a single vast unfinished plot" (19–20). Jameson's description of that plot of course comes from "The Communist Manifesto" of Marx and Engels. "The history of all hitherto existing society is the history of class struggles," Jameson argues. It is always a conflict of freeman against slave, patrician against plebeian, lord against serf, guild-master against journeyman. In this view, "oppressor and oppressed" stand "in constant opposition to one another," carry "on an uninterrupted, now hidden, now open fight, a fight that each time end[s], either in a revolutionary reconstitution of society at large or in the common ruin of the contending classes" (81). Looking a bit like Jung's notion of archetypes working through the fantasies surrounding primal instincts, this story leaves traces in the cultural manifestations of the subject that Jameson expects to find when uncovering the political unconscious in literary and other texts. In the form of criticism determined by the political unconscious, the critic's job is precisely to bring those "repressed and buried" traces to the surface in order to show the real truth of the subject or the cultural object.

Like Jung, who is compelled to establish the dominance of the collective unconscious over the Freudian, Jameson must establish the dominance of the political over the psychoanalytic notion of the unconscious. Because history is its subtending ground, Marxism dominates all other interpretative modalities simply by historicizing them. As Jameson says, Marxism subordinates other interpretations by showing that their limits "can always be overcome, and their more positive findings retained, by a radical historicizing of their mental operations." In this way, he says, "not only the content of the analysis, but the very method itself, along with the analyst, then comes to be reckoned into the 'text' or phenomenon to be explained." To show how the political dominates the unconscious in his concept, Jameson performs this historicizing on psychoanalysis. Suggesting that two of the main emphases of Freud's development of psychoanalysis were the family and sexuality, he argues that whereas Freud made each of these autonomous, "qualitatively different," features of a *private* biography of the subject, the two in fact belong to a larger *social* process. Freud especially emphasizes sexuality as an autonomous sphere subsumed in a dynamics of desire existing apart from social life. But, Jameson claims, while desire and sexuality gain their symbolic (or ideal) power from isolation from the social, they, like the family, cannot be separated from the materiality of the social world and its history. Psychoanalysis, Jameson argues, can demonstrate that "overtly nonsexual conscious experience and behavior" have sexual meanings only because it has made the "sexual apparatus" into an independent system of signs or symbols by that very "process of isolation, autonomization, specialization" (36). Jameson's view is that "as long as sexuality remains as integrated into social life in general as, say, eating, its possibilities of symbolic extension are to that degree limited, and the sexual retains its status as a banal inner-worldly event and bodily function" (64). In other words, says Jameson, the possibilities of sexuality as a symbolic field depend on its not belonging to the social—and therefore historical—field. But, for Jameson, the historicity of sexuality, as studied by such scholars as Michel Foucault, becomes evident in the ways "primitive sexuality" is transformed into modern sexuality in "the symbolic trajectory that leads from tattoos and ritual mutilation to the constitution of erogenous zones in modern men and women" (64). By such arguments, Jameson reverses the priority of his two terms: the political (meaning the social and historical) is made more determinative in human life than the unconscious. The adjective, again, dominates the noun. The 'political' is more important than the 'unconscious.'

4

> It is, of course, no accident that today, in full postmodernism, the
> older language of the "work"—the work of art, the masterwork—has
> everywhere largely been displaced by the rather different language of
> the "text," of texts and textuality.
>
> —Fredric Jameson, *Postmodernism*, 77

All these adjectival versions of the unconscious have, as it were, an
unconscious or a repressed element in common. Collective, optical,
political—all depend for their conceptual existence on a notion of
texts/textuality. With the concept of text, textuality has become perhaps the dominant figure in a poststructural, postmodernist age for all
sorts of social and intellectual activities. (For theorists or critics
engaged in discussions of text and textuality, see Barthes, Derrida,
Ducrot and Todorov, Jameson, Kristeva, McGann, Mowitt, and
Rorty.) If Freud's archeological metaphor derives from a modernist age
of history and historicization, textual metaphors emerge in a postmodernist age of semiology and semiotics. According to John Mowitt, there
are two basic notions or traditions of text, the "philological" and the
"semiological." It is the semiological tradition, with help from phenomenology, that drives postmodern reconceptualizations and extensions of
the notion. "From the philological tradition," Mowitt writes, "the text
has retained the notion of material boundaries, or what within the tradition of textual criticism was understood as the definitive edition or
version." Philology was concerned with an "original" text, one in
which writers inscribed their "intentions." But "it nevertheless insisted
upon the material force of what the text 'said.'" It was this "material
force" that semiology took from philology, but in doing so it eliminated "its idealist account of a fixed meaning." The "constitutive force
of interpretation" enters from phenomenology. In the phenomenology
of reading, says Mowitt, theorists such as Wolfgang Iser and Paul
Ricoeur focused on how readers engaged themselves with texts in
ways that brought to bear their subjectivity in producing meaning. In
making the interpreter the "bearer" of a writer's meaning, this tradition not only raises ethical issues but also "foregrounds the problem of
the subject's relation to a symbolic system which addresses him/her
from afar. Obviously," Mowitt concludes, "these inheritances undergo
profound change in the elaboration of textuality during the sixties and
seventies" (224n2).

It is the interrelation between a subject of interpretation and an
object of interpretation that gives us the semiological universe of postmodernism. In this universe, everything becomes a text, and everything

can be regarded as possessing textuality. Jameson, though seeing problems in the premise, puts it plainly. Textuality, he says, "now seems to
reorganize the objects of other disciplines and to make it possible to
deal with them in new ways which suspend the troublesome notion of
'objectivity.'" Nothing seems to escape the label *text* or *textual*.

> So it is that political power becomes a "text" that you can
> read; daily life becomes a text to be activated and deciphered
> by walking or shopping; consumers' goods are unveiled as a
> textual system, along with any number of other conceivable
> "systems" (the star system, the genre system of Hollywood
> film, etc.); war becomes a readable text, along with the city
> and the urban; and finally the body itself proves to be a
> palimpsest whose stabs of pain and symptoms, along with its
> deeper impulses and its sensory apparatus, can be read fully as
> much as any other text. (*Postmodernism* 186).

With Michel Foucault's concept of '*épistème*,' it becomes plain that
every age, defined by its ways of knowing, redefines essential concepts
within its dominant metaphorics. In the postmodern, as Jameson says,
the dominant metaphor has become text or textuality. In postmodernism, everything, not merely the unconscious, becomes text and operates through an overt or a covert grounding in textuality. With the
epistemological reorientation wrought by textuality, when we review
Jung and Krauss and Jameson, we inevitably find it. Indeed, the unconscious grounding of the optical, the collective, and the political unconscious is a textual unconscious. In Jung, we find the unconscious
textuality of the collective unconscious in the means by which Jung
"proves" the existence of the collective. This proof we find in "The
Structure of the Psyche." There, Jung begins by recounting the mysterious symptoms of a young officer who suffered from pain around the
heart, a choking sensation in the throat, and pains in his left heel.
Analyzing the officer as a patient, Jung found that the symptoms began
when the youth's fiancée jilted him for another man. Though the officer
denied the importance of the story he told Jung, upon the telling the
first two symptoms disappeared almost immediately, because they had
a "textual" dimension, the conventional heartache of failed love and the
lump in the throat resulting from swallowed tears. The bodily symptoms, that is, simply became signs for actual verbal messages the young
man was unwilling or unable to express in words until the occasion of
the analysis with Jung.

The pain in the man's heel, likewise, has a textual origin. As the
necessary information about the other two symptoms came to Jung

through the man's account of his dreams, so came information about the painful heel, for he had dreamed he had been bitten there by a snake and paralyzed. In claiming the existence of the collective unconscious, Jung argues that the serpent came not from any image in the man's personal experience, but from a collective one. But I suggest that in fact it is in the textual that the experience is collective. As Jung himself shows, its actual roots are sunk in literary texts, and these texts tie his being lamed to women, not only his fiancée, but also his mother. In those literary texts, as in his dream, women and serpents belong together. "We are evidently dealing here," says Jung, "with that same old serpent who had been the special friend of Eve." The text he has in mind is the biblical one: "And I will put enmity between thee and the woman, and between thy seed and her seed; it shall bruise thy head, and thou shalt bruise his heel" (Genesis 3:15). What is more, this text echoes one even older, an Egyptian hymn carrying much the same message. Here, it is Isis who exacts vengeance upon a god, but she does so by creating a serpent from earth and the god's spittle.

> The mouth of the god trembled with age,
> His spittle fell to the earth,
> And what he spat forth fell upon the ground.
> Then Isis kneaded it with her hands
> Together with the earth which was there;
> And she made it like a spear.
> She wound not the living snake about her face,
> But threw it in a coil upon the path
> Where the great god was wont to wander
> At his pleasure through his two kingdoms.
> The noble god stepped forth in splendour,
> The gods serving Pharaoh bore him company,
> And he went forth as was each day his wont.
> Then the noble worm stung him [...]

Whereas Jung focuses here on use of this example as proof of the collective unconscious, in fact it is in a text that this unconscious exists. It lives in textuality. "The patient's conscious knowledge of the Bible was at a lamentable minimum," says Jung. "Probably he had once heard of the serpent biting the heel and then quickly forgotten it. But something deep in his unconscious heard it and did not forget; it remembered this story at a suitable opportunity. This part of the unconscious evidently likes to express itself mythologically, because this way of expression is in keeping with its nature." Thus the "mythological" to which Jung adverts is, as any Lacanian would recognize, actually the textual, a judgment implied as well in Jung's own way of founding the collective unconscious on a "symbolical or metaphorical"—thus textual—"way of expression" (*Portable Jung* 33).

More than Jung, Jameson, in his discussion of the political unconscious, is aware of the link between textuality and his concept. As a Marxist, Jameson regards history as the ultimate ground of human existence, but though he recognizes that textuality lies within its orbit, he does not regard history as a text. It is for him—as for Althusser, to whom he adverts in this argument—that which Spinoza calls an "absent cause." As such, he says, it is "not a narrative, master or otherwise," but it can become available to us "only in textual form." Connecting the concept to Lacan's notion of the Real—which, as Jameson quotes from Lacan's Seminar 1 (66), "is that which resists symbolization absolutely"—Jameson argues that "our approach to it and to the Real itself necessarily passes through its prior textualization, its narrativization in the political unconscious" (35). But as Lacan does not claim that the Real is the unconscious, neither can Jameson claim that history is the unconscious either. Thus if all we know of the Lacanian unconscious is a text, it is therefore textual. Likewise, if all we know of history is a text, then the unconscious Jameson calls "political" is surely at the same time textual as well. This conclusion seems inevitable when we examine his lament about the way the current generation has repressed historicity in its major cultural artifacts. If modern readers, says Jameson, are "bored or scandalized by the roots [...] texts send down into the contingent circumstances of their own historical time, this is surely testimony as to [...] resistance to [their] own political unconscious and to [their] denial [...] *of the reading and the writing of the text of history within [themselves]*" (34; my emphasis).

That conclusion is equally clear in Jameson's discussion leading toward those claims regarding the Real, the absent cause, and textuality. Earlier, Jameson had argued that the political unconscious belonged to "the object," that is, to the text being interpreted. He used there the notion, from Althusser, of 'expressive causality' as a concept of local cause much like those operating within history enabling him to bridge the gap between method and object, interpretive code and functioning model. By equating expressive causality with "allegorical master narratives" (such as, he would contend, the Freudian and, equally, as I would contend, the Marxist), Jameson unintentionally suggests that it becomes impossible to separate either narratives or causality from the texts in which they operate. Expressive causality, in effect, becomes textuality. The fact is, says Jameson, "if interpretation in terms of expressive causality or of allegorical master narratives remains a constant temptation, this is because such master narratives have *inscribed themselves in the texts as well as in our thinking about them.*" Indeed, he says, "such allegorical narrative signifieds are a persistent dimension of literary and cultural texts precisely because they reflect a fundamental dimension of our collective thinking and our collective fantasies about history and reality" (34). In statements such as these, it seems especially plain that the common denominator in expressive causality, allegorical master narratives, and, perforce, the political unconscious is the text, the textual, textuality itself. In short, as this view of Jameson's concept suggests, any notion of the unconscious eventuates in the idea of the textual unconscious.

In Krauss's argument, the textuality of the optical unconscious lies in the very grid—the semiotic rectangle—Krauss employs to structure the field of modern art: the grid itself is that unconscious text subtending modernism's options. Since Krauss has used Jameson's idea of the political unconscious to formulate her concept of the optical, we may note that in his book Jameson rather effectively describes the process Krauss adverts to in her study. The "very closure of the 'semiotic rectangle,'" says Jameson, "affords a way into the text." It does so "not by positing mere logical possibilities and permutations." Rather, it does so "through its diagnostic revelation of terms or nodal points implicit in the ideological system." But because these "have, however, remained unrealized in the surface of the text," and likewise "have failed to become manifest in the logic of the narrative," "we can therefore read [them] as what the text represses" (*Political Unconscious* 48). Krauss at times seems to understand that modernism represses that which is found in the grid, that in fact the grid textualizes. Thus the grid becomes a text, the text of modernism. Moreover, as opticality in Krauss becomes textuality, Krauss's argument begins to suggest precisely why we have to "see" the unconscious as "textual."

Like the optical unconscious, the textual unconscious rests on a ground defined by grids or matrices. These include matrices defined not only by the semiotic axes and the semiotic square but also by topographies such as Freud's id, ego, and superego. In Lacan, for whom the unspoken concept of the textual unconscious was always on the verge of utterance, the matrices include a plethora of models and schemas and formulas and knots and structures and tables and graphs and algorithms. Taken together, these seem so important that we may say, No textual matrices, no Lacan. In "Introductory Talk at Sainte-Anne Hospital," Jacques-Alain Miller suggests as much. Providing a model of his own—Reading/Writing, Speech/Writing, one that mimics Lacan's

S/s—Miller says, "You speak in analysis, and it is as if you were read-ing—reading a text better and better. This would make of the uncon-scious a text, and analysis would not be a matter of what you mean, but a matter of reading well" (235). Lacanians such as Miller mimic Lacan's matrices not simply because of their explanatory power but because Lacan's very textuality is grounded in or founded upon all those grids, graphs, schemas, topologies, and the like. In truth, when Lacan thinks about the unconscious he thinks by means of them. Some of them represent little more than binary relations (as in $ \lozenge D$, repre-senting his "matheme" for the drive), and in S/s, representing both his algorithm of signification and what he calls "the topography of the unconscious" (*Ecrits: A Selection* 163). There are also various triads (Imaginary, Symbolic, Real; the elements in the Oedipus complex; the Symbolic "third" element, the other, that breaks Imaginary dualities such as mother and child). Moreover, there are complex, sequential graphs, such as those of desire, but they represent narratives rather than structures as such. The best—most useful, most easily appre-hended—graphic figures in Lacan are those that essentially only double the binaries to form quaternary matrices. Because these are structural, they represent "wholes" such as the topology of the subject rather than mere parts or functions. They are, as well, the ones that have legs, that is, that have theoretical carryover both within Lacan's own thought and to others who try to use Lacanian theory. These include Schema L (in two versions, each of which is quaternary), the structure of both metaphor and the paternal metaphor, and the struc-ture of the four discourses.

Despite Lacan's warning that we must not "forget in an intuitive image the analysis on which it is based" (332), these work, in part, because they do in fact provide something "intuitive" that others can grasp as readily as Lacan and because they represent both structures and potential narratives. Moreover, despite frequent dualisms and triads, it seems quite plain that the core of Lacan's thought, the heart of his way of thinking, is quaternary. It is not an accident that structural-ists took up Lacan. In his ever-developing theory, lower-order struc-tures evolve toward quaternaries. He likes binary dualisms, and, as structuralism has taught us, these are basic. As for triads, when they appear in Lacan they tend to be stages in an evolutionary (essentially narrative, rather than structural) process: that is, perhaps because triads tend to mark points in a series, they evolve into quaternaries that sug-gest a structure. It is quaternary structures that serve Lacan as end game, integrative schemas because they are more stable than triads and more productive intellectually than dualisms. Dualisms very effectively initiate a first level of analysis, but quaternaries emerge because they multiply relations (not doubly, but triply) and thus both complicate and sophisticate thought. For subjectivity, the multiplication achieved by a simple splitting of dualities is necessary. In "Kant *avec* Sade," Lacan himself says: "a quadripartite structure has, since the introduction of the unconscious, always been required in the construction of a subjective ordering" (774).

We see Lacan acceding to this tendency in his late, late work on the topology of Borromean knots. He speaks first about the Borromean ring or knot in *Encore*, the seminar of 1972–1973. He theorizes it more fully in the seminars of 1974–1975 and 1975–1976. As a triadic schematic, his Borromean knot lasted through just three seminars. By the fourth one, he recognized a need to augment the triad with a fourth ring whose function, he said, was to tie together the three original rings. The fourth ring was the *sinthome*. He had introduced the notion of *sinthome* to his general theory in the seminar of 1974–1975, *RSI* (an acronym for Real, Symbolic, Imaginary, his original triad of orders). In 1975–1976, in the succeeding seminar, on *le sinthome* itself, he redefines it as in fact a fourth order or register. In this clarification, it seems plain that, though by this time he is old and infirm and his mental lucidity seems to be failing rapidly, his thought is evolving toward another quaternary schematic, toward, almost surely, another version of Schema L.

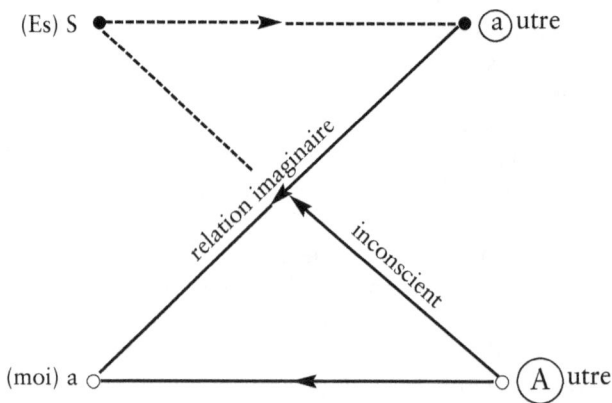

Fig. 2. Lacan's Complex Schema L

Lacan had invented the original, more complex schema L two decades before, in Seminar 2, on the ego, 1954–1955. This version, it happened, was popularized in the 1970s among Anglo-American scholars by way of an essay from the seminar on Poe's "Purloined Letter." Among Lacanians, when Derrida attacked the essay in "The Purveyor of Truth," it became such a *cause célèbre* that, in the brief reign of deconstruction, in the debate it ignited between and about Lacan and Derrida, it perhaps did more than anything else to familiarize scholars with Lacanian ideas.

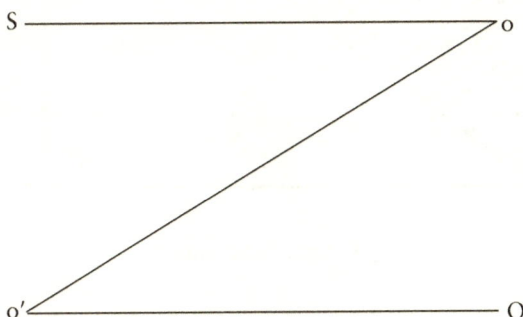

Fig. 3. Lacan's Simple Schema L

In 1955–1956, in Seminar 3, "The Psychoses," Lacan simplified Schema L. The simple form then appears in an essay summarizing ideas from the seminar (see *Ecrits: A Selection* 193). But then, in the same seminar, he immediately complicated it yet more radically by inventing Schema R (see 197). Schema R was designed to account more directly for what he called at that time "the field of reality." Heretofore less theorized than either Imaginary or Symbolic, this "field," the real, had already been designated an order by 1953 and was eventually to be called, simply, the "Real." Though schema R gives an immediate appearance as a quaternary schematic, the fact is that it functions as a triad. Its triadic nature is clear in Lacan's discussion of it (197–99, 223–24n18), where he speaks of its three parts—two triangles sandwiched around a quadrangle, all inscribed within a larger quadrangle. While it is the containing quadrangle that makes us assume Schema R is just another quaternary, like schema L, in its attempting to represent relations among the orders of the Imaginary and the Symbolic (inscribed in triangles) and "the field of reality" (inscribed in a quadrangle situated between the other two orders), it is actually a direct precursor of his Borromean topology. One sees this relation simply by eliminating the other figures and superimposing rings over each of the orders.

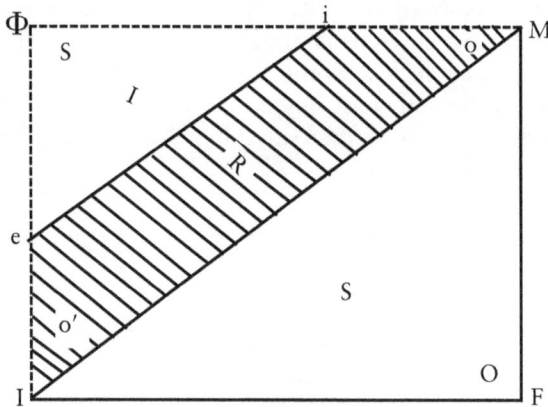

Fig. 4. Lacan's Schema R

Indeed, his Borromean topology begins as three overlapping rings designated as Imaginary, Symbolic, and Real. The triad evolves into a potential quaternary structure when in *Le sinthome* (Seminar 23, 1975–1976), he designates *sinthome* a fourth register. In the four rings—and four orders—of his ultimate Borromean topology, he generates the conditions of possibility of a new four-sided schema on the precise model of L. What is more, in a very significant way, Lacan's late, late acknowledgment of *sinthome* as an order or register finally makes good sense of those earlier versions of Schema L. Lacan's actual claims were that his ultimate topology is comprised of the three Borromean knots "tied" together by a fourth ring. While he preferred to believe in a distinction between his schemas, L, especially, and his topology formed by Borromean rings, in whatever number (three or four), the distinction is one without a difference. On the one hand, he claimed that the schema is merely "metaphorical" and thus only "represents," descriptively, "the symbolic order and its interactions with the real and the imaginary" (Evans, "Borromean Knot"). On the other, he claimed that the topology formed by Borromean knots is non-metaphorical and thus not merely representational or descriptive: "rather than simply *representing* structure," Evans summarizes, "topology *is* that structure." But such a distinction is absurd on the face of it. Lacan may wish to claim the topology "is" the structure of subjectivity or whatever

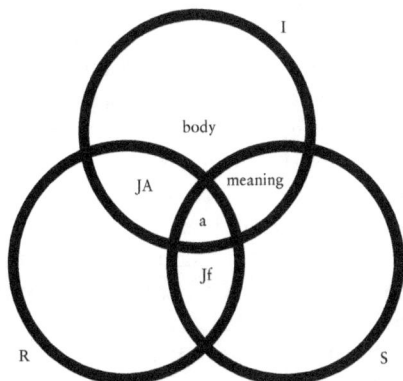

Fig. 5. Lacan's Three-Ring Borromean Knot

because, perhaps, a knot "looks like" gnarly convolutions of an actual brain. But, no, it cannot be that very Real thing. The brain is one thing, topology is another, albeit something meant to be "like" or to represent the brain. Thus, the Borromean topology is no less "metaphorical" or "representational" than Schema L. That said, except for his not yet having actually worked it out, there is simply no compelling reason for Lacan not to have revised his simplified version of Schema L to reflect his new thinking not only about a "structure" of subjectivity but also about interactions, within subjectivity, of the four registers. Thus, the bottom line, in any case, is that, as Lacanians versed in these matters conclude, the schemas of the 1950s do indeed foreshadow or lay a groundwork for ring topology coming in the 1970s. But whether triadic or quaternary, the one is no less textual than the other.

Across the years, the consistency of Lacanian theory thus lies not so much in unchanging terms (since we know that terms evolve from time to time) as in its persistent grounding in textuality. With this thought in mind, we may wonder, What would an ultimate quaternary of subjectivity look like? Lacan's thought of the final years, 1974 and after, clearly was facilitated through the triad of his Borromean knots. But as dualisms split into quaternaries and previous triads evolve into them, so it would seem inevitable that any final or ultimate schematic of subjectivity must be quaternary. Surely, it would become a new L with the four registers in appropriate relations. The tricky part is defining "appropriate." In my view, the essential first question is where to put the Real. Once that is determined the others begin to fall into place. To be consistent with all of Lacan's comments about the Real, we may put it only at or in the bottom right quadrant, in the site where Lacan has always put those elements (Unconscious, Other, Father, Name of the Father) that are either beyond representation as such or that simply ground or anchor or subtend all other elements. For instance, as in both original versions of Schema L, Lacan placed the big Other (capital A Autre) at the bottom right of his square, so in an ultimate L it seems consistent with earlier thought to place the Real there too. As Autre, in the Symbolic, subtended or anchored (as, perhaps, in *points de capiton*) the subject or subjectivity, so in that same site would the Real anchor the subject or subjectivity but in a traumatic, "impossible" way (the Real is the impossible). The more Lacan moves toward a material grounding of his late theory, the more it becomes necessary to assume that the Real, the "Impossible," is his subtending ground.

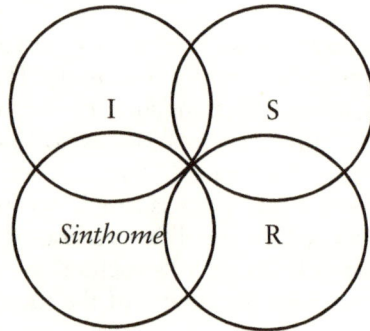

Fig. 6. A Four-Ring Borromean Knot

Since in this new schematic it seems almost certain that Imaginary and Symbolic must stand opposite each other, their placement appears mandated. That leaves only the *sinthome*. With the other three in place, there would seem to be no question about where to locate *sinthome*. But, simply in the terms about which Lacan speaks of it, we can still ask where it must go. He says, for instance, that "the *sinthome* is what 'allows one to live'" (Thurston, "Sinthome"). As the ego once had done, it ties together Real, Symbolic, and Imaginary and "allows the subject to cohere," and yet, here in the late theory, where trauma and impossibility reign, that function is "beyond meaning." "Since meaning (*sens*) is already figured within the knot, at the intersection of the symbolic and the imaginary," Luke Thurston explains, "it follows that the function of the *sinthome*—intervening to knot together real, symbolic and imaginary—is inevitably beyond meaning." In the *sinthome*, the subject simply has to be content "to *be*." In the new L, then, it seems that *sinthome* must go where "a" or "ego" or "ego-ideal" once went, as subtending or complementary to the Imaginary subject, and as contradictory to the ordinary Symbolic. It is in this location that *sinthome* makes comments Lacan made about it appear most consistent.

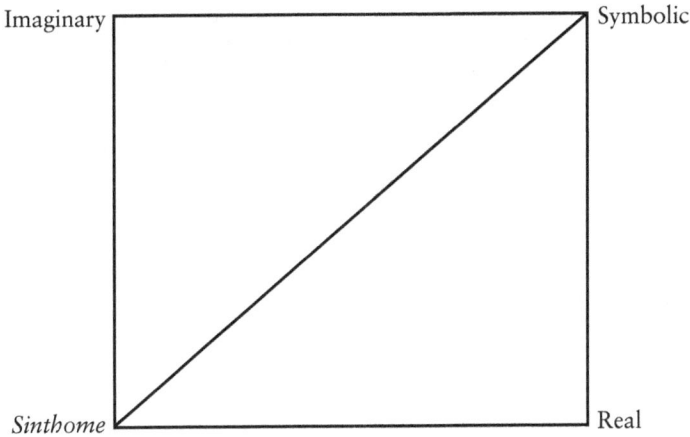

Fig. 7. An Ultimate Schema L

　　Thus, the ultimate schema involves a square at whose points (clockwise from top left) will be Imaginary, Symbolic, Real, and *sinthome*. Given such a square of logical implications functioning like a conventional Greimasian square, this new L generates Lacan's typical ways of thinking through oppositions, contradictions, and complementaries. Indeed, it is the implications of the square that perhaps best explain why Imaginary and Symbolic take positions at top left and right, respectively. Virtually by definition, any critical procedure the squares entail must begin with a "given" (of a culture, an ideology, a psyche). For Lacan, this given has to be an "imaginary" that subjects presume runs their lives (and that, of course, does run them, in ordinary, unreflective, "pathological" life). Against this Imaginary register, by implication of a "contrary," stands a not-imaginary. Since neither *sinthome* nor the Real seems to work as a contrary to Imaginary, we must look to the Symbolic. In the ultimate L, this not-imaginary can only be the Symbolic. In the procedure thereafter, in the implication of a "contradictory" opposed to the Imaginary (below and across from it in the square) stands the Real; finally, in a contradictory opposed to the Symbolic (again, below and across from it in the square) stands *sinthome*. In such an ultimate L, we now have an Imaginary that is contrary to Symbolic, complementary to *sinthome*, and contradictory to the Real, this latter being especially appropriate in a commonsensical way (the Imaginary ought to contradict the Real and, of course, vice versa). Now, too, then, we have a Symbolic contrary to Imaginary, contradictory to the Real, and complementary to *sinthome*. In Lacan's comments, and in the representation we observe in the ultimate Schema L, we must understand both just how radical, and how unchanging, is Lacan's revision of his thought. Where once it was the relation of Imaginary to Symbolic that determined the entire structure of subjectivity as posited in the 1950s, in the late, late theory of the 1970s, Lacan gives over that function to the relation of *sinthome* to the Real. And yet,—and yet—it hardly changes anything. In the Real, it simply gives over the role of the big Other to something just as enigmatic and powerful as once Lacan considered the Other in the Symbolic. Thus not very much actually changes once we see the registers configured in a set of relations represented by a square, with all its implications of contraries, contradictions, and complementaries. Whether early or late, Lacanian theory of the subject, subjectivity, and the human psyche remains grounded in a textual matrix and the unconscious remains a textual unconscious.

5

L'inconscient, c'est le discours de l'Autre. ('The unconscious is the discourse of the Other.')
                                                              —Jacques Lacan, *Ecrits*, 16

Discourse [. . .] is quintessentially a *mediative* enterprise.
                                        —Hayden V. White, *Tropics of Discourse*, 4

   So the unconscious is textual. What does that entail for literary interpretation? Here, we must move from textuality to *inter*textuality. Interpretation, of any sort, moves, reciprocally, between one text and another. Thus as we interpret literature, so also do we interpret the unconscious—and, of course, vice versa. Although literary texts are not "the" unconscious, they possess an unconscious that is necessarily textual and are interpreted intertextually. How this process of interpretation works is perhaps best understood within the tradition of text defined, as John Mowitt suggests, by semiotics and semiotic analysis. In the context of the movement toward acceptance of the notion of the textual unconscious, ideas expressed in an essay by Michael Riffaterre become particularly useful. In "The Intertextual Unconscious," Riffaterre, like Jonathan Culler, addresses both literary and textual unconscious. Like Culler, but without employing the concept of 'transference' to identify a reader's relation to a text, Riffaterre uses the notion of intertextuality to elucidate psychoanalytic interpretation of literature. Riffaterre begins with an unassailable premise, that literature is as "open to psychoanalysis as is any other form of expression" (211). Like some adherents to semiotics, Riffaterre needlessly worries about the "literariness" of literature, that which "differentiates [it] from other linguistic utterances." But the fact is, any text, whether specifically intended as literary or not, may be regarded as literary and subjected to psychoanalytic or any other type of analysis, perhaps not very fruitfully, of course, but subjected, yes.

Concerning analysis of literary texts, Riffaterre is certainly correct about the intertextual nature of interpretation and how a text's verbal features enable it. Ultimately, the features he adduces, though he names them differently, are the same as those Freud and Lacan endorse. In his generic terminology, Riffaterre suggests that psychoanalytic interpretation must begin with a reader's "scanning" a text for "signs pointing to the unconscious" (213). While, in this activity, interpretation involves no "competence" necessarily beyond that of any putative common reader, it is evident that the more expert a reader the more successful in identifying signs. What readers search for (though Riffaterre does not use the term) is anomalies in a text. They look for "words or phrases that cannot be understood with the sole help of their context and of our familiarity with grammar, lexical distribution, and the descriptive systems that subordinate the mimesis of reality to the mythologies and ideological commonplaces of our society" (213). The "signs" readers search for "point to the unconscious inasmuch as they repress a meaning in the process of conveying one" (213–14).

It is here that Riffaterre comes to intertextuality. Intertextuality occurs in signs readers find in one text that point them to signs in other texts. Though he calls this action "dual," it is essentially no more than the reciprocal process all hermeneutic activity involves. While intertextuality "is tantamount to mimesis of repression," Riffaterre says, "the application of psychoanalysis to literature needs more than a description of that mimesis." It does so because "the mimesis, rather than a represented object or referent (or even its signifier outside the text), is the starting point of reading and the sole guideline to interpretation. If this is true of all literary representations, it must also be true of the sign that represents the suppression of another, intertextual, referent" (214). Still, he warns, "Recovery of the intertext does not in itself constitute a discovery of the unconscious, but it directs the analyst toward it, and the more such 'bearings' are collected along the written line, the easier it is to pinpoint the location of the repressed."

What Riffaterre presents lies at the heart of any intertextual method of psychoanalytic reading. In a densely detailed analysis of passages of *Remembrance of Things Past*, he focuses on two types of verbal features or "signs" that operate on the two different levels essential to intertextual analysis. As in Kristeva's argument and Culler's adaptation, these are defined, in Roman Jakobson's terms, by language's two axes, the vertical (paradigmatic) one of selection and the horizontal (syntagmatic) one of combination. At the level of the word (where Jakobson stresses selection along the paradigmatic axis), Riffaterre discusses syllepsis (a trope that he concedes is essentially the same as Freud's "condensation" [215]). At the level of narrative (where Jakobson stresses combination along the syntagmatic axis), Riffaterre discusses embedded or scattered but "fully developed narrative units" (220). A "special case of intertextuality," Riffaterre says, "Syllepsis is a trope consisting in the simultaneous presence of two meanings for one word." In Jakobson's conceptualization, it is as if one word sits, vertically, above another word it thereby suppresses. The apparent meaning comes from immediate context and would generate an ordinary interpretation. As such, "the meaning required by the context represses the one incompatible with that context." But, as Jakobson's model of language suggests, when one has located a word/meaning on the one axis, immediately, that selection may foster an associative process operating on the second axis. Thus, repression, operating along this axis, Riffaterre suggests, "entails a compensation": in puns, modifications, paraphrases, or other substitutions, a repressed word "generates a syntagm or even a text in which the repressed meaning reappears in various guises" (215).

In his analysis, what seems peculiar is that Riffaterre never admits that the "signs" of the unconscious in Proust's text are recognizable as such signs because of a code, precisely the code determined by the Freudian interpretation he invokes. It is as if the unconscious of Riffaterre's text is Freudianism itself. But once we understand that code, the details of his interpretation of Proust become quite clear. Thus, as we interpret Riffaterre's remarks, we activate the reciprocal process of semeiosis, the shuttling, proper to all interpretation, between our codes and our texts. These are moves Freud identifies as condensation and displacement, Lacan as metaphoric substitution and metonymic association, the two sets, in either case, following principles schematized in Jakobson's axes of language. If, by and large, what Riffaterre calls "syllepsis" functions through individual words (as, Lacan says, metaphor is one word for another), the second way in which signs point to an intertextual unconscious functions through units of narration. In this process, "fully developed narrative units [...] are imbedded in the main narrative and sometimes scattered through it. Whereas a syllepsis straddles the text and an intertext outside of it (sometimes simply the sociolect itself), here the text-intertext pair is present in its entirety within the text—a case of intratextual intertextuality" (220). In either syllepsis or narrative units, an interpretive reader, using a code, detects signs pointing, because of repetitions, both to a textual and an intertextual unconscious. In Proust, it is plain, for instance, that asparagus, the object-sign Riffaterre examines, would be of little interpretive consequence if it did not recur so frequently as to be thought "obsessional." Moreover, in this and in other, narrative, aspects, he suggests, writers revise texts, and readers reread them in ways that suggest "an exploratory, inquisitive, questioning approach quite like psychoanalytical procedures." Further, he says, when writers, in particular, constantly revise or generate variations, they do so because of a "repetition compulsion" (221). This view may be a bit extreme, but whether repetition along the paradigmatic axis of selection/substitution or along the syntagmatic axis of combination/association, there is no question that it is vital to the hermeneutic process in literature or, indeed, any text that requires interpretation.

In preparation for any Freudian-cum-Lacanian interpretation, it is important to note two features of Riffaterre's conclusion to "The Intertextual Unconscious." One is language, the other, spatiality. Regarding the first, without ever adverting to Lacan, and, quite unaccountably, seeming to assume that psychoanalysis operates other than through language and intertexts, Riffaterre makes an important Lacanian point that therein effectively endorses not only the notion that interpretation is intertextual but also that the unconscious must be textual.

> By replacing purely psychoanalytical techniques with the tools of an analysis based on words, we assure relevancy, a pertinence defined by textual features themselves. While it is true that the interpretations thus obtained are accessible only through a detour outside the text, this detour never goes beyond language, and the absent referent is still clearly outlined by elements of the text that need the complementarity or the opposability of an intertext to be units of significance.

> While meaning is wholly present in the text, significance rests
> on the inseparability of a visible sign from its repressed inter-
> textual homologue. (225)

On the second matter, Riffaterre stresses spatiality, the synchronic. Like
Rosalind Krauss, who defines a textual grid subtending modernist
painting that applies equally well to the textuality grounding the
unconscious, Riffaterre also speaks of a type of grid, a "hypogram."
"The intertextual unconscious that the reader maps out by bringing to
light, step by step, successive intertextual correspondents of what troubles him in the text may be seen as *a vast hypogram* coextensive to the
text" (emphasis added). Riffaterre explains this synchronic or spatial
figure in terms quite consistent with how Jakobson schematizes language along two axes, one nonnarrative (the paradigmatic and substitu-
tional), the other narrative (the syntagmatic and combinative). He
explains, that is, that there is "a fundamental difference" between the
two verbal layers, the text and the intertext: "the text is narrative, the
intertext is not." This observation indicates that when we cross reference from one to another, it really does not matter where we begin.
Reference from one direction is as valid as that from another.
Moreover, regarding his favorite trope, Riffaterre says, that "syllepsis
works as well whether we read it from the text to the intertext or
reread it from language to literary discourse." Such is the case, he suggests, because time is not a feature of the hypogram: "[T]he intertext,
the verbal unconscious, lies outside of the time dimension no less than
does the unconscious of psychoanalysis" (225). Outside time means in
space, where the intertext of our interpretive code exists synchronically.
Ultimately, Riffaterre's hypogram is just another way of suggesting that
the unconscious is textual and that in texts there is a textual unconscious, and, if we have a code, we know how to interpret *that*. Thus the
next question for Lacanian interpretation perhaps becomes, Which
Lacan?

CHAPTER 2

Which Lacan?

> Broadly speaking, there are two main ways of misrepresenting
> [Lacan]. On the one hand, some commentators present the develop-
> ment of Lacan's thought in terms of dramatic and sudden "epistemo-
> logical breaks" [...] On the other hand, some writers [...] present
> Lacan's work as a single unfolding narrative with no changes of direc-
> tion, as if all the concepts existed from the beginning.
> —Dylan Evans, *An Introductory Dictionary*
> *of Lacanian Psychoanalysis*, x

1

> There is [...] a single ideology of which Lacan provides the theory.
> —Jacques-Alain Miller, *Écrits: A Selection*, 327

Even though Lacan works through dyads, triads, and quaternaries,
squares, circles, and graphs, knots, schemas, and algorithms, the
textuality underlying his theory has given no easy answer to one
major question: Which Lacan? Reduced to form (and, considering the
theoretical issues involved, one could just as readily ask "Which
Freud?") the question becomes, Is there "a" Lacan, or are there
"many" Lacans, one seamless fifty-year career or several well-defined
periods of Lacan? From the beginning, two contradictory views have
prevailed, often, quite unexpectedly, within the views of the same commentator. On the one hand, there is just one; on the other, there are
many. Or, of we want to be a wiseacre, we can say, on the third hand,
there are both. That third way opens up because, as Dylan Evans suggests, both of the others seem likely to misrepresent in important
respects. As with Freudians, with Lacanians there is a powerful clinical
and theoretical motivation to retain both the periods and the overall
unity of the teachings. After all, you do not want to confess that your
guru, though okay now, was merely a crackpot in that other time.
Early on, say up to the 1950s, it was easy enough to adopt the unitary

view. Indeed, the earliest commentators seem to have assumed unity, what David Macey calls "the Final State" or Stephen Michelman "the timeless system" (125). Some, like Jacques-Alain Miller, do take the third hand and have it both ways, a unity but stages within it. In "Lacan's Later Teaching," Miller sees continuity but sees also a "cut" at Seminar 11 ("The Four Fundamental Concepts"), where a second stage begins, and another cut at Seminar 20, "Encore." Still, Miller's basic premise stresses continuity, one based on "logic," Lacan's "devotion to reason. When one is devoted to reason for thirty years," Miller says, "we might suspect that cuts are not significant. It is precisely the continuity that gives his teaching its topological structure" (5).

Those who feel no need to justify unity but happen, like Miller, to see changing states or systems, do so in different ways. Some simply segment the career in a binary fashion, into an early and a late period. Bruce Fink, author of two important introductory studies of Lacan, informs us without argument in the preface of one, "The Lacan I am presenting is not the 'early Lacan'—that is, the clinician of the 1950s—but rather the later Lacan of the middle to late 1960s and the 1970s" (*A Clinical Introduction* xiii). But some do employ an explicit conceptual basis to describe whatever phases they postulate. In "Inventing Lacanian Theory," I used a tropological approach to the emergence of what I characterized as a specifically Lacanian theory (as opposed to a more generically Freudian one). Like others, I address a linguistic Lacan, but not Lacan as a linguistics theorist. Rather, I argue that a truly Lacanian theory emerges in the 1950s, most directly in 1957's "The Agency of the Letter," and has its roots in a metaphor of linguistics, linguistics used as a metaphor. My essay, to complete the confession, is a precursor of the argument in this book that in any Lacanian theory all the deeper roots lie in a textuality beyond linguistics. Roberto Harari, like Fink, also sees more than one phase. Somewhat reflecting a new, postmodern, historical epoch, the new conceptual paradigm shifts from a dialectical one to one based on "vortex." Such shifts, indeed, reflect what Foucault calls "epochal *épistèmés*." The earlier dialectical model, Harari argues, rests on a "substantialist, predicative, and antinomial" logic, the vortical on a logic of the "undecidable." Specifically, Harari suggests that the vortical model, in adapting Gödel's theorem, expresses an epistemological indeterminacy characteristic of a postmodernist science that suggests any truth-value in axioms is ultimately unverifiable. In this vortical paradigm, Lacan uses a rhetorical strategy of paradox to "articulate" "the undecidable." Foreshadowing a critique of Slavoj Žižek's philosophy of paradox (see chapter 8, below), Harari suggests that Lacan's new paradigm "no longer produces meaning." Rather, it "fragments it, obliterates it, does away with it" ("The *Sinthome*" 47). Well, that sure sounds like Lacan.

Okay, so which Lacan of many? Most of those interested in periodizing Lacan's teachings focus on his addition of new concepts or development of older ones. How about the Imaginary Lacan, or the Symbolic Lacan, or, better yet, the Real Lacan? One of the most persuasive models divides the career precisely into phases of the Imaginary, the Symbolic, and the Real. As Dominiek Hoens and Ed Pluth tell us, Lacan himself seems to endorse this periodization: "I began with the Imaginary, I then had to chew on the story of the Symbolic, with this linguistic reference for which I did not find everything that would have suited me, and I finished by putting out for you this famous Real in the very form of the knot" (*Le séminaire* 22, *RSI*; qtd. in Hoens and Pluth 14n4). For their part, and citing more precise dates, Hoens and Pluth report that, indeed, "Lacan's work is often divided into three periods: the Imaginary (1936–1952), the Symbolic (1953–1962), and the Real (1963–1981)" (2). Neat. But too bland? How about the *jouissant* Lacan? Many note a decided break between an early Lacan and a later that occurs when Lacan began to stress *jouissance* as opposed to desire. Sounding a bit like Virginia Woolf on the advent of modernism, Néstor Braunstein says that "the history of psychoanalysis," not merely of Lacanian theory, changed on a day in March 1959 when Lacan introduced the concept of *jouissance*.

> [F]rom that day on it became a term rich in nuances, a term that would get progressively more complicated, multiplying and defining itself until it was transformed into the foundation of a new psychoanalysis: a "notion" without which all else becomes inconsistent. Together with the topological elaborations of the same epoch, the concept of *jouissance* became a fundamental cornerstone of Lacan's thought. ("Desire and *Jouissance*" 102)

But even as he regards introduction of *jouissance* as a cataclysmic break in the teachings, Braunstein nonetheless seems reluctant to divide Lacanian theory into multiples, preferring, like Miller, to regard the theory as an ultimate whole. At the end of his essay announcing that historical fissure in psychoanalysis, Braunstein puts back together the pieces marked "desire" and "*jouissance*."

In part, when Braunstein objects to what he calls a "Manichean split" between a first Lacan and a second, he does so on political (or perhaps simply class) grounds. He resents the "forced choice loaded with hidden agendas" on which some base the split. The choice seems to be, Do you want to be smart or dumb? (Not quite the dilemma posed in Lacan's favorite Jack Benny joke: "Your money or your life?"—"I'm thinking, I'm thinking.") If one chooses the first Lacan of desire and the signifier, one chooses a "primitive" or "archaic" Lacan, and in the choice the chooser becomes equally retarded. If one chooses the second Lacan, one makes the smart choice by choosing "the Lacan of *jouissance* and the *objet a*" and thus "the desired one, a point of arrival that only 'advanced' Lacanians could reach" (114). Politics or class snobbery aside, Braunstein insists that theoretical content must remain paramount. At bottom, going for the unitary Lacan, he takes the two concepts, 'desire' and '*jouissance*,' as two sides of a single ethical issue. Do you choose anxiety or love? These are the two choices "between *jouissance* and desire." And the choice between these "two modes of passage," which sounds easy enough, is one that must be made by both a subject and "the psychoanalytic experience." Counter to his unitary stance here, however, in "Deciphering *Jouissance*" Braunstein seems to place himself among the chosen who do in fact see more than one Lacan, an old and, especially, a new, the latter emerging with the concept of *jouissance* after all. Consistent with what he claims above, he says that "a reading of the 'old' Lacan [. . . is] centered on the spoken word and the signifier" (75). But with the new, it becomes necessary to regard the unconscious as "an intermediary point of connection on the path of deciphering between the system of inscriptions that precede it and the dialogue, with its fullness of meaning, that follows it." In this view, the unconscious seems to become merely a pathway to something more important, as, Braunstein says, "it is an intermediary state in the deciphering of *jouissance*." In fairness to Braunstein, it should be pointed out that the apparently snobbish choice occurred in 1995, before so many others had jumped on the bandwagon, but, in the spirit of solidarity among all Lacanians (no matter how slow), he seems to have disavowed it in the essay of 2003.

Regardless of inconsistencies even within the views of a single commentator, it is clear that a division of Lacan's career into multiple phases is popular. Still, as Hoens and Pluth warn us as they speak of the three phases stressing, respectively, Imaginary or Symbolic or Real, "This periodization is somewhat arbitrary and thus open to debate" (2). That said, they find another way to employ Lacan's registers for periodization: they run the three across a single "recurring problematic" in Lacan. Appearing "throughout Lacan's work," this recurrent issue is that there is always "a certain point where the signifying chain, or the Symbolic as such, could be said to close itself off." In the different phases, this point must be examined within the context of the particular register appropriate to the phase. In the "early work," for instance, this point of closure, considered "in terms of the Imaginary," "would seem to be the function of the sign." Here, the sign, in contradistinction to the signifier, "would be Imaginary insofar as it does not depend upon a reference to other signs in the way that a signifier depends upon other signifiers." In turn, this point of closure is subjected to the terms of Symbolic and Real, as well as the *sinthome*. They suggest, for example, that "the notion of the Real was a solution to a theoretical problem connected to the Symbolic, and [...that] the *sinthome* is a reopening of the [recurrent] problem and at the same time a new answer to it" (14n6). Like Lacan's use of *jouissance*, a term that typically remains untranslated but means something like (but also vastly more than) "enjoyment" of a sexual or bodily nature, *sinthome* is a term that generally remains italicized in English and untranslated because, though it connotes "symptom," Lacan intends for it to add a considerable conceptual heft to it. On that "recurring problematic," Hoens and Pluth suggest that, conceptually, *sinthome* develops a sense beyond "the line of thinking" associated with the three original registers. "The *sinthome* represents a further development," they suggest, because although it "seems to be a point where the symbolizations of the Symbolic come to a stop," this point itself is neither Symbolic, Imaginary, nor Real. For them, then, *sinthome* functions to suggest there indeed is "a split in the late Lacan," one they would locate in 1975, when Lacan introduced the term itself. With *sinthome*, they conclude, "Lacan is ultimately led to think of an element that does not fit neatly into any of the three orders involved in his teaching prior to 1975. This is why it is legitimate to speak of a split in Lacan's last period, corresponding to the thought of the *sinthome*" (2). But like other commentators, Hoens and Pluth both giveth and taketh away. Let us not adopt a multiple Lacan just yet. Despite their claims regarding a split within the late work, they still seem to prefer to think of Lacan in rather unitary terms, of Lacan as "one" rather than "many." Their rationale for waffling on "many" is simply that whatever split or gap or break *sinthome* introduces, it still addresses that "recurrent problematic" and, moreover, still focuses on "Lacan's teaching concerning the Symbolic order" (3). Because the split, they insist, "specifically concerns the Symbolic" (2), it may not be a split at all. Oh, okay.

How about the late Lacan? After all, he is dead. Of late, the furor over which Lacan focuses on a "late"—or, in some circles, a "final"—Lacan, but, of course, we care only because the teachings are still very much alive. Illustrating how confusing periodizing can be, this Lacan may commence anywhere from 1959–1960 (Seminar 7, *The Ethics of*

Psychoanalysis), or 1962 ("Kant with Sade"), or 1964 (Seminar 11, *The Four Fundamental Concepts of Psychoanalysis*) to 1971–1972 (Seminar 19, *Ou pire*), or 1972–1973 (Seminar 20, *Encore*), or even, as we have seen, 1975–1976 (Seminar 23, *Le sinthome*). Most designations of a late Lacan, wherever that may begin, intend only to indicate that his theory undergoes an epistemological shift of considerable consequence somewhere along that time line between 1959 and 1975, but, given the remarkable fluidity of the demarcations, there is little interest in positing precisely dated earlier periods. "Early" is everything back to medical school. By his death, Lacan was indubitably late. In English, two recent books tout a final Lacan beginning in 1975 at Seminar 23 (Lacan's "*Séminaire*," as he called it, ended at 27, appropriately named "Dissolution," in 1980, about a year before he died, in September, 1981). Both books appeared in 2002, but because it had appeared in Argentina in Spanish in 1995, pride of place belongs to Roberto Harari's *How James Joyce Made His Name: A Reading of the Final Lacan*. In the book, on 1975–1976's Seminar 23, Harari (who is Argentine) argues strongly for the seminar's importance in offering a distinctly new turn in Lacan's thought. For one thing, Harari says, it is "probably the last moment in the whole of Lacan's teaching where a rigorous internal unity is emphasized. What emerges there is a coherent reconceptualization of many themes that relate [...] to the clinical practice of psychoanalysis." For another, Harari points out, this seminar also belongs to a long-standing tradition in psychoanalysis, a "turn to art, in particular to literature, the aesthetic domain that is closest to the analytic experience" (*How James Joyce* 1).

The second book, also addressing Seminar 23, is *Re-Inventing the Symptom*, a collection of essays (including one by Harari), edited by Luke Thurston. Thurston's collection seems to be founded on Harari's premise that a final Lacan emanates from the notion of the *sinthome*. Indeed, Thurston's title bears a subtitle, "Essays on the Final Lacan," that virtually repeats the title of Harari's book. Whatever the changes wrought in Lacanian theory by the concept of the '*sinthome*,' a "principal reason" for producing the collection of essays is essentially political. In a shot at Miller, who controls Lacan's copyrights, Thurston argues that because of "the notorious restrictions that have been placed upon publication and translation," Seminar 23 is rather inaccessible to Anglo-American readers. Beyond that, however, the essays are meant, he says, to "unravel some of [the seminar's] enigmas and shed light on its central questions" (xiii). But not surprisingly, given all the backing and filling regarding periodization we have seen already, Thurston candidly admits that there is considerable controversy, especially in France, regarding whether in fact that seminar contributes anything worthwhile to Lacanian thought. "The last years of the famous psychoanalyst's teaching," he says, "have aroused widely divergent responses among his French interpreters." While some "have eulogized this period as his grand finale—his work on the topology of knots and his new conception of writing, inspired by Joyce, amounting to a crucial *alethia* ["unveiling"] that allows us to re-think the whole course of Lacanian theory," he says, "others have seen in these last theoretical adventures merely signs of an old man's decline, symptoms, we might say, of terminal anecdotage (xiii–xiv)."

Perhaps still more oddly, not every author in Thurston's collection is willing to contend that the notion of *sinthome* in the seminar offers a significant epistemological break in Lacan's teaching. As we have seen, Hoens and Pluth, whose essay opens Thurston's volume, come down on the side of Lacanian continuity rather than rupture. They insist "that the concept of the *sinthome* is present in all but name in Lacan's work before 1975, and that in fact it corresponds to a motif present throughout Lacan's teaching" (1). Further, they argue, "The difference between [ways of writing symptom or *sinthome*] appears only from a chronological point of view: the new way of writing the symptom is perhaps a reflection of a different understanding of what was always univocally called 'symptom,' and is [. . .] founded on a more radical way of conceiving the nature of the signifier's relation to the Symbolic" (2). Hoens and Pluth are not alone. In an essay focusing on one by Lacan called "Lituraterre" (1971), Dany Nobus likewise makes a case for continuity and evolution, as opposed to rupture, in Lacan's thought. But editor Thurston, for his part, avers, "If, for Dany Nobus, the idea of theoretical rupture and discontinuity in Lacan is ultimately implausible, there remains, as several of the essays make clear, the risk that in our retrospective search for continuity and consistency, we succeed in effacing nothing so much as whatever is innovative or unexpected, whatever fails to conform to our familiar, already-understood Lacan." Ah, the pain of an editor who can not get his troops to follow their marching orders. In need of authoritative support for claims regarding the cataclysmic importance of Seminar 23, Thurston turns to a Lacanian who, these days, is far and away the most authoritative one of all. "Of the late Seminars," offers Thurston, "*Le sinthome* in particular has been singled out as the introduction of an element radically *at odds* with the predominant emphases of Lacan's teaching—and by no less influential a critic than Slavoj Žižek" (xiv).

2

[Lacan] considers that his work, the work associated with his name, began in 1952: what came before counted in his mind as his "antecedents." He doesn't thereby cancel out what came before, but stresses a cut in his own intellectual development that occurred around 1952–1953.

—Jacques-Alain Miller, "An Introduction to Seminars I and II (I)," 4

Virtually from the start of his career, Žižek has insisted there are indeed two Lacans, an early one and a later. In a preface to Žižek's first book in English, *The Sublime Object of Ideology* (1989), Ernesto Laclau, shifting debate away from "Lacans" toward "Lacanians," emphasizes interpreters of Lacanian theory more than theory itself. Locating Žižek's book in a broader historical context, Laclau points to "generations" of French Lacanians. "On the one hand," Laclau says, there is "the 'old school' or first generation of Lacanians." Including Octave and Maud Mannoni, Serge Leclaire, and Moustafa Safouan, among others, they "emphasize clinical problems and the crucial role of the *symbolic* in the psychoanalytic process." They base their approach, Laclau suggest, "on Lacan's writing in the 1950s, the era of high structuralism, in which the Imaginary register is presented as a series of variants that must be referred to a stable symbolic matrix." On the other hand, a "younger generation," he suggests, includes Michel Silvestre, Alain Grosrichard, and others, all "led" by Jacques-Alain Miller. Lacan's son-in-law, Miller married Lacan's daughter Judith and in the mid-1980s became the main litigant in a contentious legal battle over "ownership" of Lacan's writings, seminar presentations, and accounts of them. Miller has borne the brunt of hostility, both French and Anglo-American, over the slow pace, about which Luke Thurston complains, of "authorized" publication and translation of Lacan's "texts" (the provenance of which is inevitably disputed because most of them emerge from public oral presentations and thus have found life in many unauthorized or fugitive publications). Besides hostility over publication as such, other hostility has been directed toward Miller because he has been perhaps the main proponent of a formalized Lacanian theory, one represented in graphs, grids, schemas, formulas, one, indeed, very consistent with my textual Lacan. Laclau, avoiding any mention of the controversy, simply remarks that this younger generation, with Miller at its head, "has attempted to formalize Lacanian theory, pointing out the distinctions between the different stages of his teaching, and placing an accent on the theoretical importance of the last stage." But according to Laclau, this last stage is based not on *jouissance* or *sinthome*. Rather, in it "a central role is granted to the notion of the Real as that which resists symbolization" (x).

There is no doubt that Žižek allies himself with this second generation. Like his French cohort, he too fell under the tutelage of Miller, in the early 1980s in Paris. His time with Miller, Žižek admits, "was my big formative experience." Miller was—is—a great teacher, Žižek avers, adding, "[w]hatever people think about" him, as if acknowledging the hostility of folks such as Thurston. "He has this absolutely miraculous capacity for explication: you have a page of Lacan which appears to you totally incomprehensible, then you talk with him and it is not only that you understand, but it is totally transparent to you, and you think 'my God, how is it that I didn't get it, it is so clear?' So I must say this quite openly that my Lacan is Miller's Lacan. Prior to Miller I didn't really understand Lacan, and this was for me a great time of education" (*Conversations* 34). What this all means, essentially, is that while Žižek is well aware of the early Lacan, only the later one much interests him. Moreover, perhaps to cloak a difference from Miller, who is regarded as a one-Lacan man, neither is he particularly consistent in placing the epistemological break between the two Lacans. Indeed, it is probably because of Žižek, whose influence since 1989's *Sublime Object of Ideology* has been immense, that there is so little interest in pinpointing absolutely the break between early and late within that time line from 1959–1960 to 1975–1976. Essentially, this imprecision, if it is appropriate so to term it, simply indicates that, yes, there is an early Lacan, the one we see emerging from the 1930s through the late 1950s. And, yes, there is the rest of the career. Practically speaking, for Anglo-American Lacanians, the early Lacan was canonized in 1977 in the publication of "a selection" of Lacan's massive *Écrits*, published in 1966. But it also seems fair to suggest that, for Laclau's "old" generation of Francophone Lacanians as well, *Écrits* likewise made canonical the early Lacan, for while some twelve of the twenty-four pieces in it came after 1957, most of these (all dated 1966) are merely prefaces or postscripts to more substantial writings from the 1930s, 1940s, and 1950s. Indeed, only one piece in the volume has significantly affected definition of a late Lacan, and that is 1962's "Kant with Sade," to which Žižek frequently adverts.

No very precise pinpointing of an epistemological break has been necessary for Miller or Žižek and his cohort of Slovenian Lacanians. These latter include Mladen Dolar, Alenka Zupančič, and Renata Salecl (who was once married to Žižek). More effectively in Anglo-American circles than Miller (who publishes in English, but not frequently), Žižek has insisted for a decade or more that Lacanians must distinguish between a Lacan he calls either "old" or "early" and one he calls either "new" or "late." Sometimes, when speaking of Lacanians, usually Americans, who are a bit slow in their uptake of the late Lacan, he will call their Lacan the one of "the current understanding." Without a doubt, since the mid-1990s or so, Žižek's case for a better understanding of a late Lacan has been the most widely accepted by Anglo-American scholars practicing Lacanian literary and cultural interpretation. Žižek argues for a shift from early-old to late-new in several ways. In one, he argues that the shift revolves around a perception that Lacan changed his views on the relative importance of desire versus drive (and related terms such as *jouissance*, *fantasy*, and *sinthome*). Žižek argues, indeed, that the laggardly "current understanding" among those Lacanians still stuck in the 1950s "always reduces Lacan to desire, prohibition, oedipalization, so that Lacan is the Lacan of desire" and a subject resistant "toward the drives." Philosophically, he says, the old versus the new is "an unending battle" ("Interview" 148) between desire's idealism (it is all in the mind) and drive's materialism (it is all in the body). At stake in the shift from the early to the late, the old to the new Lacan, and thus from desire to drive is a view of the subject and the psycho-narratives in which it is likely to participate.

Žižek and Renata Salecl once seemingly spoke with one voice, though I have no idea whether they now even speak to each other. But, whatever the case, Salecl joined Žižek to speak to interviewers, and, there, it is she who does the heavy lifting on the differences between desire and drive. "A very simple distinction," she says, "would be that desire," oriented to the Oedipus and the Symbolic order, "is primarily intersubjective," a relation of subject to subject emphasized in Lacan's formula that the subject is an other. But another distinction, founded on Lacan's dictum that desire is a metonymy, is that one cannot satisfy desire. "Desire means that the subject goes from one [metonymic] object to another and never finds the one that would satisfy him or her." By contrast to what happens with desire, Salecl says, in the drive "intersubjectivity somehow gets lost." Though it does not disappear, drive is left behind in the process of oedipalization. "Drive is what remains," Salecl says, "when the subject is submitted to the symbolic; it remains as a kind of pressure or force that constantly undermines any point of stability that the subject tries to make in relation to the social symbolic order." As a remainder (but not as the object a), drive connects not to enjoyment but to *jouissance*. Drive, Salecl says, "is the very link to the notion of *jouissance*: the boundless enjoyment, the painful

enjoyment that very much differs from desire." Whereas desire by definition remains unsatisfiable (and so becomes the cherished aim of
advertising), drive *is* satisfiable, for it has a particular object or objective. "Drive is primarily a circulation around the object, a circulation
which with Lacan mostly means that there is a deadly pressure to
which the subject is constantly submitted without wanting to be." For
social life, life within the structures of the Symbolic, desire is more salu-
brious than drive to the welfare of the subject. "The whole logic of
desire," Salecl insists, "is a kind of liberation from [drive's] pressure.
When the subject falls into desire, somehow the pressure of drive is less
present. So desire for Lacan is in some ways a better thing than drive."
In summation, Salecl suggest this: "Drive involves the satisfaction that
the subject gets, but does not want to get. Desire is the endless logic of
dissatisfaction which produces as a side effect a satisfaction, but a satisfaction that is less deadly than the satisfaction of the drive. For Lacan
every drive is a death drive and has this kind of deadly element"
("Interview" 147).

Žižek and Salecl both speak about how differences between desire
and drive have led American Lacanians more readily to the old than to
the new Lacan. Salecl, for instance, suggests that the stress on desire
found in the old Lacan is especially American not simply because
American Lacanians have emphasized Lacan's early writings (first made
widely available in English, as we know, in 1977's *Écrits: A Selection*)
but also because Americans resist drive itself. Another reason for
American acceptance of the early theory, stressing the socialization of
the subject within the Symbolic order, was its amenability to cultural
critique. "Maybe there is an inner logic here," says Salecl; whereas "the
Lacan of desire offers a much better fit for [American] cultural critics,
the late Lacan, the Lacan of drives, gives less of a ground from which
one can do traditional cultural criticism" (147–48). Likewise, the late
theory provided Americans no explicit ethical stance. "In particular,"
Salecl suggests, "the late Lacan does not give any guidance for what
kind of a social theory or ethical theory you could produce." In
America, for these and other reasons, "[t]here was a desire not to pick
up drive in the reception of Lacan." Moreover, early Lacan is also especially compatible to American scholars and psychotherapists because its
psycho-narratives, stressing desire, yield pragmatically positive out-
comes. That stress generates stories with essentially happy endings in
which the subject, the hero or protagonist in fiction as well as in "life"
and psychotherapy, accommodates to the big Other of the Symbolic
order. As Žižek says, "Basically, the problematic of desire is ultimately
the problematic of intersubjectivity, recognition, the symbolic order,

language, subject, and so on." This problematic creates a subject who desires to please the other. "If we remain within the domain of desire," Žižek says, "then the ultimate ethical, political horizon is that of what Lacan refers to as *che vuoi*?: what does the Other want from me, what am I for the Other?" In this case, Žižek suggests, psychoanalysis is charged to address those fantasies by which the subject covers a more radical, more threatening otherness. "With this Lacan," he says, "the aim of psychoanalysis" not only "is to break through fantasies" but also "to open [the subject] to that gap of the radical otherness that is concealed by fantasies" (148).

Although Žižek often seems rather fluid in pinpointing a precise moment for the break between old and new, early and late, Lacan of desire and Lacan of drive, when he does so he is likely to argue that it occurs between 1959 and 1962, between Seminar 7, *The Ethics of Psychoanalysis*, and "Kant *avec* Sade." For Žižek, the prime difference between early Lacan and late lies in a different "logic." As the narratives implied in Salecl's discussion of desire and drive suggest, the "logic" of the later Lacan is darker, more tragic than that of the earlier favored by Americans. The logic of desire yields psycho-narratives of success, integration, assimilation to the Symbolic order. Standing on the side of Eros, the side of the Freudian life drive, desire participates readily in oedipal stories, those Lacan in "The Neurotic's Individual Myth" associates with the archetypally Freudian plot of Oedipus. The logic of the late Lacan is one Žižek identifies with Freud's Thanatos and, as Lacan also suggests in the same essay, yields stories of Narcissistic inversion. In a different interview, Žižek tells Peter Canning that when "Lacan shifts [from...] pure desire, where every identification with *jouissance* means betraying desire," everything changes. With this shift, Žižek says, "the only authentic thing to do is to identify with your symptom." With desire paramount, subjects "betray" their drives. With drive paramount, however, subjects are oriented toward the death drive. "In other words, the only true desire is the death drive, the death drive precisely as accepting your symptom" ("Sublime Theorist" 88).

More and more, Žižek seems to have adopted a late Lacan that is in fact somewhat later than the one beginning in 1959 or 1962. This late-late Lacan, we might say, emerges (as Harari, Thurston, and others would agree) with Lacan's reinterpretation or reinscription of symptom in *sinthome*. Interest in *sinthome* replaces emphasis on drive to define the late-late, the "ultimate" Lacan. If, like Nobus, we want to stress continuity as opposed to rupture, then this is the Lacan of symptom-cum-*sinthome* who, emerging, as does Žižek's merely late Lacan, between *The Ethics of Psychoanalysis* and "Kant with Sade," dominates the *séminaire* beginning with 1960–1961's Seminar 8, *Le trans-fert*, becomes especially evident in 1964's 11, *The Four Fundamental Concepts of Psychoanalysis*, and 1972–1973's 20, *Encore* (from which is taken most of the material in the very influential *Feminine Sexuality: Jacques Lacan and* l'école freudienne), and eventuates, climactically, in Seminar 22, *RSI*, where the term is introduced, and in Seminar 23, *Le sinthome*, where the concept of 'symptom' itself underwent such a rad-ical transformation that Lacan made *sinthome* a fourth register, one, as I suggested in the previous chapter, that might be regarded as inevitable given how frequently Lacan's structures evolve toward sets of four.

Indeed, on the side of continuity, Žižek himself suggests that, even as early as his reading of *Antigone* in *The Ethics of Psychoanalysis*, one can detect Lacan making a new distinction between symptom, on the one hand, and fantasy, on the other. "For the Lacan of the identifica-tion with the symptom, desire as such is a compromise. The logic of desire is that you desire in order to avoid your symptom." More pre-cisely, according to Žižek, Lacan changes the emphasis in 1960's "The Subversion of the Subject and the Dialectic of Desire in the Freudian Unconscious." There, says Žižek, "It's the crucial formula of the text, and it's a radical reversal of what he was saying a few months before. He says desire is a defense against *jouissance*. [...] It's not that *jouis-sance* is a regression or a kind of coagulation that hinders or blocks the dialectic of desire, it's that desire as such is a defense against *jouis-sance*." To illustrate this point, Žižek turns to Lacan's analysis of Antigone. Indeed, Lacan's views of her actually traverse the shift from early to later theory. In *The Ethics* seminar, it seems Lacan places her largely on the side of desire, not drive. There, Žižek contends, "Antigone is still basically pure desire. By accomplishing the terrible step beyond, into the void, into Até (divine blindness), she becomes pure desire." But when Lacan comments on Antigone in his theory after *The Ethics* and "Kant *avec* Sade," says Žižek, "she is not desire—she accepts the death drive, understood precisely as the identification with your symptom, opposed to desire." But as Žižek pushes Lacan's own reading toward the later theory, he stresses the ambiguity of Antigone's relation to the Symbolic. On the one hand, Žižek says, "One way to read Antigone is to see her as suspending the big Other as embodied in social power. On the other hand, she can also be read, and this is how Lacan still reads her in *The Ethics*, as identifying her desire with the desire of the big Other." This identification, Žižek suggests, lies in Antigone's resolving to perform the burial ritual demanded by a Symbolic that for her supercedes the orders of a mere king. It is her insistence on ritual that guarantees her death. "Why does she sacrifice her life? Because she basically says: my desire, my only desire, is that ritual must be performed. That is to say, [it is] the desire of symbolic integration, of the big Other" ("Sublime Theorist" 88).

But Žižek contends further that the break between old Lacan and new becomes visible in the analyst's reading of several concepts—*objet petit a*, the two deaths, and the like—that Žižek himself says he shall elucidate in articles forthcoming at the time the interview with Canning was published in 1993 (not only focusing on a break in Lacan's career, these articles represent a stage—early?—of Žižek's work that evolved into some dozen books comprising a majority of Žižek's twenty or more books to date). "For example, who is the *objet a* in *The Ethics*? Lacan still claims that, in the perverse scenario, the victim is the *objet a*. When he speaks of the 'between the two deaths,' he uses the miracle of Sadean victims as his example. You can torture them but they always remain beautiful. Then, suddenly, in 'Kant *avec* Sade,' it's the executioner who takes the place of the object. The victim is the S barré, the subject." Lacan, Žižek insists, "totally shifts the formula." Moreover, Žižek contends that in psychoanalysis itself, when subjects (analysands) traverse their fundamental fantasies and go through their divisions (the very split within subjectivity itself), they enter a domain of *jouissance* and themselves become objects. The subject *becomes* object when it merges with its drive. While it is possible to argue that Antigone herself makes that move into *jouissance*, the *other* desire, Žižek puts Lacan's most explicit, if "mysterious," discussion of these notions in 1964's *Four Fundamental Concepts of Psychoanalysis*.[1] In that seminar, Žižek argues, Lacan

> says that when you go through fantasy, *la traversée du fantasme*, you lose desire, you become pure drive. Again, when people talk about the truth of desire, they simply overlook that. In *The Four Fundamental Concepts*, Lacan defines the final, concluding moment of analysis as the one when you step out, when you don't have desire any more, in this sense. You become the being of the drive; you pass from the side of the divided subject to the side of the object. (89)

In sum, Žižek believes that the later Lacan will become the "ultimate Lacan" and bring along a different ethics. "[W]ith the Lacan of the drives," he says, "you get another ethical attitude." It is, he suggests, both here and in "The Spectre of Ideology," an ethics "beyond or beneath [the] horizon of spectrality" found in Derrida and a notion Žižek remarks in Levinas's concept of God as radical alterity. "All those topics that are identified with the popular reception of Lacan," he says in that interview shared with Salecl, are "suspended with reference to [the] more radical dimension [...] of drive. If desire is the desire of the Other, drive is not the drive of the other. This apparently insignificant shift from desire to drive involves the radical reshuffling, transformation of the most fundamental ethical, political, philosophical choices" ("Interview" 148).

3

> With the passage of time, I learned that I could say a little more [...]
> And then I realized that what constituted my course was a sort of "I
> don't want to know anything about it."
> —Jacques Lacan, *Encore*, 1.

Practically speaking, on the question, Which Lacan? can there be an end to the debate? Can Lacan himself end it for us? It is all well and good to consider what Lacanians might think about which Lacan, about which Lacan is *the* Lacan. What about Lacan himself? What, presumably, might he have thought? Which "Lacan" would he have chosen in a circumstance where choice might have been at stake? His comment, above—"I don't want to know anything about it"—suggests he would rather not be asked. There is, of course, an occasion where he *might* have answered. "A few months ago," Lacan said in the mid-1970s, "I examined someone who had been labeled a Freudian psychosis. Today we have seen a 'Lacanian' psychosis" ("Lacanian" 41). But Lacanian early or late? The deictic "today" refers to a moment during his seminar of 1975–1976. It is well into a period when Lacan might have invoked a late mode of analysis. But if we look at his presentation of this case of psychosis, it will become quite clear that Lacan's analysis, if not the patient's psychosis, is oriented a bit more toward early than late. Go figure, right?

To protect the identity of the patient in question, the translation calls him "Gérard Primeau." The translation comes from a transcript of an interview Lacan had with Primeau. Jacques-Alain Miller was an observer at this presentation and describes how Lacan typically conducted such interviews: "For one or two hours [the patient] will be heard, questioned, sounded, maneuvered, and finally sized up" ("Teachings" 42). Primeau, we are told, was born in 1948, the only child of a wealthy family in which the father was often away on business. He was of obvious intelligence, with a mathematical talent recognized in his youth. He was twenty-seven or twenty-eight when Lacan interviewed him during the term of Seminar 23, *Le sinthome*, in 1975–1976. He had previously been diagnosed as suffering paranoid delusions (symptoms of which, indeed, appear in the transcription). As well, he had attempted suicide, perhaps more than once, had delusions of heroically saving France from "the Fascists," and expressed anxieties about the small size of his penis. He had felt himself, psychologically, to be a woman, had engaged in sex with both men and women, and believed that he was capable of telepathy. Although interviewed during the very moment of the seminar in which Lacan of the *sinthome*—the late, even late-late Lacan—introduced himself, the patient, in 1966, when he was eighteen, had, as he tells Lacan, "tried" to read the just published *Écrits* and is thus conscious enough of concepts in Lacanian theory to try to present himself in those terms ("Lacanian" 28). Though on this matter Lacan makes no judgment, exhibiting only a wry amusement at the irony of the situation, Miller contends that Primeau's knowledge of *Écrits* "took nothing away from the authenticity of his experience" ("Teachings" 49). Nor should it. For, plainly, by the same token, educated patients of a Freudian practitioner would surely have knowledge enough of Freudian theory to present themselves as having a Freudian pathology. But what sort of Lacanian theory does Lacan himself present?

Since in his dialogue with Primeau Lacan does less than Primeau himself to provide us with a Lacanian code, it may well be that it is left to the patient to answer our question, Which Lacan? While Lacan adds that this psychosis is one "very clearly marked" as Lacanian by the presence of "imposed speeches" and by "the imaginary, the symbolic, and the real," he offers little more than that. The patient, however, is quite articulate on his problems with language and the cognitive registers, particularly the Real and the Imaginary (called by Primeau "the imaginative"):

> There is a very simple language that I use in everyday life, and there is on the other hand a language [that] has an imaginative influence, where I disconnect the people around me from the real. That is the most important. My imagination creates an other world, a world [that] would have a sense [that] is equivalent to the sense of the world that is called real, but which would be completely disjoined. The two worlds would be completely disjoined. On the other hand, these imposed sentences, to the extent that they emerge sometimes to go and aggress a person, are bridges between the imaginative world and the world that is called real.

In responses such as this one, Primeau is so aware of his "applying" Lacanian theory to his own case that, he says, he is "afraid of making a mistake" ("Lacanian" 22).

In terms of a Lacanian intertextual code, that which Michael Riffaterre might have called a "vast hypogram," the several features that make the psychosis seem patently Lacanian will seem more distinctly early Lacan than late, almost more Freudian than Lacanian in that overtly oedipal issues abound. Besides the subject's investment in language and the cognitive registers, the most significant feature lies in his relation to "the Other" and all it entails: castration anxieties, truncation of oedipal resolution, problems of gender identity, foreclosure of the Name of the Father, and the like. The pathology in the case is manifested principally in Primeau's very problematic relation to language, the Other found in speech and emanating from language. Miller, not Lacan, describes Primeau's pathology:

> When the slight separation of the enunciation from itself is amplified until it engenders individualized and thematized voices that appear in the real, when the subject feels himself transpierced by bursts of messages, by a language that speaks of itself, when he feels himself spied on in his inner core and subjected to injunctions or inhibitions whose productions he cannot annex, we then have the great 'xenophobia' that Lacan founded in the field of language with his matheme of the Other. ("Teachings" 48)

While Lacan suggests that subjects are born into a language that in effect creates them *as* subjects, "normal" subjects—by virtue of their integration of the three cognitive registers (Real, Imaginary, Symbolic)—can participate in ordinary speech and situate themselves among those registers. Because psychotics often fail in these ordinary activities, language for them, in their psychotic moments or episodes, takes on a "reality"—becoming those "thematized voices that appear in the real"—it will not have for normal subjects. For instance, Primeau suggests to Lacan that his imposed sentences provide "a kind of minitheater" where he watches them "at the same time [as] the creator and the director" ("Lacanian" 23). "It's a dream, a kind of waking dream, a permanent dream" (22). He concedes, "All speech has the force of law, all speech is signifying," but he also admits that "apparently at first [the imposed sentences] do not have a purely rational sense" (23). Besides his taking as real the world created by his imposed language, Primeau seems also to take literally elements of his very name: Gérard Primeau. For Lacan (indeed, the subject regards himself as performing "for" Lacan), the patient, operating along metaphoric and metonymic axes, "decomposes" the name into parts—*Gérard* becomes "*Geai*, a bird, *Rare*, rareness"—and invests them with meaning in the Real (20).

It is from such a decomposition that Primeau generates one of his obsessions. Thus one metaphoric theme among his "thematized voices," one that produces for him various metonymic associations, involves birds. Whereas Lacan refers to him as a "rare jay," the patient thinks in terms of bluebirds (though perhaps blue jays) and does so specifically when referring to those delusional—"imposed"—utterances. Of this delusional speech, the patient admits, "I do not know how it comes, imposes itself on my brain. It comes all at once." And then, seemingly on cue, this voice appears, accusing Primeau himself: "*You killed the bluebird. It's an anarchic system*" (20).

Later in the interview, his imposed speech inverts the threat, making Primeau a victim: "*The bluebirds. They want to get hold of me, they want to kill me*" (31). To American readers of a certain age, the way this voice suddenly intrudes will remind of similarly intrusive voices in the comedy of Jonathan Winters or, more recently, Robin Williams. But the difference is that in the comedy, we—and Winters and Williams—know that the voices are drawn, deliberately, from a domain nearly unconscious, and we know as well how they are related to our ordinary, Imaginary, circumstances in a real world. Moreover, though Winters was famously in analysis, the comics in performance can control the "emergence." Although Lacan's patient is aware that his intrusive speech comes from his unconscious (see 20), he has no control over it. The voices simply appear, "imposed," an "emergence" from a realm beyond his cognitive control, all because, in Lacan's terms, he has foreclosed the regulatory function in the Symbolic.

What he has foreclosed, of course, is a normal relation to the Other of the unconscious, the one that comes with proper repression in resolution of the Oedipus complex. When a subject has not resolved his oedipal problems, speech admits to no limits, no boundaries. If Primeau's imposed speech suggests delusions, then play upon that surname suggests yet more. When the patient transforms *Primeau* into *Prime Au* (20), regarding himself as primal, a singularity, we see not just delusions at work but delusions of grandeur. Investing his names, which belong in the Symbolic, with "Real" significance, he links both his Christian name and his surname to his notions of personal grandeur. With the Christian, he places the *geai rare* "in the imaginative world" he himself understands as belonging to Lacan's Imaginary register, but with his surname he invokes the locus of the Other in the register of the Symbolic. He starts from his name in the real: "The Gérard Primeau is the world commonly called real." Then he says that "in the imaginative world, I am *Geai rare prime au.*" Finally, he takes a piece of the deconstructed name and projects it into an authority in the Symbolic. From his word *Prime*, "which is the first," he says, he posits himself as "the one which codifies, which has force." In his delusion, it is he, not the father, who sets down the law. His delusional sense of himself as codifier, giver of law, source of signification or at least of signifiers, relates to two aspects of his psychosis. On the one hand, as the *prime one*, he sees himself as "the solitary center of a solitary circle," "the solitary center, a kind of god, the demiurge of a solitary circle." But on the other, because "this world is walled in, and [he] cannot make it pass into everyday reality," he must try to transform it into such a reality through autoerotic fantasy, through "everything which masturbates," he says, or, better—"correcting" himself— through activities "at the level of the interior dream" (23).

"Early" Lacan, as Miller reminds us, is still closely connected to the "Freudian Field." As early as 1951–1952, Lacan had offered a seminar on Freud's Dora case, following it in 1952–1953 with another on Freud's Wolf Man. These led, in 1953–1954, to Lacan's inaugurating the "official" (transcribed) seminar on the premise that he was merely "returning to Freud" by explicating for his auditors specific texts of the Viennese. "From 1953 to 1963," Miller says, "Lacan was reading Freud in his seminars, at the rate of one or two texts per year. For twelve years he presented himself as but a careful reader of Freud" ("Introduction" 6), dropping the practice only in 1964 with Seminar 11, which came to be called "The Four Fundamental Concepts of Psycho-Analysis." Thus it is not surprising that early Lacan appears more Freudian, especially in its oedipal orientation, than Lacanian. Primeau's clinical problems fit early Lacan because they arise largely, if not exclusively, from an oedipal failure. Whatever else might trouble him, it is the "family romance" located in the oedipal passage that manifests much of his pathology. As the "only son" ("prime one"?), he would be expected to propagate the father's name and authority. But despite his intellectual gifts, he dropped out of *maths superieures* just two months after starting because of his romantic "problem with a girl," one the translation, for privacy and symptomatic reasons, dubs "Hélène Pigeon." But his problem is not the girl as such but that of the oedipal resolution and his assumption of gender identity. Instead of desiring the mother and identifying with the father, the patient identifies with the mother and unwittingly desires the father. This is to say, in desiring to *be* the mother and *have* the father, he exhibits a very ambivalent sexual identification. Apparently, however, even as he desires to be his mother, he at the same time fears—or thinks that he should fear—that desire. To displace the fear, he suggests that, like the imposed speech, identification with the mother comes to him from outside and without his bidding. Still, by his assuming the mother's gendered role and thereby failing to achieve an ordinary oedipal relation to the father and the sense of law or limits or boundaries attendant upon it by submission to "the No of the Father," he becomes a being left with no protective boundaries. Thus, penetrated from without, Primeau thinks surely that along with her gender he absorbs his mother's anxiety, absorbed by osmosis or contagion, by sheer contiguity: "She was anxious, her mental state was contagious," he says. "It is not a virus but concerns the environment. Thus I was brought up by this mother, very anxious, hypersensitive, exposed to family fights with my father when he came home for the weekend. The atmosphere was tense and anxiety-provoking. I think that by osmosis I myself was very anxious" (25).

Branding his psychosis as particularly Lacanian is Primeau's persistently dysfunctional experience of language. This results from his foreclosure of the paternal function. Of the problems, one is simply Primeau's imagining that he can communicate telepathically. It seems through telepathy that he communicates with various figures of his "imagination," figures Lacan would regard as part of his dialectic of the Imaginary. Not surprisingly, given his intellectual pretensions, many of those Imaginary figures with whom he identifies and "communicates" are poets or philosophers. He believes in metempsychosis—transmigration of souls—and believed at one time he was a reincarnation of Nietzsche, at another of Artaud. He identifies with Artaud because, Primeau explains, the writer died early in the same year, 1948, in which the patient was born. Primeau also communicates with public figures who appear on radio shows. Apart from the metempsychosis, it is figures of the airwaves to whom, with a prowess he carefully distinguishes from *clairvoyance* (35), he communicates in his flights of telepathy. He believes thoughts emitted from him can be heard by others who are themselves speaking on the radio. To illustrate for Lacan this power of his thought, he tells two brief anecdotes.

> There was a program called "Radioscopie." I was reflecting...[sic] They talked for a moment, and they laughed together as though they understood something, and I was talking, I no longer remember what I was saying, but finally, they said, "That is what I want to say to an anonymous

poet." It wasn't exactly that, it was an indifference [that] is not indifferent; indifference did not exist. They spoke of an anonymous poet.

Of course, that anonymous poet they address he believes to be himself. The second anecdote also refers to "Radioscopie." While his delusion of power to broadcast over the airwaves remains the same, this time one of the motifs is connected to his grandiosity as "rare bird."

> Another time on "Radioscopie" there was another guest who was Roger Fressoz, the editor of *Canard Enchaîné*. It was after my suicide attempt. Just at the end of the interview they were talking of anticlericalism, and I said "Roger Fressoz is a [female] saint." They burst out laughing, both of them, on the radio, in a way that had no relation with what they were saying, and I heard, somewhat softer, "He could work at *Canard Enchaîné*." (36)

Again, the "He" Gérard takes to be himself. Of Lacan, nonetheless, Gérard is sensible enough to ask questions about such behavior and thought processes. "Is that the pure fruit of my imagination, or did they really hear me?" he asks. "Were they both receptor telepaths, or is it pure imagination, a creation?" (37). But in the transcription of his speech, it seems evident that he remains convinced, just as he originally had thought, that he can—and did—make contact through the airwaves with those personalities.

While the assumption of telepathic communication expresses Primeau's delusions of special powers, other aspects of his experience of language express several different but related problems: multiple anxieties regarding penetration, sexual ambiguity, discomfiture with ordinary uses of language, and bodily fragmentation. In his delusion of penetration, for instance, he conflates two words that function well to suggest his feelings of attack or persecution from the domain of the father, of any figures of authority. He tells Lacan of his word *assastination* and explains that in it he fuses *assistant* and *assassin/assassinate*. 'Assistant' identifies those persons we would call "hospital orderlies," those who control patients in psychiatric wards. The conflation suggests his apparent sense that such assistants are agents out to assassinate him because of his rare ability to be *of* the air. As Lacan would speak of it, the "sliding" of the signifiers 'assistant' and 'assassinate' into each other occurs, as Primeau says, "spontaneously, in bursts" (29). But, not a good thing, these bursts represent Primeau's sense of vulnerability, permeability, his being without boundaries. His anxiety

regarding gender ambiguity is suggested in another conflation, one in
which he combines Venus and Mercury into *Venure*, a word, joining
female and male figures. Some of his conflations or contractions seem
simply to signify his inability to rest no more comfortably in ordinary
language than in a gender identity. Of these, one of the more symptomatic becomes associated with a singer named Béatrice Sarmeau, whom
he seems to have known or at least to have seen perform. He recounts
to Lacan that he was to see her at a particular theater on a specific
date. The singer's given name and the date become associated with a
saint, the "feast of Saint Béatrice [which] is February 13." Because, he
says, the singer had asked him to come back to see her again, he formu-
lates a wish he tries to convey in one of his conflations (the French as
symptomatically incoherent as the English translation).

> I had written a wish: "From the place where I read you, didn't
> Beatrice festive" [*De l'èspace ou je vous lis, ne s'est pas
> Béatrice en fête*]. I had written *dixt*, ten days: at the same time
> the fact I was wishing for ten days, the distance between thir-
> teen and twenty-three, ten, and the formulation, I had not said
> [*dit*] it, because the ten [days] did not pass without there being
> a feast. (30)

It is with a fragmented body that the fragmented language seems
especially associated. Such tortuous logic and word play (found
throughout the interview) seem to connect the patient's pathology to
early Lacanian themes associated with the mirror stage and the notion
of the *corps morcelé*, the body in pieces. Normally, when subjects pass
through the mirror stage, they find there an integration of their body
images. Primeau seems not to have found an integrated body. Indeed,
one reason he so troubles Lacan (and us) is how he perceives his body
image. He clearly needs a specular other, a mirroring image to anchor
those floating body parts. For him, at least in the moment of the interview, Lacan might seem to be that other, but in truth he is just another
receiver. In his obvious "playing" on sounds of words, Primeau knows
he imitates wordplay for which Lacan (like that satirical magazine, to
which Primeau refers, known as *Canard Enchaîné*) is already famous.
Moreover, since Primeau knows of this fame, he is playing "to" Lacan
as well. But when Lacan avers not to understand that complicated
wordplay we see above, Primeau offers Lacan additional examples of
such contractions suggesting more than linguistic creativity or playful-
ness. Critically significant to analysis of Primeau, they powerfully display the extent of his psychotic condition by revealing his variety of
contradictory states. These include his sense of being both contracted

and expanded, of being neither male nor female, though venerated nonetheless as both, and of having made a life choice that invokes a fall, no doubt a fearful image for a "bird man" who suffers from floating unanchored in space and time. When Lacan asks Primeau to explain his anomalous use of the words *festive* and *feast*, Primeau's answer demonstrates why there is no Lacanian psychosis if there is no textual unconscious. Only a text enables us to "see" the problem:

> It was the feast. In the wish there was this word which was contracted. There is another word like *écrasété*, which is at the same time "crushed" [*écrasé*] and "exploded" [*éclaté*]. I had written a poem that I called "Venure," which is a contraction of *Venus* and *Mercure*. It was a kind of elegy. But I do not have it here, because . . . [sic] There was also a word "to fall" [*choir*] which I used to write *choixre*, to express the notion of falling and the notion of choice [*choix*]. (29–30)

The more Gérard speaks, the more one sees that his dominant problem lies in his relation to the Other, the Father of Law, the phallic signifier. For one thing, he has displaced his sense of a creative or procreative function toward language itself. But even then it is a language, like his identity, that exists without a defining, delimiting authority, the Law of the Father. Admitting no interdiction, Primeau's created world is devoid of the no/*non*, if not the Name/*nom*, of the Father. When Lacan points out, for instance, that the verb *to create* has a meaning, Gérard responds in words—"it emerges from me"—suggesting his gender problem, that his identification lies in the feminine, not with the father but with the mother. "At the moment that it emerges from me," he says,

> it is a creation. It is a little like that. One must not become intimate. The fact of speaking of these solitary circles and of living without boundaries; there is no contradiction. In my mind I do not see a contradiction. How can I explain that? I am in a solitary circle because I am broken off from reality. It is for that I speak of a solitary circle. But that does not prevent living at an imaginative level, without boundaries. It is precisely because I have no boundaries that I have a tendency to explode a little, to live without boundaries, and if one does not have boundaries to put a stop to this, you can no longer struggle. There is no more struggle. (33–34)

Interpreted within an early Lacanian paradigm, Gérard Primeau's critical problem is that he has not accepted, has not internalized, oedipal law, the "No" or the "Name" of the Father. He has not, that is, accepted the gap, the hole, the negation that splits normal subjects, and, in that splitting, constitutes them as subjects capable of sustaining discourse in our ordinary, everyday world. Without a sense of negation, of limits, and without the splitting, the psychotic subject cannot participate in normal repression. It is precisely his inability to accept the strictures of the Law of the Symbolic Father, the Other of the register of the Symbolic, that determines Primeau in his psychosis. The Symbolic may speak *through* him, but he does not speak *from* the Symbolic. In describing Gérard's suffering from the "imposed speech," Miller suggests that the problem is that such speech "intruded into the sphere of his private cogitation." (Talking with Primeau would be like trying to converse with Robin Williams in the middle of a performance.) The general problem here, the one determining the pathology as psychotic, is that Gérard "could not recognize himself as its speaker, even though the speech most often assigned him the place of grammatical subject of the statements. Each phrase he heard demanded that he complement it with a phrase of another kind, 'reflexive,' which he knew himself to be emitting. In contrast to the 'imposed' statements, he did not figure as the subject of the 'reflexive' statements." While these imposed speeches come, as it were, from out of the blue, of course they actually come from the domain of the Other, the unconscious itself. Thus, says Miller, it is in these imposed speeches that Gérard "witnessed [...] the emergence of the discourse of the Other" ("Teachings" 49). Sadly, Gérard is thus as problematic in relation to the Real and the Symbolic as the classic Freudian-cum-Lacanian psychotic, Judge Schreber, about whom Primeau would have read in 1966 in *Écrits* (see *Écrits: A Selection* 188–92, 199–221).

For Lacanian psychoanalysis, herein lies the crux of the matter Gérard Primeau illustrates. On a higher rhetorical plane, the imposed speech and the disappearance of the subject (the "I") from his speech reveal how Gérard fails. It is a failure to integrate the law of the Oedipus complex. He has not assumed as his own the value of the Other, the authority of the phallic signifier, the Law (of the Name) of the Father. "From there," says Miller, "we move to the transformation that poses the question of madness." For Gérard, it is a question Lacan, acknowledging the paradox of sanity and madness, has asked even of normal subjects. "How do we not sense," Miller quotes Lacan as saying, "that the words we depend upon are imposed on us, that speech is an overlay, a parasite, the form of cancer with which human beings are afflicted?" For his part, Miller says, "If we identify ourselves with the psychotic, it is insofar as he is, like ourselves, prey to language, or better, that this is what he teaches us" ("Teachings" 49). But of Primeau, Lacan implies no more than that, because of the many problems with the "imposed speeches," "the imaginary, the symbolic, and the real," he does not expect Gérard to "get out of it. There are," he muses, giving us just a hint of the power of drive, the death drive, when a subject is given over to it, "suicide attempts that end up succeeding." Although Lacan says that "this is a clinical picture which you will not find described, even by good clinicians," and concludes that the case of Gérard Primeau is one "to be studied" ("Lacanian" 41), we are left to wonder why Lacan himself did not make more of it either in general Lacanian terms or, especially, within the terms of his current seminar on *le sinthome.*

It is then that the interview with Primeau becomes significant to us largely *because* Lacan himself gives no answer to the question, Which Lacan? Providing virtually nothing in the way of interpretation as such, he both assumes that his audience will understand the case and by his own silence forces interpretation upon others. As we have seen, an interpretation—working from the details presented in Lacan's interview, details drawn out if not interpreted by Lacan himself—seems necessarily to come down on the side of "early Lacan." That Primeau's—and thus Lacan's—terms are clearly "early" Lacan's (certainly they are neither the Lacan of the Real nor of *le sinthome,* as we might reasonably have anticipated) suggests that, ultimately, so long as we think Lacan when we interpret, it does not matter "which Lacan" we choose. What matters is that, heuristically, we allow details of a case or an object of any interpretation (story, novel, cultural artifact, whatever) to determine direction in our interpretation. This conclusion does not mean that there is no early or late Lacan or that there is only a unitary, monolithic "career," only that any "truth" of Lacan is a contextual truth, one contingent on facts and details available. Thus what remains as a truth of interpretation, Lacanian or otherwise, is that it must occur in the intertextual space between an object of analysis, here "a Lacanian psychosis," and elements of a Lacanian theory—early or late or something in between—that "fit" them.

4

[B]y a curious twist, Lacan's fortune in the English-speaking world was due to literary critics or to writers dealing with visual culture.
—Jean-Michel Rabaté, *The Cambridge Companion to Lacan,* xv

Generally, while Žižek has been very successful persuading Lacanians of just two Lacans, there is, in a sense, a third Lacan for which he does not quite account. Many Lacanians, perforce, have "used" early Lacan and then, assimilating the late Lacan fostered by Žižek and others, have effectively generated a theory in use somewhere between early and late. We find this third- or middle-way Lacan in many of the practical applications of the theory since Žižek began making his case for the two in the late 1980s. Although no critics actually posit a "middle phase" as such, in effect there is one, but it lies in our reception of Lacanian theory rather than *in* the theory itself. That is, as critics, largely Anglo-American, have assimilated a theory legendary for its difficulties, more often than not they began as early as the late 1970s, well before Žižek's influence, to amalgamate allegedly early and allegedly late theory. The reason is simple enough: Alan Sheridan's translation of a selection of major essays from *Écrits* gave us texts of Lacan that are almost universally acknowledged as early, and Sheridan's translation of 1964's Seminar 11, *The Four Fundamental Concepts*, gave us one almost always regarded as late. Both translations appeared in 1977 and inevitably led many Anglo-American Lacanians to fuse early and late theory, particularly since at that time Žižek was not advancing a late Lacan superior to an early one.

Still, as we have seen, not much was made of either early or late theory until Žižek's *Sublime Object of Ideology* began in 1989 to draw a following and prompted a few others to stress modulations from one to the other, perhaps also with preference for the late. Žižek's take on late Lacan came from Jacques-Alain Miller, with whom he studied in Paris in the early 1980s. Miller himself seems to have belonged to both the camp of One Lacan and that of Many Lacans. While Lacan was alive, Miller seems to have fostered a unified Lacan. After Lacan's death in 1981, Miller established his own seminars and seems thereafter, though not without ambiguity, to gravitate toward Many. From Miller it seems likely that Žižek drew the notion of early and late. To found their theory of late Lacan, the Lacanian seminars Miller and Žižek stressed ranged widely, from Seminar 7, *The Ethics of Psychoanalysis*, and Seminar 11 (which, as noted, is Lacan's first to forgo explication of specific texts of Freud), to Seminar 20, *Encore*. Because English translations of the seminars have been slow in coming (*The Ethics of Psychoanalysis* did not appear in English until Dennis Porter's translation in 1992, and while selections of *Encore* appeared in *Feminine Sexuality* as early as 1983, Bruce Fink's translation of the whole seminar appeared only in 1998), it has been left to those such as Miller, Žižek, Renata Salecl, Joan Copjec, Juliet MacCannell, and others to persuade Anglo-American Lacanians of the relatively greater importance, if not mere currency, of a late Lacanian theory. In the meantime, many Lacanians, especially those of us with a bent toward application rather than theorization, tended to conflate early and late. Only gradually succumbing to the valorization of the late theory, Anglo-American reception has thereby, in effect, formed a Lacan neither early nor late but somewhere between: to wit, a *middle* Lacan.

In the readings of fiction that follow in chapters 3 through 7, this is precisely where I would fit myself. All my readings of literary texts reflect my assimilation of Lacan's theory since the early 1990s. This means that the readings reflect influences different from those observed in my *Using Lacan, Reading Fiction* of 1991. Since that book, the Lacanian texts most influencing me have been *The Ethics of Psychoanalysis* and *The Four Fundamental Concepts of Psychoanalysis*, both regarded as late Lacan, and by far the Lacanian most influential on me, as these days on many other Lacanians, has been Slavoj Žižek, especially his early books *Looking Awry* (1991) and *Enjoy Your Symptom!* (1992), along with the widely influential *Sublime Object of Ideology*, in all of which we find advanced a late Lacanian theory of drive, *jouissance*, the two deaths, the Mother-Thing, and oedipal and primordial fathers. Since all my readings necessarily reflect my reception of the theory, however, and as I have continued to draw upon certain earlier texts from *Écrits* and elsewhere (such as "Desire and the Interpretation of Desire in *Hamlet*"), *my* Lacan remains a Lacan cooked, shall we say, rather than raw. I think, indeed, that this is the truth of Lacanians: that we are all cooking our Lacan, early, late, or middle, as best we can from the ingredients at hand.

Part II

Lacanian Exemplifications

CHAPTER 3

Invisible Man: The Textual Unconscious and a Subject beyond History

[E]ach great instinctual metamorphosis in the life of the individual will once again challenge its [ego's] delimitation, composed as it is of a conjunction of the subject's history and the unthinkable innateness of his desire.

—Jacques Lacan, *Écrits: A Selection*, 19–20

In *Invisible Man*, Ralph Ellison concretizes the reality of a textual unconscious precisely at a historical moment in the 1940s and early 1950s when the concept was emerging from unstated theoretical presupposition and before it effectively disappeared as a vanishing mediator. In the novel, it connects directly to one of its brilliant features, the way Ellison opens what appears to be merely a technical problem. The technical problem is the one caused by how his narrator (the memoirist, the invisible man) presumes to be what Jacques Lacan calls *"le sujet supposé savoir,"* usually translated as "the subject supposed to know" or, better yet for reading Ellison's novel, as "the supposed subject of knowing" (Schneiderman vii). When a narrator who is also the subject of a narration supposedly knows all in advance—that is, as Ellison's narrator puts it, from a place where "the end was [...] the beginning" (571)—one might ordinarily expect such a narrator-subject to have nothing about which to be in suspense in his or her recounting of a tale. On this matter, there is a technical and a psychoanalytic answer. On the level of technique, as Fitzgerald does in *The Great Gatsby*, Ellison first appears to solve the problem at its simplest level by the device of a split narrator who suggests in so many words at many crucial moments, "But I did not know then what I came to know later." Second, still at the level of technique, he solves the problem more complexly by using recurrent tropes—figures of speech and patterns of images—whose meanings are constantly immanent but are directly exposed only at moments of climactic insight. This second technique especially abets a psychoanalytic reading. In this reading, one knows in advance that in Ellison's or any other novel, because to Lacanian psychoanalysis it is true of life itself, there can be no subject who "knows." There is only a supposition that there is a subject who knows, a subject, which Lacan identifies as the Symbolic, who is supposed or presumed to know.

The essence of the Lacanian Symbolic is interpretation. It is grounded on a notion of textuality, an assumption that the unconscious is textual and is interpreted intertextually. Thus, Ellison's novel, though it shares a fact of narrative with all other narrative, exhibits more directly than most this essential of Lacanian theory. Technically and psychoanalytically, Ellison's masterpiece rests on the void of this supposition of knowledge and thus has a hollow center around which Ellison's narrator's language circles in an effort to fill or encompass it. Indeed, what makes Ellison's novel so special to psychoanalytic reading is how its very structure exemplifies a subjectivity posited by Lacan, one that is split between a Real of being and a Symbolic of meaning or knowledge. Thus the problem of Ellison's narrator-as-subject is precisely that of all human subjects. It is a problem of seeing and, of course, being seen in one's invisibility. Inevitably, it takes place in those arenas—Imaginary, Symbolic, and Real—Lacan regards as the registers of perception. Since according to Lacan the subject can never see itself except as mirrored or projected in others, Ellison's narration involves objects or persons whose purposes are precisely to make the invisible visible, to fill or reveal the central void. In "The Meaning of Narration in *Invisible Man*," Valerie Smith puts the issue in a nonpsychoanalytic way: "One might describe the story of Ellison's protagonist as the quest for an appropriate identity" (27).

For Lacan, that appropriate identity, though not so consciously sought as to be described as the object of a quest, may well be simply the normative one found by any subject whatsoever. While the details always vary in the psychogenesis of a normal subject (which in psychoanalysis probably does not exist as such), its structure remains the same. The story Lacan outlines recounts the subject's movement through a series of identifications in the register of the Imaginary to ones in the Symbolic that confer subjective 'maturity' (another concept, like 'normal' and even 'identity,' that Lacan would never exactly endorse). These traversals thereby encompass the ordinary subject's passage through what Lacan calls the "mirror stage" as well as what he and the traditional Freudians call the "Oedipus complex." Finally, as the Lacanian subject both finds itself retroactively, as the subject it *will have been*, and does so, inevitably, through a *méconnaissance*, a misunderstanding, so does the subject of *Invisible Man* find himself. As Slavoj Žižek suggests in "The Truth Arises from Misrecognition," the notion of the subject's retroaction, its discovery of its self or ego or ego-ideal retroactively, after the fact, is connected to a paradox of the unconscious, the fact that a subject's knowledge of itself is always already present in the unconscious and so a discovery about one-self in the future is always merely an unveiling of something already past. Thus a paradox of *Invisible Man* is that its narrative recounts a journey backward through time that ends beyond history. In a process of writing that serves nonetheless as a historical *act*, Ellison's subject finds himself in a future constructed upon a misunderstanding, a failure precisely to understand until his act of writing the meaning of a message that has lain in his unconscious from the very beginning.

1

In order to know how to reply to the subject [..., one must] recognize first of all the place where his ego is, the ego that Freud himself defined as an ego formed of a verbal nucleus [... Otherwise], there will be the risk of a misunderstanding concerning the desire that is there to be recognized and concerning the object to whom this desire is addressed.

—Jacques Lacan, *Écrits: A Selection*, 89

The message from the unconscious lies in words the invisible man's grandfather had uttered on his deathbed. But the mystery surrounding the grandfather is so "visible" in the text that one begins to wonder if in fact it is not a lure, a cover for some deeper, more threatening or psychoanalytically repressed theme or meaning. It is. It has to do with what Lacan, in *The Four Fundamental Concepts of Psychoanalysis* (209–14), calls the *"vel"* of alienation associated with the mirror stage and the register of the Imaginary. Thus the mystery in the novel has to do not with fathers but with the mother and mothers. The clue to this mystery, ironically, comes in one of the most frequently discussed images in the text. The image is pervasive in the criticism not only because it is important in the novel but also because it is important in the history of African Americans. Discussed at article's length by Virginia M. Burke, this image is a figure of "the veil." The figure first appears in a context loaded with the narrator's critique of fathers and father figures, including his own grandfather, the college Founder, the college's current president (Dr. Bledsoe), and, eventually, the war vet-eran inmate of the Golden Day asylum. The figure's first appearance— which, like most others concerned with the more covert theme of history, benefits from the memoirist's proleptic perspective—refers to

the college's statue of the Founder and evokes the narrator's concerns
about his ability to understand himself and his life. Looking back upon
his life from his warm hole underground, the narrator tells us:

> It's so long ago and far away that here in my invisibility I
> wonder if it happened at all. Then in my mind's eye I see the
> bronze statue of the college Founder, the cold Father symbol,
> his hands outstretched in the breathtaking gesture of lifting a
> veil that flutters in hard, metallic folds above the face of a
> kneeling slave; and I am standing puzzled, unable to decide
> whether the veil is really being lifted, or lowered more firmly
> in place; whether I am witnessing a revelation or a more effi-
> cient blinding. (36)

Now, we know that the veil is one of the most persistent and powerful tropes in the historical experience of African Americans and the
literature of social revolution. Thus, while Ellison could easily have
borrowed the image from his African American racial heritage, he
could just as easily have taken it from Karl Marx and so from the
European social revolutionary. In *The Riddle of History,* Bruce Mazlish
points out the importance of this image in the writings of Marx:

> As it develops, the breaking of the fetters is metamorphosed
> into the image of the tearing of the veil. Before we can act, we
> must *see* the reality of life. To anyone who has read the
> *Manifesto,* examples leap to mind. Interestingly enough Marx
> credits the bourgeoisie itself with the initial rending of the veil:
> it has "torn away from the family its sentimental veil";
> "stripped of its halo every occupation"; and, "for exploita-
> tion, veiled by religious and political illusions, it has substi-
> tuted naked, shameless, direct, brutal exploitation." (242)

But as any Americanist knows, the *fin de siècle* black writer W. E.
B. DuBois uses the veil as a recurrent motif in *Souls of Black Folk.*
While we know that Ellison had a flirtation with Marxism and was
knowledgeable of DuBois, in fact the easiest source for this image lies
in his own personal history, for while a student at Tuskegee he saw it
on an actual statue there commemorating another African American
authority figure: Booker T. Washington. Regardless of where he found
it, Ellison chose it because the image is historically resonant and the-
matically crucial to *Invisible Man.* It is crucial because it represents a
structural relation between a signifier and a signified, between an
"object" (image, sound, whatever) and its "meaning." Lacan suggests
this structure in the algorithm—S/s—that he discusses at length in the

1950s, in the early years of his seminar. In Lacan's psychoanalytic terms, the algorithm has to do not only with the structure of language but also with the development of the subject in its separation from the mother. It is a separation that comes in the normal subject's recognition that it *is* separate from her (that she *is* separate), and, thus, its acceptance that its "identity" is founded upon a void. (In Hitchcock's *Psycho*, it is Norman Bates's refusal to accept separation from the mother that defines him as psychotic.) Coming in the crucial moment of what Lacan, in *The Four Fundamental Concepts*, calls "the veil of blindness" (208) at one place and at another "the *vel* of alienation" (211), the subject enters the either/or of being and meaning. In this dilemma, which expresses the puzzling void of identity, a subject must choose one or the other. It can not have both. The game is not one of both/and. To choose being is to lose meaning. But to choose meaning is to lose life and meaning. This is the paradox, that a subject may subordinate life itself to a meaning given it by an object such as money or a memento or a cherished doll or, on another level, to a concept such as 'honor' or 'loyalty.' It is recognition of such an ambiguity, not merely one having to do with perception itself (the visual conundrum, as it were, of rabbit or duck in the shadow figure), that explains the powerful resonance of Ellison's image of the Father symbol's lifting the veil from—or placing it on—the face of the woman slave.

But there is more at stake than this that emerges upon the belated reappearance of the image in the text. The stakes have to do with the slow movement of the narrator-as-emergent-subject from the dominance of what Lacan calls the "register of the Imaginary" to dominance of the register of the Symbolic (it is important we understand that no register simply drops away like the stages of a launched rocket). In the space between that first crucial appearance of the veil and the next appearance, the narrator reorients himself from the simpler identifications and aggressions of the Imaginary to the more complex acceptance of the cognitive ambiguities and arbitrariness of the Symbolic. Since that space occupies half the novel, it is necessary to trace the long path to the next occurrence of the veil. The veil resurfaces in the memory of the narrator rather late in the narrative, after he has begun to learn about history by taking an active part in its making. When that image at last again recurs, much of his own personal history seems to culminate in it. Between times, however, following his departure from college and before he begins his political activism, it is as if he has no personal or historical identity whatsoever. Like the subject in that void Julia Kristeva dubs "the *chora*" occurring before the advent of the mirror stage, he is largely a passive receptacle for experiences in the world. In that *vel*—the either/or of being and meaning—he is caught on the side of being alone. What has forestalled his ability to act on the world is his inability or unwillingness to perceive meanings behind appearances—significances beneath signifiers. The problem here, perhaps, lies in the structure of the sign itself, for that structure is built upon a bar, across a gap, around a void. For Lacan, the relation between the signifier and the signified—represented in the algorithm S/s—is best explained as a matter of letters. For him, in analysis, "the letter" is always important, for while as a metonym of the sign itself the algorithm seems to represent univocality or a one-to-one relation between a "thing" and a "meaning," it necessarily represents how the relation of thing and meaning in fact is always arbitrary, is always structured by a bar or gap. Revealing why Derrida, in "The Purveyor of Truth," so fixates upon Lacan, the bar between signifier and signified shows that full significance, as in Derrida's notion of *différrance*, is a matter of difference and deferral and that ultimate signifance must therefore always be held in abeyance.

While for Lacan the tale that models the indeterminacy of the letter is Poe's "Purloined Letter," which he discusses in perhaps his most famous essay, "The Seminar on 'The Purloined Letter,'" he might well have worked with Ellison's novel, for letters are just as important in *Invisible Man*. The narrator, as many critics have noted, carries around several varieties of written documents in his briefcase. All are vouchers—signifiers—of an ego or self he thinks he possesses or at least desires to possess. To various people in New York, he takes, for example, reference letters Bledsoe had given him, but when he realizes no success with them he is compelled to learn that "reference" is as problematic in these letters as we know the concept to be in Lacan's analysis of Poe's tale. To imagine that there is a simple, one-to-one correlation between a sign and its meaning is to operate in the Lacanian Imaginary. Indeed, that is where the invisible man operates at this time. He does not yet see that the letters—no more than *the* letter—never simply refer to a significance; rather, they always exist—or, Lacan's word, *insist*—within a complex, a system of similarities and differences. They signify a social or cultural system whose meanings are immanent in the system but never directly manifested in any one signifier from that system. The letters reify, even if one does not understand, that system.

Thus the "lesson" the invisible man learns exemplifies Lacan's view of the sign, reference, and relation of desire to one's subjectivity. He learns that those letters of apparent reference yield precisely the same meanings as those in the dream he had of his grandfather. Simply put, they keep him running, running from one site in the system to another.

Bledsoe's letter enjoins the man named Emerson to keep secret from the narrator his actual expulsion from college since Bledsoe assumes, rightly, that the narrator will desire to return to that apparent site of full, unmediated meaning. But even if the narrator were to be allowed to go back, he would learn only how impossible is such a return to full meaning or original plenitude or the origin itself of one's being. The letter in Lacan is an image of the little object of desire, the *objet petit a,* and it is that object that represents desire, the impossibility of fulfilling desire, of recapturing an original object that, paradoxically, never existed because it in some fashion is always identified with/as the Phallus, a concept that in Lacan is simply lack itself. In his typically impenetrable language, Lacan says, "The *objet [petit] a* is something from which the subject, in order to constitute itself, has separated itself off as organ. This serves as a symbol of the lack, that is to say, of the phallus, not as such, but in so far as it is lacking" (*Four Fundamental Concepts* 103). Desire, circulating through this lack, keeps the subject running, just as the narrator's letters keep him running. Though he does not know what they mean, the narrator easily imagines the *effect* of those letters and, by Lacanian extension, *the* letter. "My dear Mr. Emerson," goes Ellison's narrator's imaginary reconstruction of the letter from that "humble and obedient servant, A. H. Bledsoe": "The Robin bearing this letter is a former student. Please hope him to death, and keep him running" (194).

In Lacan, to mature from the Imaginary to the Symbolic is to traverse the moment of the oedipal encounter. For Lacan as for Freud, the oedipal moment involves the eternal triangle, the family romance, the psychical contest of the subject with the father "for" the mother. The mother has been the great absence in *Invisible Man.* Because she has been hidden by all the figures of the father, it is really the mother who is returned from the repressed when the image of the veil recurs. Ellison's narrator is now prepared for that significance—and more—in the image when it does recur. The figure surfaces in his memory during the eviction of an old black couple from their rundown apartment building. This eviction culminates a series of encounters the narrator has had with what for him are ambiguously meaningful racial images. There are the relics, emblems, and symbols from his heritage and history as an African American. There is the exchange—presented in chapter 9—with the "blues man," who reminds the narrator of the vets at the Golden Day and whose rhymes the narrator had learned in childhood but has now forgotten. There is the little scene in the drugstore where the narrator asks for toast and orange juice instead of the pork chops and grits he really wants. To drink the pulpy juice, he thinks, is "an act of discipline, a sign of the change that was coming over me and which would return me to college a more experienced man" (178). There is the episode, in Emerson's office, where he learns he will not be allowed to return to college after all and is reminded of the artifacts of African American history he has seen in a museum at the college: "I recalled only a few cracked relics from slavery times: an iron pot, an ancient bell, a set of ankle-irons and links of chain, a primitive loom, a spinning wheel, a gourd for drinking, an ugly ebony African god that seemed to sneer [...] , a leather whip with copper brads, a branding iron with the double letter MM." Though he remembers these relics, he admits that he prefers to think of other times, the days just after the Civil War, "the times close to those blind Barbee had described" (181). There is, finally, the sequence recounted in chapter 13, when, out of a job, out of the hospital, and back in Harlem, the narrator recognizes how closely his own personal identity is connected to the historical identity of his people. In part, his awareness comes to him in such ironic signs as the advertisement proclaiming "You too can be truly beautiful [...] Win greater happiness with whiter complexion. Be outstanding in your social set" (262). But, most of all, it comes in his sacramental consumption of a hot sweet potato. Eating it, the narrator experiences coming over him "an intense feeling of freedom" (264). When the yam peddler calls him "one of these old-fashioned yam eaters," he avows, "They're my birthmark. [...] I yam what I am!" (266).

The *more* that we shall see associated with the figure of the mother lying behind the veil is race. Given the subject's entrapment in the *vel* of alienation between being and meaning, race would seem to exist on the side of being. It lies in the site where—like the mother—the subject's physical existence lies. With his feelings of racial identity restored by all these experiences, he arrives at the scene of the old couple's eviction. There, the images that Ellison's hero encounters induce perhaps the most powerful perceptual epiphany in *Invisible Man* because they link his racial heritage to the image of the mother who has been displaced from consciousness and thereby virtually eliminated from the novel. The scene of the eviction is a type of primal scene, for not only does it involve the repression of a racial trauma, but it also involves the repression of a subject's psychoanalytic trauma—the subject's confronting the desire of the mother. In the oedipal complex, that desire is blocked by the father, not, Lacan would say, by the real father, but by the Law of the Father founded on the Name of the Father. In this novel, the subject's desire of his racial heritage is likewise blocked by the Father, the Law of a culture that makes black invisible, albeit it is a Law whose potency is threatened by all those black sons who represent a prepotent sexuality that may overcome the Father. All these oedipal implications become manifest in an eviction scene whose significance turns on a sign that names an originary provider, a primal father, a "Primus Provo" who signifies—*is* a Signifier *of*—the narrator's racial heritage. While in the beginning of the scene, the people who have gathered to watch the eviction are as unwilling to see what is going on as he himself has been to see it, he soon realizes just how symbolic it is for all: "Now I recognized a selfconsciousness about them, as though they, we, were ashamed to witness the eviction, as though we were all unwilling intruders upon some shameful event; and thus we were careful not to touch or stare too hard at the effects that lined the curb; for we were witnesses of what we did not wish to see, though curious, fascinated, despite our shame" (270).

As it should be since the oedipal encounter is involved, the meaning of the scene begins with a figure of the mother. The old woman whose "mind-plunging crying" envelops them all is perhaps of the same generation as the narrator's grandfather and partly for that reason begins to make the eviction personal for Ellison's hero. Whereas the relics from the past he remembers displayed in the college's museum are far distant from him and his life, the "clutter of household objects" piled by white men in the street begin to restore to him his own past. He says,

> I looked down to see looking out of an oval frame a portrait of the old couple when young, seeing the sad, stiff dignity of the faces there; feeling strange memories awakening that began an echoing in my head like that of a hysterical voice stuttering in a dark street. Seeing them look back at me as though even then in that nineteenth-century day they had expected little, and this with a grim, unillusioned pride that suddenly seemed to me both a reproach and a warning.

He sees other details—"A pair of crudely carved and polished bones, 'knocking bones,' used to accompany music at country dances," "a straightening comb, switches of false hair, a curling iron," "a faded tintype of Abraham Lincoln" (271), and finally "a fragile paper, coming apart with age, written in black ink grown yellow." Reading the paper, he begins to achieve a real and moving consciousness of his patrimony: "FREE PAPERS. *Be it known to all men that my negro, Primus Provo, has been freed by me this sixth day of August, 1859. Signed: John Samuels. Macon.*" Without knowing why, he is very moved by what this paper reveals to him. "My hands were trembling," the narrator says, "my breath rasping," "as if I had run a long distance." Even more troubling, it is, he says, "as if I had [. . .] come upon a coiled snake in a busy street" (272). But he must not be too quick to say what this image might mean, for it means both more and other than what he might at first surmise.

This snake is another letter, an S, as it were, standing as a sign of the Sign, as a sign of the phallic signifier itself. So chilling in its affects, the serpent clearly evokes an archetype of transgression that is as much oedipal as it is Christian (indeed, if Freud is right, is oedipal before Christian). While the specific evil signified by the snake is another S, slavery itself, the snake, by evoking the dialectic of the master and the slave, also signifies the violation of Law, the transgression toward freedom of the created subject who operates under the authorization and the interdiction of the Father. The authorizing Father Ellison's hero invokes is Abraham Lincoln, the one who within human law played God and let the narrator's people go. But there is no simple Imaginary relation here between real existential freedom and a proclamation claiming emancipation. In the domain of the Symbolic, into which Ellison's narrator, as subject, is being absorbed, meanings are complex, triangulated, immanent in a structure, but beyond total capture. As a subject beginning to realize his subjectivity, his being as castrated, as one who cannot have or be the signifier (the Phallus, in Lacan's terms), the narrator undergoes a perceptual revolution that shifts dominance from the Imaginary to the Symbolic. The eviction, psychoanalytically, is an ambiguous scene of desire and castration, of wanting and losing, and as such it clearly thrusts the narrator toward the *post*oedipal. In the beyond of this crisis, the narrator is able to confront both the mother and race beyond desire, beyond Eros, and therefore on the side of Law and, yes, Thanatos. The crisis shows the narrator that while he has run a long way to escape the authority of the Phallus (represented as the grandfather), rather than escaping it—and him—he has simply returned to him and his words. Now, retroactively and by way of *méconnaissance,* he shall become, because of his grandfather's words, the man he will have been.

What he really sees where that serpent lies is not only the historical fact of chattel bondage, but also the oedipal fact that all subjects are bound under the Law of their culture, the Symbolic Law of the social structures within which they persist as subjects. The background of this double realization may well be Freud's myth of the primal horde, the band of brothers who murder the primal father. Whatever the case, wanting to resist the lesson, the narrator thinks in dismay, "*It has been longer than that, further removed in time.*" And yet, he realizes, "I knew that it hadn't been" (272). Such a realization, whether expressly oedipal or limited to a historical event, brings with it a sense of dispossession, one shared by all African Americans of course, but by all human beings who have faced their limitations as subjects in a symbolic world ruled by the signifier. Ready now to operate under Law, he sees again the veil and the figure of the mother who stands behind the veil that had covered the face of the slave in the statue of the Founder. All the manifold significances of the scene of the eviction are evoked in the conjunction of the various *objets* and the vision of the mother. First come the objects: "And with this sense of dispossession," says Ellison's narrator, "came a pang of vague recognition: this junk, these shabby chairs, these heavy, old-fashioned pressing irons, zinc wash tubs with dented bottoms—all throbbed within me with more meaning than there should have been." Then, in an italic font to suggest its significance, comes the maternal vision:

> And why did I, standing in the crowd, see like a vision my mother hanging wash on a cold windy day, so cold that the warm clothes froze even before the vapor thinned and hung stiff on the line, and her hands white and raw in the skirt-swirling wind and her gray head bare to the darkened sky— why were they causing me discomfort so far beyond their intrinsic meaning as objects? And why did I see them now as behind a veil that threatened to lift, stirred by the cold wind in the narrow street? (273)

That of which heretofore the narrator had been dispossessed is his mother and his race. Although of course, as Lacan insists, not everything can be restored, his experience now with the old couple and along with it his memory of his mother begin to restore something of that which heretofore had been lost to him. Almost for the first time, he begins to engage in a work of memory that, on the one hand, Freud calls "*Nachträglichkeit*" and identifies as the return of the repressed and, on the other, that Lacan calls "*rémemoration*" (much as Toni Morrison, in *Beloved*, calls it "rememory"). As the narrator's mind loops back to his own life, he recognizes those people—and especially the one person, the mother—in it who have given him being and made it meaningful. The more he looks backward to the past encoded in all those historically symbolic objects—in the museum, cluttering the sidewalk, in his briefcase—the more he recaptures signifying images from his own lived past, his past as a psychoanalytic subject always threatened by *aphanisis,* a subjectivity fading in the gap situated between meaning and being.[1] While that past, he begins to understand, is indeed represented for him in his mother, it is more effectually represented in his social life by the old people who signify both race and bondage.

They are his past, and their eighty-seven years, he realizes, are the years that have made him a "freak [neither] of nature, nor of history" (15). More than anything else, the scene of the eviction, the scene of primal racial identification and oedipal transformation, shows the way in which Ellison's narrator has moved from narcissistic entrapment of Imaginary identifications to the ambiguous oedipal "freedom" of the Symbolic. In this freedom, in Lacanian terms, he realizes himself as a subject.

2

> The father, the Name-of-the-father, sustains the structure of desire with the structure of the law—but the inheritance of the father is that which Kierkegaard designates for us, namely, his sin.
> —Jacques Lacan, *Four Fundamental Concepts*, 34

If the struggle of the first, Imaginary phase of the novel largely involves a personal identification with the other as mother and, in her, with race, the struggle of the second, Symbolic phase of *Invisible Man* largely involves introjections of the father and acceptance of the Name-of-the-Father. These come about through an engagement with a figure of the ego-ideal that leads to an enlarged consciousness of the Symbolic. In the changing subjectivity of the narrator, the Symbolic is made evident in his orientations toward figures of the Symbolic Other. These take two forms. One includes persons in whom he finds symbolic projections, and a second includes the substitution for the father of a signifier—history-as-*History*—that he comes to understand in a Symbolic way. Not separated from the first, Imaginary, phase in any schematic way, this second, Symbolic, phase (kept apart from the decidedly Symbolic commentary in the prologue) begins as early as the first chapter's second paragraph. In accord with Lacan's notion of a secondary narcissism, the narrator's secondary struggle begins in a long statement that provides one of the most important Symbolic Others through which the narrator can view those experiences that make up the only personal history he can have. The passage is the well-known one about his grandfather. His grandfather is the narrator's first figure of the Other, the subject supposed to know. "My grandfather," the narrator admits, "is the one" (16).

But as the first phase of the novel's constitution of the subject involved the structure (S/s) of the sign, so this second phase involves the reading or interpretation of it. The Symbolic is hermeneutic, so the narrator's persistent inability to fathom the figural mystery of the words, overheard, that his grandfather uttered upon his deathbed inhibits his growth as a normative subject. The grandfather's words have to do with the reality that the narrator—as a child—thinks he has seen around him: "Son," the old man says to the narrator's father,

> "after I'm gone I want you to keep up the good fight. I never told you, but our life is a war and I have been a traitor all my born days, a spy in the enemy's country ever since I give up my gun back in the Reconstruction. Live with your head in the lion's mouth. I want you to overcome 'em with yeses, undermine 'em with grins, agree 'em to death and destruction, let 'em swoller you till they vomit or bust wide open." (16)

While the old man's words suggest to the youth that there is another, more authoritative reality within which he exists, so long as he is caught in the register of the Imaginary, he himself cannot see it. From within the Imaginary, this Symbolic reality is as invisible to the him as he later discovers himself to be to others. Thus the grandfather's words have set the boy running after some mystery just as surely as had those white people who wrote the message—"Keep this Nigger-Boy Running" (33)—the youth reads in his dream, well elucidated by Joseph Trimmer, about the old man after the "battle royal" episode.

The basic narrative problem of *Invisible Man*, as it is related to the interchange of the cognitive orders of the Imaginary and the Symbolic, is suggested by the narrator's contradictory motives for flight. While we may say that the grandfather's counsel makes of the African American the white man's symptom, a sign of the pathology that defines him, the symptom of the invisible man is flight, the very sign that must be read or interpreted. Flight covers the real problem the narrator must interpret, that is, the problem of interpretation itself. At the heart of the problem lies a dilemma regarding how—within the Symbolic—to reconcile competing, contradictory constructions of "reality" and "history." In the novel, one construction of reality and history resides in the Lacanian Imaginary, the other in the Real. The narrator sees how interpretation occurs in both registers on the occasion of Homer Barbee's recitation of the legend of the Founder. Belonging to the simpler, largely binary domain of the Imaginary, the legend, Ellison's tour-de-force creation of oral traditional narration, belongs to a history imposed upon African Americans that they are supposed—expected as well as presumed—to accept. Though the recitation covers some dozen pages, the narrator's tropes encapsulate the significance of Barbee's legend at the outset. First, he enfigures within the language of theater, ritual, and religion. "Here upon this stage," he says, the black rite of Horatio Alger was performed to God's own acting script, with millionaires come down to portray themselves; not merely acting out the myth of their goodness, and wealth and success and power and benevolence and authority in cardboard masks, but them selves, these virtues concretely! Not the wafer and the wine, but the flesh and the blood, vibrant and alive, and vibrant even when stooped, ancient and withered. (111)

Here, the narrator's tropes are metaphoric (based on the structure of the algorithm, S/s, "this equals that") and, most crucially, belong to a tradition of romantic, pastoral, Christian imagery suggesting how those millionaires are shepherds to the flocks of black people who come under their purview. In the narrator's basic trope, the signifier, S, is "the same" as the signified, s. Indeed, as signs these are described (but of course metaphorically), as if they were "iconic" ones. The "cardboard masks" do not hide a thing different from its meaning; no, they are "themselves" "the virtues concretely," "the flesh and the blood," not merely the "wafer and the wine," "vibrant and alive," however contradictory the physical embodiments in men "stooped, ancient and withered."

In contradistinction to this version of black life in the ordinary social Imaginary is another, metonymic version. This one irrupts upon the narrator's consciousness in the register of the Real. Lacan says frequently (and consistently throughout his work) that the Real is "the impossible" (*Four Fundamental Concepts* 167) or that it is "that which resists symbolization absolutely" (*Freud's Papers on Technique* 66). Practically speaking, this dictum means that the Real comes to us in objects or events unframed within familiar metaphors, if within metaphors at all. Typically, it comes in metonymy, objects connected within a temporal or spatial context rather than an enfiguring, mediating metaphor (which, requiring interpretation that may yet be ambiguous, thus belongs to the Symbolic). In the novel, in the context of the "black rite" of the legend of the Founder, the narrator immediately contrasts a romantic, pastoral, sacramental, metaphoric enfiguration to another. This other is indeed "the other" to that received story by which these black youths are to be socialized. This other is demonic and terrifying and stands in stark contradiction to the validity of that "rite" so staunchly defended by those who "belong to this family sheltered from those lost in ignorance and darkness" (111). It is, however, a representation entirely consonant with one that the narrator has encountered before, that of the dying grandfather. Like ghosts or phantasms or revenants in horror tales, these *others* appear to the narrator as the Real—the horror—of a black life unexplained by the legend of the Founder. In effect, they embody a reality buried beneath the signifiers of the legend. In ordinarily socialized, malleable, pacified black life, these others are the symptom—indeed, the trauma—that defines it. It is they who situate the narrator in the paradise of the legend. "And I remember too," the narrator says, in one enormous sentence,

> how we confronted those others, those who had set me here in this Eden, whom we knew though we didn't know, who were unfamiliar in their familiarity, who trailed their words to us through blood and violence and ridicule and condescension with drawling smiles, and who exhorted and threatened, intimidated with innocent words as they described to us the limitations of our lives and the vast boldness of our aspirations, the staggering folly of our impatience to rise even higher; who, as they talked, aroused furtive visions within me of blood-froth sparkling their chins like their familiar tobacco juice, and upon their lips the curdled milk of a million black slave mammies' withered dugs, a treacherous and fluid knowledge of our being, imbibed at our source and now regurgitated foul upon us. (112)

These two passages enfigure interpretation as a problem not because of the obvious differences between them, but because the narrator, at the moment in the narrative when they occur, does not grasp what to make of them. They simply remain as contradictory. But the problem does not lie in the first, the legend. In the register of the Imaginary, he knows he is expected both to understand and to accept its meanings. Rather, the trouble the narrator must face lies in those spectral, traumatic others irrupting from the domain of the unsymbolizable Real. As a representation of the hard reality of race, they emanate from the same register as the narrator's mother, evoked here in "a million black slave mammies' withered dugs," the very source of a "knowledge of our being." Those parts of the human physiognomy—chins, lips, vomit, blood-froth, withered dugs—represent the tragic division in which they are involved, the mechanistic process that grinds them up, and the radical ideology that rests upon them. Clearly, while the rhetoric of the narrator here suggests he believes the dangerous enfiguration of history-as-tragedy more than he believes the cheerful history-as-pastoral romance, it is equally clear that he does not yet know how to see beyond one or the other. Those, like the grandfather, who would put the lie to the romantic, Horatio-Alger dreams of future

glory of the sort symbolized by those white visitors are as invisible—
"unfamiliar in their familiarity"—to the college youths as the narrator eventually discovers himself to be to white America. Still, at the
moment he hears those words the narrator only dimly perceives that
this world, from another reality, belongs to another register, the Real,
that at historical moments requires of the social Symbolic that it
adjust its significations. From the contradictions of the one by the
other, the narrator will be driven to constitute a new Symbolic in
which he can believe.

Much in the manner of the textual unconscious to which, in chapter 1, I connected Fredric Jameson's notion of the political unconscious
revealed in contradictions in the social Symbolic, these contradictions
of interpretation, of knowledge and understanding, slowly emerge from
the unconscious and begin to lift a veil from the eyes of the invisible
man. What they reveal is precisely how the register of the Symbolic
accounts for them. In this process, which defines the larger structure of
Ellison's novel, the most important lesson the emergent subject must
learn is that *the* Symbolic does not supplant but, rather, interrelates in
structures with the Real and the Imaginary. For the subject, these registers, will he or nil he, are constituted, just as is the subject itself, *with*
the Symbolic but not *by* it. Thus he must learn that no Symbolic such
as history—not even his own lived history—is a simple, objective
datum in a putative Real. In his interpretation of these radically contradictory enfigurations of history he has begun to go beyond "history."
Not merely something in reality—in the Real—revealed to one's per-
ceptions, it is, rather, an "object" constructed by cognition within the
register of the Symbolic. Ellison's narrator gets, in short, his first lesson
in philosophy of history, in 'history' as a concept, of history as something captured only in words, in figures. It is history, in short, as what
the philosopher Ernst Cassirer calls a "symbolic form" or as what
Lacan (and, now, postmodernists) would call a "master signifier." The
narrator has used the word *history* before this point in the narrative,
but always, except in the prologue (where it is largely proleptic,
recounting, in Lacanian terms, "what will have been"), in the context
of narration when he looks back over the experiences about which he
tells. But now the word appears in a dramatic context that shows us
how his understanding has grown right up to the time he begins to
write of his life. The next lesson in his understanding of history within
the register of the Symbolic is that no understanding is ever really final.
To think so is to return to the illusory stabilities of simple identifications and antagonisms within the Imaginary. Ironically, this lesson
comes from one who has accepted the master signifier defining history

for the Brotherhood (Ellison's fictionalization, as is well known, of the Communist Party). That one is Brother Jack.

As a member of the Brotherhood, Brother Jack has already taken history as a signifier. Because he has seen how our hero had aroused a crowd to violence in order to stop that eviction of the old folks, he hopes to recruit him to his ideology. "The old ones," Jack tells him, are "agrarian types, you know. Being ground up by industrial conditions. Thrown on the dump heaps and cast aside. You pointed it out very well. 'Eighty-seven years and nothing to show for it,' you said. You were absolutely correct" (290). But despite Brother Jack's efforts, Ellison's narrator eventually learns another, contradictory lesson. Though he at first assents to the claim Brother Jack makes because these old people, whether they have ever lived on a farm or in the rural South, *are* agrarian types, the narrator cannot finally accept the ramifications of Brother Jack's model of history. Jack is right in saying that "*History*"—as a signifier—"has been born in your brain," but he is wrong in his assumption that the narrator is in the process of shedding his "old agrarian self." In fact, the situation is just the reverse, for the narrator (as we have seen) has constructed his ego identity *through* that old type, that past experience of his people, and, above all, he has finally realized, "[T]hey reminded me of folks I know down South. It's taken me a long time to feel it, but they're folks just like me" (291). Thus, if his Imaginary involvement in the political actions of the Brotherhood causes him to forget his roots for a while, the involvement nevertheless leads to a real achievement. Eventually, he solidifies his determination by the Symbolic in his acceptance not only of those old people but also of his mother and his race as the Symbolic Others who will make possible his reconciliation with the grandfather who comes to stand with yet another figure for the Name-of-the-Father in the Symbolic.

3

> First of all, there is [...] a narcissism connected with the corporeal image [...that] makes up the unity of the subject [...T]he second narcissism [...] is identification with the other.
> —Jacques Lacan, *Freud's Papers on Technique*, 125

In the register of the Symbolic, the narrator's involvement in history as a signifier in—and of—the Symbolic must go beyond his engagement with the old people, the mother, and the grandfather. Oddly, it must go through narcissism. In Lacan there are two narcissisms, one associated with the subject's primary, mirror- phase investment in the ideal ego of

Imaginary identification, the other its secondary investment in the ego-ideal of Symbolic identification. The first is a narcissism that establishes a bodily unity in the subject during Lacan's mirror stage. The second is crucial to resolving the oedipal complex. "That," says Lacan, "is what enables him to see in its place and to structure, as a function of this place in his world, his being" (*Freud's Papers* 125). In effect, to put the issue too simply, the function of secondary narcissism is to move the subject toward a mature relation to the world and others in it. Thus, it becomes plain that Ellison's narrator must engage not a figure of the ideal ego (Freud's *Idealich*) but one of the ego-ideal (*Ichideal*). In the Lacanian quaternary structure of the subject (enfigured in Schema L, reproduced in my chapter 1), the ego-ideal serves as a relay to the authority of Law, the Father, the Name-of-the-Father. In Ellison's novel, the figure of the ego-ideal, the identificatory "other" on the plane of the Symbolic, cathects with parental imagoes and engages the narrator in the investigation of history and the self in yet another way.

The two—history and ego or self—are linked in the trope of brotherhood. By definition, brotherhood—as a band of equals—must exist within the Imaginary, and its identifications must therefore be subject to dissolutions founded on antagonism. Even while Ellison's hero rather scrupulously performs his duties as a unit of "the" Brotherhood, he has serious doubts about the concept of history—and brotherhood—imposed upon him by that organization. These doubts become focused upon—and resolved in—his friend Tod Clifton. As a relay point between Imaginary and Symbolic, Clifton represents not only a figure of the Imaginary ideal ego (or, in Freud, *Idealich*), but also the figure more crucial to maturation of the ego-ideal, Freud's *Ichideal*. At first Tod seems only the identificatory other of the Imaginary, the specular double of the mirror phase who establishes a sense of unity in the ego.[2] But, later, more than all others, Tod becomes a figure (the figure is synecdoche) representing to the narrator a concept of human subjectivity transcending a mere organization called "the Brotherhood." As a figure of Lacan's second narcissism, Tod becomes an identificatory other in whom the part may find itself whole, a brother in and of the Symbolic in whom more truly the narrator can see himself, an ego projection whose actions in the present relate personally and ideologically to his finding his place in the world.

This double-sided relation between Tod and the narrator is quite plain. The narrator's Imaginary relation, both dualistically identificatory and aggressive, to the ideal ego, alter ego, or *Idealich* is exhibited in a variety of ways. In the fight, for instance, with Ras the Exhorter, Tod and the narrator sympathetically reinforce one another, the narrator knocking out of Ras's hand the knife with which he threatened Tod's life and Tod knocking Ras down later on when the Exhorter gets verbally abusive. But despite their mutual defense against Ras, the two cannot easily cast aside Ras's words and ideas about race and the relationship of black men to white. And Tod, if not the narrator at this time, begins to believe that the policies of the Brotherhood may not be entirely satisfactory. Tod's thoughts about history, then, become an expression of the unconscious doubts the narrator himself has repressed. Though he can admit that Ras "was an exhorter, all right, and I was caught in the crude, insane eloquence of his plea" (374), the narrator nonetheless tells Ras his thinking will get him—and them— "lost in the backwash of history" (375). It is with some shock, however, that the narrator responds to Tod's anguished remark, "I suppose sometimes"—as Ras has done—"a man *has* to plunge outside history." The narrator's naive response at the time is to think, "Maybe he's right." Thus he is "suddenly very glad" to have "found Brotherhood" (377). But on the day Tod Clifton is killed, he has no such easy response, and his relation to Tod begins to shift from the specular Imaginary to the deeper Symbolic, from ideal ego in the Imaginary to ego-ideal in the Symbolic. On that day, the narrator discovers Tod in the city hawking a grotesque Sambo doll the narrator regards as "an obscene flouncing of everything human" (434–35). There, Tod's behavior and his refusal to recognize the narrator are convincing evidence that Tod too had "chosen—how had he put it the night he fought with Ras?—to fall outside of *history*" (434). Inside history, Tod is merely an Imaginary other, an ideal ego. Outside it, where he moves into the unconscious itself, he becomes an ego-ideal, an Other signifying the narrator's assumption of Law in the Symbolic.

As ego-ideal, Tod, dead and mourned, exerts a powerful impact on the narrator. Lacan addresses such an impact in "Desire and the Interpretation of Desire in *Hamlet*." There, Lacan suggests that mourning breaks down the subject and requires it to reconstitute itself in a reassumption of the authority of the Symbolic. The "object of mourning derives its importance for us from a certain identification relationship," Lacan says, one "that Freud attempted to define most precisely with the term 'incorporation'" (37). The relation between Tod, as ideal Other, and the narrator accounts for the trauma Tod's death yields because for a time it disintegrates the narrator's sense of the integrity of the Symbolic itself. Thoughts of Brotherhood are merely Imaginary and simply will not erase the narrator's existential anguish upon confronting the Real of death once the policeman has slain Tod Clifton. So the narrator's own mind begins "to plunge" in the way that Clifton's must have, and while going down into a subway all he can do is ask himself questions. "Why should a man deliberately plunge outside of history," he wonders. "Why should he choose to disarm himself, give up his voice and leave the only organization offering him a chance to 'define' himself?" (438). And more than that, "Why did he choose to plunge into nothingness, into the void of faceless faces, of soundless voices, lying outside history?" Then, really for the first time, thoughts about what might have motivated young Clifton prompt the narrator to form ideas of his own about history. History, he realizes, may be a signifier, but it is still arbitrary. Even an invisible man can define it; he too can play the game in which signifiers rule. In these thoughts, he lifts another veil of the Imaginary covering the Symbolic. The uninformed, he realizes, believe "history records the patterns of men's lives." That is what "they say." "All things," they also say, "are duly recorded—all things of importance, that is. But not quite," he realizes, "for actually it is only the known, the seen, the heard and only those events that the recorder regards as important that are put down, those lies his keepers keep their power by" (439).

The grim tragedy of Tod's death forces the narrator to probe yet deeper into the notion of history and the domain of the Symbolic. He starts with one of the basic tenets of the Brotherhood. He asks, Is history a force in nature that can be understood only by the Brotherhood's doctrinal scientists? Around him after Tod is dead he begins to see others—identificatory others—who in their own ways would deny history as violently as Clifton finally had. These others help him see a larger, more transcendent, Symbolic truth. If history is a signifier, he wonders, what relation does it have to the lives of those others—"familiar in their unfamiliarity"—he sees around him? For his history to be an adequate signifier, it must include the outsiders, the alienated, the marginal in ways the Brotherhood does not. While Ellison's hero still clings to the idea of Brotherhood, he is also beginning to think seriously about lives other than his own. The zoot-suiters, for instance, also undermine any standard conception of history. Like himself, they are invisible men whom "everyone must have seen [...] or perhaps failed to see [...] at all." Like Tod, they are "men outside of historical time, they were untouched, they didn't believe in Brotherhood, no doubt had never heard of it; or perhaps like Clifton would mysteriously have rejected its mysteries; men of transition whose faces were immobile" (440). Moreover, the narrator, in the midst of these speculations, has an even more disconcerting thought. They may be more consequential than he has imagined: "who knew but that they were the saviors, the true leaders, the bearers of something precious? The stewards of something uncomfortable, burdensome, which they hated because, living outside the realm of history, there was no one to applaud their value and they themselves failed to understand it." But then the narrator has what is perhaps his most disturbing thought of all. What if the Brotherhood's notion of history as something rational and analyzable by scientific methods is wrong? "What if history was a gambler," he asks,

> instead of a force in a laboratory experiment, and the boys his ace in the hole? What if history was not a reasonable citizen, but a madman full of paranoid guile and these boys his agents, his big surprise! His own revenge? For they were outside, in the dark with Sambo, the dancing paper doll; taking it on the lambo with my fallen brother, Tod Clifton (Tod, Tod) running and dodging the forces of history instead of making a dominating stand. (441)

Playing the history game, Ellison's hero begins to modify the Brotherhood's concept of history so that it will embrace goals of his own toward which he cautiously moves. But at this stage, his ruminations remain tied more securely to Imaginary identifications than to Symbolic ones. At first, for instance, he tries to protect his identification with the organization. While he decides the idea of Brotherhood is still valuable, he also sees that it contradicts the notion that history as a machine must grind up people—old or young—who stand in its inexorable path. He can see these people as persons now, but rather than joining them in their underground world, ostensibly outside time and history, he determines to bring them into a historical realm still defined by the Brotherhood. "They'd been there all along," he realizes, "but somehow I had missed them. I'd missed them even when my work had been most successful. They were outside the groove of history, and it was my job to get them in, all of them." But such resolves lead him to other questions that undercut the Brotherhood and yet do not release its hold entirely. For instance, he wonders what might be the content and medium of history as he passes a record shop and hears a recording of the blues. He ask himself, "[W]as this all that would be recorded? Was this the only true history of the times, a mood blared by trumpets, trombones, saxophones and drums, a song with turgid, inadequate words?" (443). Thus, while he decides that Tod's death must be put to some political use, the only use at this moment he can imagine remains one serving in behalf of the Brotherhood. Once told by the party leaders that the individual is meaningless in the work of the organization, he thinks, "The shooting was all that was left of [Tod] now. Clifton had chosen to plunge out of history and, except for the picture it made in my mind's eye, only the plunge was recorded, and that was the only important thing" (447). To use Tod's death, the narrator thus plans to show Harlem that "the meaning of his death was greater than the incident or the object that caused it." He would use that death as a way to avenge Tod and to prevent other deaths like his. But, still in thrall to the Brotherhood, he also plans to use it as a way to attract members lost from the Brotherhood back into it. "It would be ruthless," he realizes, "but a ruthlessness in the interest of Brotherhood, for we had only our minds and bodies, as against the other side's vast power" (448).

Although the narrator plans to use the funeral to further the ends of the Brotherhood, in fact it does two other things crucial to his own development. First, it reifies the importance both of Tod Clifton as a Symbolic ideal and of the register of the Symbolic itself. In "Desire and the Interpretation of Desire in *Hamlet*," Lacan suggests that funeral rites "fulfill our obligation to what is called the memory of the dead," but they also invoke "the entire play of the symbolic register" (38). While their function is to "fill that hole in the real" created by the loss of the beloved or the identificatory other, the only means by which to do this is through the Symbolic register, "the totality of the signifier." Thus, it is through "logos," the Word, that this function is achieved, in the face of the extreme "disorder that is produced" when "signifying elements" have become inadequate "to cope with the hole that has been created in existence," when, indeed, a death has "impeached" the total "system of signifiers." In Lacan, the Symbolic is the domain of the word, the logos, *the* word that undergirds signification. One reason that many people faint or become momentarily—or, even, more than momentarily—disoriented upon learning of the death of a loved or otherwise identificatory personage is that this is knowledge of the Real itself and such knowledge may rip our cognitive foundations from the Symbolic. Mourning, of the sort that Tod inspires in the narrator, functions to return the dead to the domain of the word and, in the process, reconstitutes the Symbolic in the subject and thereby reconstitutes subjectivity itself. In the text, the narrator's funeral oration serves these functions. As a figure of the dead, Tod represents a relay between the unconscious that grounds the subject and the Symbolic that frames a subject's ordinary—Imaginary—life as it is played out. Thus, rather than reinforcing the power of the Brotherhood, the speech leads the narrator to Symbolic authority in the Law of the Other who resides in the place of the dead.

In ironic fact, then, the funeral oration leads the narrator to a clearer sense of himself, his ego, in relation to the collective power of the social order. The speech he makes at the funeral and the music he hears as part of it lead him not to collective brotherhood but to an epiphany about the synecdochic relation of the individual as part to its social Other as whole. Picking up the blues theme about which he has given much thought, the narrator says of the song sung by an "old, plaintive, masculine voice" (452) accompanied by a euphonium horn: "the song had aroused us all. It was not the words, for they were all the same old slave-borne words; it was as though he'd changed the emotion beneath the words while yet the old longing, resigned, transcendent emotion still sounded above, now deepened by the something for which the theory of Brotherhood had given me no name" (453). Moreover, after his own irony-laden speech, followed by a feeling of failure because he "had been unable to bring in the political issues," he finally arrives at a satisfying revelation. It comes when, taking one last look at Tod Clifton's coffin, it a signifier of the mourned dead, he sees "not a crowd but the set faces of individual men and women" (459). His revelation is that the one, a subject, an individual, has a Symbolic—not merely an Imaginary and therefore only specular—relation to its defining, determining, empowering Other. The Other may speak through us, he realizes, but we may also speak in the name of the Other as well when the two—ego and Other—operate in the normative way in an ordinary subject. This fusion of ego or ego-ideal and Other is as close as a subject comes to going beyond the Other, beyond the Phallus, in a beyond that is really nowhere since, Lacan says, there is no Other of the Other. But since that impossibility seldom stops the subject from positing—supposing, that is—such a beyond, we must ask, What does this ultra-Other become in *Invisible Man*?

4

> It is the truth of what [his] desire has been in his history that the patient cries out through his symptom, as Christ said that the stones themselves would have cried out if the children of Israel had not lent them their voice.
>
> —Jacques Lacan, *Écrits: A Selection*, 167

We may say that the main conflict in *Invisible Man* lies in the narrator's need to define himself against a backdrop of signifiers of race, family, and social life. The resolution of that conflict must come in the narrator's accepting his role as authoritative, Symbolic being, as the one supposed to know or as the father speaking in the Name-of-the-Father (on self, naming, the proper name, see Neighbors). All of these elements have revolved about the notion of history. In addressing a thematics of history, Ellison's novel participates in a movement of sorts that includes many important novels from the late 1940s into the 1970s, including, for instance, Norman Mailer's *Naked and the Dead*, Saul Bellow's *Herzog*, William Styron's *Confessions of Nat Turner*, and John Updike's *Centaur*.[3] In such novels, "history" has become the battlefield, but the battle is not so much between troops as among tropes, among, that is, figures of speech, enfigurations, or symbolizations. It is, in short, a battle that takes place within the Symbolic. In Ellison, once the narrator through Tod Clifton establishes a firm ego-ideal, and so resolves that conflict (oedipal), he then must engage the representation of the Imaginary other of ideology. To do that his emerging concept of history must replace that of the Brotherhood. In personal terms, given the sense of the worth of the individual that Clifton, the zoot-suiters, and the crowd at the funeral lend him, Ellison's hero realizes he must fight the party leadership. Since he has himself taken "personal responsibility" for organizing and conducting Tod's funeral, he finds that he must defend theorizing his own inchoate historical philosophy. For this reason he tells white Tobitt, married to a black woman, to ask his wife "to take [him] around to the gin mills and the barber shops and the juke joints and the churches, Brother. Yes, and the beauty parlors on Saturdays when they're frying hair. A whole unrecorded history is spoken there, Brother" (471). Still, he does not want to leave the Brotherhood. While he believes that the life he is living is the "only historically meaningful life" (478) he can live, he yet believes that to be outside the Brotherhood is to be "outside history" (499). But that feeling changes during his discussions with Brother Hambro about the organization's "new directives" and his role in carrying them out, for he finds nothing there to equal the satisfaction effected by his projection into his ego-ideal, Tod Clifton, and thus the sense of union and wholeness he had felt with the crowd at Clifton's funeral, the same crowd that Hambro asks him to "sacrifice for the good of the whole" (502). Nor can he quite accept Hambro's notion that progress comes from the machinations of the organization. He feels he is simply being asked to put the brakes on "the old wheel of history." "Or," he wonders, ironically, "is it the little wheels *within* the wheel?" (504).

From all these engagements, he comes to a series of conclusions. A major conclusion involves generally what every human subject learns, but more particularly concerns his role in the Brotherhood and his place in its conception of history. "Well, I *was* and yet I was invisible, that was the fundamental contradiction. I was and yet I was unseen" by the Brotherhood. Suffering this realization, he determines *one* meaning implicit in his dying grandfather's words: "I saw that I could agree with Jack [and the Brotherhood] without agreeing. And I could tell Harlem to have hope when there was no hope. Perhaps I could tell them to hope until I found the basis of something real, some firm ground for action that would lead them onto the plane of history. But until then I would have to move them without myself being moved" (507). Further, while he calls this plan "a Rinehart," it is, alas, essentially the same procedure the Brotherhood uses and the same one he thinks he at last is denying when he pretends to accede to its demands. In the meantime he determines another conclusion in the face of his invisibility. "I was my experiences and my experiences were me," he insists, "and no blind men, no matter how powerful they became, even if they conquered the world, could take that, or change one single itch, taunt, laugh, cry, scar, ache, rage or pain of it" (508). All those others who "set themselves up to describe the world" (507) and who—like those "reality instructors" we find in Saul Bellow's *Herzog*—try to force their "picture of reality upon" him will have no power over him again (508).

But there is another important lesson, one providing a gloss on his grandfather's message, that must be learned before he can assume his final place beyond history. Ellison's hero must learn that the methods he attempts to use to help his people, whether they are the methods of a Rinehart or of a Brotherhood, simply cannot work. They make him as blind to others as he is invisible to them, and they allow him ultimately to be used by those whom he must defeat. He comes to this realization in the midst of the riot started by Ras the Destroyer: "Could this be the answer, could this be what the committee had planned, the answer to why they'd surrendered our influence to Ras?" he asks himself when he hears the dread words, "race riot." Immediately, he begins to see the strategy clearly: "It was not suicide, but murder. The committee had planned it. And I had helped, had been a tool." As a "tool" adapted to a finely tuned machine of historical process, doing what it demands, he is made, he realizes, a "tool just at the very moment I had thought myself free. By pretending to agree I *had* indeed agreed, had made myself responsible for that huddled form lighted by flame and gunfire in the street, and all the others whom now the night was making ripe for death" (553). His revelation imposes a heavy responsibility that sticks with him as tenaciously as that briefcase which comes to represent—almost to *contain*—his very identity.

This negative interpretation of his grandfather's message, however, is not the ultimate conclusion about history. Ellison's hero must continue to search for a signification of it that is appropriate to his own emerging "picture of reality." That he finds it and where he finds it probably account for the enormous appeal *Invisible Man* has for Americans of every race. His Signifier, his History, is made in *America*. Moving through a concept of communal history to one of personal identity, he recognizes, he says, "the simple yet confoundingly complex arrangement of hope and desire, fear and hate, that had brought me here still running, and knowing now who I was and where I was and knowing too that I had no longer to run for or from the Jacks and the Emersons and the Bledsoes and Nortons, but only from their confusion, impatience, and refusal to recognize the beautiful absurdity of their American identity and mine" (559). He argues for diversity, long before the term achieves its current signification. "America," he says in the epilogue, "is woven of many strands; I would recognize them and let so remain." He says, moreover, "Our fate is to become one, and yet many—This is not prophecy, but description." To accept our racial history, our ethnic origins, is not to succumb to racism. When perverted ethnicity becomes racist it brings with it a moral reversal that affects racism of any sort. "Thus one of the greatest jokes in the world," he says, "is the spectacle of the whites busy escaping blackness and becoming blacker every day, and the blacks striving toward whiteness, becoming quite dull and gray. None of us seems to know who he is or where he's going" (577).

What the invisible man arrives at, finally, is an affirmative interpretation of his grandfather's deathbed advice. It is an interpretation of American history that affirms the Law, the Name-of-the-Father, not the father or other figures of the real or Imaginary. In doing so, he goes beyond the father and seizes his power to speak in the Name—the principle—of the Father, in, really, the names of the Founding Fathers: "Could he have meant—hell, he *must* have meant," says the narrator, "the principle, that we were to affirm the principle on which the country was built and not the men, or at least not the men who did the violence" (574). Those who do the violence—men such as the Jacks and the Emersons, the Bledsoes and the Nortons and the Rases—will create only a universe of blood. Such is the narrator's meaning when he tells these men in his dream at the end of the novel's final chapter, "*there's your universe, and that drip-drop [of blood] upon the water you hear is all the history you've made, all you're going to make*" (570). Once he plunges through that open manhole and into the underground realm where, like Tod Clifton and the great mass of others around him, he plunges outside history-as-it-is-known, he recognizes that he too must finally eschew violence.

There, in that underworld, he is left with one meaningful conclusion beyond history, one self-affirming, life-changing act outside history that he can perform. Thus, at the end, we return to our beginning, as

Ellison's narrator reaches the precise point where he is prepared to begin the act he has just completed. *He writes his book.* To write the book is to reify the power of the Symbolic, to produce a signifier that displaces the father and stamps oneself *as* Father, though not *of* himself, as the vet had enjoined, but *for* others who might take him as *le sujet supposé savoir*, the subject supposed to know. Lacan's concept, considered at some length in *The Four Fundamental Concepts of Psychoanalysis* (224–25, 230–43), refers to the Other, the "great" Other who is supposed (by a subject) to know all. In religion, this Other is often called "God"; in philosophy, it might be the "Idea"; to a Marxist, it is "History." In psychoanalysis, in the relation of the analyst and analysand, the role of such an Other is created in the transference and is assigned to the analyst. But in fact, Lacan says, this Other that knows, whether, God, Idea, History, whatever, is actually always only the subject's unconscious, for only the unconscious really knows the subject. In analysis, through the transference, the analysand attributes to the analyst knowledge that is already present, though repressed, in the unconscious. Analysis, through the technique of association, in the talking cure, may uncover the repressed material. Possibly in ordinary life (as in journal keeping) and certainly in literature, the act of writing may produce a self-knowledge of the sort that comes in psychoanalysis. It is this act that allows Ellison's narrator to approach an Other who/which knows. But as a Symbolic, this who or which never speaks a message that is beyond interpretation. Thus the narrator's book, as a signifier, as a manifestly textual unconscious, casts narrator and readers into what Lacan calls the "defiles of the signifier." Once more—and inevitably, since there is no Other of the Other—the book ambiguates the role of interpretation—and the Symbolic. As much as the narrator himself, the book participates in the *vel* of alienation, the either/or of being and meaning. But it plays mainly on the side of being, on the side of the body and the act lying outside history. As John M. Reilly has said, "[L]iterature—an imaginative variety of historical interpretation and reinterpretation—is always [...] a realm of conscious, deliberate action" ("Reconstruction" 3). But while the "memoir" the invisible man constructs surely represents such a deliberately assertive act, it cannot fail but to end up as just another object, just another signifier that "history" must interpret. Thus, whereas Ellison's book is indeed a historical act, its meaning, like meaning in any domain, is still—and will always be—open to interpretation in and by the Symbolic. Hence, if the novel leaves us with any message, it is the constancy of the battle for both being and meaning and the constancy of our fading into one or the other in the determining but indeterminate universe of a Real beyond history.

CHAPTER 4

Méconnaissance: "Saint" Flannery, Sexuality, and the Culture of Psychoanalysis

The saint [...] occupies the place of *objet petit a*, of pure object, of somebody undergoing radical subjective destitution.
—Slavoj Žižek, *The Sublime Object of Ideology*, 116

W riting *Wise Blood* at the same pivotal historical moment in the theoretical life of the textual unconscious as was Ralph Ellison when composing *Invisible Man*, Flannery O'Connor consciously rejects a presupposition Ellison embraced. O'Connor offers an interesting case of the relation between a culture and a subject within it, between cultural text and literary text, between an unconscious that is textual and conscious disavowals of psychoanalysis as such. Because she was a Christian writer who suffered considerably from a painful and debilitating disease, died young, and left a legacy of remarkable stories and novels, critics of many persuasions have canonized her in ways few writers have been canonized. Since it is hard to argue with a saint, the vast majority of readers, acting as if there were neither unconscious nor textual unconscious, have capitulated to O'Connor's pronouncements on how to read those works. Several critics—myself among them—have reminded us how effectively O'Connor has set the terms of the discourse about her. Working in the modernist period, she thought herself not a modernist but a throwback to an earlier age. Consequently, one of the more interesting, but generally ignored questions about Flannery O'Connor is how to periodize her work. Whatever her claims, it is clear she is modernist in important ways. We see that in her use of myth, for example, and in how she uses the devices of lyrical or "poetic" fiction such as powerful controlling metaphors and recurrent image motifs to knit together a form in place of traditional emplotments. In her practice, moreover, she is a modernist easily allied with New Criticism. Of O'Connor's adherence to its tenets, Frederick Crews says, "As she freely admitted, she came into her own as an artist only after undergoing a full New Critical initiation at the University of Iowa's Writer's Workshop under the tutelage of Paul Engle and Andrew Lytle, with Brooks and Warren's then ubiquitous *Understanding Fiction* providing the models" (144). Indeed, says Crews, "Even the most impressive and original of her stories adhere to the classroom formula of her day: show, don't tell; keep the narrative voice distinct from those of your characters; cultivate understatement; develop a central image or symbol to convey your theme 'objectively'; and point everything toward one neatly sprung ironic reversal. No one ever put it all together with greater deftness" (144–45).

But if O'Connor herself might have conceded those affinities, she adamantly opposed herself to modernism in her intended themes. Indeed, her themes as she sees them reflect a distant time, and her insistent pursuit of Christian, specifically Catholic, values makes her dream of another time that might best be described as medieval. She could have been Henry Adams longing for the epoch of the Virgin, a time when the Church stood as the regnant power in a world universally perceived as spiritual, as one in which spirit and matter were fully united, not split as O'Connor saw them in her century. While apparent from early adulthood, O'Connor's interest in this split was fueled in 1954 by William F. Lynch's "Theology and the Imagination," an essay addressing modernist Manicheanism and that bane of religion, psychoanalysis. Discussing aspects of O'Connor's rejection of modernism, M. A. Klug focuses on the Manichean split between spirit and matter. "Flannery O'Connor," writes Klug, "made no secret of her contempt for the modern age. Her antagonism to it goes far beyond the artist's conventional scorn of science, technology, middle-class values, 'the smell of steaks in passageways.'" Because of the Manicheanism she laments so often in her essays and letters, says Klug, "she attacks the central assumptions of literary modernism as vigorously as those of our social and economic life" (303).

O'Connor understands of course that her viewpoint is different and insists it must be that way because, as a Christian author, she has a different concern. Many letters of hers collected in *The Habit of Being* address this and related issues. "I don't think you should write something as long as a novel," she writes in one to novelist John Hawkes, "around anything that is not of the gravest concern." For her, that concern "is always the conflict between an attraction for the Holy" with which she identifies "and the disbelief in it that we breathe in with the air of the times" (349). Thus, she recognizes that if her own ideological position is not manifestly self-divided, it is certainly contrary to that of her own epoch. To illustrate the difference between her and the modernists, she tells Hawkes that whereas readers of *The Violent Bear It Away* will identify with young Tarwater's uncle (the schoolteacher Rayber, a rationalist and empiricist), she herself identifies with the boy's great-uncle Tarwater, a prophet in the ancient biblical mold. "The modern reader will identify himself with the schoolteacher," she says, "but it is the old man who speaks for me" (350). While there is no question O'Connor relishes her contrary position, there remains a question, one I have previously addressed, whether her statements tell the whole story. As I suggested in "Flannery O'Connor's *Others*" (and as Michael Kreyling likewise contends), O'Connor had a love and hate relation to the ideology represented by Rayber, one she calls "psychology," but one that seems more properly identified as "psychoanalysis" and metonymically located in the person of Sigmund Freud. But in that essay I argued that she opposed Freud because psychoanalysis threatened to destroy religion. As, later, I began to suggest in the conclusion of "Framed in the Gaze," I now am convinced Freud stands for something in O'Connor's universe both different and more complicated. While for O'Connor religion remains an issue, her fear lies in the entanglements of modernism with the culture of psychoanalysis and its attitudes toward sexuality. My argument is more complicated but resolves to this: O'Connor disavowed modernism because of psychoanalysis, but she disavowed psychoanalysis because in her own unconscious it touched fears—cloaked through a pervasive *méconnaissance*—regarding sex, gender, desire, and identity.

1

[W]e enter the symbolic order the moment a feature functions as the index of its opposite.
—Slavoj Žižek, *The Abyss of Freedom*, 39

Like it or not, O'Connor found herself embedded in modernist culture. However defined, that culture has undeniable, if not always clear, relations to psychoanalysis. In *Freud and the Culture of Psychoanalysis*, Steven Marcus argues that Freudian theory is virtually indivisible from modernism or "modernity." Moreover, he suggests that the work of Freud most implicated in modernity is *Three Essays on the Theory of Sexuality*. "In my view," says Marcus, "no work of its kind or scope is more important for the understanding of how modernity—or the generally recognized modern point of view—came into being or was brought about. As one reads it, one can almost see

certain vital parts of modernity in the very processes of disclosure, formation and construction" (2). In effect, this modern point of view and
the processes Marcus names give modernism its character, define the
modern as a culture of psychoanalysis, and, what is more, construct for
us *modernist* reading. Opposed to the accretive method of textual exe-
gesis found in Judeo-Christian traditions, modernist reading, in looking
for a hidden meaning below the signifiers of a text, follows the model
of Freudian reading. Indeed, though it need not be explicitly Freudian,
"interpretation" as a standard activity of readers became established in
this century largely because Freud's notion of a relation between a
manifest and a latent content made sense of interpretive activity.

In *Making Meaning*, a book on film interpretation with implications
for all interpretive activity, David Bordwell defines two modes of interpretation as such and a mode of interpretation that presumes not to
interpret meaning at all. In his triad "explicit," "implicit," and "symptomal," the symptomal signifies more than the psychoanalytic alone. "If
explicit meaning is like a transparent garment," Bordwell says,

> and implicit meaning is like a semiopaque veil, symptomatic
> meaning is like a disguise. Taken as individual expression,
> symptomatic meaning may be treated as the consequence of
> the artist's obsessions (for example, *Psycho* as a worked-over
> version of a fantasy of Hitchcock's). Taken as part of a social
> dynamic, it may be traced to economic, political, or ideologi-
> cal processes (for example, *Psycho* as concealing the male fear
> of woman's sexuality). (9)

Rejecting even the possibility of explicit meaning as the only meaning,
modernist reading of the variety called "formalist" or "New Critical"
falls into the category of the "implicit" and that of the self-consciously
ideological variety into the "symptomal." The project called "modernist" is to find that other reading (whether implicit or symptomal)
below the manifest. For reasons I shall soon address, that modernist
project is one O'Connor almost desperately denies.

In her denial of psychoanalytic reading, O'Connor exhibits symptoms that lead to other interpretations distinctly more interesting, if not
more true, than her overt ones. Despite O'Connor's defense of an
explicit text conveying theological meanings, and despite her objections
to the psychoanalytic, her way and the modernist method of the psychoanalytic, as Kreyling, Satterfield, and I have argued, are readily conflated. One of the best critics writing on O'Connor, Frederick Asals, in
one essay, has made a point like this. The subject of Asals's essay—the
use O'Connor makes of the figure of the double—is itself symptomatic

of the modernist reading. "Now," says Asals, "we might conclude quickly that her distinctive contribution to the modern tradition of the double is to give the motif a weight that is theological rather than psychological or simply moral." Such a contribution O'Connor herself claimed. But Asals is no more content to stop there than I am. Neither does he agree that her "art is [...] so univalent." Contrary to O'Connor's expostulations in her letters and speeches, "introducing the theological," he says, "does not demand expelling the psychological." Indeed, says Asals, the matter is entirely "the reverse: the revelations in O'Connor's works, so often precipitated by those double figures, come only when the consciousness of the protagonist, with all its presuppositions and defenses, is finally overthrown and deeper awareness forces its way through" (76).

Although Asals well summarizes the premises of a modernist reading, he seems to fall into the trap that O'Connor sets for us in her positing the theological as the only valid reading of her fiction. His comments, as in the following, while they appear to valorize both the psychoanalytic and the theological, in fact make the theological dominant. His embedded figures (of lower and higher) make plain that O'Connor's theological is the hegemonic reading. "O'Connor clearly saw the human unconscious not only as, say, the repository of repressed sexual urges," says Asals,

> but as a realm of inherent theological dimension from which could come intimations of the demonic and the divine. Those potent doubles thus embody the link between the unknown within the self and the unknown beyond it, between the "other" hidden inside and that Other dimension which transcends the self, between the deepest roots of one's being and the furthest reaches of Being. As *Doppelgängers* they thereby themselves acquire a double reference, pointing at once to the denials of the opposite numbers they face and to an unsuspected world beyond. (76–77)

Such claims, which O'Connor generally denied, lead Asals to two others that would also be anathema to her. One is that "O'Connor's doubles all spring from the same region of her creative mind and emerge with a Dionysian force that is anterior to whatever theological role they are asked to play" (77). The second: "The double in O'Connor's fiction represents an ineluctable human dualism, the divided self that is the inheritance of fallen man who is thereby doomed not only to incompleteness but to rending conflict" (81). From O'Connor's perspective, Asals is probably more correct when he

suggests that when her fiction seems almost to "demand a 'psychological' reading," it may actually be "parodying the very material she is
exploiting" (67). But parody, far from truly denying the prior—psychological—modality, actually helps to authenticate its existence.

A Freudian reading of *Wise Blood* by James C. McCullagh will
serve to show how firmly entrenched in psychoanalytic theory is modernist reading. McCullagh helps me make two major points. One is that
in his effort to accommodate O'Connor's expressed position regarding
how to read her, McCullagh almost inevitably attempts to integrate the
psychoanalytic and the theological or Christian hermeneutics. His
opening gesture is accommodation. "Flannery O'Connor in 'The Role
of the Catholic Novelist,'" McCullagh points out, "has acknowledged
the difficulty of writing religious fiction for a largely secular audience."
His second gesture, therefore, is to find a way to have both—religious
and secular—modalities of reading. O'Connor "surmounts this aesthetic hurdle in *Wise Blood*," he suggests, "by articulating a symbolic
mode which necessitates and justifies a blending of psychological and
theological concerns." A third gesture "explains" why, within that
"symbolic mode," the combination is possible. The reason is cultural.
"Before eternity can reveal the significance of events in time, the basic
struggle must take place on the psychological level but in a psychology
that has been exposed to a religious temper" (43). While the "psychological," McCullagh implies, may be independent of any cultural context, the religious cannot. Hazel Motes suffers religious obsessions
because he has grown up where he has. While O'Connor herself would
not agree with this unstated premise, it is one on which McCullagh's
argument seems to rest.

The second point lies in how McCullagh demonstrates the hegemony of the modernist culture of psychoanalysis. He is so totally
embedded in this culture that he does not need Freud. He never actually quotes or even needs to quote a text of Freud. One infers from the
absence of recourse to Freud or Freudians that McCullagh assumes—
quite correctly, no doubt—readers know through cultural or "tacit"
knowledge all they need of Freudian theory. He knows that readers
will know. Since the essay relies entirely on tacit knowledge of psychoanalytic theory, it of course focuses on the most standard element—the
emplotment of the family romance as named in the Oedipus complex.
"The concrete symbolic patterns and motifs which O'Connor invokes
in the novel," says McCullagh, "involve a fictional transfiguration of
Jesus (Christ as Southern 'cracker'), the figure of Maria Cross (mother
as the cross), the Oedipal theme Christianized, and a strategy of visual
imagery suggesting the ambiguous nature of 'seeing through' to

Christ" (43–44). As this summation of his essay suggests, however, McCullagh, while building on the Freudian, chooses throughout to subordinate the psychoanalytic to the Christian reading. He suggests, for example, "In *Wise Blood* there exists a complex relationship between Hazel Motes' efforts to break away from his mother and his attempts to blaspheme his way to Christ. In simple terms this is an ambitious manifestation of the Oedipal theme Christianized; Christ and the mother are linked in the impressionable psychology of the protagonist" (44).

As he must, McCullagh focuses largely on O'Connor's representations of dreams. In the novel, two are found in chapter 1 and a third in chapter 9; a fourth passage, in chapter 3, has the effect of dream as it deals with a flashback to Hazel's trip to a carnival. McCullagh claims that at the same time they integrate the religious elements, these dream scenes are the obvious Freudian sites in the text. The two critical modes, religious and psychoanalytic, seem to meld in a treatment of death. "That [Hazel] is tied to his mother and to Christ," he says, "is made clear by the dream sequences," for there the text's "symbols merge with the fact of death" (47). The theme of death surfaces clearly in the first dream, the one taking place on the train to Taulkinham. It appears in the dream's literal content. "Once he is in the sleeping berth," McCullagh reminds us, "[Hazel] has a series of numbing dreams about the deaths of his father, grandfather, brothers, and mother." The superficial content of these dreams might "dramatize the young man's morbid fear of and fascination with death," but the dreams have other meanings as well. Most important of these is the way, in the passage focusing on the mother, "it dramatizes just how closely Haze is tied to" her (47–48). While McCullagh's analysis is more intricate than I suggest, the main thrust of the argument is to link death and mother to Haze's feeling of guilt. That guilt, McCullagh argues, is tied to the family romance, the child's erotic desire for the mother.

This desire becomes evident in the novel in chapter 3, where, in a dreamlike flashback, Haze recalls the moment at a carnival when he, then a boy of ten, claiming twelve to the barker, sees a naked woman on exhibit in a coffinlike black-lined box and then goes home to be punished by his mother. At home, upon her punishment, as the novel tells us, he replaces "the guilt of the tent for the nameless unplaced guilt that was in him" (*Wise Blood* 63). "It seems obvious," says McCullagh, "that the 'unplaced guilt' Haze experiences is a direct result of the Oedipal urge" (51). Though the association of mother, carnival exhibitionist, and coffinlike box suggests that women in general are connected

to death, his guilt seems precisely connected to his desire for his
mother. "When he returns home from the fair," McCullagh says, Haze
"sees his mother as a conscious reminder of his guilt but, out of desperation or desire, he imagines her in the box in the tent." In his fantasy
vision, "What he has seen [...] is his mother naked in the coffin."
Moreover, says McCullagh, sex joins death here because Haze's father,
at the carnival, had "connected the carnival woman with death." Thus,
argues McCullagh, "there is every reason to believe that Haze" either
wishes his mother would die or "wishes to join her in death."
Moreover, McCullagh suggests, while its religious dimension makes
more of it, it at least seems "likely that the 'unplaced guilt' is a reference to his unconscious sexual appropriation of his mother" (52). In
order for Haze to surmount his guilt, he will have to reject his desire
for his mother; to redeem the mother herself he will have to transform
her, somehow, into the instrument of his own redemption. That
redemption, McCullagh argues, will be tied to Haze's ability to see the
world properly. "The rejection of his mother and the subsequent renunciation of his quest mark the first time he is able to see clearly" (55).

Combining the religious and psychoanalytic themes, McCullagh
suggests that the "mother who has haunted [Haze] becomes, in some
respects, the instrument of his redemption." Her function outlines that
of the archetype of "Maria Cross." Haze's mother becomes the "cross"
who will be "his salvation." The results of his severing "the Oedipal
chain," a severance inferred from his having resisted all those women in
the novel who try to "mother" him, are that he ceases his blasphemy
and becomes "ready for Christ" (56). He reaches Christ, however, only
because a policeman destroys the beloved Essex that Haze hopes to
drive while carrying his ministry beyond Taulkinham. Bereft of this
object, Haze finds himself in a blighted world so dead he suddenly realizes "where his profane mission has been taking him. There is no more
need for blasphemous rhetoric since it neither helped him forget his
mother nor get to Christ. For these reasons it is not surprising that he
abandons his arrogance and blinds himself," an act that represents "an
exaggerated form of his childhood penance," his walking with shoes
full of stones after the episode of the carnival. But to justify Haze's acts
of self-immolation, McCullagh turns neither to a Christian nor to a
specific psychoanalytic rationale. Though he might explicitly have used
features of either, he begs the question of rationale in two ways. In one,
he turns to the notion of paradox. "Paradoxically," he claims,
"O'Connor suggests that true vision might come only through death,
mortification, and denial" (57). Thus, where McCullagh seems most to
have needed some master narrative taken from one or the other of his

selected modes of reading, he turns to what seems merely a lame, formalist, perhaps New Critical–inspired invocation of paradox. In the second way, McCullagh simply takes—on faith, shall we say—that Haze rests finally in spiritual peace and has indeed given up his desire for his mother and his quest for a new jesus. "Given the nature of his blasphemous quest and his relationship to the mother," writes McCullagh, "there is little reason to suspect that his final comfort is not of a truly spiritual kind" (58).

2

> Misrecognition represents a certain organization of affirmations and negations, to which the subject is attached. [...] There must surely be, behind one's misrecognition, a kind of knowledge of what there is to misrecognize.
> —Jacques Lacan, *Freud's Papers on Technique*, 167

McCullagh's "Christianized" Freudian reading of *Wise Blood* demonstrates that, indeed, one can read O'Connor's texts according to Christian or psychoanalytic theory and that, moreover, the one need not eliminate the other. So why does O'Connor resist the Freudian and psychoanalytic and, in that resistance, resist her own time, the age of the modern that constructs her and the reception of her works? To answer these questions, I shall shift focus from Freudian to Lacanian theory. While O'Connor is smart and knowledgeable about her own and the ways of her time, she exhibits much that Jacques Lacan would call *"méconnaissance"* in her representations of her ideological position. For Lacan, *méconnaissance* signifies an illusion of the autonomy of ego and consciousness that cloaks an unconscious perception of one's fragmentation, of one's self or ego as in fact alienated from or divided against itself (see, for example, *Écrits: A Selection* 6, 15, 42, 138, 282). The term does not suggest delusion or stupidity or some character flaw. Because it suggests that what we think we know may also contain an unconscious dimension we do not perceive, the concept is absolutely central to psychoanalysis. In O'Connor, one reason for the *méconnaissance* is precisely her denial that the unconscious even exists. But its existence nonetheless becomes apparent almost instantly in her own epistemology, the one that reveals itself, implicitly, in the title of *Wise Blood*. For it is rather plain that notions in a letter she calls a cognitive "blood-business" and "head-business" (522) exactly replicate ordinary distinctions between the unconscious and consciousness. That which drives both Enoch Emery and Hazel Motes in the novel is the unconscious, "blood-business"; that which they feel they must resist is the too rational, merely conscious "head-business." *They* do not know that, but O'Connor does, for she recognizes that the *méconnaissance* of the two reflects her own orientation toward the modernist age. Still, while she understands them, she does not understand herself—that her orientation exhibits ways she is divided against herself as much as against her age. The main split she exhibits is that between what Raymond Williams calls the "residual" and the "dominant," in O'Connor the split between the residual culture of fundamentalist Christianity and the dominant culture of psychoanalysis.[1] As we shall see, this self-division shows itself in her letters in a variety of contexts. In particular, it shows itself in her comments about Hazel Motes and the composition of the novel *Wise Blood.*

At perhaps the most overt level, O'Connor's *méconnaissance* shows through in her desire to remain free of the impositions of her modernist culture. The one imposition that seems most troubling to her is psychoanalysis itself. As a number of critics—myself included— have observed, her denial of psychoanalysis and with it the culture of psychoanalysis is quite direct. On a very conscious level, where the head business occurs, O'Connor knows that psychoanalysis offers a way of reading her work that will seem more accessible to most read- ers than the way she intends or thinks she intends. In a bit of humor, she expresses such awareness in comments about the book that will become *Wise Blood.* In a letter to fellow novelist Robie Macauley, she says, "Me and Enoch are living in the woods in Connecticut with the Robert Fitzgeralds." But before that, O'Connor had lived briefly in New York City, the center in America of the culture of psychoanalysis and a place where popular lore has it everyone may be as loony as Enoch himself. "Enoch didn't care so much for New York," she tells Macauley. "He said there wasn't no privetcy [sic] there. Every time he went to sit in the bushes there was already somebody sitting there ahead of him" (21).

When we examine such comments in the context provided by the story and its place of publication, they reveal the nature of O'Connor's illusion of her and her work's autonomy within a dominant culture. What is that context? The story in which Enoch Emery first had seen print, "The Heart of the Park," appeared in the *Partisan Review* (vol. 16, February 1949) and is reprinted in *The Complete Stories.* Revised slightly, it became chapter 5 of *Wise Blood.* Both story and book chap- ter recount Enoch's voyeuristic, obsessive-compulsive behavior. In the remark to Macauley, O'Connor's allusion to the bushes refers to the way Enoch hides in abelia shrubs and spies on women who come to

swim at a park that also includes a zoo and a museum figuring prominently in Enoch's preoccupations. Having discovered some object at
"the dark secret center of the park" (*Complete Stories* 83; *Wise Blood*
82) where the museum sits, Enoch awaits an unknown someone to
whom he must show that secret object. Enoch feels "[h]e had wise
blood like his daddy" (*Complete Stories* 81; *Wise Blood* 79), and it is
that which drives him toward the secret object and the unknown other
with whom he must share it.

Given the psychological quirks Enoch exhibits in his display of religious compulsion, one must conclude that surely O'Connor recognizes
the irony of the story's publication in, of all places, the *Partisan
Review*. She knows the review has been *the* journal of the New York
intellectuals. As Alexander Bloom has shown in *Prodigal Sons*, the
review, largely because of Lionel Trilling, became virtually the house
organ of the culture of psychoanalysis. What is more, O'Connor reveals
her *méconnaissance* yet further in her acknowledgment of the journal.
Ending her letter's little fable, O'Connor tells Macauley that Enoch
"was very nervous before we left and somebody at the *Partisan Review*
told him to go to an analyst. He went and the analyst said what was
wrong with him was his daddy's fault and Enoch was so mad that anybody should defame his daddy that he pushed the analyst out the
window" (21). The comic fable may all be in good fun, but, whether
O'Connor means to, it indicates she is well aware of the psychoanalytic
orientation of the journal in which her story appears. Moreover, with
that knowledge, she must realize that an oedipal hermeneutic will
inevitably be applied to Enoch's "case." Indeed, in defending her story
against psychoanalysis, the fable reveals some of its best humor in her
nearly perfect representation of the psychoanalytic transference Freud
makes the cornerstone of analysis. As conventional analytic patients
transfer their problems to the analyst and act out the feelings attendant
upon them, so, in her fable, Enoch transfers his problem—his father—
to the analyst and throws him, in place of the father, through the
window. Thus while entertaining enough, O'Connor's defense ends up
less a defense than a confession of her knowledge of *Partisan Review*,
psychoanalysis, and the power the culture of psychoanalysis will have
over interpretation of her work, if not indeed over the creative energies
out of which it emerges.

O'Connor's *méconnaissance* may be just as crucial, though subtler,
in her comments elsewhere about the other major character of *Wise
Blood*, Hazel Motes. Through humor, O'Connor displaces her ambivalent resistance-cum-attraction to psychoanalysis in her remarks to
Macauley. But to another correspondent, Ben Griffith, she displaces in

another direction. She simply *misconstrues* a query and assumes any question about Oedipus must be one of sources rather than implicit psychoanalytic significance. She calls such questions by readers "source-itis." But the name O'Connor gives the "disease" is only a symptom of what really troubles O'Connor—her own ambivalence toward psychoanalytic theory. On the one hand, she dismisses Griffith's source hunting: "I don't know how to cure the source-itis except to tell you that I can discover a good many possible sources myself for *Wise Blood* but I am often embarrassed to find that I read the sources after I had written the book" (68). But, on the other, she also admits to the ways in which her mind, like anyone's, processes materials that might go into her fiction. "I have one of those food-chopper brains," she tells Griffith, "that nothing comes out of the way it went in."

That food chopper might account for any assimilated influences—however unconscious, however Freudian. But when she seems on the verge of confessing about the importance to her of the Freudian Oedipus, she nonetheless backs off. As an influence, "The Oedipus business comes nearer home," she admits. "Of course Haze Motes is not an Oedipus figure but there are the obvious resemblances." Those resemblances to which she seems to refer, however, would be to the original, the Sophoclean Oedipus, not the Freudian *concept*. She feels she can prove this claim because of the context within which she finished the novel. "At the time I was writing the last of the book," she says, "I was living in Connecticut with the Robert Fitzgeralds. Robert Fitzgerald translated the Theban cycle with Dudley Fitts, and their translation of the *Oedipus Rex* had just come out and I was much taken with it." While in all apparent candor she can admit, "Anyway, all I can say is, I did a lot of thinking about Oedipus," in fact she admits very little that is revelatory. For no reasonable reader ever assumes that Haze Motes, despite the self-blinding, is a representation of Oedipus. The question is only, Does Haze—or Enoch, for that matter—represent an Oedipus *complex*? Acting out the purest *méconnaissance*, O'Connor dodges that question entirely. Her final bit of defense against the Freudian intimations is a simple dictum: "My background and my inclinations are both Catholic and I think this is very apparent in the book" (68). But that hardly settles the question.

Living and writing within a culture of psychoanalysis, O'Connor finds she must defend herself in other ways. But these ways also exhibit her *méconnaissance*. One important way has to do with her overt references to Freud and psychoanalytic interpretation. Several critics have offered Freudian interpretations or discussed her responses to the claims of others that she fosters Freudian interpretations (besides Asals and McCullagh, see for instance Kreyling, LeClair, and Satterfield). Suffice it to point out here that regarding the way others associate her work with Freudian theory, she seems always to deny so vehemently as to make one wonder what the truth really is. She admits to knowing some Freudian (and Jungian) theory and, especially, to having read an article comparing the thought of Freud to that of St. Thomas Aquinas: "Guess who comes out on top?" she jokingly asks one correspondent. But O'Connor confesses to her a wary ambivalence toward Freud. "As to Sigmund," she writes, "I am against him tooth and toenail but I am crafty: never deny, seldom confirm, always distinguish. Within his limitations I am ready to admit certain uses for him" (110).[2]

But to others in her letters she speaks as if use of psychoanalytic theory would be the thing most remote from her mind. She explodes, for example, on Cecil Dawkins, who apparently had thought that the main character of "The Lame Shall Enter First" somehow "represents Freud." If indeed that is Dawkins's reading, one has to agree with O'Connor's puzzlement, but one has also to feel that O'Connor reacts too strongly to the error. "There's nothing *in* the story that could possibly suggest that Sheppard represents Freud," she insists. "This is some theory of which you are possessed." But having established that psychoanalytic assessment, O'Connor ends with an expression that suggests it is she, not the critic, "possessed" by Freud. "I have just read a review in the Chicago *Sun* about *Wise Blood* in which I am congratulated for producing a *Lolita* five or six years before Nabokov—so Freud is dogging my tracks all the way" (490). The image she calls up here—"dogging my tracks"—suggests to a reader of her fiction the various figures of Jesus that likewise dog so many of her characters, especially *Wise Blood*'s Haze and young Tarwater, of *The Violent Bear It Away*. That she may have detected the unconscious self-allusion could also account for her abrupt change of tone toward Dawkins. "I really have quite a respect for Freud when he isn't made into a philosopher," she says. "If I can lay hands on it, I will send you an article about him and St. Thomas in which they are rowing in the same boat. You probably hear a lot about Freud at Yaddo [the writers' retreat]. To religion I think he is much less dangerous than Jung" (490–91). All in all, indeed, one begins to feel that Freud dogs O'Connor in precisely the same way Christ dogs her redemption-starved characters. The question is why? Why, apart from her defense of her Christianity, does O'Connor so vehemently deny psychoanalysis and Freudian constructions of meaning?

3

> When Lacan says that the "secret of psychoanalysis" consists in the fact that "there is no sexual act, whereas there is sexuality," the act is to be conceived precisely as the performative assumption, by the subject, of his symbolic mandate.
>
> —Slavoj Žižek, *Tarrying with the Negative*, 276n38

One answer is O'Connor's fear for religion's future, but the more precise answer is sex and sexuality. Neither sex nor sexuality has been a major theme of O'Connor's critics, but J. O. Tate and D. G. Kehl, among a few, have offered discussions bearing on my interests. In "Framed in the Gaze," I have also taken up some of these issues. In that essay, I offer a postmodernist reading of O'Connor through Lacan that separates from culturally controlled 'sexuality' the rawer primality of sex itself. These concepts pivot on the difference between what the Lacanian critic Slavoj Žižek, in matters I will address more fully in later chapters, often stresses as the "oedipal" versus the "anal" or "phallic" fathers. In the oxymoronic contradictions common to postmodernist Lacanian interpretation, Hazel Motes focuses both the oedipal and, especially, the phallic "fathers." In "Framed in the Gaze," I suggest, "Haze is the terrible, anamorphotic, phallic thing that symbolizes O'Connor's horror not of sexuality (for that is constituted and controlled in our discourses), but of something more primal—of sex it*self*" (69). In O'Connor, it is clear, I think, that sex and sexuality bind themselves to the issues surrounding psychoanalysis per se because Freud presumed to make sex the absolute foundation of his theory. If O'Connor seems self-blinded about the relation between religion and psychoanalysis as philosophies, she seems especially obtuse about questions of sexuality raised by Freudian theory. That naiveté is as evident when she talks about herself as about her characters.

A passage in one of her letters suggests the multiple ways O'Connor handles—or mishandles—sexuality. In the first place, this letter is to the correspondent Sally Fitzgerald, editor of *The Habit of Being*, designated "A" for Anonymous. Beginning their correspondence in the summer of 1955, "A" became O'Connor's most frequent correspondent and favored confidante. After her death (by suicide after a long history of depression), "A," it was revealed in 1998, was a woman named Betty Hester. Hester not only was an aspiring writer but, at the time her correspondence with O'Connor began, was also a Catholic (much to O'Connor's distress, she later left the Church). The two of them shared ideas about both writing and religion, and both wrote book reviews for the Catholic magazine called *The Bulletin*. While it seems unlikely the identification was merely one-sided, for O'Connor, in Lacanian terms, Hester clearly represents an Imaginary, identificatory, very positively charged other to whom she unconsciously divulges more than she might suspect. One sees, for instance, how O'Connor, imagining Hester as a woman perhaps as beautiful as St. Catherine of Genoa (113–14), saw her at the same time as a self more whole and beautiful than her lupus permitted O'Connor to imagine herself at the time. In such identifications there is always a latent erotism (potentially but not necessarily homoerotic) of the sort found, especially, in adolescent identifications between same-sex pairings. In this context, there is an oddly appropriate irony in Sally Fitzgerald's identifying Hester as "A." While the letter is meant to stand for "Anonymous," it lends itself as well to perhaps the most famous letter in American literature, the *A* associated with Hester Prynne of Hawthorne's *Scarlet Letter*. Then, to compound an irony that O'Connor would have appreciated, when it turns out that "A" is also named Hester, the confluence of letter, name, and identificatory themes becomes totally unexpected when we examine the particular significance given the letter *a* in Lacanian terminology, for there *a* has resonances that fit idealizations of the sort O'Connor finds in Betty Hester. While uppercase *A* in Lacan is designated "the big Other" he associates with the unconscious as well as the paternal signifier (among others, the Father), he designates "the little a" in the formula *l'objet petit a* as the signifier of the object of desire, itself in relation to the subject also the *autre*/other representing an Imaginary identification found in the ideal ego. Disregarding the disproportionate burden the letter *A* may bear for Lacanian readers, Betty Hester, whatever else she may represent for O'Connor, certainly fits the bill for an identificatory other found in an ideal ego.

There is no doubt that Hester, in that role, forced O'Connor to address topics, such as sex and sexuality, she preferred to avoid. From one letter's opening, we are left to infer that Hester had previously asked some question about the absence of positive sexual relations in O'Connor's fiction. "You are in many ways an uncanny girl," O'Connor confesses, "and very right about the lacking category." Then she adds that this "reminds me that Chekhov said 'he-and-she is the machine that makes fiction work,' or something near. Of course I think it is too exclusive a view." But whether O'Connor's fiction stresses sexuality—the he-and-she machine—is not the only issue. There is the more important issue of her attitude toward it. For her, is it inevitably associated with guilt and sin? Hester seems to have claimed that, yes, in O'Connor sexuality itself is sinful. But in response O'Connor immediately displaces what seems a personal question toward something impersonal—church doctrine. Though she at once identifies sex-as-sin with a Jansenism influencing her youth, she denies having consciously accepted that doctrine. "You are right that this is the category lacking but wrong that I don't associate it with the virtuous emotions. I associate it a good deal beyond the simply virtuous emotions; I identify it plainly with the sacred. My inability to handle it so far in fiction may be purely personal, as my upbringing has smacked a little of Jansenism even if my convictions do not." Indeed, contrary to the Jansenist view, hers, claims O'Connor, is in keeping with more traditional Catholic doctrine. In its proper forms, sex is a sacrament, but it is one O'Connor does not feel prepared to represent in her fiction. She tells Hester that "there is also the fact that it being for me the center of life and most holy, I should keep my hands off it until I feel that what I can do with it will be right, which is to say, given" (117). *Given?*

In this letter's observations about sexual themes, O'Connor persists in the obfuscation, the misunderstanding—in short, the *méconnaissance* one comes to expect. Its issues extend to questions of gender and gender differences. In these contexts, one must ask, what does that word *given* mean? Does it mean that she will represent it when it is "given" her by the object of her faith—when, that is, God speaks through her creativity? Or does it mean that she will be able to represent sex positively only when she has experienced it in a proper way, presumably within marriage? Whatever our answers, O'Connor yokes expressions of sexuality to questions of gender. On the side of the female, she yokes them to the Christian virtue of purity. "Purity," she tells Hester, "strikes me as the most mysterious of the virtues and the more I think about it the less I know about it" (117). Then, to suggest to Hester that she does write about such matters, she claims to her friend that it is on this question of purity the story called "A Temple of the Holy Ghost" focuses. But while purity—or sexual innocence— may be an issue in the story, it hardly seems the main theme around which it revolves.

"A Temple of the Holy Ghost" is about a young girl who suffers confusion (somewhat like the child Hazel Motes) over reports by two older and wiser girl friends from the church school who have seen a hermaphroditic "freak" at a local fair. But as we find in a story such as Katherine Anne Porter's "The Grave," which likewise focuses on children, especially also a young girl, O'Connor's story seems more essentially about sexual initiation, the "Fall" as sexual knowledge, and puzzlement about gender differentiation than it seems about preserving or defining an abstract sexual purity. Its ending, for instance, uses the information that the law has shut down the fair and its exhibition of the hermaphrodite as a reason for suggesting the sacramental imagery one finds at the end that is so typical in O'Connor when salvation—the redemptive choice—is at stake. The shutdown of the fair suggests that the community has been redeemed; its means (the Host) and its path (a country road) to heaven are clearly marked in the story's rapturous language: "The sun was a huge red ball like an elevated Host drenched in blood and when it sank out of sight, it left a line in the sky like a red clay road hanging over the trees" (*Complete Stories* 248). Although in her letter to Hester O'Connor says that the only way to salvation is "acceptance of the Crucifixtion [sic], Christ's and our own" (124), the implicit question the story answers is, "What in human life comprises that crucifixion?" The story suggests clearly that, at least for the female, it is a cross constructed of sex and gender.

Given the questions of sex, gender, and gender differentiation O'Connor raises here, she is perhaps most disingenuous of all, in the context of sexual *méconnaissance*, in telling Hester that Ben Griffith, the same Griffith of the Oedipus question, had seen sexual displacement at work in O'Connor's story called "A Circle in the Fire." For not only will readers see sexual displacement in that story; they will also see how O'Connor differentiates gender vis à vis sexuality. Griffith, she says, "remarked that in these stories there was usually a strong kind of sex potential that was always turned aside and that this gave the stories some of their tension" (118–19). In this story, he suggests, "there is a strong possibility that the child in the woods with the boys may be [sexually] attacked—but [instead] the attack takes another form" (119). The form it takes is the boys' setting fire to the woods. However important to the story and the boys, and however symbolically *sexual* the burning may be, the story is not really about them; it is about the girl and her mother. Because the girl is as sexually innocent as the one in "A Temple of the Holy Ghost," the major event in "A Circle in the Fire" is not the fire, but the girl's observing the naked boys' bathing in a cow watering trough and then running about the field, "the sun glinting on their long wet bodies" (192).

In "A Circle in the Fire," it is through this freely expressed *jouissance* of the body that O'Connor tellingly differentiates her genders. For her females, there is no such *jouissance*. Since the mother, for example, is as sexually repressed as the girl is innocent, for her the woods fire, about which she had constantly worried, is the main event. It represents—as O'Connor surely must realize—the threatening sexuality the mother has so long suppressed. Ending as it does for mother and daughter, the story can be "about" nothing other than sexuality, sexuality-as-fall, about an experience of castration—a "new misery"—suffered by females but in the child's fantasy imagery one seemingly escaped by males, at least these three males. "The child came to a stop beside her mother," O'Connor begins the story's final paragraph, "and stared up at her face as if she had never seen it before. It was the face of the new misery she felt, but on her mother it looked old and it looked as if it might belong to *anybody*" (emphasis added). But, clearly, it won't belong to just any *body*, only to the female body. For the woman, there will, apparently, be no joy, no *jouissance*, such as that to be experienced by those males. Ending that paragraph, O'Connor writes, "She stood taut, listening, and could just catch in the distance a few wild high shrieks of joy as if the prophets were dancing in the fiery furnace, in the circle the angel had cleared for them" (193). As "prophets," the boys announce an experience of joy for which angels have cleared a space in the circle of fire but only for those males. In the context of the story's conclusion, in short, were it not for her usual *méconnaissance*, O'Connor's admission about Griffith's observation of "sex potential" would hardly seem credible: "I really hadn't thought of it," she says, "until he pointed it out but I believe it is a very perceptive comment" (118–19). But if this story suggests nothing else, it does at least suggest why O'Connor felt such reservations about gender and the relation of sexuality to it.

4

> In the identity of man and God, my personal experience of being abandoned by God [...] overlaps with the despair of Christ himself at being abandoned by the divine Father.
> —Slavoj Žižek, *Metastases of Enjoyment*, 40–41

That O'Connor innocently or willfully fails to see or accept the psychoanalytic dimensions of her work has acute importance in another direction. Her *méconnaissance* obscures from her the deep roots of her fiction in her own psyche. Because the themes are all intertwined, O'Connor was as disingenuous about the revelatory relation of an author to her work as she was about sexuality and the psychoanalytic hermeneutic. As she often would do later on, Hester had apparently addressed the relationship in letters to O'Connor virtually from the outset of the correspondence. In one early letter (the seventh, 24 September 1955), Hester seems to have said that an author divulges much of herself in her writing, but O'Connor's view—naturally, one begins to surmise—is much more guarded. "Your comments on how much of oneself one reveals in the work are a little too sweeping for me," she tells her confidante. "Now I understand that something of oneself gets through and often something that one is not conscious of." Moreover, she adds, "to have sympathy for any character, you have to put a good deal of yourself in him." But possibly because of the vow of distance and objectivity she took with her formalist professors at the School for Writers of the State University of Iowa, O'Connor claims that a good writer does not reveal herself naked in her work. "[T]o say that any complete denudation of the writer occurs in the successful work is, according to me, a romantic exaggeration," she expostulates. "A great part of the art is precisely in seeing that this does not happen." While her concluding comment on this subject is succinct and on the face of it expresses her philosophy simply enough, it harbors, nonetheless, a revealing ambiguity regarding cause and effect. "Any story I reveal myself completely in," she concludes, "will be a bad story" (105). But what she does not explain is whether it will be bad because it reveals her secrets or because the revelation itself corrupts form, theme, or content. Given her penchant for willful misunderstanding, one surmises that, if she understood these alternatives, the former problem, the unveiling of self, would bother her more than the latter, the disruption of form.

Just how powerfully O'Connor herself is implicated in these questions of sex, sexuality, the psychoanalytic, and an author's literary creations she reveals in this same letter to Hester in which Hester addresses sexual themes in her friend's fiction. The passage to be probed here follows hard upon the remarks about Chekhov, Jansenism, and the purity of sanctified sex. From an analytic perspective, the significant issue is the thematic drift, the way—almost as if metonymic free association were at work—in which O'Connor moves, first, from the implied topic of sexual love to her creative relation to her "others" Enoch Emery and Hazel Motes and, second, from there to her severe affliction by lupus erythematosus (a disease whose name and nature O'Connor had not yet divulged to Hester; she would do so only after a full year's correspondence). The tropological basis of these shifts suggests how viscerally charged the cluster of topics must have become for O'Connor. She bridges between the topic of sexual love and the two characters in *Wise Blood* in this statement: "I suppose what you work hardest on is what you know least" (105). Though the statement apparently means that she works hard to represent sexuality in her fiction because, she admits, she does not know the subject well, in fact she does not at all represent sexuality often, so the associative turn to the characters raises questions. But that she links this category "lacking" in her fiction to these characters in *Wise Blood* suggests they are indeed invested with significance for her self in ways connecting sexuality and her own definition as a subject.

In Lacanian theory, that which is implicated in sexuality and must be found "lacking" in the constitution of the subject is known as the phallic signifier. Thus, the point of intersection between Haze and his creator is the role of the signifier in the formation—and expression—of one's identity. O'Connor's comments about him and the text of *Wise Blood* suggest Hazel himself plays for O'Connor the role of a phallic signifier representing her identity at its most unconscious. As the originary symbol of *Symbolic* signification, the phallic signifier functions in the same way as any tabooed object or word. It functions best—perhaps only—behind a veil, a screen. Though absent in a context where it might be expected to appear, paradoxically its presence may most appropriately be inferred from its effects on behavior. Indeed, Lacan would point out that the metonymic, associative turn in O'Connor's letter to Hester concerning sexuality in the fiction turns on a missing signifier that connects to O'Connor's own identity. To begin with, this signifier, in the letter, is simply a word. While evidently the main topic of the letter, the word *sex* is never used in it. But, eventually, this specific, absent-but-present signifier points to the determinative role of the signifier associated with the function (oedipal) determining a subject's ego identity. That identity implicates itself in the subject's desire and thus shows where the phallic signifier transforms itself into Lacan's *objet petit a*, the object that causes desire and in causing desire constitutes the subject.

Read as closely as one would read a literary text, that one letter to Hester offers many suggestions. To begin, for O'Connor, it suggests that Hazel is that signifier transformed into the *objet a*, a piece of the real in the body tied to one's deepest "self," that "thing" more myself than myself. As such, in Lacanian theory, it is characterized by absence as much as presence, by a hole or something missing as much as by a real thing actually present. Moreover, it is around this hole that subjectivity is constituted and revolves. We see O'Connor circulating around this absent presence in the different ways she speaks of Hazel and Enoch. For her, Enoch exists in the Imaginary, but Hazel exists ambiguously—problematically—in both the Symbolic and the Real. In terms of Lacanian textuality, the relations between Enoch and Haze are best envisioned within the structure of Schema L, for it is perhaps the best—certainly the most direct—figure Lacan uses to show the structure of "subjectivity." (Since Schema L is included in "From Freud to Jacques Lacan and the Textual Unconscious," for this discussion of *Wise Blood* please refer to the schema there.) Using these relationships,

I would locate Enoch along the top (with "I" and "ideal ego"), where identifications are rather conscious. I would locate Hazel along the bottom (with "ego-ideal" and "the Other"), where they are usually unconscious. O'Connor's levels of awareness of the symbolic dimensions of Enoch and Hazel are pretty clear. As we have seen, she talks freely in her letters about Enoch and his perversion (voyeurism). Suggesting how comfortable she is with Enoch, she admits there that she wrote the episodes involving Enoch very easily. The letter to Hester shows that, moreover, Enoch's role is easy to construct because, in Lacanian terms, it lies in the Imaginary. She says to Hester, "I never had a moment's thought over Enoch." In fact, she says, "Everything Enoch said and did was as plain to me as my hand" (117). But as a figure of the Imaginary, identificatory other, Enoch is not the other who is more herself than herself, the signifying *objet a* through which one reaches toward the self one cannot reach and, moreover, that represents one's most secret desire as well as the guilty pleasure (*jouissance*) attendant upon it. Nor is Enoch the *objet* that, because it is always separable, can be lost. Least of all is he the object of one's secret desire that may also serve as the subject of one's severest punishment.

Hazel is something else, however. O'Connor admits that she labors over him. For her, Haze becomes a signifier pointing to some piece of herself that lies much deeper than anything Enoch signifies. In the beginning, Hazel is the one who, says O'Connor, "I struggled over" (117). He is the signifier who for her conscious, speaking "I" mediates between her ego-ideal, on the one hand, and, on the other hand, the great Other. The one is the ideal "I" implicated in imagos of the parents (here, one must assume mainly her father, Edward O'Connor), and the second the master signifier that settles all meaning, the one who, for O'Connor, is the Holy Trinity—Father, Son, and Holy Ghost, the Three-Person God of her Christianity. We find these, as Lacan insists, by identifying the "underlying" meanings "intended" by the subject in the tropes or figures of speech or language. Lacan stresses the tropes of metaphor and metonymy, the former as the figure in which a sign stands in place of another, the latter as that in which a sign signifies in a context that is left unnamed. Analyzed closely through an understanding of both metaphor and metonymy (the latter especially), that letter to Hester ultimately shows why Haze plays between the Real and the Symbolic. As a metaphor of the phallic signifier, Haze is implicated in the Oedipus resolution and symbolic castration. On the one hand, he focuses desire, guilt, and the punishment that in the Oedipus structure is always castration, and, on the other, he suggests whatever redemption there may be for O'Connor.

But Hazel, he of the ambiguously gendered name, carries another significance for O'Connor. This one seems in fact to be the issue of gender. Her attitude toward gender O'Connor discusses in another letter to Hester. "What you say about there being two [sexes] now brings it home to me," she writes. "I've always believed there were two but generally acted as if there were only one. I guess meditation and contemplation and all the ways of prayer boil down to keeping it firmly in sight that there are two. I've never spent much time over the bride-bridegroom analogy. For me, perhaps because it began for me in the beginning, it's been more father and child" (136). Besides the child, another image of the human that for O'Connor apparently escapes sexuality is the angel. In her claim to have believed in angels all her life and to have wished to be one, O'Connor finds yet another way to escape gender and sexuality, to find just one sex in the face of the sex that is not one. But for O'Connor the child remains the dominant image of the sexless, innocent, ungendered human being. She plainly wants to have remained a child. To Hester, in comments ostensibly about her childlike outlook on the world, O'Connor seems equally to be concerned about sexual maturity. She says,

> The things you have said about my being surprised to be over twelve have struck me as being quite comically accurate. When I was twelve I made up my mind absolutely that I would not get older. I don't remember how I meant to stop it. There was something about "teen" attached to anything that was repulsive to me. I certainly didn't approve of what I saw of people that age. I was a very ancient twelve; my views at that age would have done credit to a Civil War veteran. I am much younger now than I was at twelve or anyway, less burdened. The weight of centuries lies on children, I'm sure of it. (136–37)

Her feelings about herself—her own loss, the punishment seemingly meted out to her—are ultimately, albeit unconsciously, worked through in her final burst of creativity regarding Hazel Motes. She explains that, largely because of her difficulties in creating him, she took five years to write the novel and even after finishing felt it a failure. Worse, near the end of it, when she was still struggling to settle Haze's fate, she suffered that onset of lupus, her "energy-depriving ailment," as she regularly names it to Hester and others. For the lupus, she says, she "began to take cortisone in large doses and cortisone makes you think night and day until I suppose the mind dies of exhaustion if you are not rescued." Though rescued, she adds that "during this time I was more or less living my life and H. Mote's [sic] too and as my disease affected the joints, I conceived the notion that I would eventually become paralized [sic] and was going blind." In these feelings no doubt projecting onto Hazel, O'Connor finds him a representation of her own body and its pain. She either used the book, as she says ambiguously, to "spell out" her "own course" or "the illness [...] had spelled out the book" (118). Whatever the case, her feeling was that God (for her that ultimate big Other) had "rescued" her from herself. Consequently, one must infer that the assumption of faith one sees Haze act out through self-blinding and other bodily tortures in *Wise Blood* expresses a redemption O'Connor herself must have desired. It would come only when she conquered her fear that in the disease-as-punishment God had renounced her. In conquering that feeling, she will find her own sense of redemption.

If we find most of these suggestions in her metaphoric ("I am like him") identification with Haze, we find that last suggestion—the assumption of redemption—in a predictable metonymic (associative) shift. In her discourse to Hester, she expresses her deepest feeling of resolution not in a discussion of Haze but in a shift to another character of her fiction—Guizac in "The Displaced Person"—whose story also invokes Christian redemption. Since in the letter redemption had not been a topic till now, the shift to it suggests what in fact is most on O'Connor's mind. In this letter, when shifting her attention to "The Displaced Person," O'Connor suggests in the very shift itself that she may have shared both the feeling of abandonment suffered by Guizac ("the Pole," himself "the displaced person") and some sense of the story's theme of redemption. Contrary to the Pole's own judgment, O'Connor in the letter to Hester insists that Guizac achieves redemption. How? Why? For Guizac, redemption comes, paradoxically, in his very despair at feeling abandonment. The Lacanian critic Slavoj Žižek, in *Metastases of Enjoyment*, asks, "How do I, a finite mortal, concretely experience my *identity* with God? I experience it in my own radical despair, which—paradoxically—involves a *loss* of faith" (40). Again, paradoxically, he suggests that our humanity rises toward the divine when our "personal experience of being abandoned by God [...] overlaps with the despair of Christ himself at being abandoned by the divine Father" (40–41). In O'Connor's view, it is precisely this sense of abandonment that links Guizac to Christ, makes of him a Christ *figure*, a human figuration of Christianity's great Other. Guizac, O'Connor says, achieves redemption in the very sharing of Christ's own sense of abandonment by God, for that is a feeling Christ also poignantly expressed on the cross. "This," she says to Hester, "is where we share

Christ's agony." We share it most "when He was about to die and cried out, 'My God, why have You forsaken Me?'" (118). If O'Connor likewise feels abandonment—and how at times could she not have?—might not she also have accepted its paradoxical redemption?

The textual evidence of O'Connor's letters—and that one letter to Betty Hester in particular—suggests that O'Connor worked through some sense of guilt and punishment, transgression, abandonment, and redemption in the final transfiguration in *Wise Blood* of Hazel Motes into what, in another letter, she herself calls "a kind of Protestant saint" (69). Given her powerful identification with Hazel, particularly in what Žižek calls "radical subjective destitution" (*Sublime Object of Ideology* 116), O'Connor might well have shared in that sense of sainthood. But even if she did not, it is clear that, knowing of the physical tortures of her life and of her accomplishments amidst suffering, many of her readers have sainted her as much as she felt she sainted Hazel. Indeed, it has been what I have dubbed her sainthood that has suppressed investigation of the intricate relations among modernism, psychoanalysis, gender, sexuality, and identity in her fiction and the letters. Nevertheless, though I am not sure anyone can understand fully all that is going on in O'Connor's multiple, contradictory, identificatory linkages to Hazel Motes, I finally want to have suggested how powerful are those linkages. Though I believe Hazel's experience in the novel represents something of O'Connor's own experience of religious doubt and resolution, I mainly want to insist that my reading of some of O'Connor's letters not only casts revealing light on *Wise Blood*, but that it also helps to explain why O'Connor seemed so opposed to psychoanalytic interpretation of her work even though much of it virtually begs for such reading.

Ultimately, while her explicit objections to Freudian readings sometimes have had the effect of bringing them on, I insist that *that* was surely something she must at least unconsciously have desired. Without her fictions' potential for being read within the dominant modernist paradigm of the culture of psychoanalysis, they would hardly have found the place they have come to enjoy in the contemporary interstice between modernism and postmodernism. The absolutely most desirable kind of reading of her work, from her perspective (conscious or otherwise), surely would be a psychoanalytic one (such as Asals's or McCullagh's) that embraces as well the Christian. For such readings not only would allow her to find her place in the modernist pantheon (as, indeed, she has), but of course they would also allow her to defend her most strongly felt ideological convictions. "Christianized" Freudianism allows O'Connor to eat her cake and to have it too. But it takes, I think, a Lacanian reading of *Wise Blood* and some of her letters to reveal the reasons why this is the case.

CHAPTER 5

The Forced Choice: *Le Père ou Pire* in Glaspell's "Jury of Her Peers"

[W]hat is this feminine depression that suspends the causal link, the causal connection between our acts and external stimuli, if not the founding gesture of subjectivity, the primordial act of freedom, of refusing our insertion into the nexus of causes and effects?
—Slavoj Žižek, *Metastases of Enjoyment*, 122

As subjects within the cultural Symbolic of a patriarchal society, what choices have women? How can a woman oppose patriarchy when, in the phenomenon Jacques Lacan in his late work calls the "forced choice," its very structure coopts her opposition? Are all her oppositional choices forced choices? The notorious Freudian question, What does a woman want? might be better put as What does a woman do? If the historical abuses of women were not problem enough, then the pervasive double binds trapping their actions seem more than enough to drive women mad. In literature, the madwoman is so common that it has become almost a convention within recent feminist and earlier protofeminist narratives. As the figure of "the madwoman in the attic" attests, women writers have often turned to the literal or figurative psychotic to free themselves of the Symbolic of their times and to change it for later ones. While such figures, as Gilbert and Gubar suggest, may point to the "schizophrenia of authorship" (78), they may also represent a larger political agenda. By making the madwoman a figure of cultural dissidence, women writers have set in motion changes in the cultural Symbolic that may someday produce those different subjects desired by dissidence or rebellion or revolution.

But if psychosis is a choice, is it not also a forced choice? Answers to this and other social and political questions may come from a Lacanian examination of literary works such as Charlotte Perkins Gilman's "Yellow Wallpaper" or Susan Glaspell's "Jury of Her Peers." In the last two decades or so, both of these have become very effective show pieces for feminist and other social readings of the plight of women in patriarchal cultures. In Gilman, the madwoman seems largely a danger to herself, but in Glaspell the woman's psychosis leads to an almost archetypal act of murder-as-liberation.[1] Because they both deal with social life, realistic stories such as these attest to the social and personal problems attending women who take a dissident subject position. While Gilman and Glaspell suggest the high cost of female heroism when battling the cultural Symbolic, recent readings of their most famous stories well address the psychic costs but not necessarily the ambiguities inherent in them. Though the protagonist of Gilman's "Yellow Wallpaper" rejects her husband and thereby rejects the confinement imposed upon her by both matrimony and nineteenth-century medicine, at the same time she nonetheless falls ever deeper into psychosis. When Minnie Wright, of Glaspell's "Jury," murders her husband and likewise rejects the abusive, soul-killing authority of a cruel mate who stands in for an equally cruel and abusive patriarchal "law," she too suffers from an apparent psychotic breakdown. So what does a woman do?

As it has become a text noteworthy for affirming the possibility of a woman's social dissidence, "A Jury of Her Peers" suggests that the socioeconomic conditions of women on the American farm frontier at the turn to the twentieth century virtually demanded that women resist the cultural Symbolic, even if it meant—especially if it meant—pursuing a desire on the side of narcissism contrary to the desire emanating from oedipal law. These conditions are exhibited in the murder case on which Glaspell bases the play *Trifles* and the story it became.[2] In writing about the case, Glaspell followed all the conventions of sensationalism found in the journalism of the time. Early on, she seems to have taken the side of the state against the accused, Margaret Hossack, but after she had apparently made a visit to the woman in the presence of law officers she seems to have softened her attitude. In her reports thereafter, Glaspell makes of the woman a victim of circumstances much more like those she would create in her play and the story some fifteen years later. Moreover, as details of the relations between the wife and husband came out, Glaspell learned that Mrs. Hossack had been seriously mistreated by Hossack for many years. Indeed, the couple's children supported the mother in the case largely, Linda Ben-Zvi infers from the evidence, because of their sympathy for the mother and antipathy toward a brutal father. According to Ben-Zvi, the case illustrated for Glaspell "the process by which juridical attitudes toward, and prosecution of, women are shaped by societal concepts of female behavior, the same concepts that may have motivated the act of murder" ("Murder" 22).

The Hossack case demonstrated to Glaspell, after years of reflection, that, in such situations admitting of little legal recourse or few practicable solutions, women might well be driven to murder, but thereafter they would find neither public sympathy nor mercy in a system of justice blind to women's plight within a patriarchal culture. For Glaspell, then, the question became, How does a woman find a jury of her peers? or, alternatively, What indeed would *be* a jury of a woman's peers? For answers, women must turn to other women. In the midst of patriarchy, however, that means reverting to the lure of the mother and valorizing narcissistic desire.[3] While some (by no means all) recent readings of "A Jury of Her Peers" suggest that the woman's solution appears to have avoided the double bind of patriarchy, a reading founded on Lacan suggests that the story's heroic pair—Mrs. Hale and Mrs. Peters—actually end by supporting patriarchy in ways they may not fully comprehend. Because the dissident woman may only choose the worse by rejecting ordinary patriarchal law, such a reading suggests just how risky and potentially tragic is the woman's choice and why a story that has seemed so affirmative ends in a dissidence at best ironic, a victory only Pyrrhic.

In our critiques of social life and literature, how do we get at the ironic, often paradoxical underside of such acts of dissidence? Although we will neither arrive at some indisputable truth nor perhaps even a more satisfactory reading, we may begin to see the costs, the ambiguities, by following a "newer"—"other" or "later"—Lacanian theory that focuses not on desire, the Imaginary, and the Symbolic (oedipal) Father, but the drives, *jouissance*, and the (M)other of the Real. Even so, a late Lacanian approach does not ignore the Imaginary or the Symbolic, desire or the father; rather, as it is exemplified in many of the essays of Slavoj Žižek, it typically analyzes some or all of these elements in a series of moves that culminates by showing how they rest on the unfathomability of the *objet a*, the horror of the Real, and the danger to the subject of das Ding. This late Lacanian focus not only enables and often embraces the findings of nonpsychoanalytic readings, but it also reveals the dark, even tragic, underside of even the most laudable dissidence. A late Lacanian protocol, calling for a series of moves traversing Imaginary, Symbolic, and Real, will show how "A Jury of Her Peers" illustrates the paradox of the forced choice faced by women in patriarchy whatever the form—overt or covert—their rebellion takes.

1

In short, "subject" designates this primordial impossible-forced choice by means of which we choose (or not) to be "in the world"—that is, to exist as the "there" of being.

—Slavoj Žižek, *Metastases of Enjoyment*, 185

The relations of subjects to the register of the Imaginary automatically invoke the human social bond. That bond begins with the mother in the subject's passage through the mirror phase. As illustration of the basic Lacanian plot, Glaspell's story repeats the subject's assumption in the Imaginary of an ideal ego (Idealich) found in the image of the mother and on the side of narcissism. Says Lacan, "[By] dependence on her love, that is to say, by the desire for her desire, [the child] identifies [it]self with the imaginary object of this desire in so far as the mother herself symbolizes it" in the signifier of the Father (*Écrits* 198).[4] The "desire of the mother," Lacan says in *The Ethics of Psychoanalysis*, "is the origin of everything." It "is the founding desire," the desire that founds "the whole structure" he associates with subjectivity (283). But when adults repeat the desire of the Mother, they bring an element of transgression, of violation of oedipal law, and thus they bring questions of crime, guilt, and punishment. What is more, in Lacan's theorization of the subject, such repetitions also raise questions of ethics rooted in the relation of moral choices to law and the subject's desire, a desire that Lacan posits as a "metonymy" of the "subject's being" (321). Adult repetitions of the desire of the Mother, therefore, are very complex. They represent, Lacan suggests, something other than the oedipal transgression Freud posits in the "murder of the father, the great myth that he places at the origin of the development of civilization." Indeed, says Lacan, they represent something yet more primal, an "even more obscure and original transgression for which he finds a name at the end of his work, in a word, the death instinct, to the extent that man finds himself anchored deep within to its formidable dialectic" (2).

As a story of this more primal transgression, of a return to the desire of what, because the mother is the first other, Lacan will now call the (M)other, "A Jury of Her Peers" raises questions not only about desire and the subject's relation to others and to the law, but also about the subject's anchoring in that "formidable dialectic" of Eros and Thanatos, life and death, Oedipus and Narcissus. As such a story, Glaspell's suggests that the plot of Imaginary identifications comes fraught with potentially tragic implications that Lacan, in the seminar on ethics, localizes in Sophocles' Antigone. As a story of women's transgressions in the domain of the Imaginary, "A Jury of Her Peers" is like *Antigone*, but without its tragic denouement (on Lacan's reading of *Antigone*, see my "*Other* Desire"). Glaspell's story embeds gender themes within the broader themes of crime and law (see also Hallgren, Makowsky, and Mustazza's "Gender"). As a murder mystery, the story itself involves a crime. Someone has murdered a farmer, John Wright.

He died in his bed with a rope knotted around his neck. The chief suspect is the wife, Minnie Foster Wright. In the crime, it is clear that ordinary human law has been violated, but Glaspell makes much more of the thematics of law than this simple event would presuppose. This thematics is implicit in the main subjectivity through which the story represents matters, the Mrs. Hale played by Glaspell in the dramatic performances. As would any married woman, Martha Hale bears a mark of the law—of Symbolic law—because she participates in the cultural law that constructs her as married. What is more, as would be characteristic of that time and place, Glaspell almost always refers to her in the text as *Mrs.* Hale, rarely as Martha or Martha Hale (and she never gives her maiden name). As Sherri Hallgren notes, moreover, "The men in the story truly believe that a woman is married to the law, that *Mrs.* Hale and *Mrs.* Peters are essentially bonded to their husbands, and, through their husbands, will owe allegiance to the patriarchal structure of the world" (216).

The thematics of law is yet more overt than this, however. It occurs in the dominating presence of law enfigured in the sheriff and county attorney come to investigate the crime. But Glaspell complicates the relation of Mrs. Hale to signifiers of the law by suggesting that such signifiers are not always male and may cross gender lines. In the story's opening scene, in the investigation of the scene of the crime, Mrs. Hale joins specific male signifiers of the law—the sheriff (Mr. Peters, he of the phallic surname) and the county's prosecuting attorney (Mr. Henderson). More important to Mrs. Hale, however, is the Imaginary other she seizes upon in a process of narcissistic identification. This "other" woman, Mrs. Peters, is also the sheriff's wife. "She had met Mrs. Peters the year before at the county fair," the narrator tells us of Mrs. Hale, "and the thing she remembered about her was that she didn't seem like a sheriff's wife." Because she "was small and thin and didn't have a strong voice" (279), she does not fit well the signifying image conventionally associated with law and authority. But a woman could fit such an image. The demands of the stereotypical image are met by the wife of the previous sheriff. In contrast to Mrs. Peters, that woman, Mrs. Gorman, "had a voice," Mrs. Hale thinks, "that somehow seemed to be backing up the law with every word." Likewise, the narrator reports, the commonplace image fits Mr. Peters quite adequately: "[I]f Mrs. Peters didn't look like a sheriff's wife, Peters made it up in looking like a sheriff. He was to a dot the kind of man who could get himself elected sheriff—a heavy man with a big voice, who was particularly genial with the law-abiding, as if to make it plain that he knew the difference between" (280). Whatever other significance these exhibitions of the arbitrariness of cultural signifiers of law may have, they clearly suggest a direction to the struggle regarding law and gender engaging Mrs. Hale.

Though not fitting exactly Mrs. Hale's preconception of a sheriff's wife, Mrs. Peters—Martha Hale's Imaginary Nebenmensch—represents woman's gender situation more emphatically than Mrs. Hale. Indeed, the cultural—Symbolic—paradigm of married women fits Mrs. Peters doubly. As "wife," she, like Mrs. Hale, is constructed under the law, but, as the wife of a sheriff, Mrs. Peters is also "married *to* the law." Glaspell makes much of this notion in the story. She especially emphasizes the phrase in the context of a male chauvinism that throughout the story has denigrated women and women's things and activities. Moreover, she places all instances of the phrase toward the story's end, at the very moment when the two women are on the verge of rebellion against a law that is blind to their threat. "Married to the law" first occurs when the county attorney picks up an apron that the women intend to take to Minnie Wright, who is in custody in jail. His remark suggests that because women and their things can hardly be dangerous, the two are no threat to liberate Minnie from imprisonment. The attorney disregards in the same way some quilt blocks the two women had recognized as evidence of the state of mind that might have led Minnie to murder her husband.

As a signifier of the lawful Symbolic, the county attorney illustrates how ignorant of its subjects the Law can be. Oblivious to the fact that with his hands on those blocks in Minnie's sewing basket he is virtually in possession of the most critical evidence against Minnie, he is equally blind to a dissidence he might have read in the evidence of Mrs. Hale's eyes. "Her eyes felt like fire," the story tells us. "She had a feeling that if he took up the basket she would snatch it from him." But there is no need, for the attorney, comfortable in his dismissal of women's things, merely laughs and says, "Mrs. Peters doesn't need supervising." After all, "a sheriff's wife is married to the law. Ever think of it that way, Mrs. Peters?" (305). For his part, the sheriff himself enjoys the phrase so much that, chuckling, he repeats it—"Married to the law"—before moving off to more "important" matters. The final use of the phrase may be the most ironic. It occurs precisely as the two women make their decision to harbor a woman they know to be a criminal according to ordinary law. Doing that (albeit, they never literally speak what they know), they themselves violate ordinary law. Moreover, becoming a law unto themselves, they provide a jury of peers to one whose social demand acting on unconscious desire had come to transcend the laws of men.

2

This is how the tautology "law is law" has to be read. The first law ("law is...") is the universal law in so far as it is abstractly opposed to crime, whereas the second law ("...law") reveals the concealed truth of the first: the obscene violence, the absolute, universalized crime as its hidden reverse.
—Slavoj Žižek, *For They Know Not What They Do*, 34

When we examine social or literary subjects in relation to the register of the Symbolic, we find the father and law. In "Jury," the phrase *married to the law*, as it occurs in the context of the violation of ordinary, "oedipal" law, draws us toward the Symbolic and makes explicit the form that the dissidence of the female subjects shall take. More even than male subjects, women—and yet more particularly married women—exist under a "social contract" in what Slavoj Žižek views as a "forced choice." In choosing to belong to a "symbolic community," the subject accepts two paradoxical conditions, one, a subjectivity that "does not exist prior to this choice" and, two, a subjectivity that is then "constituted by means of" the choice (*Enjoy* 74–75). As Žižek says, there is a further paradox: "The choice of community, the 'social contract,' is a paradoxical choice where I maintain the freedom of choice only if I 'make the right choice': if I choose the 'other' of the community, I stand to lose the very freedom, the very possibility of choice" (75). In a social contract, the choice always focuses on the culture's symbolic law. In Glaspell's story, the rebellion against that forced choice is a rebellion against law as such. That rebellion drives the plot in which Mrs. Hale and Mrs. Peters act in complicity. They rebel against law because they perceive that as its subjects they have been given nothing in return for what they have given up.

As subjects under the law (like all subjects, both male and female), they are ruled by what Žižek describes as "the oedipal father," "the symbolic-dead father, Name-of-the-Father, the father of Law who does not enjoy, who ignores the dimension of enjoyment" (*Metastases* 206). This is the blind, ignorant "Father" who knows them not and recognizes not at all what they have forsaken—namely, the maternal object of primal desire. As Žižek says, "What is sacrificed in the act of choice is of course the Thing, the incestuous Object that embodies impossible enjoyment," this choice being like the forced choice creating the communal subject in that it involves a paradox, "the fact that the incestuous Object *comes to be through being lost*." In short, the being of this "lost" object "is not given prior to its loss" (*Enjoy* 75). In "A Jury of Her Peers," we find the lost maternal object eventually in Minnie

Foster (that is, Minnie before marriage to Wright), and we find the
blind, ignorant father in two particular ways: discomfiture with "the
law" as such and in expressions of an almost literal blindness in figures
identified with or as the law.

Discomfiture with the law has been visible, albeit faintly, from the
beginning of the story. For instance, at the start of the journey out to
the Wright farm, when Mrs. Hale thinks about Sheriff Peters as a powerful representative of the law, she finds little consolation. Rather, the
thought, coming like a "stab" (280), makes her anxious—perhaps for
herself, but certainly for Minnie Wright. Later, anxiety about the law
becomes more a suspicion about its origins. When Mrs. Peters says to
her that "the law is the law," Mrs. Hale responds in a way that
removes law from the empyrean of abstractions and places it in the
domain of man-made things. Supposing that "the law is the law," Mrs.
Hale turns to the kitchen stove and notes that its fire is not "much to
brag of." In that modest fire she finds her metaphor to explain what is
wrong with the law. "The law is the law—and a bad stove is a bad
stove" (294). What's more, having questioned law, she begins to question the matter of crime as well. If law, like that stove, is man-made
and potentially dysfunctional, might not crime be just as much a construction, a matter of construal within a context? When Mrs. Peters, in
her "tight little way," says, "The law has got to punish crime, Mrs.
Hale," Mrs. Hale replies by drawing attention to an image of the
"criminal." She says, "I wish you'd seen Minnie Foster." She wishes
this woman who is married to the law had seen Minnie before she
chose marriage, "when she wore a white dress with blue ribbons, and
stood up there in the choir and sang" (303). Could that woman, she
wonders, ever be a criminal?

Moreover, if law and crime are matters of construal, of human
judgment or construction, then guilt and responsibility are likewise just
such matters. Who is the guilty, who the responsible person? Early in
the story, Mrs. Hale had begun to share responsibility for Minnie's
plight. At the door of the Wright's farmhouse, she had experienced "a
moment of feeling she could not cross that threshold" (280). The feeling came from her realization that since she had not crossed it in better
times, why should she do so now? "Time and time again it had been in
her mind," writes Glaspell of Mrs. Hale. But for the twenty years
Minnie Foster had been Minnie Wright "there was always something to
do and Minnie Foster would go from her mind." Thus, when Mrs.
Hale thinks, later, of Minnie singing in her white dress and blue ribbons, this "picture" of the girl whom she "had let [...] die for lack of
life" becomes too much to bear. Thereupon, she redefines crime and,

with it, guilt and responsibility. The real crime, she implies, is that she had so rarely visited Minnie. "That was a crime! That was a crime!" she expostulates. "Who's going to punish that?" (281). When Mrs. Peters tries to console her and cautions her toward silence by a fearful look toward the place where the men are located, Mrs. Hale not only refuses to be silenced but also insists on a knowledge the women share that is beyond the capabilities of the men. "I might 'a' *known* she needed help! I tell you, it's *queer*, Mrs. Peters. We live close together, and we live far apart. We all go through the same things—it's all just a different kind of the same thing! If it weren't—why do you and I *understand?* Why do we *know*—what we know this minute?" (303).

Here, as this woman's recognition raises again issues of gender and patriarchy, we see how the law and the Symbolic may be interpolated in a discourse from its underside, from the side of opposition or abjection or the subaltern. We find this other discourse, this discourse by the other of patriarchy, in Glaspell's description of female interpolation in the midst of the blindness of the Symbolic (oedipal) Father as exhibited through male—and patriarchal—arrogance. Speaking of this interpolation as a "double voice," Susan Lanser notes how the women in Glaspell's story communicate "in 'women's language' under the watchful but unseeing eyes of the Law" (618). Clearly, female reading and the blindness of the Law of the Symbolic Father form a tandem in the text. In Mrs. Hale's recognition, Glaspell makes it plain that these women derive their knowledge from their experience within the constructions—and constrictions—of gender. Because they are women, as Minnie Wright is, they know what she has undergone. In their virtually unconscious search for evidence of extenuating motive in the murder of John Wright, Mrs. Hale and Mrs. Peters begin to recognize that they have all experienced abjection under male dominance. As women, they are as invisible to the men as the clues read by the women in a signifying chain of "women's things."

What is more, male arrogance represents a constant reminder of women's abjection within a patriarchal culture. This arrogance is indexed at first in minor ways. One index is male laughter. For instance, we read in one place as the women consider whether Minnie was going to quilt or knot her log-cabin pattern, "There was a laugh for the ways of women" (295). In another, we read how the women worry that the men would laugh were they to know that the women were all wrought up about a dead canary. In yet another, mentioned already, we read how the county attorney laughs when he considers that the women were planning to take to the jail an apron for Minnie Wright. Not a very "dangerous thing," he jokes. The male laughter is simply an index to the arrogance with which the men regard women, providing they regard them at all. In the matter of reading evidence, for example, the men assume that the women would not "know a clue if they [came] upon it" (289). But, in general, the men do not assume that women's things could contribute anything worthwhile to the investigation anyway. They look around Minnie Wright's kitchen, for instance, and decide there is "nothing important" there that can help them. "Nothing here but kitchen things," the sheriff said, "with a little laugh for the insignificance of kitchen things." Likewise, when the county attorney looks into Minnie's cupboard, he finds only a "nice mess" made by jars of fruit preserves that had frozen and cracked during the night before the investigation. When Mrs. Peters explains that Minnie had worried about just such an accident's occurring with her in custody and the fire left to die out, each man in turn offers a dismissive response. Sheriff Peters merely laughs and says, "Well, can you beat the women! Held for murder, and worrying about her preserves!" Then the attorney quips, "I guess before we're through with her she may have something more serious than preserves to worry about." Finally, Mrs. Hale's husband, "with good-natured superiority," weighs in with, "Oh, well, [...] women are used to worrying over trifles" (287).

But it is precisely in the pursuit of trifles, those trifles that name Glaspell's play, that interpolation within a female discourse uncovers the motive behind Minnie Wright's crime. Following a chain of signifiers that present themselves at first at the level of the unconscious of the women, Mrs. Hale and Mrs. Peters discover a prior crime—the "murder" of Minnie Foster. The chain of signifiers is constituted of female "things." First, they notice that many tasks around the house, especially in the kitchen, have been left undone. Mrs. Hale notices that the cover is off a bucket of sugar and that beside it, suggesting an act partly finished, is a half-full paper bag of sugar. Likewise, she notices "a dish-towel in the middle of the kitchen table." The table itself is half wiped, one side clean, the other messy, it signifying to Mrs. Hale "things begun—and not finished" (293). She finds yet further evidence of unfinished things in the blocks Minnie had started for a quilt. Most of the blocks are finely done, "nice and even," but one "looks as if she didn't know what she was about" (295). "The difference was startling" to Mrs. Hale. "Holding this block made her feel queer, as if the distracted thoughts of the woman who had perhaps turned to it to try and quiet herself were communicating themselves to her." When Mrs. Peters finds a bird cage and notices that its door is broken, the two women begin quickly to read other pieces of evidence. Shortly, they come upon the bird that belongs to the cage. It lies dead, entombed in a tiny box Minnie has placed among her sewing things: "Somebody wrung its neck," says Mrs. Peters (297).

Because the two women see in it the evidence of the brutal, desire-denying male who has "killed" the innocence of their identificatory object, the dead bird has a chilling effect on them. They have already associated Minnie herself with a bird: "She—come to think of it, she was kind of like a bird herself. Real sweet and pretty, but kind of timid and—fluttery" (299). Further, they recognize that to Minnie Wright the canary had been a signifier of her own desire and identity. In an otherwise very astute reading of this story, Hallgren makes the mistake of regarding the motive behind the murder the killing of the canary in itself, an act she calls "pet-ricide" (213). But Mrs. Hale and Mrs. Peters see deeper than that. Instead, they perceive that Minnie had strangled her husband because he had murdered a symbolic thing dearer to her than her own life. This thing Mrs. Hale equates with a child, that thing which for women, Lacan suggests, represents the Phallus. "I wonder," Mrs. Hale says, "how it would seem [...] never to have had any children around?" Then, her eyes taking in the kitchen and recognizing what the canary had meant to Minnie, she opines, "No, Wright wouldn't like the bird," because it was a "thing that sang. She used to sing. He killed that too." Finally, when Mrs. Peters cautiously observes, "Of course we don't know who killed the bird," Mrs. Hale's answer is precise: "I knew John Wright" (302). Such knowledge brings them an understanding that John Wright, in killing the bird, has just as surely killed the last object of desire possessed by his wife. Moreover, they see that in so doing he has effectively murdered her as well. In those paired recognitions, the two women judge Minnie's crime a justified homicide. Or, more radically, they judge it no crime at all. As women, they are her peers, they form her jury, they interpret the evidence, and, with no recourse to law other than the law of their own desire, they absolve her.

3

[T]he Real is defined as a point of the immediate coincidence of the opposite poles: each pole passes immediately into its opposite; each is already in itself its own opposite.
—Slavoj Žižek, *The Sublime Object of Ideology*, 172

A third move, one that Žižek, in *The Sublime Object of Ideology*, claims is most symptomatic of late Lacanian analysis, calls for examination of a social or literary object from the perspective of the Real.

The Real engages us with paradoxical relations, situations, meanings. The "immediate coincidence of opposite or even contradictory determinations," notes Žižek, "is what *defines* the Lacanian Real" (171). Reading "A Jury of Her Peers" from or for the Real entails recognizing paradoxical conjunctions or contradictory meanings. The paradoxical or contradictory we see immediately in the women's interpolations of the chain of signifiers that constitute the evidence absolving Minnie Wright. In judging Minnie, they surely have decided that events in her married life with John Wright have driven her insane. But in Lacanian terms, insanity—psychosis—occurs precisely because the "foreclosure" of the Symbolic enables the enactment in the Real of the subject's most primal desire. In the seminar *The Psychoses*, Lacan shows that Freud's concept 'Verwerfung,' the term Lacan translates as "foreclusion" and English yields as "foreclosure," identifies the way in which the psychotic subject has eliminated the prime orienting signifier—the Other—from its place in the structure of the psyche. "At issue is the rejection of a primordial signifier into the outer shadows," Lacan says, "a signifier that will henceforth be missing" in the subject's behavior (150). Likewise, in the seminar *The Ethics of Psychoanalysis*, Lacan says that "the moving force of paranoia is essentially the rejection of a certain support in the symbolic order." That support, Lacan says, provides the subject with the means to function around the split or defile caused by the primal "Real" Lacan calls "das Ding." It is, says Lacan, "that specific support around which the division between the two sides of the relationship to *das Ding* operates" (54) and without which ordinary subjectivity collapses into pathology. Thus "foreclosure" does not deny or diminish the importance of the Symbolic in the constitution of subjectivity. Rather, the foreclosure for ordinary life produces consequences that make us more aware of the Symbolic's value in suppressing the more dangerous Real.

It is the Symbolic, anchored not in the Imaginary other of ego identification but in the Other of the Law, that enables the subject to experience ordinary reality. It is inside the "primordial body" of the Symbolic, says Lacan, that "Freud posits the constitution of a world of reality, [one that] is already punctuated, already structured, in terms of signifiers" (*Psychoses* 150). Without this body, this Symbolic Other, the subject drifts, rudderless, unable to distinguish between dream or hallucination and the representations of reality structured by a shared Symbolic system. We know, as do the two women investigating Minnie Wright, that Minnie's psyche has lost contact with reality because her acts and speech do not accord with structures of law—those rules, protocols, assumptions, understandings operating in ordinary cultural life.

The evidence they uncover is as much evidence of the role—and, yes, power—of the Symbolic as it is of her dementia. In the story, Glaspell shows the force of the cultural norms found in the Symbolic in the opening two paragraphs. There, the subject involved is Mrs. Hale, one of the normative subjects against whom Minnie will be judged. Glaspell tells us that although this farm woman is being called away from her house because of the most extraordinary event in the history of her county, she is nonetheless upset that she has to leave home with things in disorder. "As she hurriedly wound [her scarf] round her head her eye made a scandalized sweep of her kitchen." Even faced with what she knows already is a grisly murder, her consciousness is governed by cultural norms. What she notices, Glaspell tells us, is "that her kitchen was in no shape for leaving: her bread all ready for mixing, half the flour sifted and half unsifted." Rushing out of the house to join the others in the journey to the Wright farm, Martha Hale still thinks of how she ought to have left things: "She hated," writes Glaspell, "to see things half done" (279).

In valorizing norms such as these, Mrs. Hale and the sheriff's wife recognize a pathology that leads us to the Real of the primal object. They are permitted to detect that something is *not* right with Minnie Wright. Abandoning the sugar bucket uncovered and the sugar sack unattended to, leaving the kitchen table half wiped off, failing to finish off those quilt blocks in the proper way—all this suggests to the two-woman jury that Minnie has lost her culturally determined psychic moorings. Other behavior they learn about leads others to judge likewise. In his account of discovering the crime, Mr. Hale notes that Minnie does not behave in ordinary ways, "as if she didn't know what she was going to do next." When Hale asks her if he can see her husband, she merely replies, "No." When Hale ask if he's home, "'Yes,' says she, 'he's home.'" When Hale asks why he cannot see her husband, she says, "Cause he's dead" (284). When asked how he died, she replies, "He died of a rope around his neck," and, Hale says, she "just went on pleatin' at her apron" (285). While this behavior may be "normal" enough for someone who has just strangled her husband, one other bit of behavior seems to a reader strange in any circumstances. Though Mrs. Hale and the sheriff's wife apparently agree that Minnie has placed the dead canary in the pretty little box in order to bury it later, the pattern of evidence regarding her mental condition suggests strongly that she has no such intention. Rather, she has placed it where she means it to stay—in her sewing basket. There, in the tradition to which Faulkner's Miss Emily of "A Rose for Emily" also contributes by saving her lover's unburied remains, the entombed bird will remain as a memorial—a *memento mori*—to a self she has seen destroyed. Minnie's attitude toward her dead husband (he is home, but, at the same time, not home) suggests she has lost her orientation toward signifiers of life and death. Her attitude toward the dead bird suggests likewise.

While the dead bird becomes a signifier for the two women in the way clues are signifiers in detective mysteries, Minnie Wright becomes a signifier of a very different sort: she becomes a signifier of that toward which the two women will reorient not only their personal relationship, but also their relationship to the paternal signifier itself. Though Minnie Wright has lost her orientation to the paternal signifier (the Law located in the Name of the Father), she, unlike the dead canary, is to the two women a signifier strictly in language, for unlike the canary she is actually absent—elsewhere—throughout the story. She, like John Wright as well, is present only in the words of those who speak of her. In their words, the two women suggest she signifies their own essential desires. As their Other, she dramatizes their mutual dissident fantasies and the object cause—the *objet petit a*—of their desire. Having foreclosed the orienting structures of the Symbolic, Minnie Wright—in her identificatory relationship to that entombed canary—has returned to Lacan's primal Real of das Ding, "the beyond-of-the-signified" (*Ethics* 54) that, for Freud and Lacan, is the primal Other, at once the forbidden Father-Thing and the forbidden (M)other-Thing who embodies the engulfment of the subject representing psychic, if not physical, death. More important, in her psychosis repeating for the two women their deepest desires, Minnie signifies to them their return in fantasy to das Ding, the imaginary refinding of the first object of desire, the return to the primal (M)other. While she signifies the violation of oedipal law to the representatives *of* the Law (the sheriff; the county attorney), for the two "detectives" who become Minnie's jury she signifies the (M)other lost to them—lost, indeed, to all subjects who have passed through the oedipal resolution and who have not, as Minnie has, suffered a lapse into psychosis.

In their search for an other opposed to culture's ordinary signifiers of law, the two women move toward a psychic event more fundamental than the murder Minnie Wright commits. In psychoanalysis, the dominant story of the normative subject is the oedipal. But in its repetition of the story of the subject's Imaginary identification with the first other, "A Jury of Her Peers" repeats the union of the subject with the (M)other forbidden to it by the law of Oedipus. Thus as a recrudescence of the story of the anti-Oedipus, Glaspell's takes us back across all our moves, from Imaginary identifications, to Symbolic contrarieties, to Real contradictions. In the Imaginary, its most interesting development lies in how the story shows the repetition of the forbidden desire of the (M)other in what must be called a "love story." At least one critic has noted this element: says Hallgren, "The language Glaspell uses to describe [their] collusion is nearly erotic" (214). Indeed, not "nearly," but extremely erotic, Glaspell's language offers a story of female identification transgressing Symbolic law in the uncovering of the signifier of the lost (M)other of the Real, the lost object, the (M)other as the lost or repressed object of every subject's primordial desire. One way to think of this love story is to regard it as a communion of women, a story in which two women separated by space and the norms of their community form a community of two in support of a third who symbolizes their shared condition as subjects under patriarchal authority.

While "A Jury of Her Peers" is in fact quite a chaste story of Imaginary identification, it exhibits the sense of threat to patriarchy that female desire, especially lesbian desire, may arouse. Glaspell activates this threat by using a language of romantic encounter that she weaves around the reading of evidence undertaken by the two women (as a detective story, the tale may indeed remind readers of the film and television convention of the sleuthing couple). In this romantic layer of Glaspell's story, developments occur through the women's physical movements toward each other and through a language of eyes. The first physical move bringing the two women closer occurs just after the county attorney raises the question of a possible motive for Minnie's murdering her husband and immediately following his reference to the "nice mess" made by the broken jars of Minnie's preserves. Here, Glaspell writes, "The two women had drawn nearer." The next move occurs following Mr. Hale's reference, "with good-natured superiority," to the way women worry over "trifles." "The two women," Glaspell writes, "moved a little closer together. Neither of them spoke." Still, since the course of "love" is not always smooth, to move toward each other they must overcome a series of obstacles. As in many conventional love stories, the real obstacles lie within themselves. While Mrs. Hale has seized on Mrs. Peters as an Imaginary other with whom she can identify (and in whom she can find her ideal ego), she has a moment of disenchantment when, examining the shabby clothes Minnie possesses, she talks about John Wright's stinginess and how it made Minnie withdraw from the community because she must have felt inadequate. "I think maybe that's why she kept so much to herself," says Mrs. Hale. "I s'pose she felt she couldn't do her part; and then, you don't enjoy things when you feel shabby. She used to wear pretty clothes and be lively—when she

was Minnie Foster, one of the town girls, singing in the choir. But
that—oh, that was twenty years ago" (287).

As a signifier, the psychotic woman triangulates the desires of the
two women much as the paternal signifier triangulates subjects in the
Oedipus complex. Because Mrs. Hale's sense of identification with
Minnie Foster is powerful here, it is incumbent on Mrs. Peters to share
that identification. But Mrs. Hale is not certain yet that she does.
Tenderly folding Minnie's "shabby clothing" at the kitchen table, Mrs.
Hale looks at Mrs. Peters and finds "there was something in the other
woman's look that irritated her." Her inference is that Mrs. Peters
"don't care" and that it makes little "difference [...] to her whether
Minnie Foster had pretty clothes when she was a girl." But, happily,
this moment of uncertain connection is followed by another in which
Mrs. Hale begins to suspect more identification. Looking at Mrs. Peters
again, she sees that the other "had that shrinking manner, and yet her
eyes looked as if they could see a long way into things." When Mrs.
Peters, in her timid way, takes down a shawl for Minnie and speaks of
how an apron would make the woman "feel more natural," Mrs. Hale
"suddenly" takes "a quick step toward the other woman" and asks the
crucial question, "Do you think she—did it?" (292).

Hereafter, because of the movement of the women toward each
other signaled in exchanges of gazes and therefore through the language of eyes, Glaspell's becomes a story that, occurring in subversion of the Law, takes place beneath—and beneath the notice of—the
men. In a moment suggesting upper versus lower, dominant versus
dominated, the story makes the subversion explicit in one passage.
On the one hand, "The two women stood there silent, above them the
footsteps of the men who were looking for evidence against the
woman who had worked in that kitchen." On the other, "That look
of seeing into things, of seeing through a thing to something else, was
in the eyes of the sheriff's wife now" (294). From this moment, the
language of eyes tells a story of uninterrupted desire and subversion.
When the women notice that those quilt blocks are not done properly, for instance, Glaspell writes, "Their eyes met—something
flashed to life, passed between them; then, as if with an effort, they
seemed to pull away from each other" (295). Next, when the two
women discover that the canary's cage door is broken, Glaspell
writes, "Again their eyes met—startled, questioning, apprehensive.
For a moment neither spoke nor stirred" (297–98). Likewise, when
the two discover the corpse of the bird, its neck broken, Glaspell
writes, "And then again the eyes of the two women met—this time
clung together in a look of dawning comprehension, of growing

horror. Mrs. Peters looked from the dead bird to the broken door of the cage. Again their eyes met" (300).

Psychoanalytically, much more is going on here than, as it were, meets the eye. In the register of the Imaginary, the objective of those identifications found in love stories is to apprehend that kernel of the Real of one's being that escapes knowledge. It is to find or—really—refind "[one's] innermost, intimate kernel called by Freud *Kern unseres Wesen* and by Lacan *das Ding*." It is, adds Žižek, "that strange body in my interior which is 'in me more than me,' which is radically interior and [at] the same time already exterior" (*Sublime* 180). Mrs. Hale has an apprehension of this kernel. It speaks, in the moment following Mrs. Peters's recognition that in the canary Minnie had seen her own kernel of self and that Wright's killing the bird was an act of soul murder. When Mrs. Peters admits how awful it would have been for Minnie to lose "a bird to sing to you," Glaspell writes of Mrs. Hale: "It was as if something within her not herself had spoken, and it found in Mrs. Peters something she did not know as herself" (302). The climax of this story occurs when, amidst much talk of law, of being married to the law, the two women come together in their subversive pact, in submission to their desire to have *it*, to have the lost object, the (M)other in the Real lost in the oedipal assumption of the Symbolic Law. In this moment, *it* lies with Mrs. Peters. She has finally yielded resolutely to the desire, now shared, to put the (M)other in the place of the Symbolic Father.

In its focus on aspects of the gaze, the story suggests that it is Mrs. Hale's gaze—the gaze of the identificatory other—that makes "her turn back. Her eyes made her turn back." These eyes represent those of the "other woman" who is one's identificatory other. Thus, "Slowly, unwillingly, Mrs. Peters turned her head until her eyes met the eyes of the other woman. There was a moment when they held each other in a steady, burning look in which there was no evasion nor flinching." Then the gaze of this other leads Mrs. Peters to the object that represents the "thing itself," the bodily presence of the (M)other, the Thing of one's material reality. "Then Martha Hale's eyes pointed the way to the basket in which was hidden *the thing* that would make certain the conviction of the other woman—that woman who was not there and yet who had been there with them all through the hour" (306). In hiding the bird's little coffin, the women not only protect the figure of the (M)other (with them not just "through the hour," but in fact always), but they also conceal their desire for the thing hidden, the Thing Itself, das Ding that is, Lacan says, the abyssal "beyond-of-the-signified."

We may say that these two women, by concealing what they know, have committed a crime against ordinary social law. Indeed, they have. But there is more. To psychoanalysis, their crime is yet more primal. In their installing the abjected woman in the place of the Law, the place of the Other, these two women repeat—or attempt to repeat—the subject's most fundamental desire, the desire of incest. "What we find in the incest law," says Lacan, in *The Ethics of Psychoanalysis*, "is located as such at the level of the unconscious in relation to *das Ding*, the Thing." But as such that object is precisely the one that can be attained neither in the Imaginary nor in the Symbolic. "The desire for the mother cannot be satisfied," says Lacan, "because it is the end, the terminal point, the abolition of the whole world of demand [. . .] that at its deepest level structures [the human] unconscious." This terminal point is always an abyss, a dead end, as it were, for if one enters it one enters—as Minnie Wright herself does—the domain of psychosis, where the subject-as-subject disappears and loses any perception of itself as "enjoying" that which it has sought. In the other direction—in the direction of the Other of the Oedipus—lies the Symbolic. In his analysis of Freud's notion of the pleasure principle, Lacan suggests it is this principle, in its underpinning of desire, that makes the quest of the (M)other impossible by its forming the oedipal law. "It is to the extent that the function of the pleasure principle is to make man always search for what he has to find again, but which he never will attain, that one reaches the essence [of human culture], namely, that sphere or relationship which is known as the law of the prohibition of incest" (68).

Thus it seems the story Glaspell tells in "A Jury of Her Peers" is transgressive less because in its use of language it suggests a story of some forbidden lesbian love than because, as fundamentally a story of the desire of and for the (M)other, it is the most forbidden (psychoanalytic) story of all, a story of narcissistic subversion of the oedipal patriarchy. *This* story thus suggests both the contradictions of desire and the double bind of any subject's transgressions of hegemonic patriarchal Law. At bottom, when the story shows that at the point where the two women enter the abyss of das Ding and find the little death object, the canary's perverse sarcophagus, they ally themselves with another law. Ultimately, in hiding the death object and with it hiding their transgressive desire, they experience—as do readers in their identifications—a momentary triumph, the triumph of the desire of *the* (M)other over the patriarchal law that tolerates maternal desire least of all. Their moment of triumph occurs in the irony of the story's virtual last words—"knot it" (306). As much as these words enfigure in metonymy the noose Minnie Wright has pulled around her husband's neck, they are also phonically identical to a denial, to "*not* it." Thus at some unconscious textual level, these two words mean that the signifier of patriarchal law is *not*, is most especially not *it*. *That* thing—the Phallus, the signifier of the Father, the Law of the Father—is not it. Whatever these words may mean on whatever level, the presumably "happy" ending they give the story suggests that, at least momentarily, the desire of Narcissus—in the battle against Oedipus—has won out.

4

> The usual critique of patriarchy fatally neglects the fact that there are two fathers.
>
> —Slavoj Žižek, *Metastases of Enjoyment*, 206

But have these women "won"? As the analyst knows, Culture—with a capital C—is oedipal, not narcissistic. Because the Other of Law comes from culture, and our culture is patriarchal, any woman's apparent victory is likely to be fleeting. Moreover, for those same reasons, it may be a victory shadowed by terror and burdened (as Lacan's *Ethics of Psychoanalysis* suggests) by the troubling questions of ethics it raises. In this feature, the story raises the very same questions every change in the social Symbolic entails. For, indeed, every real change must establish a Symbolic within which the signifiers of the new order will be taken as Law. It need only be evolutionary change in the Symbolic. As Glaspell's story suggests, the change need only be to establish the (M)other not in the place of the Law of the Father, but to establish the (M)other along with the Father, as equal to the Father so that we may, unselfconsciously, speak in the Name of the Mother as readily as in the Name of the Father. That, essentially, is the argument of much feminist thought. For many, Carol Gilligan offers a philosophical alternative to ordinary Western patriarchy. Gilligan's thought is very cogently connected to Glaspell's story by Sherri Hallgren. "In contemplating their cover-up," says Hallgren, "Mrs. Hale and Mrs. Peters are about to overturn the system not simply of justice but of conventional values, instituting a female system of ethics for that of the patriarchy." That system, as in Gilligan, would place more value on making the world safe than on punishing those who transgress its rules. In a world ruled by female ethics, care giving would be more important than ruling. Says Gilligan, "[I]f aggression is tied, as women perceive, to the fracture of human connection, then the activities of care [. . .] are the activities that make the social world safe, by avoiding isolation and preventing aggression rather than by making rules to limit its extent" (Gilligan 43;

qtd. in Hallgren 209). Says Hallgren, "Mrs. Peters and Mrs. Hale, then, in their empathy and their desire to help Minnie Wright—their 'activities of care'—are doing more to 'make the social world safe' than are the sheriff and attorney who seek to see Minnie punished." But, what is more, they find a way to judge John Wright's crime: "[I]f fracture of connection is the dangerous activity, then [his] 'crime' in this female version of an ordered and safe world is, first, his isolation and emotional abandonment of his wife, and, finally, his destruction of what did constitute her connection with something that would communicate with her—her canary" (209). While Hallgren points out that within this maternal ethics the two women judge themselves as guilty, too, the larger guilt in the story must lie in a culture that refuses to incorporate maternal values into the Law of the Father, the rule of the cultural Symbolic. If a dissident reading demonstrates anything at all, it must demonstrate that the cultural Symbolic to which the Law is anchored must be regarded as neither unfailing nor totally closed to change. As Law seems to be articulated in a fictional world such as that we find in, say, Jane Austen, maternal and paternal values—narcissistic *jouissance* and oedipal desire wedded as equals—may in fact be incorporated into the Law of the Symbolic that dominates normative lives.

But, unfortunately, "A Jury of Her Peers" shows that things rarely are this simple. Moreover, looking at the ideological base of the story through a late Lacanian perspective, one sees why things are never so simple, why a story such as Glaspell's, contrary to many readings, may paradoxically reinforce, rather than weaken, patriarchal ideology. "The aim of the 'critique of ideology,' of the analysis of an ideological edifice," says Žižek, "is to extract [the] symptomal kernel which the official, public ideological text simultaneously disavows and needs for its undisturbed functioning" ("Re-visioning" 19). Within the premises of Lacanian theory, ideological critique of Glaspell's story shows that the liberating change in the Symbolic order will not occur unless we understand how complicated is the relationship of subjects to Symbolic Law and, especially, of the moral suasion of ordinary oedipal law and the violence of the obscene superego law of the primordial father that Žižek so frequently emphasizes in his writings. We may go back to that tautology "law is law." In it, Žižek says in *For They Know Not What They Do*, "We can sense this concealed dimension of violence already apropos of the everyday, 'spontaneous' reading of the proposition 'law is law.'" He asks whether this phrase is not "usually evoked precisely when we are confronted with the 'unfair,' 'incomprehensible' constraint that pertains to the law? In other words, what does this tautology effectively mean if not the cynical wisdom that law remains in its most fundamental dimension a form of radical violence which must be obeyed regardless of our subjective appreciation?" (34). In the relation of Minnie to John Wright, we may see how the suasion of ordinary law depends upon the obscene law and its forms of violence. This relation suggests the double bind, the catch-22, in which the human subject finds itself. Because all normative subjects are split, all subjects, not women subjects only, are caught in what Žižek repeatedly stresses as a late Lacanian notion of the "forced choice" between two evils, *le père ou pire*, the father or worse: on the one hand, the oedipal or ordinary father of normative patriarchal subjection and, on the other, the anal or obscene or superego father identified with the terrifying narcissistic *jouissance* of the *objet a*.

In Glaspell's story, if ordinary law has its representatives in the sheriff and the county attorney, the primordial, superego law has its in John Wright. In these representatives, we see clearly how the ordinary (oedipal) rests fundamentally upon the primordial (narcissistic). We see it precisely in that male laughter so pervasive in the text. That laughter suggests an enjoyment in the scene of the crime that can only connote the complicity of the one law with the other. "This strain of enjoyment," says Žižek, "is crucial for the 'normal' functioning of power." In a brief story, he tells how, in "a most distastefully enjoyable way," a "personal experience" reveals to him "this inherent obscenity of Power" ("Re-visioning" 18). In his story, Žižek tells how he and a group of other soldiers laughed derisively at another's unsuccessful attempts to masturbate to enable a medical officer to evaluate a physical complaint of the soldier. The derisive laughter—"distastefully enjoyable"—showed Žižek how the law—embodied in the officer—could at once rule and solicit the complicity of the ruled (the soldiers). "This scene brought about in me an experience of quasi-epiphany," says Žižek.

> *In nuce*, there was everything in it, the entire apparatus of Power: the uncanny mixture of imposed enjoyment and humiliating coercion; the agency of Power which shouts severe orders, but simultaneously shares with us, his subordinates, obscene laughter bearing witness to a deep solidarity; the grotesque excess by means of which, in a unique short-circuit, attitudes which are officially opposed and mutually exclusive reveal their uncanny complicity, where the solemn agent of Power suddenly starts to wink at us across the table in a gesture of obscene solidarity, letting us know that the thing (his orders) is not to be taken too seriously, and thereby consolidating his power. (18–19)

The laughter of the men in "A Jury of Her Peers" illustrates precisely the same relation of complicity between the ordinary law and the
law of the obscene, superego, primordial father found in John Wright.
The "law," it is clear, demands John Wright. He is the bogeyman who
scares all but the most courageous women into line with the relatively
less violent demands of patriarchy itself. The relation of law to John
Wright, indeed, suggests why, historically, law has been so lenient
toward abusive husbands. As through violence they show women that
men have the upper hand, they leave the ordinary male nothing to do
but say, "Ain't it a shame." Thus, John Wright shows why, when
women are given a choice, it is likely to be a choice between evils, *le
père—ou pire*, "the Father—or worse."

So, given the forced choice all subjects—but, within patriarchy,
especially women subjects—must make between two evils, what choice
have Mrs. Hale and Mrs. Peters made? The two dissident women
appear to support Minnie because she seems to have found an escape
from the dilemma of the forced choice. They see she has found a desire
outside her husband (he the oedipal-cum-primordial father) and
demonstrates a willingness to perform any act, however violent, to
prevent his seizing it or, as is usually the case, to rip it from him if he
has it already. They see the meaning of her violence. "At its most radical level," says Žižek, "violence is precisely an endeavor to strike a
blow at this unbearable surplus-enjoyment contained in the Other"
("Re-visioning" 18). But if Minnie Foster Wright escapes the forced
choice by "choosing" a third way, her two jurors must finally decide
whether her way is truly the better choice. In choosing the way of her
desire and the denial of the Symbolic bond upon which society
depends, Minnie is "free," but she purchases her freedom at a vast
cost. What is the cost of psychosis?

It is, says Žižek, "the psychotic [...] who has refused to walk into
the trap of the forced choice and to accept that he has 'always already
chosen': he took the choice 'seriously' and chose the impossible opposite of the Name of the Father, i.e., of the symbolic identification which
confers us a place in the intersubjective space." But, as Lacan argues,
the descent into madness *is* a choice, involves an ethics, and demands a
judgment. This choice, Žižek suggests, "is why Lacan insists that psychosis is to be 'located within the register of ethics': psychosis is a mode
'not to give way as to our desire,' it signals our refusal to exchange
enjoyment for the Name of the Father" (*Enjoy* 77). Thus if Minnie
holds to her enjoyment, it is surely to be at the cost of her personal
freedom and a judgment on her ethics. So she leaves her jurors with the
decision—"*père ou pire*," Father or worse. Because they do not reveal

to the law what they have uncovered, they do nothing to change Minnie's fate nor to affect their own—except in "fostering" their own enjoyment at secretly tweaking the nose of the law. Ultimately, they too enjoy. They too wink at each other as they share silently a critique of blind Law. But, as Žižek says of subjects in general, they do no more than enjoy their own symptom, their own suppression. To fully understand "A Jury of Her Peers," then, we must understand that they do indeed finally choose "Father." To choose otherwise, alas, is only to choose the worse.[5]

As troubling as this reading of "A Jury of Her Peers" may be to readers who desire a happier ending to it, there is in our history since Glaspell's time a more positive note to be sounded. While, clearly, it is difficult to change the cultural Symbolic, it can be changed. If Lacan is the messenger of the forced choice, he also is, according to Jacques-Alain Miller, the messenger of change. In his portion of "The Other Who Does not Exist and His Ethical Committees" (coauthored with Eric Laurent), Miller argues that while the Freudian epoch that embraced the time of Glaspell's story took the Other as real (in, for example, God or Science), in the Lacanian epoch, our epoch, the Other is only a *semblant*, a seeming, a fiction, a fabrication. The Other as *semblant* does not change the structure of subjectivity, for subjects must still "use" it: "*One can make do without the Name-of-the-Father on condition that one make use of it*" as if it were real, Miller stresses (18). But this thesis of Lacan, says Miller, does suggest a change in the dynamism within the structure of the subject. In this change, Lacanian theory offers a role to the Imaginary—and thus to the subject's identifications with the Mother—stronger than it had during the Freudian epoch to which the work of the earlier Lacan was largely devoted. This more potent role is illustrated, for instance, in the relation of the Imaginary to the Symbolic within Lacan's Schema L. When Miller argues that "the contemporary symbolic [...] is far from being up to puncturing, crossing the imaginary" (21), he suggests that the Symbolic of the Lacanian—or postmodern—epoch no longer so simply dominates the Imaginary as once upon a time.

Indeed, Miller suggests that the late Lacan relativizes both the Oedipus and the concept of 'subjectivity.' The late Lacan offers a new, normative subject who may in fact find its *semblants* of the Other in images of the mother as readily as in images of the father. Further, this late Lacan Miller describes accords feminism and the gay and lesbian movements a considerable role in changing postmodern subjectivity. While he merely wonders what might be the changes wrought on the homosexual subject when "the social Other henceforth greets it in a

completely different way," he makes a more definitive claim for feminism: "[T]he identification with the signifier *to be a woman*," he says,
"has led to the juridical and political emancipation of women, up to the
specifically ethical revolt of feminism, the incidence of which makes
itself felt at all levels of the new *American way of life*" (23). While such
claims for the new subject uncovered by the late Lacan will not remove
the forced choice from social life, they do acknowledge openings for
change in the relation of subjects to the cultural Symbolic that have not
always been recognized by opponents of Lacan or psychoanalysis. For
the project of the psychoanalysis of culture and society, this is good
news indeed.

CHAPTER 6

Oedipus, Narcissus, and the Maternal Thing in Fitzgerald's "Winter Dreams"

That Lacan may have [. . .] elaborated the Freudian [oedipal] myth, up to the point of formalising it on the linguistic model of metaphor, does not mean that he had ever neglected its relativity.
—Jacques-Alain Miller, "The Other Who Does Not Exist and His Ethical Committees," 25–26.

Although Jacques-Alain Miller, especially, and several others— including Joan Copjec, Renata Salecl, and Juliet MacCannell— have been important Lacanian revisionists, the most effective advocate of a late Lacan has been Slavoj Žižek. Žižek typically disparages early or old Lacan as merely a "current" understanding. This "current critical approach to Lacan," he argues, "reduces Lacan to desire, prohibition, oedipalization, so that Lacan is the Lacan of desire." For critics as well as clinicians, a shift from current-old to new-late Lacan shifts critical focus from desire to drive and to a different (but certainly not new) set of concepts. "Basically," says Žižek, "the problematic of desire is ultimately the problematic of intersubjectivity, recognition, the symbolic order, language, [and the] subject," whereas, invoking the Real, "drive introduces the materialist notion of impenetrability, that which resists symbolization" ("Interview" 148). While in the early Lacan oedipalization seems to have enabled the Symbolic to produce a stable subject who directs its own actions, the later Lacan undermines such notions and gives us objects who are merely subjects of the forces of drive and *jouissance*. Julia Kristeva, for one among several feminist theorists critical of traditional Freudian notions of the unconscious (theorists including Parveen Adams, Elizabeth Grosz, and MacCannell), comes down strongly on the side of drive and *jouissance* when she stresses the strong pull on the subject to "regress" toward the domain of the mother, the source of subjectivity in the "semiotic." For her and other feminist theorists, this opening back toward the primal mother (often expressed in experimental art and literature) is a means toward freedom from the patriarchal Symbolic posited by both Lacan and Kristeva (and observed in its merely Pyrrhic victory in "A Jury of Her Peers"). But in the context of those late Lacanian interpretations of culture and psychoanalysis by Žižek and those he has influenced (Adams, Copjec, MacCannell, Salecl), the most critical issue for us lies in the deeply paradoxical situation of the subject, the paradox Freud identifies in the drives, Eros and Thanatos. From a strictly Lacanian perspective, regression to the *jouissance* of the maternal Thing must remain dangerous for the subject.

Analysis of F. Scott Fitzgerald's "Winter Dreams" may begin to show us the shape of a late Lacanian reading that deals with such issues. Fitzgerald's story illustrates how we may read the dialectic of desire (Oedipus versus Narcissus) not only in the context of oedipal authority—installation of the Lacanian Law of the Symbolic Father— but also in that of maternal *jouissance* (residing somewhere, in Lacan's Real, certainly, and perhaps in notions that surely attach to it: Torok and Abraham's "crypt" and that semiotic *chora* Julia Kristeva posits). But even as a reading of this dialectic in Fitzgerald's story facilitates understanding of much post-Freudian psychoanalytic theory, not to be disregarded is how such reading also explains something about the story critics have often sought and generally missed. Exhibiting features of Freud's family romance and regarded by scholars as a forerunner of *The Great Gatsby*, the story involves a young man of modest origins who aspires to a better, wealthier, more powerful life—and, with it, a grander ego or self or identity. Written in 1922 and published first in December of that year, "Winter Dreams" appeared in Fitzgerald's collection *All the Sad Young Men* (1926). With "Absolution" (written in June 1923 and published in 1924), "The Rich Boy" (written in 1925, as a sort of spin-off of *Gatsby* and published in 1926), and "The Sensible Thing" (written in 1923 and published in 1924), "Winter Dreams" is often regarded as part of a "Gatsby cluster" adumbrating plots, themes, or characters of the 1925 novel. "Indeed," Matthew J. Bruccoli tells us, "Fitzgerald removed Dexter Green's response to Judy Jones's home from the magazine text and wrote it into the novel as Jay Gatsby's response to Daisy Fay's home" (217).

These days, some critics take "Winter Dreams" seriously largely because its main characters (the youth and the girl who grows up to be a femme fatale) prefigure Gatsby and Daisy Fay Buchanan and because the story is an early enunciation of Fitzgerald's dominant theme, the loss of illusions. "The dream-and-disillusion motif in the story," says Clinton S. Burhans, "appears in varying forms and degrees from its intermittent emergence in *This Side of Paradise* to its central exploration in *The Last Tycoon*; it is Fitzgerald's major theme" (412). Despite a paramount interest in the novel, however, many still regard "Winter Dreams" as among Fitzgerald's best. John F. Kuehl (64) places it in Fitzgerald's top eight. Bruccoli says it is the best of the Gatsby cluster (217). Anthologized in James H. Pickering's popular college text *Fiction 100* for more than thirty years, it was in the 1960s the most assiduously discussed of all the stories. Virtually all focused on the story's ending. Robert Sklar, Henry Dan Piper, James E. Miller Jr., Burhans, and Arthur Mizener, for example, all offered one interpretation or another of what precisely it is Dexter feels he has lost and cries for at the story's end. The answers range from Sklar's claim that it is immortality to Piper's argument that it is the past, Miller's that it is beauty, Mizener's that it is the ability to feel deeply, and Burhans's that it is the dream itself. Germane to my interests, one critic does attribute "psychological" dimensions to Dexter's loss. Saying "Dexter had been manipulated to a startling degree by psychological factors of which he had been unaware," Alice Hall Petry suggests that what he cries for is himself (137). All these readings of the story are valuable, but by hiding the story's light under the bushel of *The Great Gatsby* or by making the loss canonical in Fitzgerald's fiction or even by attempting to make the theme unique to "Winter Dreams," many—Petry notwithstanding—fail to see the fundamentally psychoanalytic reason the story appeals deeply to virtually every reader, male and female alike.

Plainly, whatever Dexter cries for, the story itself cries for a new psychoanalytic reading, one from the perspective of a late Lacanian theory, especially as filtered through Slavoj Žižek and others. This reading must focus on the story's sometimes intrusive but typically misconstrued oedipal elements. Because of its role in determining human subjectivity, the oedipal complex illustrates the dialectic of desire versus drive so critical to developing subjectivity. In the formation of the "normal" subject, the resolution of the Oedipus complex is determinative. According to Lacan, the Oedipus in Freudian theory is one of two basic myths; the second is that of Narcissus ("Neurotic's Individual Myth" 407, 423). While pivoting between Narcissus and Oedipus, oedipalization embraces the roles of both mother and father, of desire and drive, and desire and *jouissance*. At the same time, moreover, as a process, it invokes the Imaginary of the mirror phase and the Symbolic assumed during oedipalization itself. As one might surmise, the two myths are oriented differently: in the oedipal, the subject is oriented toward desire and the paternal, but in the narcissistic, toward drive and the maternal. Because of these orientations, the one myth for the subject is clearly good, and the other bad. In its orientation toward desire

and intersubjectivity, the basic oedipal plot of maturation exhibits the
normalizing trajectory of mirror-phase narcissism moving through the
resolutions of oedipalization. "[T]he very normalization of [...] maturation," says Lacan, is "dependent [...] on a cultural mediation as
exemplified, in the case of the sexual object, by the oedipus complex"
(*Écrits: A Selection* 5–6). In short, in the oedipal plot, when the subject
shifts orientation from Mother to Father, as it were, he or she resolves
identity—including gender identity—by acceding to the authority of the
Other within the Symbolic order. Ultimately, if not immediately, in
making the shift to the paternal, the oedipal plot operates in the order
of the Symbolic. Its basic *mythos* or story of course is that of Oedipus.
The Oedipus story exhibits the vicissitudes of the subject's recognition
and, normatively, acceptance of a symbolic castration signified by
limits placed on primal drives. Its plot structure thus turns on the subject's accession to the rule of law localized, typically, in figures (potentially either male or female) who come to signify the law of the
Symbolic: the laws, rules, conventions, and the like of a given culture.
While Lacan often identifies the Symbolic as the Law of the Name of
the Father, in his later years he recognized that feminism has rightly
expanded the notion of law to include the role of the female as well as
the male. Because the pivotal force in this type of story is authoritarian
prohibition or interdiction, such stories begin in a desire that challenges
it ("I want that"). They end not only in a failure ("I cannot have that"),
but, more important, in a resignation ("I will live without it") that
shows how the subject has internalized the law. Whereas the basic plot
of the myth of Narcissus creates stories of law that foreground drive,
the one of Oedipus creates stories of desire that foreground law.

1

> Desire means that the subject goes from one object to another and
> never finds one that would satisfy him or her.
> —Renata Salecl, "Interview," 147.

Fitzgerald's "Winter Dreams" not only almost perfectly illustrates
the features of the psychoanalytic oedipal plot as posited in Lacanian
theory, but it also allows us to revisit the plot of Narcissus in the context of postmodern psychoanalytic theory influenced by such post-
Lacanian theorists as Julia Kristeva, Jacqueline Rose, Renata Salecl,
Juliet MacCannell, and others. Not universally accepted by feminist
Lacanians, Kristeva, coming down strongly on the side of drive and
jouissance, stresses the pull on the subject to regress toward the narcis-

sistic domain of the mother, the source of subjectivity in Kristeva's "semiotic." For her, as for many other feminist theorists, however, this opening back toward the primal mother (a pull often expressed, Kristeva argues, in experimental art and literature) is a means, although typically only ephemeral, toward freedom from the patriarchal Symbolic as it is posited by Freudians, including both Lacan and Kristeva herself. Jacqueline Rose, an early Anglo-American Lacanian, in "Julia Kristeva—Take Two," suggests that the notion of the semiotic is the "least useful aspect of Kristeva's work." Rose claims so because Kristeva's "maternally connoted and primitive semiotic is [...] first defined as the hidden underside of culture"—an image, Rose says, in which "we can recognize the proximity [...] to the classical demonic image of femininity"—"and then idealised as something whose value and exuberance the culture cannot manage and has therefore had to repress," this latter, she suggests, "a simple reverse of that first image which makes femininity the ideal excluded instance of all culture" (154). In fact, however, despite Rose, it is easy enough to absorb Kristeva's notion into Lacanian notions—paradoxical, of course (as Žižek invariably contends)—of the two aspects of "mother," for these connect to and form a symmetrical pairing with antithetical aspects of "father," as well. In Lacanian theory, especially as Žižek advocates it, there are both good mothers and fathers and bad mothers and fathers. And, often, the twain do meet.

Like Jay Gatsby, the protagonist of "Winter Dreams," Dexter Green, spends his life seeking to satisfy a desire represented for him in the figure of a woman. Gatsby of course seeks the object of desire in Daisy Fay, Dexter in Judy Jones. Since the object is never attainable, both Gatsby and Dexter approach it (as do most subjects) from the side, for, in the beginning, they focus not on the woman as such, but on the accouterments of wealth with which they associate the woman and in which they display their right to her, the one who symbolizes their fantasies. This displacement from woman to things is exhibited in the image that gives the story its title, for Dexter imagines his desire as "winter dreams." Perhaps entertained by any youth in the process of oedipalization, *winter dreams* seems a precise metaphor for heroic fantasies of attaining the object of desire. Since the oedipal myth typically ends in resignation, the metaphor works very effectively, for while 'dreams' express the potency of desire, 'winter' suggests that it may have a boundary to it. Suggesting the bittersweet resolution of the oedipal complex, the metaphor initiates Dexter's recognition (with apologies to the Rolling Stones) that while you can not always get what you want, once you have accepted the law of the Oedipus you can get what you need to function in the world. In working out its oedipal implications in surprisingly complex ways, "Winter Dreams," in an adult repetition of a childhood phenomenon, shows how for at least one subject the Oedipus resolution eventuates.

In the story, the titular phrase first occurs in a context that does not immediately explain its meaning. When he is about fourteen and working as a caddy at the local country club, Dexter abruptly quits his job. Seemingly unaccountable, the boy's decision has something to do with the girl—Judy—who ostensibly represents Dexter's love object. But at the beginning of the story, Judy is just eleven, and the boy does not know the child, in a sexual or any other sense. Though he knows who her father is, Dexter does not quite understand why his first encounter with Judy causes him suddenly to walk away from a job he really loves, loves in large part because it places him among those in whom he finds his narcissistic being both loveable and admirable. But what is at stake is oedipal, not narcissistic. Indeed, the narrator's language describing the event begins to suggest a psychological trauma. "The enormity of his decision [to quit] frightened him," Fitzgerald tells us, but while "[Dexter] had received a strong emotional shock" and "his perturbation required a violent and immediate outlet" (220), still, nothing concrete seems attached to either the event or the affect. Thus, agreeing with the narrator's contention that this explanation is insufficient, readers are led to ask, What is the "emotional shock," and why does it require "violent and immediate outlet"?

Early in the story there simply is no adequate explanation of the tremendous gap between the apparent precipitating event and its affect within the boy. All that happens is that Dexter has watched Judy, as the prepubescent *enfant terrible*, throw a temper tantrum because her nurse-chaperon cannot find an available caddy. Though Dexter ostensibly is available, he is under instructions not to take anyone out until his caddy master returns. But returning while Judy is assailing her nurse, the caddy master seemingly solves the dispute by assigning Dexter to the twosome. Still, Dexter will not go. Sounding a little like Melville's Bartleby ("I'd prefer not to"), the reluctant Dexter simply says, "I don't think I'll go out to-day." Moreover, when the caddy master orders him to go, Dexter quits his job on the spot (220). Readers have every right to wonder why. Fitzgerald makes it clear that Dexter's reasons, if not obvious, are complex. "As so frequently would be the case in the future," the narrator says, "Dexter was unconsciously dictated to by his winter dreams" (220). But what do those dreams entail?

While Fitzgerald is not very specific about them, his language has an immense Lacanian resonance that prompts several observations.

First, of course, the dreams are not at all limited to winter. They are the generic label for Dexter's fantasies of desire. When Lacan says, as he often does, that "desire is a metonymy," he means that while desire wraps itself in "objects" and becomes identified with them through the tropological principle of association or contiguity, desire does not cease when the actual objects are obtained. When Fitzgerald says that "the quality and the seasonability of these winter dreams varied, but the stuff of them remained" (220), he seems literally translating Lacan's notion that no matter how the metonymic objects (the seasons or the temporal instances) change, desire persists because the "stuff" (or energy or motility) of desire remains.

Second, though Fitzgerald seems to imply that Dexter might well satisfy his desires, his winter dreams, by capturing the objects themselves, the fact is—and Fitzgerald surely recognizes it—that Dexter cannot so satisfy them. The narrator's fantasy, however, is to suggest that Dexter somehow can dissociate desire from its objects, that one may distinguish or distill some essence from its corporeal manifestations. Speaking as if snobbery focuses on essences, the narrator says, "But do not get the impression, because his winter dreams happened to be concerned at first with musings on the rich, that there was anything merely snobbish in the boy." Somehow, it is more pure to desire the things: "He wanted not association with glittering things and glittering people—he wanted the glittering things themselves" (220–21). But for Lacan the simple fact is that the "association" is all we can have. Where desire is concerned, there is no capturing it, even if one captures *das ding an sich* in "the things themselves."

Third, we have finally reached some hint of what the story is really about. Whether it is possible to capture desire itself, Dexter's effort to capture those most desirable things signifying those winter dreams is imbricated in a network of prohibitions that, as Fitzgerald himself suggests, can only be unconscious, in this case unconscious because they are profoundly oedipal. "Often," says the narrator, "[Dexter] reached out for the best without knowing why he wanted it—and sometimes he ran up against the mysterious denials and prohibitions in which life indulges." The story is about these aspects of Dexter's life. "It is with one of those denials," says the narrator, "and not with his career as a whole that this story deals" (221). Indeed, once explained, the "denials and prohibitions" can make sense of a story that over the decades has almost endlessly puzzled readers.

All those denials and prohibitions revolve around a series of annunciations—of Judy Jones to Dexter Green. Dealt with briefly already, the first is that of Judy at eleven to Dexter at fourteen.

However subtly, this first one establishes the oedipal prohibitions of the
story, as, in Lacan's language, interdictions against "having," not
"being." As might be expected from the story's title, the interdictions
focus largely on Judy as the object of Dexter's phallic desire. The story
turns on the subject's desire to have an other because that other is presumed to have what one lacks. That "thing" of course being the
Phallus, it is the signifier the subject in the mirror phase assumes the
mother has. Thus, in an apparent paradox that is not easily understood, the Phallus or the metonymic objects that come to stand for it
will first be associated with the mother and then, later, with the father.
Indeed, in our culture (and presumably in others as well) this association makes of the woman—especially the beautiful woman—another
signifier of the Phallus, a sign of that which every subject, male or
female, desires. It is as such an incipient, beautiful, phallic object that
unwittingly Judy first announces herself to Dexter. Fitzgerald's narrator
says that while the "little girl" of eleven who had prompted Dexter to
quit his job was ugly, she was, paradoxically, "beautifully ugly."
Moreover, since in her the "spark" of beauty's force was already "per-
ceptible," she is one of those "little girls [...] who are destined after a
few years to be inexpressibly lovely and bring no end of misery to a
great number of men." Thus, as the incipient phallic object, she seems
prepotent, transcendent, capable in her ungodly godliness of the creation of life itself. "There was a general ungodliness," Fitzgerald writes,
"in the way her lips twisted down at the corners when she smiled, and
in the [...] almost passionate quality of her eyes." Of her even at the
age of eleven, the narrator says, "Vitality is born in such women. It was
utterly in evidence now, shining through her thin frame in a sort of
glow" (218).

In Judy's second annunciation, Fitzgerald no longer needs to conceal pedophilic phallic desire in oxymorons such as "beautifully ugly."
At eleven offering only a glow hinting at later realizations of the phallic
object, at twenty Judy seems the real thing when Dexter at twenty-three
next encounters her. But since the Phallus is never real, from the beginning Judy wears a halo of desirability because of her metonymic association with a place—and, eventually, a subject—of wealth and power.
As he had first seen her on a golf course, and, what is more, not just
any course, but the local Sherry Island Golf Club frequented by the rich
and powerful, so years later he again sees her playing at the very same
club. In the intervening years, Dexter had changed as much as Judy.
Since in the meantime he has accomplished some of his youthful
dreams and become a monied player in other venues of the rich and
famous, he now comes there not as an employee but as a guest.

Examining her closely in this second annunciation, Dexter finds in her the fulfillment of the earlier promise. "The quality of exaggeration, of thinness, which had made her passionate eyes and down-turning mouth absurd at eleven," Fitzgerald writes, "was gone now. She was arrestingly beautiful." As before, in her beauty Dexter sees the generative powers of life, but, proleptically, he also sees something else more fleeting and darker that may contravene those powers. "The color in her cheeks," writes Fitzgerald, "was centered like the color in a picture—it was not a 'high' color, but a sort of fluctuating and feverish warmth, so shaded that it seemed at any moment it would recede and disappear. This color and the mobility of her mouth gave a continual impression of flux, of intense life, of passionate vitality—balanced only partially by the sad luxury of her eyes" (222). If beauty is in the eye of the beholder, then perhaps that "sad luxury" lies in Dexter's more than Judy's. While *luxury* may mean "desirable," it also may mean "costly and hard to get." Even without Judy, Dexter has realized much of what he imagines comprises his winter dreams, but there is some further desire that he has not yet satisfied and that Judy seems to represent. The questions are, What is it, and at what cost will it come?

2

> So desire for Lacan is in some ways a better thing than drive. Drive involves the satisfaction that the subject gets, but does not want to get.
> —Renata Salecl, "Interview," 147

By the time of the third annunciation of Judy to Dexter, Dexter has begun to experience himself as lacking, as alienated, as in need of something he thinks Judy can supply him. In Judy's presence, Dexter is experiencing the bifurcations of desire. In desire, says Lacan, there is alienation because it is first experienced in another or as the possession of another. "The human being," says Lacan, "only sees his form materialised, whole, the mirage of himself, outside himself" (*Freud's Papers* 140). Putting it in one of his formulaic sayings, Lacan repeats many times, "Desire is the desire of the Other" (*Four Fundamental Concepts* 235, for example). But, as if that experience of otherness were not alienating enough, desire alienates further because it turns on castration, on the subject's recognition of a lack where all desire begins: "All human desire," says Lacan, "is based on castration" (118). Consequently, to study the subject as psychoanalysis does is to engage "the central lack in which the subject experiences [it]self as desire." That study, says Lacan, "touches on sexuality only in as much as, in the form of the drive, it manifests itself in the defile of the signifier, in which is constituted the dialectic of the subject in the double stage of alienation and separation," the two found, respectively, in the mirror phase and the oedipal resolution (265–66).

It is in Judy's third annunciation that the story's oedipal elements become much clearer. The third occurs on the same day as the second. It is marked by insistently oneiric elements that highlight psychoanalytic themes. It occurs in the evening as Dexter lies on a swimming raft in a lake dreamily listening to music wafting across the water. In the bosom of water and darkness and sound, Dexter experiences a moment of enjoyment, of what Lacan calls "*jouissance*," an ecstasy suggesting an at least momentary satisfaction of all one's desires. Fitzgerald tells us that the sound of the tune played on a piano across the water "precipitated in him a sort of ecstasy and it was with that ecstasy he viewed what happened to him now. It was a mood of intense appreciation, a sense that, for once, he was magnificently attune to life and that everything about him was radiating a brightness and a glamour he might never know again" (223). In this context, when Judy appears this third time, she opens desire not as satisfaction but as a gap, a fissure in the oceanic oneness, or, in Lacan's terms, as a defile (like the wake of a motor boat) left by the disappearance of the signifier.

Judy opens desire almost explicitly as the Phallus that Lacan says signifies the impossibility—the empty defile—of human desire. Here, Fitzgerald's language is almost shocking in its directness. Arriving virtually as the phallic object itself, Judy emanates from "a low, pale oblong" that detaches "itself suddenly from the darkness of the Island, spitting forth the reverberate sound of a racing motorboat." Like a veritable Aphrodite arising from the waves, she seems to come from "white streamers of cleft water [that] rolled themselves out behind." The boat was "almost immediately [...] beside him, drowning out the hot tinkle of the piano in the drone of its spray." When the craft does not come to him at this pass, Dexter raises himself and becomes "aware of a figure standing at the wheel, of two dark eyes regarding him over the lengthening space of water—then the boat had gone by and was sweeping in an immense and purposeless circle of spray round and round in the middle of the lake. With equal eccentricity one of the circles flattened out and headed back toward the raft" (223). When the "nose of [her] boat" bumps the raft on which Dexter lies, the raft tilts "rakishly" and precipitates Dexter toward Judy. It is from "different degrees of interest," writes Fitzgerald, that "they recognized each other" (224). But desire, as Lacan repeatedly says, is the desire of the other. And, instead, at the moment he sees himself as the object of her desire, he sees his own desire looking back at him.

As a representation of the phallic (*jouissant*) object of Dexter's desire, Judy invokes in Dexter the dilemma of human subjectivity— alienation or separation. That dilemma regards whether, on the one hand, to remain outside ("beyond") the pleasure principle by retaining the *jouissance* of the mirror identification with the (M)other or, on the other hand, whether to obey the paradoxical limits of the pleasure principle by moving to the homeostasis of desire that follows the oedipal resolution. In Lacan, *jouissance* belongs to primal drive, the psychic energy—for want of a better term—that exists in Kristeva's "semiotic *chora*." Taking her term from Plato's *Timaeus*, Kristeva says it is a "receptacle [...], unnameable, improbable, hybrid, anterior to naming, to the One, to the father, and, consequently, maternally connoted" (*Desire in Language* 133). In theorizing the *chora*, Kristeva makes one of her major contributions to Lacanian theory. Given no name in Lacan (but in Freud regarded as the preoedipal libido), the *chora* is the site Kristeva posits as the origin of "meaning" in the subject (Lechte 142). It exists before the creation of either desire or subjectivity itself, the two, Lacan insists, occurring simultaneously (as a chicken-or-egg phenomenon). Within this psychic scenario, desire seems antithetical to drive, not to *jouissance*. *Jouissance* is the object of drive, pleasure the object of desire. Says Alan Sheridan, translator of the essays in *Écrits: A Selection*, "Pleasure obeys the law of homeostasis that Freud evokes in 'Beyond the Pleasure Principle,' whereby, through discharge, the psyche seeks the lowest possible level of tension. '*Jouissance*' transgresses this law and, in that respect, it is *beyond* the pleasure principle" (x). When Lacan speaks of alienation and separation, he typically means the alienation of the subject recognized in the mirror stage and the separation of that subject from *jouissance*, a separation incurred by the symbolic castration accepted ("I will live without it") at the resolution of the Oedipus complex.

Invoking the Oedipus complex, when Judy situates Dexter within the dialectic of desire, she places him between the polarities of desire and *jouissance*, alienation and separation, Oedipus and Narcissus. While she opens the problem of *jouissance* and mirror-stage alienation within Dexter, it is more important in a story of oedipal resolution that she also raises the attendant problem of separation and the conciliations of desire. Finding himself in the image of Judy, Dexter is caught up in an Imaginary, mirror-stage duality in which, if the rule of the father never intercedes, the play of *jouissance* will proceed unchecked. But as the phallic object, Judy inevitably draws Dexter toward the separating role of the oedipal father. If she *is* the maternal Phallus of preoedipal *jouis-sance*, then she is also that which belongs to the Father of Law. For Dexter to separate from *jouissance*, he must move from a dualistic or dyadic relation to Judy into a triangular one, one adding a third entity who is—or at least represents—the father. We can see the oedipal triangle forming in the very moment, during that third annunciation, when she in fact announces herself to him. When she says, "My name is Judy Jones," she assigns herself a Symbolic value that comes from a third party, one who inevitably represents the father, even if he is not the Father in fact. "I live," she says, "in a house over there on the Island, and in that house there is a man waiting for me." This man, she tells Dexter, "says I'm his ideal" (224). Since her word "ideal" shifts the subject from the Imaginary to the Symbolic, the Lacanian aura it brings is critical to Dexter's oedipal separation from *jouissance*. As the identificatory object ("I am that"), Judy would be for that man who waits (the lover, father, whoever) what, following Freud, Lacan calls "the ideal ego." But since this ideal ego is often, if not always, associated with the mother, this image of Judy must almost inevitably—again, by association—also invoke the father.

3

> The two fathers, imaginary and real, are what is left over once pater-nal symbolic authority disintegrates.
> —Slavoj Žižek, *The Fragile Absolute*, 75

In the father, the subject may find what Lacan, again following Freud, calls the "ego-ideal" (Ichideal) that in the oedipal resolution emerges in the "second narcissism" (as Lacan, in *Freud's Papers on Technique*, calls it). For Lacan, the meaning of the ego-ideal is ambiguous. On the one hand, it is the figure who represents "the privileged signifier," the figure who allows the subject to "feel himself both satisfactory and loved." But, on the other, it is the "privileged object" that introduces death, the ultimate signifier. For human beings, says Lacan, "because [they know] the signifiers, sex and its significations are always capable of making present the presence of death" (*Four Fundamental Concepts* 257). Even as the ego's ideal on the side of law, the father begins to be associated with denial and death, with the limit of desire (that is, castration) rather than its limitless possibility (that is, *jouis-sance* beyond the pleasure principle). In "Winter Dreams," it is quite clear that this father—he representing the ego-ideal—is Judy's father, Mr. Mortimer Jones. It is he whom Dexter wishes to emulate and he under whose gaze Dexter imagines himself "satisfactory and loved." At the beginning of the story, before "winter dreams" has been used at all, but in the midst of concrete exemplifications of those dreams, Fitzgerald gives us a Dexter who loves autumn and makes "brisk abrupt gestures of command to imaginary audiences and armies," a Dexter who imagines himself a golf champion defeating the local star "in a marvelous match played a hundred times over the fairways of his imagination." Further, imagining himself "stepping from a Pierce-Arrow automobile, *like Mr. Mortimer Jones*," he will be a Dexter who "strolled frigidly into the lounge of the Sherry Island Golf Club" or one who is "surrounded by an admiring crowd" as he gives "an exhibition of fancy diving from the spring-board of the club raft" (my emphasis). More important, as he imagines himself doing these things perhaps as Jones, he also imagines himself under Jones's admiring gaze. "Among those who watched him in open-mouthed wonder," writes Fitzgerald, "was Mr. Mortimer Jones." Even better, perhaps because it is an event in reality that confirms those dreams, "one day it came to pass that Mr. Jones—himself and not his ghost—came up to Dexter with tears in his eyes and said that Dexter was the - - - - [sic] best caddy in the club, and wouldn't he decide not to quit if Mr. Jones made it worth his while?" (218).

But Mortimer Jones is implicated in why Dexter has quit in the first place, for the reason the fourteen-year-old boy quits is his unconscious desire for the man's eleven-year-old daughter. That conclusion may not be transparent because Fitzgerald's text begins later than his story. Since in the moment he quits Dexter apparently has realized his oedipalized desire (to have Jones's admiring recognition), his decision to quit seems to make as little sense as the reason he gives Mr. Jones for his doing so. At fourteen, he says, "I'm too old." But while the answer seems at first peculiar, it finally is exactly right, for if the oedipal resolution is a matter of sexual maturation, then he is in fact "too old" for what the scene with eleven-year-old Judy entails—not desire, but *jouissance*. Though Fitzgerald's text begins at a point concerning the business about Dexter's imagination and his admiration of Mr. Jones, Dexter's story had already begun before that point, and it had begun with the child, Judy. Through his relation to Judy, Dexter reencounters the structure and—will he, nil he—the object of the oedipal triangle, the *jouissant* desire of the child for the mother or for that which, in its symbolic transformation, the mother represents—the Phallus of *jouissance*.

As the representation of what the subject believes the father has (both the Phallus and *jouissance*), it is Judy who raises the specter

(Jones as "ghost," perhaps like the ghost of Hamlet's father) of that second father, the ferocious superego figure of the primordial father of Freud's Oedipus myth. Of the primordial father, it is enough to say that the oedipal father is a better, more life-giving bargain that he. As Lacan says in a late seminar (and as discussed in my chapter on Glaspell), the choice lies between *le père ou pire*, the (oedipal) father or worse (the primordial). But in the context of his desire to have what the primordial, *jouissant* father has, Dexter projects onto Judy all the power of the mother as phallic signifier. That projection explains his quitting his job. His reason for doing so makes sense not as answer to the question, "Why won't you caddy for her?" but as answer to another, unconscious, sexual question that later in Dexter's life does in fact arise in a disguised form: "Why won't you sleep with [marry] her?" Since in Lacan (and Freud) a child is typically thought of as a representation of the mother's desire and thus as a signifier of the Phallus, Judy's age at this point is irrelevant. Because she is what Mr. Jones has, she signifies that which Dexter lacks—the Phallus—and thus desires.

Because in Dexter's Symbolic order Judy fits in the place of the mother in relation to the father, she draws down the oedipal prohibition against incestuous desire. Whereas Dexter cannot admit desiring her, he can, however, desire the father or, what is more appropriate for the "normal" subject, desire to be the father and to play the father's role. While, normatively, it may be true that Judy is too young to be desired at this moment, the truth in the order of the Symbolic is indeed that Dexter is "too old." He is no longer a child. He must put away childish things. As Fitzgerald might have had Dexter's later avatar Jay Gatsby phrase it, he must be about his father's business—about, that is, the business engaging *the* Father. If Dexter's—or any subject's—desire were ultimately reduced to wealth and power, Dexter's story would have shown him as perfectly contented, for, matching one aspect of the image of his ego-ideal, Mortimer Jones, he becomes quite wealthy. Moreover, if Dexter's—or any subject's—desire were defined by the sexual other who seems to epitomize all desire, then Dexter's story might well have been happy enough, too, for there is a moment when Dexter "has" Judy—and has her, as it were, right under the nose of Mr. Mortimer Jones. How so?

4

For Lacan every drive is a death drive and has this kind of deadly element.

—Renata Salecl, "Interview," 147

Between Judy's third and fourth annunciations to Dexter, about two years pass. After Judy and Dexter go their separate ways following that third, summertime, annunciation, Dexter becomes engaged to another woman—Irene Scheerer, who, quite explicably, seems more like Dexter's mother than like any lover (see 228). In the fourth encounter, even while Judy knows of his engagement to Irene, she flirts with Dexter nonetheless. When he takes her home, she appears once more under the aegis of her father, for his house, in Fitzgerald's language, at the same time reminds Dexter of him and represents the object of Dexter's desire. "The dark street lightened, the dwellings of the rich loomed up around them," Fitzgerald writes, when Dexter

> stopped his coupé in front of the great white bulk of the Mortimer Joneses house, somnolent, gorgeous, drenched with the splendor of the damp moonlight. Its solidity startled him. The strong walls, the steel of the girders, the breadth and beam and pomp of it were there only to bring out the contrast with the young beauty beside him. It was sturdy to accentuate her slightness—as if to show what a breeze could be generated by a butterfly's wing.

Though Dexter has not come to this place expecting to enter it, in the presence of all that the house represents in his imagination, he can hardly resist when Judy offers herself—and it—to him. She, if he will have her, offers to marry him. "A million phrases of anger, pride, passion, hatred, tenderness fought on his lips. Then a perfect wave of emotion washed over him, carrying off with it a sediment of wisdom, of convention, of doubt, of honor. This was his girl who was speaking, his own, his beautiful, his pride" (232). When she, as it were, offers him the keys to his kingdom, he can hardly do otherwise than accept.

Accepting the authority of the oedipal father, however, he learns that this kingdom is something he cannot have. Since it is Judy's role to function as the Phallus, the object symbolizing the subject's unappeasable desire, Fitzgerald's story is the stronger because of the way it shows the separation of the subject from oedipal desire. For it is Judy, not Dexter, who breaks off their engagement. She does so, she says, because it would not be right to "'take him away' from Irene" (233). If instead Dexter had broken off, he might ever after have told himself, "But I *could* have had her." The story makes plain, however, that Dexter accommodates the loss of Judy entirely for what she represents symbolically. As a symbol of the Phallus, she represents something beyond desire. In that role, she connects Dexter to a primal drive, one that antedates her enactment of it. "It did not," Fitzgerald tells us, "take him many hours to decide he had wanted Judy ever since he was a proud, desirous little boy" (226). As that symbol of satisfaction, Judy is self-contained, self-absorbed, something that exists prior to and quite apart from Dexter. Indeed, Fitzgerald makes plain her primality. He tells us that, for whatever reasons—"so much youthful love, so many youthful lovers"—Judy "was entertained only by the gratification of her desires and by the direct exercise of her own charm." As if she were a force of nature or an organism of satisfaction, she had become able "to nourish herself wholly from within" (227).

But as a symbol of desire, she also represents its infinity, its unappeasability. In such a kiss as occurs everywhere in Fitzgerald's fiction documenting desire, Dexter has a premonition of its limitlessness from the first moment he kisses her. "A lump rose in Dexter's throat," Fitzgerald tells us of that moment, "and he waited breathless for the experiment, facing the unpredictable compound that would form mysteriously from the elements of their lips." Hoping that the kiss would create the attainable object itself, the mysterious compound, Dexter sees instead a more mysterious, more paradoxical fulfillment, one that leaves him wanting more. "Then he saw—she communicated her excitement to him, lavishly, deeply, with kisses that were not a promise but a fulfillment." As "fulfillment," however, those kisses do not eradicate his emptiness. They make him more aware of his lack. "They aroused in him," writes Fitzgerald, "not hunger demanding renewal but surfeit that would demand more surfeit." Like "charity, creating want by holding back nothing at all," her kisses represent only the paradox of desire: they reify lack itself by reinforcing the truth of the subject's castration (226).

The truth Dexter admits is the law of the oedipal resolution. For him, Judy affirms desire as, in words from Lacan, the subject's castration, its "absolute condition" (*Écrits: A Selection* 265). As the symbol of that which the subject wants but cannot have, she invokes castration in the prohibitions of the Law of the Father. That Law comes to Dexter in stages. At first, he thinks the prohibition or obstacle lies in him or in something he does. When his "first exhilaration" became "restlessness and dissatisfaction," he reacts as an addict, his "helpless ecstasy of losing himself in her" becoming "opiate rather than tonic" (227). Wanting her, assuming still that she could remove the lack in him, he continues at first to want "to take Judy Jones with him. No disillusion as to the world in which she had grown up could cure his illusion as to her desirability" (228). Eventually, however, he recognizes there is some other reason he cannot have her. The recognition comes with the passage of the seasons, of the passing of spring and summer into the autumn that presages the winter of his dreams. Recognizing both that "[s]he had brought him ecstatic happiness and intolerable agony of spirit" and that her relation to him was marked by an "utter indifference," Dexter faces the radical truth of desire. Ultimately, he cannot have its object. "When autumn had come and gone again," writes Fitzgerald, "it occurred to him that he could not have Judy Jones" (229).

The submission to oedipal authority becomes plainer in Fitzgerald's text when, as it were, Judy appears to Dexter the last time. There is no annunciation of Judy to Dexter in the end. Rather, she is enunciated: spoken, she comes to him in the speech of others. At the end, Dexter hears that she is married and mother of children of her own. That she had been for him an idealized object, the fantasied object of desire, the other in whom the subject first recognizes itself and what it wants or lacks and thus desires, becomes very plain in the language of desire and castration and death that permeates the final paragraphs of Fitzgerald's narrative. Hoping that with "nothing else to lose" he might be made "invulnerable at last," he finds that he can still lose "something more." In the fading of Judy's beauty, he finds that he can lose desire itself. He loses her. That loss opens up in him a hole where death lies. Not actually dead, Judy nonetheless signifies the gap, the *béance*, the emptiness of mourning and melancholia that comes with such losses. "The dream was gone," Fitzgerald writes. "Something had been taken from him. [...] And her mouth damp to his kisses and her eyes plaintive with melancholy and her freshness like new fine linen in the morning. Why, these things were no longer in the world! They had existed and they existed no longer." In mourning for what she had been, Dexter as subject also mourns for himself, for all that the subject desires but can never possess. The thing lost is some dream of himself that now can never be fulfilled, will never be in the world. "For the first time in years the tears were streaming down his face. But they were for himself now." For the subject, the self mourned stands for all loss. It is he himself who is lost. "For he had gone away and he could never go back any more" (235).

But he cannot properly mourn that loss because there is yet a prior loss. "Even the grief he could have borne was left behind in the country of illusion, of youth, of the richness of life, where his winter dreams had flourished" (235–36). But the loss of those dreams, Fitzgerald makes plain, is also tantamount to the loss of the Phallus itself, that "thing" in which one's desire and one's subjectivity are symbolized and the loss of which is castration. What, in Lacan's words, Dexter has faced, as must every castrated subject, is loss itself. He faces what

Lacan calls "the power of pure loss" (*Écrits: A Selection* 287) that comes from knowing that no "proof of love" can ever satisfy, can ever restore the thing lost, can ever make the subject whole again. The last words in Fitzgerald's story capture the very essence of castration, of the oedipal resolution, of the fate of desire and the Phallus under oedipal authority. "Long ago, [...] long ago, there was something in me, but now that thing is gone. Now that thing is gone, that thing is gone. I cannot cry. I cannot care. That thing will come back no more" (236).

5

> [T]he strongest challenge to Freud's unconscious [is] the feminist power to question whether the unconscious representations of "the other scene" which articulate it to the social order can be altered in response to changing material conditions of women in ways that preclude the (by now) utter predictability of the oedipal formula.
> —Juliet MacCannell, "The Unconscious," 443

A reading of "Winter Dreams" from the perspective of the later Lacan sees Dexter's story not only as about desire but also about drive, *jouissance*, and related concepts, all subsumed within the Real. Though I have not elaborated on the "other" myth, the plot of Narcissus, I began with Lacan's notion that with Oedipus it provides one of the two essential myths of psychoanalysis. Because Oedipus stresses the accommodations of desire to Narcissus and the depredations of *jouissance*, there is a sense in which the main function of the Oedipus complex and its attendant plot is to prevent the postoedipal subject's finally collapsing back into the bosom of Narcissus. As Juliet MacCannell has written, "This is where feminism takes issue with the Freudian unconscious" ("Unconscious" 442). She points out that a major project of feminist theory has been to define alternatives to this Freudian "other scene." Among those, each suggesting a sort of "'reserve' of signifiers or metonyms," each particularly "linked to the mother rather than the father" (443), are Kristeva's "semiotic" *chora* and Torok and Abraham's "unconscious 'crypt'" in the ego. Both these, which Lacan would regard as belonging to the Real, are domains of "the semiotic" where signification originates (see also Adams, "Of Female Bondage"). Kristeva's semiotic, says Elizabeth Grosz, in analysis not only of Kristeva but also of Lacan, "threatens to undermine and de-stabilize the rule-governed operations of the Symbolic, resisting its rules and norms. Governed by the primary processes, which seek immediate gratification of what may be anti-social impulses, the semiotic is the raw data of corporeal forces and energies organized by the law-abiding and rule-governed secondary-process activities of the Symbolic" ("Kristeva"195). Rooted in the maternal and the ground from which are launched attacks on the Symbolic of patriarchy, the semiotic, Grosz suggests, "remains incompletely contained by the Symbolic, and is manifested in the 'physicality' or 'materiality' of textual production: it is a materiality that, like the primary processes or the repressed, threatens to return, disrupting signifying conventions" (195–96). Thus, if the subject in the preoedipal stage is to be assimilated into the Symbolic, thereby becoming a normative one, either masculine or feminine, the "semiotic must be renounced and transcended." Even so, however, even for the normative subject, "this subsumption of the semiotic in the Symbolic is never complete or finalized" (196).

Thus, because any normative subject is on the verge always of collapsing into neurosis (or worse), the two plots and their narrative trajectories may finally be conflated one into the other. We may see that conflation, as Miller or Salecl or Žižek might suggest, if in "Winter Dreams" we recast the story of the dialectic of the subject's desire in late Lacanian terms, in ones stressing *jouissance*, Autre, das Ding, and the *objet a*, each attached to the Maternal Thing and subsumed within Lacan's notion of the Real. In its melancholy Weltschmerz, the ending to Dexter's story seems both right and touching. But readings stressing the resolutions of oedipalization never fully address issues—mother, maternal *jouissance*, drive, the death drive, thanatic narcissism, and the like—raised by some Lacanians and many feminist psychoanalytic critics. While, as Jacqueline Rose acknowledges in her "Introduction—II" to Lacan's *Feminine Sexuality*, Lacan inevitably is "implicated in the phallocentrism he described" in his teachings, there is no denying the role he assigns to language and the Symbolic. Indeed, Rose argues, the issues of the unconscious and of sexuality "cannot be referred back to a body outside language, a place to which the 'feminine,' and through that, women, might escape." Nonetheless, Rose contends, "The 'feminine' stands for a refusal of [the phallic] organisation, its ordering, its identity" (56). Thus, Lacanian interpreters, in following the imperative (*Cherchez la mere*) to search for the mother in texts, discover a strong affinity with feminist critique.

In part, this critique means looking also for the oedipal story of women characters typically relegated to the background. To that end we must note that in the exchange between Dexter and Judy, we must also see that Judy herself has an oedipal story. For Dexter, the thing lost is, ultimately, primal maternal *jouissance* itself. But the "Thing that will come back no more" (236), the thing for which Judy herself is the substitute, is the Lacanian *objet a*. While I, like other critics, make much of Dexter's oedipal story, there is much that might also be said of Judy's, for there is, perforce, one for her in "Winter Dreams" as well. That Judy later marries and has children suggests she has resolved her oedipal complex successfully. Still, it is plain enough in the story's details that Dexter does not participate in the family romance from his side alone; Judy also participates from hers. She clearly understands that she represents the everything for Mortimer Jones that Lacan calls the "Phallus." It is Mortimer who shadows that man who, in her words, calls her his "ideal." Indeed, in the vague hints of an incestuous relation between father and daughter, Judy and Mortimer may well adumbrate the incestuous abuse by Devereux Warren of his daughter Nicole, who becomes mentally ill as a result of the abuse and later both wife and patient of protagonist Dick Diver in Fitzgerald's *Tender Is the Night* (1934). It is certainly the case not only that Judy has a very ambiguous relation to Dexter Green but also that this relation suffers because of her own powerful oedipal attachment to her father. Judy finds it impossible to marry Dexter because—both in Dexter's oedipal structure and in her own—she fits into the same place, the place of the mother. But, as a consequence, because Dexter fits too incestuously into the place of the father in Judy's, Judy is obliged to reject him in turn because of the threat of symbolic incest he poses. For Judy, then, the reasons she must reject Dexter are precisely the same as Dexter's for rejecting—or, as his language suggests, "losing"—Judy. In each, the bottom line is incest-cum-castration, a trajectory that inevitably leads us back to the lost object of desire, the mother herself.

Besides searching for the oedipal story of the daughter, as it were, we must also search for the mother. To find the female in a canonical literature largely male and stressing oedipalization of the male, we must often focus either on figures nearly invisible or on the qualities of language itself. A powerful influence on feminist theory, Kristeva is important in part because of her emphasis on the preoedipal *chora* and subjectivity as a process always implicated in that maternal domain she calls "the semiotic," that ur-region wherein she contends signification originates. Says John Lechte of Kristeva's theory, "The semiotic[,...] equated with the feminine *chora*, [...] is roughly the unrepresentable place of the mother. It is a kind of origin, but not one that is nameable; for that would place it squarely within the symbolic realm and give us a false notion of it." Rather, he says, "Like the feminine in general, the *chora* is on the side of the material, poetic dimension of language" (142). In "Winter Dreams," when we ask, Where—apart from Judy Jones—is the mother? it is in the semiotic resonances of Fitzgerald's

poetic language that we find her. When in the story we find the semiotic *chora*, the mother, the maternal other, we may see more clearly
how and why oedipalization itself can never be about the father only
but must inevitably be about both the father and the mother. In the
text, the role of the mother comes up in a strange passage (there may be
a rule that the invisible *chora*, because it lies in the semiotic, must
always occur in strange passages). In a typical boy-dating-girl situation
following upon that third annunciation of Judy as phallic object of
desire, Dexter has gone to Judy's house and waits for her to come
downstairs to go out with him. There, though at first his imagination
works as that of an ordinary lover, eventually it works more as that of
a father. Awaiting Judy, "Dexter peopled the soft deep summer room
and the sunporch that opened from it with the men who had already
loved Judy." Because "[h]e knew the sort of men they were" (224), he
surely knows what they want. But though his imagination puts him in
competition with these men, it takes a turn that makes him not Judy's
father, as we may expect, but the father of those men who love her.
Therefore, since he is one of those men who love Judy, his imagination
makes him not only a father but his own father. "He had seen," writes
Fitzgerald, "that, in one sense, he was better than these men. He was
newer and stronger. Yet in acknowledging to himself that he wished his
children to be like them *he was admitting that he was but the rough,
strong stuff from which they eternally sprang*" (224–25; my emphasis).

Moreover, having imagined himself in the paternal role, he next—
and almost inevitably—imagines himself in a relation to his own
mother. In the only mention of her in the text, the logic of his feeling
himself as son and father ought to make him husband and lover in relation to her. But since he has already displaced his desire from her
toward Judy and Mr. Jones, he does not recognize himself in a relation
of desire to his mother. Rather, in a plain repression of that desire, he
imagines her in a role like that of the nanny in the scene at the country
club with the eleven-year-old Judy. In short, he imagines his mother as
a social inferior but as one whom the child has risen above only
because of her sacrifices, the sacrifices that constitute her as—in
Kristeva's language—"abjected." The signifiers of difference between
his abjected mother and his idealized father, Mortimer Jones as ego-
ideal, are clothing and manners (after all, this is Fitzgerald). Dexter
knows what he must have to fill the defile the mother primally represents. "When the time had come for him to wear good clothes,"
Fitzgerald tells us, "he had known who were the best tailors in
America." Thus, meeting Judy on that first date, Dexter wears a suit
made by "the best" and comports himself with a "particular reserve"

acquired from his university. "He recognized the value to him of such a mannerism," Fitzgerald reports, "and he had adopted it; he knew that to be careless in dress and manner required more confidence than to be careful. But carelessness was for his children. His mother's name had been Krimplich. She was a Bohemian of the peasant class and she had talked broken English to the end of her days. Her son must keep to the set patterns" (225).

While the abjected mother—the Bohemian peasant Krimplich—has made him what he becomes, she has also constructed in him a desire for something better found in a social class higher than hers or his, one represented by the Joneses. In them or in keeping up with them, she seems to have taught Dexter, he can have "it," the *it* here not the objectives of desire but the pure satisfaction of *jouissance*. For Dexter or any other subject, however, the resolution of the oedipal encounter is the knowledge that "it" is precisely what one cannot have, whatever "it" is—whatever symbolizes the Phallus or whatever the Phallus symbolizes. In gaining such knowledge, the subject finds the abjected mother's role to be as significant as that of the father. But the story abjection tells is darker than the simpler oedipal tales of "growing up." As Kristeva says in "Approaching Abjection," "The abject is the violence of mourning for an 'object' that has always already been lost. The abject shatters the wall of repression and its judgments. It takes the ego back to its source on the abominable limits from which, in order to be, the ego has broken away—it assigns it a source in the non-ego, drive, and death." Still, there is a "happy" ending here. "Abjection," Kristeva says, "is a resurrection that has gone through death (of the ego). It is an alchemy that transforms death drive into a start of life, of new significance" (15).

In "Winter Dreams," the roles of both the nearly invisible mother—on the side of *jouissance*—and the barely more visible father—on the side of law—are involved in substitutions Freud would attribute to the family romance. One aspect of the family romance is the subject's imagining itself as the child of other parents, ones more beautiful or powerful or successful than its own. Clearly, for Dexter, the Joneses offer this other family. But even to Dexter this substitution is certainly almost conscious. In the unconscious, however, the substitutions are more complex and, except to analysis, much less accessible. The mother or mother figures evoke the mirror phase, the father or father figures the Oedipus complex. On the one hand, in the mirror phase, the mother or, really, Lacan says, the desire of the mother substitutes for the *jouissance* that Freud calls "primal, presexual libido." On the other, in the Oedipus complex, the Law of the Father substitutes for the desire of the mother. In the process of such substitutions, says Lacan, is born the subject's use of or attachment to or even constitution within language. The substitutions have the form of metaphor, one thing in place of another. Jacques-Alain Miller, in "To Interpret the Cause," calls this metaphoric substitution, "this substitution of the law of the father for the desire of the mother," the "adequate sequence" because it explains not only the concept of the 'Phallus,' but also concepts of 'castration' and the 'Oedipus complex.' "The consequence," says Miller, "is that we suppose we know, after the installation of this metaphor, [...] why the mother does not always stay near her child." In Freud and Lacan—but also in feminists Kristeva and Rose, Grosz and Salecl—the reason why is the Phallus. Moreover, it is the metaphor—the substitution, "the formula," as Miller calls it, of the father's law substituted for the mother's desire—that "unifies the oedipus theory and the castration complex" (46) by establishing the sexual relationship as a relation not of one sex to another, but of each to a signifier, the Phallus.

Thus, strange as it may seem to ordinary thinking, the relation between Dexter and Judy is not sexual. Indeed, Lacan claims that there is no sexual relation, "that in the case of the speaking being the relation between the sexes does not take place" (*Feminine Sexuality* 138; see also *Encore* 66, where Fink translates the passage as: "that no relationship gets constituted between the sexes in the case of speaking beings"). The reason Lacan says so frequently there is no sexual relationship, in the ordinary, presumptive, intuitive sense, is that the relationship is not of sexes but of each sex to something else, the Phallus, that substitute for the mother's desire. As Miller explains the relation, the Phallus ultimately signifies the unknown "X," the unknown thing—which Lacan also calls "das Ding"—that the mother is presumed to have. But, explains Miller, "We do not know [...] the cause of her desire" nor "do we know what and where she enjoys. The meaning of the phallus," therefore, Miller suggests, "is, precisely, to give an answer to this X." In this answer, the *jouissance* is made phallic and as such is made into meaning, significance. As Miller puts it, "the meaning of the paternal metaphor, of the Freudian Oedipus as inscribed by Lacan, translates itself as from an unknown *jouissance* to the phallusization of *jouissance*, that is, to a significantization of *jouissance*." Miller points out, however, that at this very primal level, the substitution is significantly and, to some extent, even conceptually different. "What we saw before," he explains, "was the substitution of one signifier for another." But at this different conceptual level, where in Lacan we find the paternal metaphor, a nonsignifier is put in place of a signifier. This,

says Miller, "is the secret of the paternal metaphor in Lacan, the secret
to oedipus. It is not only what had always been repeated as the father
substituted for the mother." Rather, it "is that it enables *jouissance* to
be inscribed in the symbolic order" (47). The importance of this
inscription, which occurs upon the installation of the Oedipus complex,
is that because *jouissance* now belongs to a signifying system and has
meaning, it is not simply some primal, uncognized, drive-bound being.
Because the Oedipus complex gives *jouissance* meaning, sexuality itself
changes, for as biological sexuation is transformed into "significance,"
the process creates a psychical—Symbolic—"sex" to go along with—
and that afterwards always overlays—the biological.

In Miller's reading of Lacanian theory, the Freudian libido becomes
Jouissance, the uppercase *J* indicating its universalized significance. For
subjectivity to develop, Miller suggests, something must substitute for
libido or primary *jouissance*. That something, which Miller, with
Lacan, calls the "Other" or "Autre" and abbreviates *A*, is actually language itself. In this Other Miller finds a "generalized linguistic
metaphor which articulates the relation between A as language or as
the place of the signifier, and capital J as primary *jouissance*, primary
libido, what Lacan calls *das Ding*." Miller suggests that Lacan uses the
German das Ding for primal *jouissance* because, coming before language, it can in some sense have no name. It is only a "thing," or, properly, *the* thing. But as the substitution involved in metaphor always
effaces that for which it stands, the substitution of the Other for *jouissance* means that *jouissance* is always already lost to the normal, oedipalized subject. While the subject can certainly orient itself in the
direction of the lost thing, it cannot recapture that thing once—and
because—it has entered language. "And it is in this sense of *das Ding* as
before the signifier," says Miller, "that gives a sense of what would
come before the capital A. As such, it is already lost because, from the
outset, we are into language. So, this *jouissance* is already a missing
jouissance, a *jouissance* of which we know nothing but that we have
lost it because of language" (47)

For its sophisticated rendering of such complex themes, "Winter
Dreams" is particularly valuable. Moreover, this value is increased by
its repetition—and, when read properly within Lacanian terms, *correc-
tion*—of the oedipal myth, arguably literature's most visible if not most
important plot. In the headnote to "Winter Dreams" in *The Short
Stories of F. Scott Fitzgerald*, Matthew Bruccoli says that at the end of
the story Dexter "grieves for the loss of his capacity to grieve" (217). In
Lacanian terms, Bruccoli's comment may well be translated to mean
that Dexter has truly become the postoedipal subject, for he has
resigned himself to loss, loss not of grief or of Judy but of that which

every oedipalized subject loses—the Phallus. To begin with, this resignation means that the subject has given up the *jouissance* Lacan associates with the maternal other, the (M)other, and has accommodated to
desire as it is limited by the pleasure principle. As says Miller, "[T]he
mother is always linked to *jouissance*, to enjoyment. And that is why
[...] what appeared in Freud as the father prohibiting access to the
mother appears in Lacan as speech interdicting *jouissance*" (44).
Miller's comment suggests that the major problem in both the creation
of subjectivity in the mirror phase and the resolution of gender issues in
the decline of the Oedipus complex is neither the father nor the mother
as such, but *jouissance*. It is not that Dexter must foreswear "having"
Judy because Judy "becomes" his mother and tosses him into incestuous competition with the father. It is, rather, that if Dexter is to become
a normalized postoedipal subject, he must foreswear Judy because she
introduces the specter of the forbidden enjoyment of some thing—the
(M)other Thing—beyond or prior to *jouissance*.

In any oedipal story, finally, it appears that the ultimate problem
is not the Father after all but the lost object. Whatever specifically the
object may be for any particular subject, it is always primally connected to the mother. As Neil Hertz contends regarding Kristeva's
claims in "L'Abjet de l'amour," narcissism of the sort found in
Fitzgerald's story is

> a means of covering over—to mask, but also to protect—the
> *vide* [or emptiness] or separation that offers the infant the
> possibility of speech and individuation; without this complic-
> ity or, as Kristeva puts it, this "solidarity" between the
> infant's narcissism and the *vide*, "chaos will take away all
> possibility of distinction, of a trace and of symbolization,
> leading to the confusion of the limits of bodies, of words, of
> the real and the symbolic." (*End of the Line* 232; Kristeva 20;
> trans. Hertz)

Indeed, in the Lacanian theory on which Kristeva bases much of her
work the oedipal is merely a cover for the narcissistic plot, the Father
merely an always-threatened substitute for the Mother, and desire
always a less threatening alternative to drive and the easeful bliss of
thanatic *jouissance*. If the Oedipus plot seems literature's most important one, it is so—as feminist critics such as Rose and Kristeva, Grosz
and Salecl, as well as Jessica Benjamin, Nancy Chodorow, and Luce
Irigaray, have begun to establish—only because it effectively effaces the
plot of Narcissus, the maternal story that provides the very ground for
human subjectivity itself.

CHAPTER 7

Hart's *Damage*, Lacanian Tragedy, and the Ethics of *Jouissance*

In the last years of Lacan's teaching, [...] the accent was shifted from the split between the imaginary and the symbolic to the barrier separating the real from (symbolically structured) reality.

—Slavoj Žižek, *Looking Awry*, viii

Among the most horrifying images in recent film occurs in Louis Malle's version (1993) of Josephine Hart's novel *Damage* (1991). It is that of a naked father (Jeremy Irons) cradling his fully dressed, dead adult son (Rupert Graves). The two form a perverse pietà of grieving parent and dead child. The image horrifies even more within the narrative context than outside it because while viewers know the father as a physician, a member of Britain's Parliament, the chair of a powerful health-services committee, and a possible candidate for prime minister, they also know that he has had an affair with the son's fiancée (Juliet Binoche) and that the son has died from a two-story fall precipitated by his discovering father and fiancée in flagrante delicto. Occurring in both the film and the novel, the scene opens onto powerful themes of postmodern life that yield especially well to analysis based on concepts from the late theory of Jacques Lacan. Apart from Lacan's own so-called late works, those beginning, approximately (see "Which Lacan?"), with Seminar 7, *The Ethics of Psychoanalysis*, this aspect of Lacanian theory becomes a focal point for a cadre of psychoanalytic critics of culture. These, we may say, are led by Jacques-Alain Miller and, especially, Slavoj Žižek. They include, among others, Joan Copjec, Mladen Dolar, Renata Salecl, Elizabeth Cowie, Parveen Adams, Alenka Zupančič, and Juliet Flower MacCannell. These critics form no school of which I am aware, but several traits identify them as a cohort. There are, of course, their links to Miller and Žižek, but some, such as Copjec, once a senior editor, have as well a link to the journal *October*. Several have published in book series edited by Žižek, including Duke's Sic, Verso's Wo Es War, MIT's Short Circuits, and Analecta in Slovene.

Moreover, in the last fifteen years, Žižek's readings of Lacan, probably more even than Miller's, have influenced others in this cadre—as well as Lacanians in general—perhaps as greatly as has Lacan himself. Mainly what makes them seem a cohort, if not a cadre, is that they emphasize Lacan's late notions of drive, *jouissance*, and the Real at the expense of his early concepts of 'desire,' the 'Imaginary,' and the 'Symbolic.' But besides this, they typically interest themselves in cultural studies and elements of popular culture more than in literature alone. Further, most construe the universe as ironic, tragic, or perversely paradoxical (so that everything contains or is canceled by its opposite), and because they color culture and its artifacts in dark tones, they are fascinated by film noir and related forms and themes.

Working through a new twist late Lacan gives to ethics and traditional tragedy, they have generated a vision of postmodern life that one may identify with a paradoxical, perhaps perverse formulation. In this vision, as Miller has argued in "The Other Who Does Not Exist and His Ethical Committees," because Freudian "universals" have become historical, we now live in a postpatriarchal, postoedipal universe where *semblants* of the Father now reign. Like Miller, MacCannell, in *The Regime of the Brother*, posits a psychoanalytic cultural theory outlining a universe beyond Oedipus. There, in place of the oedipal, patriarchal father, we now have the brother. In place of oedipal desire, we now have narcissistic *jouissance*. In place of the family structure underlying the social contract of traditional community, we have the dyad of brother and brother, founded not on the superego but on the ideal (Imaginary) ego.[1] According to MacCannell, the traditional universe of the oedipal father and mother has been replaced by a neototemic regime of bonded brothers. The brothers' law mimes not the disinterested Symbolic gaze of the benevolent patriarch who permits our oedipal (erotic, reproductive) desire but the narcissistic drive to *jouissance* of the phallic or primordial father of *Totem and Taboo*, a father who arrogates all desire to himself. Freud's late works, says MacCannell, foresee the shift from the sexual family unit to the asexual model of the artificial collective found in an "*It*," "the unconscious, the id [that] takes over from the father-superego as the model of the collective" (*Regime* 9). Though some traditional opponents of patriarchy see this shift as good news, MacCannell is less optimistic, for as the regime reconstitutes the thanatic *jouissance* of the totemic father, it may become the worse of two evils. The new father-brother offers no advantages to children, cultural others, or women—for example, it disavows or denies entirely female desire, if not female existence as the sister. Thus the danger of the postoedipal universe lies in how the new order

replaces the old. By forbidding oedipal desire and demanding narcissistic *jouissance* as, in Copjec's words, a "'civic' duty" (182–83), the new
regime promotes an infatuation with death in actual or symbolic forms
that engenders what might be called "Lacanian tragedy."

Lacan offers a precise formulation of the dilemma of the postoedipal universe, a dilemma glimpsed in the horrifying image from Malle's
film. Observed already in my two previous chapters, it is *le père ou pire*
"the father or worse." Lacan expanded on this notion in Seminar 19,
1971–1972, *ou pire* "or worse." This is the forced choice left by the
shift within social life from a traditional oedipal subject founded on an
ethics of desire to a posttraditional subject founded on an ethics of *jouissance*, the one on the side of Eros and social life, the other on that of
Thanatos and the death drive. This shift is reflected in film noir. Because
the femme fatale turns desire toward *jouissance*, Lacanians such as
Copjec and Žižek find in noir a cultural vision representing the new postoedipal universe and an ethics commensurate with the shift from a subject oriented to desire (and thus constrained by castration and the
pleasure principle) to one oriented to *jouissance* (and thus denying con-
straints of castration and aiming beyond the pleasure principle). But the
same noirish vision is accessibly articulated in Hart's novel. Not only
does Hart's language exemplify the figures in MacCannell's regime of
the brother, but the novel also reveals the ethics grounding postoedipal
social life and Lacanian tragedy. Reading Hart's *Damage* through late
Lacanian theory, particularly as articulated by Copjec, Žižek, Zupančič,
and MacCannell, one may illuminate the implications of the historical
shift—described by Copjec, Zupančič, and MacCannell—from an ethics
of desire to one of *jouissance*. In event, character, and especially language—a language of paradoxes (perhaps less "Lacanian" than
"Žižekian," as we shall see in "Beyond Lacan") representing life and
death, desire and drive, oedipal and primordial fathers, and anaclitic
(M)others and femmes fatales within single characters—Hart's *Damage*
represents a transition to the ethics of *jouissance* that marks a postmodern epoch beyond Oedipus. Using noir elements to reveal that transition,
Damage both models the traditional oedipal subject of desire and ultimately replaces it with the new narcissistic subject of *jouissance* to
reveal the ethics of Lacanian tragedy.

1

Desire sustains itself by remaining unsatisfied. As for the drive, the
fact that it "understands that this is not the way it will be satisfied"

does not stop it from finding satisfaction "elsewhere." Thus in contrast to desire, the drive sustains itself on the very fact that it is satisfied.

—Alenka Zupančič, *Ethics of the Real*, 242

Damage is important in our understanding the shift from the old
oedipal order to the new narcissism, from the order of desire to that of
the drive. This shift, Copjec suggests, has a cognate move—epochal,
historical, and ongoing, neither personal nor idiosyncratic. It shifts
emphasis to concepts—either "meaning" or "being"—Lacan associates
with the *vel* of alienation. Heretofore, in that process known as "oedipalization," it has been a good thing for subjects to be oriented to
meaning (and thus to desire within the pleasure principle and oedipal
law) rather than to being (and thus to drive and *jouissance* within the
domain of the narcissistic). Modeling a traditional oedipal subject of
desire and sense before replacing it with a new subject of *jouissance*
and being, *Damage* constitutes its narrator-protagonist's subjectivity
more in Lacanian than in Freudian terms. In it, the constitution of the
subject comes with the creation of what looks like oedipal desire.
Although subjectivity appears as if it were something always already
present in the subject, it is not present at all until brought into being by
a signifier. That signifier is the other in whom the nascent subject finds
itself in the specular operation of the mirror phase. In this operation,
desire is the element—the tincture—that makes subjectivity "visible."
In Lacan, because desire is always "desire of the other," it is the specular other who provides the signifier that reveals, retroactively, the subject as subject. In his discussions of the "graphs of desire," Lacan calls
"quilting" this double movement—backward through a signifier and
then forward away from it. Describing this movement and its results,
Žižek says, "The product of this quilting (what 'comes out on the other
side' ...) is [...] the divided, split subject, and at the same time the
effaced signifier, the lack of signifier, the void, an empty space in the
signifier's network." Once the subject appears, the signifier found in
the other disappears but remains as an empty space, a lack that has
properties but is no longer a thing in itself. Adverting to Althusser's
notion of "interpellation," Žižek suggests that Lacan's initial graphing
of desire sketches in its simplest form the origination of human subjects. "This minimal articulation," says Žižek, "already attests to the
fact that we are dealing with the process of *interpellation of individuals*
[...] *into subjects*" (*Sublime* 101).

As Copjec, Cowie, and Žižek describe the concept of 'noir,' it
clearly embraces the form and themes of Hart's *Damage*. Analyzing
film noir and classic detective film in *Read My Desire*, Copjec asserts

not only that "the old modern order of desire, ruled over by an
Oedipal father, has begun to be replaced by a new order of the drive,
in which we no longer have recourse to the protections against *jouissance* that the Oedipal father once offered," but also that "Lacan has
argued that this shift describes a general historical transition whose
process we are still witnessing" (182). Though Copjec and Žižek discuss the shift from the traditional subject of desire to the new subject
of drive in classic detective films and film noir, in the postoedipal universe there is no reason it cannot appear in other film genres as well.
Cowie points out that noir can be associated with both "gothic" film
and "the woman's film" (148). In *Enjoy Your Symptom!* Žižek seems
to treat the noir universe found in film noir as if it were primarily an
element of a single genre. But in *Tarrying with the Negative*, he writes,
"[O]ur thesis is that the 'proper,' detective *noir* as it were *arrives at its
truth* [...] only by way of its fusion with another genre, specifically
science fiction or the occult" (10). So surely the logic of noir may be
expressed in, for instance, the love story. The conjunction of oedipal
desire, sense, and subjectivity Lacan posits fits well the conventions of
that traditional story.

Although it is so dark it may seem otherwise, *Damage*, as the
unnamed narrator says, is indeed a "love story" (216). In it, the narrator falls in love with Anna Barton not because she is anything in particular but because as a signifying other it is she who calls him into
existence as himself. In the love story, this moment of recognition,
when the subject is called into existence—interpellated—*as* lover has
the force, Žižek suggests (*Ticklish Subject* 130), of what Alain Badiou
calls a "Truth-Event." It is a moment, essentially unpredictable and
unexpected, that marks a break or separation between a life before
and life after. It is a *truth*-event because it reveals a truth of a subject
or situation. Situations Badiou regards as truth-events include, in politics, the French Revolution and the October Revolution, and, in art,
the atonal revolution in music wrought by Schoenberg, Berg, and
Webern (*Ticklish Subject* 167n3). For subjects, falling in love, in its
break between a past and a future, "subjectivizes." In *Damage*, the
moment in which Anna interpellates the narrator as subject is a clear
representation of a specular, identificatory moment of truth. This
moment hinges on the narrator's sense that never before has he "been"
or "had" a self or identity. As if a good Lacanian, in the novel's first
words, he speaks of this identity as one to be found extrinsically, in
another. That identity represents a "geography of the soul" for which
we search all our lives. "For some," he says, "the search is for the
imprint of another; a child or a mother, a grandfather or a brother, a

lover, a husband, a wife, or a foe" (1). Though we must take his claims metaphorically, the narrator insists he has never found that other until he meets Anna Barton. Ordinarily, one would expect an adult nonpsychotic subject to have found an identificatory other in the mother or some primal nurturer in the mirror stage. Indeed, that must have been the case with the narrator, but for reasons that shall eventually become clear he thinks of himself and his life as if that identificatory relation had never occurred for him.

That way of thinking has psychical consequences. Because he speaks of himself before Anna as a subject more alienated than even the ordinary, alienated, split Lacanian subject, the narrator seems almost to exhibit the foreclosure of the Name of the Father that structures the psychotic subject. That virtual foreclosure leaves him merely an actor, not a subject. In his life, he says, he has "traveled far," found companions in a wife, son, and daughter who love him but remains "unfamiliar" to them. "I have lived with them," he says, "a loving alien in surroundings of unsatisfying beauty." Though he has "gently and silently smoothed the rough edges of [his] being," he remains "an efficient dissembler" (2). Indeed, as "dissembler" suggests, he feels his life and identity have all been a "performance," almost as if he were endorsing Judith Butler's notion of gender and identity as performativity (introduced in *Gender Trouble* and extended in *Bodies That Matter*). He speaks of himself as a member of some "good English repertory company" who "acted those parts required of" him. But these parts or roles bring no passion with them, involve no real desire. "The passion that transforms life, and art," he says, "did not seem to be mine. But in all its essentials, my life was a good performance" (20). Nor had he suffered. Instead, because he "had obeyed the rules," he had "been rewarded." "My ambitions, in important and respected fields, had been realised. I had enough money from income, and private means, to put me beyond financial worry." Moreover, he says in summary of his life to the moment of his first meeting with Anna Barton, "Clear direction, some luck, and here I was, fifty and fully realised" (23). So, we wonder, what's the problem?

The problem lies, as Hart represents it, deep in a childhood the narrator himself suggests must have begun to prepare him for an orientation to drive—and thus *jouissance*—rather than desire. "They say that childhood forms us, that those early influences are the key to everything." His childhood begs for the sort of analysis on which psychoanalysis is founded, for his problem lies in his relation to his parents and their desire, to his passage through the oedipal complex. That means the father must play a major role. Indeed, the narrator confesses that his father and his views dominated his early life: "The combination of his unquestioning belief in his own power to dictate his life and the tall, heavy body in which this will resided, made him a most formidable man" (4). In Freudian theory, whereas the father in the role of the oedipal father intrudes between the desire of the child for the mother, but at the same time constructs a permissible desire for the child, the narrator's father seems not only to deny a permissible desire but also to deny the existence of desire itself.

In place of desire, the narrator's father puts a drive he calls will. A bit like the Schopenhauer of *The World as Will and Representation*, the father insists that the fundamental reality is a will capable of displacing anything else. The father believed that will was everything; "the total power of will" represented "his fundamental credo." The narrator says he often heard the father's words, "Will. Man's greatest asset. Underused by the majority. The solution to all life's problems" (4). In his life, the father insisted that will could govern everything from his relations with others in business to his relations with his wife (the narrator's mother), to, of course, his relations with his son. His relations with his wife are crucial in the son's construction of himself. In his account, the narrator suggests that in denying the objects of desire, his father succeeds in denying desire-as-such. In place of desire's objects, the father has "goals," and goals belong to drive, not desire, and are implicated in *jouissance*. He had made of the narrator's mother a goal, something to "win." After winning her, he set out to deny that desire had anything to do with him or her. Instead, he was determined "to ensure that any way of life she pursued did not interfere with the other goals of his life" (5). As he denies reality to desire in his own life, so he denies desire to the wife and seems to have transmitted that denial to his son as well.

This double denial has immense consequences. The father's interdiction not only of the mother to the son, but of desire-as-such creates a mystery for the son where there should remain no mystery. The mystery involves sexual desire, perhaps sexuality itself. Will having replaced desire in the relation between the parents, their relation has no grounding the son can grasp. "The nature of the attraction between them," the narrator says at age fifty, "is still a mystery to me." The mother seems neither to have offered his father any particular beauty nor to have offered him an image of the accomplished woman. For the son, her one especial talent and one that seemed perhaps to have expressed some sort of desire-not-will lay in her painting. Though, he says, "Some of her water-colours decorated the walls of my childhood home," she suddenly stops her painting sometime between childhood and the birth of the son. "I have never learned why," he says. But whatever the reason, he associates it with his father and his will: in some vague way, the son believes the father did not want her to paint. Thus not only does the mother essentially disappear from the narrative (to be represented only in those paintings), but in her place remains the mystery of the relation between the parents. "The nature of the bond between them, for it was undoubtedly there, still eludes me." It seems not, at any rate, to have been sexual. He says that he was an only child and that after his birth his parents had separate bedrooms. "Perhaps my birth had caused a trauma. Whatever the reason, there was my father's room, and my mother's room, and they were separate." Oddly, however, the son wonders not at all about the mother's sexual life or desire. It is about the father's only that he wonders: "How did that young man live his sexual life?" While he supposes that others might have had lovers, of his father he says, "I have heard no scandalous stories, overheard no innuendos" (5). Thus, in his recollections, the "facts" seem to suggest that sexual desire must not have existed for either the father or the mother. What he does not grasp until he reenacts it in his own life is that his father models not oedipal desire but drive and the narcissism of *jouissance*.

For normative subjectivity, desire—of the mother and of the child for the mother—is appropriate. Without it, the oedipal interdiction that constructs the subject does not work. In the case of the narrator, that interdiction seems to have been avoided. Though he knows something is lacking in his parents' relations and within himself, he seems thus to have been constructed in a world in which ordinary desire plays no role. From that world, he takes into manhood the lesson of drive he learned from his father's will. In his choice of a career, for instance, he seems not to have been marked by desire, but by will, not his own, but his father's. "My life as a child, and as a young boy, seems shrouded in a mist," he says, a mist "permeated by the constant power of my father's presence." His father's motto, "Make up your mind about it. Then do it" (6), becomes his own where profession is involved. He decides to become a physician. As a physician, however, he finds that no desire marks his relations to the objects of his medicine. "Though I studied the myriad ills of the body and ways to soothe them, this brought me no closer to my fellow man. I seemed not to care about him or love him, any more than if I had studied economics." Thus, he knows he lacks something. "There was something missing in me, and in my commitment" (8), he says, and while we might perceive his lack as desire as such, he does not know or feel that. Like his father, he orients himself between will and goals. He has "won" everything, has fulfilled his "ambitions," each an extension in "choice" of his will. But, still, he wonders, if he has a "good life," "whose life" is it? (9).

Whereas in a wife he might have found release from the blandness and sterility of such a life, the narrator neither finds nor looks for anything of the sort. Apparently modeling his erotic life on the one he perceives in his father's and mother's lives, he chooses Ingrid not for beauty or intelligence (albeit, she is both beautiful and intelligent), but for two negative attractions. On the one hand, "There was nothing about her that jarred or caused me pain." On the other, "She possessed in great measure the powerful seductiveness of serenity." Still, he seems to recognize, however vaguely, that Ingrid could have represented more or other, could perhaps have solved the mystery of the relations of ordinary oedipal parents. Instead, he says, "I, who had feared love, feared some wildness it might unleash in me, was soothed." Moreover, whereas an ordinary marriage based on erotic passion might have solved that oedipal mystery, his marriage to Ingrid does no such thing. Because, as he concedes, "I unfolded no mysteries with her" (10), he leaves the field of desire open to Anna Barton and what at first she appears, paradoxically, to offer to him—a *maternal* object who experiences desire and thus is an other in whom, as it were, he finds both desire and subjectivity. Both—desire and subjectivity—turn out to be stopgaps, however, for the one eventually gives way to drive, and the other reveals itself not as the oedipal subject but, eventually, as the narcissistic subject of *jouissance*.

2

> In so far as sexual difference is a Real that resists symbolization, the sexual relationship is condemned to remain an asymmetrical non-relationship in which the Other, our partner, prior to being a subject, is a Thing.
>
> —Slavoj Žižek, *Metastases of Enjoyment*, 108

We may say that the narrator-protagonist of *Damage* merely takes a detour through desire and ordinary oedipal subjectivity before becoming the problematical subject of our postuniverse. His detour goes through the femme fatale, one guise of the maternal object who experiences desire and, as Copjec says, serves as a "defense against the drive" by her relation to *jouissance* (198). As Žižek suggests in his discussions of film noir, the role of the femme fatale foregrounds the paradoxical role of "woman" in the construction of "man." That role raises issues of desire and drive. Žižek points out that Lacan's controversial claim that "Woman is a symptom" (*Feminine Sexuality* 168) of a man can be understood in two radically opposed ways because in Lacan's career Lacan himself shifted his views on the symptom. In the first, the "early"view of the 1950s, Lacan saw the symptom, Žižek says, as "a *cyphered message*," one in which therefore the "woman-symptom appears as the sign, the embodiment of man's fall, attesting to the fact that man 'gave way as to his desire'" (*Enjoy* 154). In this view as illustrated in Žižek's discussion of the noir universe, "woman is *not* an external, active cause which lures man into a fall—she is just a *consequence*, a result, a materialization of man's fall. So, when man purifies his desire of the pathological remainders, woman disintegrates in precisely the same way a symptom dissolves after successful interpretation, after we have symbolized its repressed meaning" (155).

But, Žižek asks, is there not more? "Does not Lacan's other notorious thesis—the claim that 'woman doesn't exist'—point in the same direction? Woman doesn't exist in herself, as a positive entity with full ontological consistency, but only as a symptom of man." In the second view, found in the late writings and seminars and foregrounding drive and *jouissance*, Lacan regarded the symptom "as a particular signifying formation which confers on the subject its very ontological consistency, enabling it to structure its basic, constitutive relationship to *enjoyment (jouissance)*." In this late Lacanian view, both the symptom and woman-as-symptom change. Says Žižek, "[I]f the symptom is dissolved, the subject itself loses the ground under his feet, disintegrates. In this sense, 'woman is a symptom of man' means that *man himself exists only through woman qua his symptom*: all his ontological consistency hangs on, is suspended from his symptom, is 'externalized' in his symptom. In other words, man literally *ex-sists*: his entire being lies 'out there,' in woman" (155). Žižek is especially interested in film noir because, paradoxically, it expresses both these Lacanian views of woman and symptom.

Because Hart's *Damage*, though not film noir as such, creates a radically noir universe in its handling of a love story, the figure of Anna Barton exhibits not merely one but both views. It is clear that, in terms of early Lacanian subjectivization, she may be taken as a materialization of the narrator's fall into desire and subjectivity. But, most important for our new postuniverse, the text of *Damage* seems largely to support the second, late Lacanian view—woman as focus of drive and symptom in which man exists. This is the view within which we see Anna Barton constituting the narrator as a postoedipal subject. Although from every perspective except that of the narrator, Anna Barton is clearly the femme fatale, from his she is the woman in whom

he "ex-sists." If the consequences of the first meeting of Anna and the
narrator were not so tragic and the characters themselves so much
caught up in that noir universe, we might call their meeting—"We
stood silently, I looked away. I looked back. Grey eyes stared straight
back into mine, and held them and me, motionless" (29)—a
"Harlequin moment," the moment in popular romances when lovers
first perceive each other, each seized in the mirror of the other's eyes.
But this is more than a Harlequin moment, for in the gaze of the other
the narrator identifies a Lacanian desire, Lacanian, Žižek would say,
because, paradoxically, it is desire already marked by drive. It is one
that while giving the narrator a self also gives him such a blind narcissistic drive toward satisfaction that it impels him to ignore ordinary
moral and social laws. Indeed, in this late Lacanian view of woman as
symptom, says Žižek, it is she who "embodies the death drive" (*Enjoy*
156). We, if not the narrator, may have seen the extreme noir role in
which his desire/drive has cast Anna Barton when after their first
encounter she leaves him. Walking away from him, she appears a walking knife blade as her "tall black-suited body seemed to carve its way
through the crowded room" (29). Here, clearly, the language Hart uses
defines not the surrogate of the eternal anaclitic—oedipal—(M)other,
but the castrating Other located in the femme fatale. Even so, the narrator is not willing to recognize her as such—yet.

Until the tale's climactic moment, the one marked by Martyn's
death, the narrator simply never sees in Anna Barton the femme fatale.
Much to the contrary, in his eyes throughout the virtual entirety of the
text, Anna is not the femme fatale others might see. Instead, she is the
other who has constituted him as a real subject apart from mere "performance." In this guise as (M)other, she is the ever-patient, tolerant,
loving, and forgiving mother of the mirror—the one who gives him
birth, self, identity. Thus when that Harlequin moment occurs, the narrator represents himself as not knowing who or what Anna Barton represents apart from the one who calls him into being. In the immediate
aftermath of this moment, however, he constructs her within the specular—ambiguously identificatory and aggressive—sense of self-fulfill-
ment he has found within her gaze. In a passage coming after they have
begun their perhaps inevitable sadomasochistic love games (inevitable
because of the duality of the specular relation), the narrator explicitly
describes his relation to Anna: he is like the demanding, aggressive, violent child; she is likened to the mother. The relation has begun, he says,
in a violent birth that begets violence. "I literally felt I was being born,"
he says. "And because birth is always violent, I never looked for, nor
ever found, gentleness." Surely, it is being, not sense, drive, not desire

that marks their relation. Indeed, the violence takes him—and us—into what he calls "the outer reaches of our being." There, he says, in the very definition of *jouissance*, "Pain turns into ecstasy. A glance turns into a threat. A challenge deep behind the eye or mouth, that only Anna or I could understand, led us on and on, intoxicated by the power to create our own magnificent universe"—a universe, alas, that narcissistically reflects the postuniverse of a blind, fraternal "It" desiring annihilation. If in this relation the narrator is what MacCannell would call the new phallic "brother," then Anna is the disavowed "sister-mother" permitted to feel nothing, to deny nothing. Thus, of Anna, the passive slave object in their specular sadomasochistic relation, the narrator says, "She never cried out. Patiently she suffered the slow torments of my adoration. Sometimes, her limbs locked, impossibly angled, as on a rack of my imagination, stoically she bore my weight." In the language within which that imagination constructs her, she has become "dark-eyed, mother-like, the timeless creator of the thing that hurt her" (46).

But if, as the postuniverse demands and the narrator's construction of Anna suggests, there are always two mothers, there must always be two desires or, rather, two sides of the desiring—split—subject. One, of course, is called desire, the other drive. These two psychoanalysis identifies as oedipal and narcissistic, the latter violent, aggressive, preemptive, the former persistent but tolerant, accommodating. *Damage* makes both sides of the split subject evident in that very first meeting and its reflective aftermath. There, Hart's language suggests that desire in general is the operative function in that moment. The moment marks itself in a silent, repressed passion that is entirely orgasmic. Its more extended aftermath looks postorgasmic. In this meeting with a character who in every way is unhomelike, uncanny, *unheimlich*, he still finds a repose which in the "stillness [that] descended upon" (29) him becomes *heimlich*, canny, "home." While the moment, as elsewhere, shows itself as a kind of birth, it is one represented in a mythical signifier of rebirth found in a serpent's losing its skin. "I sighed a deep sigh," he says, "as if I had slipped suddenly out of a skin" (29–30). Though he says he feels "old," he also feels "content." The moment has offered him a "shock of recognition [that] had passed through [his] body like a powerful current." The recognition he feels is precisely that which gives him a specular other in whom to symbolize himself. "Just for a moment," he says, "I had met my sort, another of my species. We had acknowledged one another." Immediate reflection tells him he "would be grateful for that, and would let it slip away." Indeed, he says, "I had been home."

He may not have had long there, but he had "longer than most people" (30).

But further reflection tells him differently and reveals a Lacanian difference. A scene marked momentarily by the language of desire's quiescence ultimately connotes a satisfaction forever to be pursued. "It was enough," he thinks at first, "enough for my lifetime." But then he corrects himself: "Of course, it wasn't enough." It cannot be enough because in Anna Barton he has discovered desire and become constituted as a real subject. No longer regarding himself an actor in a performance (and thus, in Lacanian terms, putting the lie to Butler's notion of identity as performativity), he becomes a subject split by desire. Hart's Lacanian language of splits, gaps, faults is quite clear. In its introducing the novel's titular theme, a passage of reflection following the noirish Harlequin moment suggests that the real damage done in the course of events may well have been that done to the narrator and will not have been done to the others—wife and children—more commonly perceived as his victims. "The surface remained untroubled," he says, but "damage" is occurring elsewhere, in "the ground [that] was beginning to be less firm under my feet," in a "fault long hidden [that] was being revealed," in "the smallest, briefest tremor, barely worth recording" (32). However slight these tremors, he says "the pain that shot through me was so intense, I knew real damage was now being done." While he cannot specifically locate the damage nor predict recovery, he understands that it has to do with his "identity." "Suffice to know," he says, "that I was less the man I had been, and more myself . . . a new strange self" (32-33).

The "new strange self" Anna Barton creates in the narrator seems, until Martyn's death, unable to see her in any guise other than as the specular (M)other. As Copjec says of the femme fatale in film noir, it is in this role that Anna provides the narrator a defense against drive and *jouissance*. That is, he gives over to her these destructive elements. "Having chosen *jouissance*," Copjec says,

> the noir hero risks its shattering, annihilating effects, which threaten his very status as subject. In order to *indemnify* himself against these dangers, he creates in the femme fatale a *double* to which he surrenders the *jouissance* he cannot himself sustain. That is, he tries to take some distance from himself, to initiate some alterity in his relation to himself—to split himself, we could say, not as the desiring subject between sense and being, but between knowledge and *jouissance*. Giving up his right to enjoyment, the hero contracts with the

femme fatale that she will henceforth command it from him, as levy. (199)

But if the narrator is unable or unwilling to see Anna as anything but good for him, others are perfectly capable of seeing her as a very dangerous figure. In speaking to her husband about their life, including their children, for example, Ingrid says all would be "perfect" but for Anna. "She is a very, very strange girl, don't you think?" (72). Ingrid concedes that while she detests the prattling talkiness of some of Martyn's girl friends, she worries more about Anna's relative silence. "Anna's quietness is," she says, "mysterious. She is almost sinister." While these may appear as merely a woman's—especially a mother's—intuitions, others who have known Anna longer confirm them to the narrator. The man in the text named Wilbur Hunter, a writer who has married Anna's mother, knows her well enough to point out, "Anna has brought a great deal of pain to a number of people. She is completely blameless, in my opinion. But she is a catalyst for disaster" (107). A young man named Peter Calderon, a psychiatrist who earlier in his life had been one of Anna's lovers, says of her much the same thing as Ingrid and Wilbur. Peter says, for instance, that she "provokes strange conversations," and he warns the narrator that in fact it is his son who knows Anna best of all. Martyn knows her well enough to allow her freedom to be what she is. "Your son," he tells the narrator, "allows her mysteries, her secrets, and perhaps her other loves" (164).

But perhaps Anna Barton herself provides the narrator the strongest evidence of the other role she shall play in his life. She does so when she tells her story of the suicide of her brother. Because of her role in and the attitude she evinces about the brother's death, that story might well have given the narrator pause. She tells him explicitly that her story is a warning. Why does the brother, Aston, kill himself? Anna's answer seems virtually a gloss on Lacan's premise that there is no sexual relation. "There's no such thing as a sexual relationship," Lacan says, "because one's jouissance of the Other taken as a body is always inadequate—perverse, on the one hand, insofar as the Other is reduced to object a, and crazy and enigmatic, on the other" (*Encore* 144). Her brother "suffered from an unrequited love of me," Anna says. "I tried to soothe him with my body," but she of course failed. Though amidst some pauses, she speaks quickly about the boy's "pain," her own "foolishness," and their mutual "confusion." But she also concludes rather bluntly. "He killed himself. Understandably. That is my story, simply told. Please do not ask again." Offering her tale to "issue a warning," she insists she speaks as a "damaged" person. "Damaged people," she says, "are dangerous. They know they can survive" (42).

No more than the warnings of the others does the narrator heed Anna's. Rather, at a moment when he expects that she will marry Martyn, he persists in seeing her as something else, as one who "looked so sure, so strong," one who to him is like "some goddess to whom one could safely hand one's destiny, certain that her decisions would be right, her judgement wise." Though he understands that the two of them are "colluding" in an effort to betray through adultery others whom they love, at the same time they violate the "age-old" taboo associated with acts implying a form of incest. He persists in his passionate relation with her because he must have her, what she represents. Speaking precisely of "semblance," as Jacques-Alain Miller, in "The Other Who Does Not Exist," speaks of *semblants* of the Other in our postoedipal social universe, the narrator says, "And we knew that we would continue to the end. We were designing our world, and those most closely bound to us, *into a semblance of order*. An order which would allow us our essential, blazing, structured chaos of desire" (114; emphasis added). Alas, order disappears, and chaos reigns over them when Martyn dies. As the narrator, naked, holds his dead son in his arms on the foyer floor and Anna walks toward him, he sees in a blinding flash what she really is, what she means, the role she plays. "Dressed and combed and hideously calm[,] she said, 'It's over. It's all over.' Touching me lightly on the shoulder and looking at Martyn without pity, she almost glided towards the door, and disappeared into the night" (169). Another day, another death.

3

Lacan conceives this difference between the two deaths as the difference between real (biological) death and its symbolization, the "settling of accounts," the accomplishment of symbolic destiny.
—Slavoj Žižek, *The Sublime Object of Ideology*, 135

In the noir universe in which Ingrid, Martyn, and the narrator are caught, not only are there two guises of the mother, but there are also two deaths. Ironically, neither death is Martyn's or her brother's. Most prominently in *The Ethics of Psychoanalysis*, Lacan discusses the concept of 'two deaths' in his argument concerning the place from which Antigone speaks in Sophocles' tragedy. By choosing to defy Creon and societal Law and aligning herself with a "natural" law, Antigone places herself on the side of death by virtue of denying the validity of her culture's Other, its Symbolic structure. Doing so, she becomes, in effect, one of the living dead. Her paradoxical condition as living dead is expressed when Lacan interprets her as saying, "I am dead and I desire death" (*Ethics* 281; see also Mellard, "*Other* Desire"). *Damage* provides the narrator a space from which to speak much like that given Antigone. Žižek points out the sort of narrative situation in which Hart's narrator-subject finds himself. Noir narrative, says Žižek, "is characterized by a radical split, a kind of structural imbalance, as to the possibility of narrativization." The imbalance comes because the narrator may tell his story—and thereby assimilate it to the Symbolic Other—only from the position of the end, *the* end, the position of death. Says Žižek, "[T]he integration of the subject's position into the field of the big Other, the narrativization of his fate, becomes possible only when the subject is in a sense already dead, although [like Antigone] still alive, when 'the game is already over.'" Here, says Žižek, "the subject finds himself at the place baptized by Lacan 'the in-between-two-deaths' (*l'entre-deux-morts*)" (*Enjoy* 151; *Ethics* 272).

In *Damage*, perhaps the most immediate way in which the narrator seems to exist in a state between two deaths lies in his remaining nameless. While I might have called the narrator "Stephen Fleming," as the film does, I have avoided that convenience in my discussion because of the foreclosure of the name that would be the Name of the Father. If naming is a Symbolic birth, then unnaming brings the death in the Symbolic Lacan seems to have in mind when he speaks of the second death as erasure from the Symbolic universe (*Ethics* 294–95). But Hart offers other ways to suggest the between of two deaths. Mainly, she uses the language of two deaths or of a living death or a situation between life and death. She uses these in many places where the narrator tells of the effect his encounter with Anna Barton has had on him. I have already suggested how often this man speaks of that encounter's giving birth to a self or identity he had not known. While his language of birth has to do with his constitution as a subject, this other language, a language of death, positions him as a narrator and the narration as a field of events in relation to the Other of the Symbolic. The vocabulary of "in between" begins with the fateful moment, likewise represented powerfully in the film, when the narrator picks up the telephone, a voice says, "Hello, it's Anna," and he, saying nothing else, tells her to go to her house, wait for him, and expect him there in an hour. Then, between her greeting and his terse instructions, the narrator tells us: "I waited quietly. Knowing that in my life there was now an end and a beginning. Not knowing where the beginning would end" (37).

The narrator's account of his and Anna's first sexual engagement—
primal and animalistic in its abandon—insists on the paradoxical,
Möbius-strip quality his life has assumed because of Anna. The quality
of that life as in-between appears in a nicely stylized, lyrical passage
containing the refrain "there would be time." It is the narrator who
seems to expect that the anticipation expressed in the phrase will be
realized because for him time now stands still. In that stopped time, in
his one real life between two deaths, he finds the place from which he
speaks. Although imagery of eyes made blind by flowers and ears
closed by "silken softness" seems to foreshadow the specific sexual
game the two will play at the end when Martyn discovers them cou-
pling and, in effect, dies of the shock, at this inaugural moment the narrator will focus only on his new enunciative position. "This place
'between the two deaths,'" says Žižek in *The Sublime Object of
Ideology*, "a place of sublime beauty as well as terrifying monsters, is
the site of *das Ding*, of the real-traumatic kernel in the midst of symbolic order" (135). In the real-traumatic kernel that Anna Barton represents, Hart's narrator seems to have found those terrifying monsters.
With her, there will be time also, he says, "in that dark and silent world
for the howl of the lonely man, who had feared eternal exile." In
imagery that graphically creates the sort of nocturnal monster that
must live in the in-between world Anna has created for him, he imagines himself not as the monster, but as the man who lies hidden within
such a traumatic being. "Even if we had never come together again," he
says, "my life would have been lost in contemplation of the emerging
skeleton beneath my skin. It was as though a man's bones broke
through the face of the werewolf. Shining with humanity, he stalked
through his midnight life towards the first day." Returning home after
that first, violent sexual meeting with Anna, he says he "slept through
until morning, twelve hours, a kind of death perhaps" (38). Later, summarizing his feelings about life "after Anna," he says, "And round
every meeting with her spun a ribbon of certainty that my life had
already ended. It had ended in the split second of my first sight of her."
In one of his most precise formulations of the theme of the in-between
of two deaths, he says, "It was time out of [ordinary] life. Like an acid
it ran through all the years behind me, burning and destroying" (44).

Toward the end of the narrative, the text offers other indications
that the narrator tells his story in a time out of ordinary life, in a time
situated between two deaths. After the death of Martyn, Ingrid insists
her husband should himself have died before causing the son's tragedy.
But her pain comes almost equally from the boy's death and her recognition that her husband had never really lived until he met Anna

Barton. While she says quietly, "You should have died," she expostulates in angry realization: "My God, you never really seemed alive to
anything until Anna." As for the narrator, he admits she understands
him. "You are absolutely right on both counts. I should have died. But
I didn't think of it. I never was really alive to anything until Anna"
(183). Thus in the narration later, it comes as a fulfillment of his claim
when he laments a future without Anna. What he envisions is a form of
death "looming ahead," "years of emptiness." The only way he can fill
them, he thinks, is "with every word spoken about Anna, from the day
I first heard of her existence" (187). Anna's mother—yet another
person with whom the narrator comes in contact—recognizes the previous deadness in his existence and the life that Anna had brought to
him. In response to the narrator's telling her that Ingrid had wished he
had died before Martyn's tragedy, Anna's mother says, simply, "But
then you'd never have lived at all. Would you?" The narrator's answer,
however insensitive, is a bluntly truthful, "No" (208).

Plainly, the narrator tells his story from a place where he is already
dead. That is, the spatiotemporal location of the narration occurs
between, on the one hand, a birth into a new life or self or identity that
comes with the recognition of desire-as-such and, on the other, a death
that occurs once the life-giving object (Anna Barton) disappears. In this
aspect of the novel's narration, it is particularly like the voice and location of narration in film noir. Copjec speaks of this element as "the
grain of the voice" and (giving way the meaning of her book's title)
urges, "*Don't read my words; read my desire!*" Copjec connects this
voice to desire, oedipal desire. The narrator's words, she says, tell us to
interpret them. "That is, don't take me literally (i.e., universally), but
realize that these words are the unique bearers of my desire." As bearers of desire, the narrator's words suggest something entirely private,
particular, different. Such words suppose, says Copjec, "a private
beyond, a being that does not surrender itself in speech" (189). But in
the shift from oedipal desire to narcissistic drive we find in the postuniverse of noir and the regime of the brother, "this private beyond no
longer remains hidden. What's involved in the drive," Copjec says,
alluding to *The Four Fundamental Concepts*, "is a *making oneself
heard* or *making oneself seen*; that is to say, the intimate core of our
being, no longer sheltered by sense, ceases to be supposed and suddenly
becomes exposed." It is such an exposure of drive and being we begin
to see in the narrative space of *Damage*. In the film of Hart's novel, the
"grain of the voice" is heard specifically as Jeremy Irons's voiceover
narration at the end following Martyn's death, Anna's disappearance,
and the withdrawal of "Fleming" from the world. But in the novel, this

voice is a constant, is present from the beginning and especially like that of film noir. "In film noir," says Copjec, "the grain of the voice surfaces alongside the diegetic reality. Issuing from the point of death, it marks not some ideal point where the subject would finally be absorbed into his narrative, used up; it materializes rather that which can never be incorporated into the narrative." In noir it is death that, paradoxically, gives material body "to the narrator's absence from the very diegetic reality his speech describes" (190).

Damage suggests very strongly that the narrative voice emanates from the space of death, of the living dead. One way it reveals this death in life (the narrator as the living dead) is through the subject's placement beyond desire. Any subject who is alive is a desiring subject, has or feels or experiences desire. As a sign of the narrator's being dead before Anna arrives, the text places him not only outside drive but also beyond the field of desire. A sign of his *birth* in her is the creation in him of desire, her making him a desiring subject, her making him a subject by causing desire in him. After Anna disappears from his life, almost as if she had never existed, she consigns him back to death by returning him again to a place beyond desire. As she tells him in a letter representing his only real contact with her following Martyn's death, she is taking back what she had given him. However fatal a gift she may have been to him, she shall take back herself and taking herself back shall take back his desire. She tells him he had wanted pain, and pain, along with an identity, she had given him. "I was the gift of pain which you sought so eagerly, pleasure's greatest reward. Though bound together in a savage minuet, whoever and whatever we truly are or were meant to be, soared free. Like aliens on earth we found in each and every step the language of our own lost planet. You needed pain. It was mine you hungered for." If indeed it was pain for which he hungered, desired, that hunger, that desire has been satisfied. He has had "it," *still* has it, is therefore, despite what he may believe, beyond desire or such a hunger. "But though you do not believe it, your hunger is fully satisfied," she says. "Remember you have your own pain now. It will be 'everything, always.' Even if you found me, I would not be there. Don't search for something you already have" (209). To have everything is effectively to be dead, a subject beyond desire. The narrator himself understands that idea. After reading Anna's letter, he seems to pick up on her image of aliens for his own identity, for he says in effect that as a subject he is a dead thing residing in a thing (pain, grief, death itself) lodged within a still living body. "I felt my body," he says. "This thing will need to be housed somewhere until it is finally ready for burial." He has promised Ingrid that he will live on so as to carry her grief, but he feels instead that he "need[s] a coffin" (210).

Though beginning as dead and through Anna finding life in desire, the narrator constructs himself as dead again because in the field of drive he is beyond desire, beyond Oedipus. Early in their relationship, the narrator asks Anna to explain herself, to answer the question, "Who are you?" Her answer, not surprisingly, is "I am what you desire" (41). She is the object he desires. She is desire itself. Gone, however, she takes desire from him as a subject. In the aftermath of Martyn's death and Anna's disappearance, the narrator reports, "Desire rarely troubles me." But in his recounting of an episode in which desire does manifest itself in his life, he distinguishes between his "self" and his body. The body that still lives on may occasionally respond to desire, but the subject, dead inside the body, does not. Speaking of Anna, he says, "Once [...] I laid her picture on the floor. Stretching out on it, in what I thought was a rage of grief, I found myself instead lost in a storm of the body's desperation" that emanated in "tears and semen" (214). Another time, in what may be a spectral hallucination, but in what is surely a moment symptomatic of living death, whether real or hallucinatory, the narrator says, "Anna appears before me. She moves towards me." Reversing the Harlequin moment and exhibiting the empty gaze of the living dead, Anna, he says, "looks into and beyond me as though gathering herself from me for ever. Silently, she wrestles for the part of her I still keep. She is all-powerful. It is an act of repossession." Whatever that "part," that "thing" is he retains of her, in her repossessing it she takes away the support that has kept his body going. Thus, he says, "My body seems to fall in on itself," and to be translated into, sublimated into, a sign or language, "to become a song or a scream, a sound so high, so thin, that it shatters bone and tears muscle." Her repossession of that thing, his thing, his desire, makes of him one of those alien objects that evaporates once its Symbolic support has been taken away. "I know my heart has been ripped," he says. "It is disintegrating. I fall to my knees. It is an act of worship and defeat" (215). Thus, effectively dead as a subject, he simply must await the death of the body that houses a thing already dead. Later, in his hallucination, seeing her spectre with Peter Calderon and seeing her "pregnancy" (meaning that Peter now has the thing, has the Phallus for Anna), he suffers what he calls "final thoughts" and seems to close the door on all his life. "Dying, possibly years before the idiotic mechanism of my body finally surrenders, I whisper to myself and to the silent faces [of Martyn and Anna on the pictures] in the hall, 'At least I am certain of the truth now'" (216). And that truth bespeaks not desire, pleasure or the old oedipal father but drive, *jouissance*, and the new phallic father-brother.

4

> In the modern bourgeois nuclear family, the two functions of the father [as ego-ideal and ferocious superego] which were previously separated, that is, embodied in different people [...] are united in one and the same person.
>
> —Slavoj Žižek, *The Ticklish Subject*, 313

Damage is partly about the phallic object of *jouissance* as symbolized in the femme fatale and is thus about the noir guise of the Mother-Thing that the subject does not immediately recognize. But more important, it is about the phallic father, specifically about phallic and oedipal fathers and the tension between the two, who represent drive and desire, being and sense, *jouissance* and pleasure. In this emphasis, *Damage* represents particularly well the historical shift from desire to drive noted by Copjec and MacCannell. But in Lacan both drive and desire are always present in any notion of the father. Although in *The Ticklish Subject* Žižek raises the ante to three (and I will take up this issue in "Beyond Lacan"), his most persistent claim is that in Lacan there are always two fathers. When there are three it is because one of them, the negative, splits into two versions. Žižek speaks about the more essential two in his discussion in *Enjoy Your Symptom!* of the noir universe I have extended to cover the love story found in *Damage*. Its love story expresses the logic of noir in exhibiting the dominant motifs that mark the noir universe, the femme fatale and the "other" father, the second father—not the oedipal, but the anal or phallic or demonic or primordial father (it has, like Jehovah, many names). *Damage* has the femme fatale, as we have seen, in Anna Barton, the primordial father in the narrator (and, not coincidentally, it seems in his own father). Actually, paradoxically, the narrator functions in the roles of both fathers. In his Imaginary life, the one he describes as a mere performance driven by what the social Symbolic wants of him, he plays the role of the ordinary "dead" father, the oedipal father of desire and "mere" pleasure. In *Metastases of Enjoyment*, Žižek describes the role of the oedipal father as "the symbolic-dead father, Name-of-the-Father, the father of Law who does not enjoy, who ignores the dimension of enjoyment" (206). In his "ordinary," pre-Anna Barton Imaginary life, this is exactly the role the narrator plays. In that life, he says, "I hid the awkwardness and pain with which I inclined towards my chosen outline, and tried to be what those I loved expected me to be—a good husband, a good father, and a good son." From the perspective of the ordinary world, he succeeds admirably, even spectacularly. He has a beautiful wife who admires him, a son who respects him, and a daughter who worships him. "I was a faithful, if not passionate, husband, and I acted lovingly and responsibly towards my children. I had seen them safely through to young adulthood" (2).

In a noir irony, it is the son, Martyn, who tells us how effectively his father has served as the ordinary father, the Symbolic-dead father, the oedipal father of rule, law, order, sublimated desire. In a scene when his engagement to Anna Barton is announced at his maternal grandfather's estate (Hartley), Martyn says that he and Sally had "idyllic childhoods" filled with "rituals" of travel and "holidays at Hartley" that offered "balm to the soul" (129). But pressed to explain how his parents might have failed the children, Martyn violates the classic interdiction "Be careful what you wish for. You may get it." He says that the family under the guidance of his father provided "too much order." Sounding Lacanian, he says it offered "lack," but it was "a lack of chaos and passion." Little does he know that chaos is come and awaits him. "We looked at each other from either side of the table," his father tells us: "A father who had missed knowing his son. A son who thought he knew his father" (130). The father Martyn thinks he knows is the oedipal father who in his ignorance allows him desire and pleasure. The one he does not know is the obscene, life- and joy-denying primordial father who wills his death, murders him, and chooses to become him.

There is good reason Martyn does not know his father is or has become the anal or phallic or primordial father. According to Žižek, the anal father represents the tendency in Lacan's seminar, especially beginning with *The Ethics of Psychoanalysis* (1959–1960), for every concept to have, as a Möbius strip does, an obverse, a paradoxical reverse or inner lining that contradicts or obviates it. The primordial father, Žižek writes, "is the obscene, superego anal figure that is real-alive, the 'Master of Enjoyment.'" In Freud, this primordial father is the one who is murdered by the primal horde of brothers, murdered precisely because, expressing drive, he forbids *their* desire and pleasure by taking all the women for himself. Because of the power of his drive to *jouissance*, he would murder them if necessary to prevent their desires or drives. Žižek suggests that politically, in the exchange of master for leader, the primordial father paradoxically follows the oedipal father. "In all emblematic revolutions, from the French to the Russian," says Žižek, "the overthrow of the impotent old regime of the symbolic

Master (French King, Tsar) ended in the rule of a far more 'repressive' figure of the 'anal' father-Leader (Napoleon, Stalin)." This historical pattern suggests to Žižek that in the myth of the primal horde Freud had things backward. "The order of succession described by Freud in *Totem and Taboo* (the murdered primordial Father-Enjoyment returns in the guise of the symbolic authority of the Name) is thus reversed: the deposed symbolic Master returns as the obscene-real Leader." In this account, Žižek suggests, "Freud was the victim of a kind of perspective illusion: 'primordial father' is a later, eminently modern, post-revolutionary phenomenon, the result of the dissolution of traditional symbolic authority" (*Metastases* 206).

In *Damage*, because his father unconsciously performs the oedipal father as a cover for the primordial, Martyn is in the paradoxical position of the people. Whereas they hope to get rid of the sleeping, ignorant master, they succeed only in replacing him with the life- and desire-denying "chaos and passion" of a primordial leader. Be careful what you wish for. "Only a dead-symbolic father leaves the space for enjoyment open," says Žižek; "the 'anal' father, 'Master of Enjoyment,' who can see me also where I enjoy, completely obstructs my access to enjoyment." On the one hand, it is "the symbolic father *qua dead*—that is, ignorant of enjoyment— [who] allows us to keep fantasies structuring our enjoyment at bay, to maintain a minimal distance between them and the social space." On the other, it is "the obscene 'anal' father [who] directly animates the phantasmic support of our being which thereby immediately pervades the entire social field" (206). *Damage*, in a single scene, offers us both the oedipal and the primordial. In that dining-room scene where Martyn asks for his own death and does not know it, his sister Sally's boyfriend, Jonathan, explains both in comments about his own father. Defining chaos and passion, he, in effect, defines the anal or obscene or primordial father, the father the narrator has discovered himself to be. But, ironically, in explaining the vicissitudes of Jonathan's father's life, Jonathan describes the paradigm of the oedipal father as well. As voracious womanizer, that father is the primordial. "Well," says Jonathan, "if you want chaos and passion you should have lived in our house. My father was a perfect gentleman. But it's no secret he was a constant womanizer. He and my mother had the most terrible rows. Still, she stayed with him. For me and my sister, I suppose." As an ill old man, confined to the care of his wife and effectively a living dead, he's the figure of the dead father Žižek describes. "They're very happy now," Jonathan says. "But then he's been ill for some time. It sounds cruel to say so, but she likes his weakness. He's rather surrendered to her, like a good child with a kind nurse" (130).

But, more important to Hart's novel and the historical shift from desire to drive, the narrator also represents both oedipal and primordial fathers. In the scene at Hartley of Martyn's announcement of his engagement to Anna Barton, the father performs his purely Imaginary role as the oedipal father to Martyn by refusing at this moment to give way to drive within the context of that genteel, ordinary social space. There, oedipal law both controls him and remains manifest in his behavior. While the primordial father looms in his thoughts, in his social relations up until Martyn's death the oedipal father keeps the primordial repressed. But the repression reveals its hostile underside. It is evident in many places in the narration of this extended scene, but it is almost purely evident at a moment when Martyn prattles on about his love for Anna Barton and his plans for marriage. "He smiled at me," the father recounts. "His handsomeness, his height, and his happiness all combined to make him seem like a young god striding towards his golden future." Sounds good. But for his part, the father says, "I felt like a heavy, weary attendant, doomed to watch the sun shine ever more brightly on his chosen child" (140). In such language, we see the clear outline of the god or child to be sacrificed, Adonis or Isaac the son of Abraham, the god or son to be put to death, the latter by the father as a sign of his worship of the primordial, jealous Jehovah who some day, in a New Testament guise, shall likewise demand the death of his only begotten son. Perhaps the most peculiar—paradoxical—exemplifications of the narrator's role as the primordial father occur at Martyn's death. It is not peculiar that the primordial father should somehow cause the death of the son who would steal his enjoyment. That is his job. What at first seems peculiar is that Hart's text makes the opposite or contrary of the primordial father not the oedipal father, but the eternal, shall we say "anaclitic," mother. As the following application of the Greimasian logical square suggests, that relation is appropriate.

In relation to the subject's desire (desire as good for the subject) the oedipal and primordial fathers exist not on the axis of opposition or contrariety but on the axis of contradiction. While complementary to the femme fatale (which, Lacan says, is another name for the Name of the Father), the oedipal father is contradictory to the primordial father. The anaclitic (oedipal) mother is complementary to the primordial father and contradictory to the femme fatale. Hart's text shows these relations of contrariety and contradiction very clearly. After the narrator has revealed himself and his real desire to his son as that of the primordial father, the text contrasts the father's destructive desire, hard and unyielding body to its opposites in the anaclitic mother. "The power of my body as I held him in my arms, his neck as awkward as a broken stem," says the father-now-primordial-father, "was useless in its strength. Where, where is the softness that could have cradled him?" He recognizes the need of the good-enough mother and her signifiers. "Breasts are needed," he says, "and roundness and softness, for the dead bodies of our children, as we hold them to us in the wild truthfulness of our grief." It seems that here the word *grief* in the phrase "wild truthfulness of our grief" ought to be replaced by the word *drive*. It is the obscene, destructive drive of the primordial father that the narrator's language evokes. "The hardness of my chest," he says, "gave his face no place to hide. My muscled arms felt obscene and threatening, as they tried to gather and shape the brokenness of his body to me" (168).

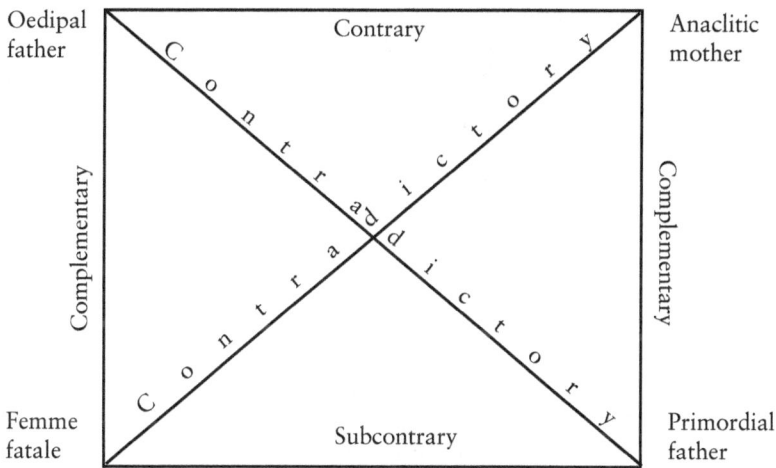

Fig. 8. A Greimasian Square of Implications

Seemingly more peculiar and paradoxical is how Hart's text further represents the role of the primordial father as the complement of the mother. A later scene in which the narrator attempts to comfort Martyn's mother, Ingrid, who mourns bitterly the death of her son, provides a motive for the narrator's turning into the jealous, vengeful, destructive, anal or obscene or primordial father. We find that motive in Ingrid's admission: "Martyn was the one for me. There is always just one person really. Anna, I suppose, for you?" (182). We may thus see how the father's drive relates to the mother's drive to remain the phallic

mother in the fantasy of the son, for the drive of the phallic mother
relates to how the oedipal mother's desire contradicts the desire of the
ordinary or oedipal father. None of this, one supposes, is mysterious
or unpredictable. Seemingly unpredictable, but entirely appropriate in
the text, is how Hart represents the father's actions regarding the son's
death as the reverse of a birth. In his language, he concedes the
mother's drive to be the phallic mother, for in it he represents her as
both birthing mother and thrusting father, himself as a maternal body
receiving a phallic insemination, not of life but of death. The language
is very graphic in the father's effort to obviate Ingrid's mourning by
taking the death into himself as a fetus to be borne—to be carried. "I
brought this death into being," he says. "Let me carry it. I will never
release myself from his death, or fly away from it. Let it slip towards
me, Ingrid. Push it towards me, push his death towards me. Breathe
deeply, Ingrid, breathe deeply. You will live after this. Push Martyn's
death towards me. You will live. Give him to me now. Give me his
death." Indeed, in the next narrative moment, following a series of
bodily throes that one might interpret as resulting from either birth or
sexual actions, Ingrid seems to yield up her son's death and pass it as a
projectile—alien—object into the body of the father. After "a terrible
silent scream" and "a sigh so deep that [the narrator] knew it was
over," he says, "Something flew towards me and seemed to invade
me" (179).

5

The fact that knowledge thus enters the picture at the very beginning
(the subject knows that the Other knows) determines that what follows will be a tragedy quite different from that of Oedipus.
                    —Alenka Zupančič, *Ethics of the Real*, 173

In cultural and literary terms, *Damage* allows two important conclusions. Culturally, it exposes the danger Copjec describes in the
shift from desire to drive and MacCannell identifies in the new postoedipal, postpatriarchal universe of the regime of the brother.
Literarily, it exemplifies the perverse twist Lacan brings to the notion
of the tragic and the ethics of *jouissance*. Specifically, it exemplifies
the cultural dilemma Lacan identifies in the forced choice *le père ou
pire*, the (oedipal) father or worse (the primordial father). To talk
about the tragic is to confront an element in Lacan's theory that is as
troubling to feminist theory as to traditional ethics because it leads
back to the notion of woman as a symptom of man. I have argued

that Anna may represent both views of the symptom, both a "cyphered message" encoding the oedipal subject's relinquishment of desire and a "signifying formation" conferring identity on the subject in relation to its narcissistic desire for the maternal thing. It is in the latter guise that Anna plays her most important role. For as femme fatale, she is the symptom in which the narrator comes to reveal his most secret, unconscious motive—the drive toward *jouissance* focused not on Anna but on his son, his son's death, and replacing his son. Her role as femme fatale, therefore, explains what may seem a mystery in the novel (and film)—why Anna Barton "disappears." In his discussion of film noir, Žižek provides a way to explain that disappearance. Once the narrator is revealed as the primordial father, he and Anna can no longer coexist. "The crucial point not to be missed," says Žižek, "is that the *femme fatale* and the obscene-knowing father cannot appear simultaneously, within the same narrative space." In the presence of the narrator as primordial father, Anna may play a role only as "woman." In Žižek's words, she must become "an *object of exchange* between father and son," the father as the one whose drive suppresses the son's enjoyment, the son as the one whose desire shall (mythically) lead to the murder of the father (*Enjoy* 160). Thus, as femme fatale, Anna must disappear into her being as a woman at the narrative's end, where, indeed, her spectre appears as both pregnant and leading a child by the hand and accompanied by a putative father, Peter Calderon.

It is Anna who, as femme fatale, determines the narrator's end. "In the classical hard-boiled novel and *film noir*," says Žižek, "the *femme fatale* is an agent of (evil) fate: the moment she appears [...] the hero's fate is sealed, events take their inexorable course." Furthermore, he says, "the 'blackness,' the '*noir*' character of the *noir* universe, is affiliated to this inexorable fate epitomized by the woman-Thing: in her face, the hero can read the foreboding of his future doom." But in Žižek's argument, as in *Damage*, the issue is yet more paradoxical. As Žižek argues that for the subject "the lowest ebb, the point of true horror, is the moment of *Versagung* when the subject finds himself face to face with the groundless abyss of his lack of being," so it is the abyss of that lack of being in his life before Anna Barton that the narrator encounters in her. Thus, as Žižek suggests more generally of the subject, the narrator's meeting with Anna Barton is a form of relief. Through her, he "eludes anew the confrontation with his lack of being. In this sense, Lacan's thesis on woman as 'one of the Names of the Father' fully applies to the *femme fatale* in the *noir* universe: the function she performs is exactly homologous to that of the Name of the

Father, i.e., she renders it possible for the subject to locate himself
again within the texture of symbolic fate" (*Enjoy* 169).

But is that fate tragic? Certainly, the narrator may seem the conventional tragic hero, for his life is marked by the topos of the fall from
power and privilege. After Martyn's death, the narrator tells us, "There
was the slow realisation by discreet visitors from my lost world that the
man before them, their old protégé or rival or colleague, was falling
faster and faster away from them; falling through layers of power and
success, through the membranes of decency and ordinariness into a
labyrinth of horror. And in its paths lurked depravity, brutality, death.
And most frightening of all—chaos" (195). But from a Lacanian perspective he is also a tragic hero. We see that tragedy in the moment in
the narrative when the primordial father seems to have realized the
jouissance of drive: he absorbs the death of the son and carries it with
him forever. However terrifying that moment, the really terrifying element that makes of Hart's novel Lacanian tragedy is this: in representing the truth of the subject the novel represents the father's acting in
what Lacan would regard as the one truly *ethical* way. The acts are ethical because the narrator does not compromise, does not "give way on
his desire."

Enacting his drive to possess Anna Barton at whatever cost, he
enacts a deeper, yet more unconscious drive to murder the son and
thereby himself to become the father-brother MacCannell describes,
"the pseudo-Oedipus [of] the Regime of the Brother" (22), the *père
jouissant* of a neototemic culture. This drive is the obverse of the oedipal desire in which, archetypally, it is the desire of the son to murder
the father to steal his *jouissance* with or in the mother. In *The Ethics of
Psychoanalysis*, Lacan insists that the true ethical position is not that
which abides by the desire of the law of one's culture, but that which
stays with the *jouissant* drive of the Other within. "When Lacan formu-
lates his maxim of psychoanalytic ethics, '*ne ce pas céder sur son désir*,'
that is, 'don't compromise, don't give way on your desire,'" Žižek
explains, "it is fidelity to one's desire itself that is elevated to the level
of ethical duty, so that '*ne ce pas céder sur son désir*' is ultimately
another way of saying 'Do your duty!'" (*Ticklish Subject* 153). Hart
reveals, in very powerful language, the narrator's fidelity to his strange,
brutal, horrifying kernel of *jouissant* desire—to carry forever that
incubus, that dead thing thrust into him by Ingrid in her grief. After
Martyn's death and following the scene in which the narrator officiates
at that paradoxical birth and insemination, he speaks of how horror
devours one. Hoping to protect Ingrid and daughter Sally from the
horror of Martyn's death, he has begged that it be given him, given not

so he can destroy it but rather so he might do otherwise. "Ingrid had borne me Martyn," he says. "And last night I had embraced his death and had borne it away from her." Chivalrously said, but his next sentence betrays the *jouissance* he experiences in his son's death. "I would," he says, "*treasure* it" (193; emphasis added).

Adding to the horror of his *jouissant* treasure is that it is not even kept secret. He exposes it, as Copjec says of the drive of the noir hero, as "the intimate core of [his] being" (190). As others have recognized Anna Barton as femme fatale, so others recognize in him the phallic drive of the primordial father. Thus while he had felt something fly into him at that earlier scene, he later finds confirmation from Ingrid that indeed she had yielded up that thing of horror and passed it to him. But it is because she recognizes the obscenity of his demand that she dismisses him from her life. It will not be the son he carries away from her, then, but the obscene kernel of his *jouissance*. "That night, that strange night when you said, 'Give him to me. Give him to me,'" she says to him, "'some terrible anger left me. It flew to you. I want it out of my life for ever. You must take it with you, and go away" (200). In the exchange when she wishes upon him what he had desired of his son, his death, one sees the most horrifying element in the father's drive. Even after the tragedy that has befallen him and all the others, he cannot give up, will not give up on his "desire," the object of his *jouissance*. When she says, "I don't mean this to sound cruel, but what a pity you didn't die, in some accident or something, last year," he replies, "My tragedy is that I don't agree" (201).

Contrary to what we as readers want—or think we want—the logic of this paradoxical ethics no doubt makes of him as much a tragic hero as Oedipus has been deemed. But, as a tragic figure, he is like neither Oedipus nor Hamlet, that other archetypally psychoanalytic figure of tragedy. In *Ethics of the Real*, Alenka Zupančič suggests that, as tragic figures defined by how knowledge relates to their acts, Oedipus and Hamlet form a triad with Synge de Coûfontaine of Claudel's trilogy (*The Hostage, Crusts,* and *The Humiliation of the Father*), among the classic tragedies (*Oedipus Rex, Antigone,* and *Hamlet*) Lacan addressed within the context of the psychoanalytic experience during Seminars 6, 7, and 8, 1958 through 1961 (170). Oedipus does not know (he has killed his father) but is compelled to act regardless. Hamlet knows (he must kill the King) but can not act. Sygne knows and acts (to save a life, that of a husband who, ironically, is also her most detested enemy). It is within Sygne's situation, says Zupančič, that "modern ethics must be situated" (256). In that Hart's narrator knows (the potential consequence of his acts) and acts anyway, he is like Sygne, but even so his is not a modern ethics. While there remains something selfless about Sygne's sacrifice of her life to save not that of her former—and still beloved—lover but that of a husband she detests, there is in the sacrifice of Hart's narrator—despite a potential nobility seen in his accepting responsibility for everything—no such traditionally tragic mitigating selflessness. Nonetheless, the brutal—Lacanian—truth of *Damage* is that the narrator *is* a figure of tragedy, but it is not because of some sanctifying form of renunciation. Rather, it is because, however horrifying the consequences of the acts he precipitates, he "does his duty." In Lacanian terms, he hews to the hard—even self-destructive—line of his drive as the obscenely *jouissant* primordial father. *Le père ou pire.* So, worse yet, for our postoedipal, postpatriarchal, posteverything universe, this is the father-*cum*-brother who perhaps hereafter will dominate our interior and social lives. The tragedy of *Damage*, which seems to represent a beyond even to Sygne de Côufontaine's, is that it may come to represent not just *an* ethics, but *the* ethics of our own *post*-postmodern age.

Part III

Beyond Lacan

CHAPTER 8

Beyond Lacan: Slavoj Žižek, Things to Die for, and a Philosophy of Paradox

> At the core of Žižek's work is a vigorous reactivation of Lacanian psychoanalysis in the service of a project at once political and philosophical.
> —Sarah Kay, *Žižek*, 1

A s Lacan became the beyond of Freud, so now there is—perhaps—a beyond of Lacan. But if that beyond is Slavoj Žižek— and this needs to be determined—he represents a critical, not a clinical, theory, a philosophical, not a methodological one. The legitimate heir of Lacan should have been Jacques-Alain Miller. Indeed, as a clinician, Miller probably is. Bruce Fink, for one, suggests in *A Clinical Introduction to Lacanian Psychoanalysis* that Miller is "the foremost interpreter of Lacan's work in the world today" (vii). But for Anglo-American Lacanians, who mostly are not clinicians, Miller neither publishes frequently enough in English to make a major impact, nor, in his writings (in contrast to his lectures), is he charismatic enough to attract a following. Further, while in his lectures he is both engaging and extremely persuasive, in his role as caretaker of the Lacanian textual legacy he has evoked considerable hostility since it is perceived that he is too slow in releasing unpublished seminars to publication and translation. Thus the one who best qualifies no doubt is Žižek, who earned doctorates in both philosophy and psychoanalysis. Besides being both immensely prolific in English and as charismatic as a revival preacher, Žižek, as we know, has been a protégé of Miller and unabashedly attests to Miller's impact on him: "[M]y Lacan," he has said, "is Miller's Lacan" (*Conversations* 34). Thus, with all irony noted, it is through Žižek that Miller gains a following. But Žižek is the man. Among dozens of prominent Lacanians, there is now no question that he is the most prominent and, more crucially, most influential.

On Lacanian theory and its applications, Žižek is usually readable, frequently entertaining, and, despite much repetitiveness, always revelatory.[1] In countless essays and at least a score of books in English since *The Sublime Object of Ideology* (1989), he rarely fails to bring new, often transformative, insights to Lacanian concepts. Moreover, mixing German idealism—especially Hegelianism—with Lacanian concepts, Žižek is extraordinarily successful in linking psychoanalytic thought to unexpected texts or films or authors or ideologues or ideologies or cultural—especially political—events. These days, his fame—even notoriety—is such that he has become a public figure whose recognition quotient has been raised—and confirmed—by profiles in *Lingua Franca* (now defunct) and *The New Yorker*. Robert Boynton's *Lingua Franca* profile, "Enjoy Your Žižek," like Terry Eagleton's earlier and similarly titled review essay in *London Review of Books* called "Enjoy!" widened Žižek's fame among academics, and Rebecca Mead's *New Yorker* profile certainly introduced him to a broadly educated readership. Under the title "The Marx Brother," Mead's profile confirms what we already know, that "a philosopher from Slovenia" has become "an international star" (38).[2] Without disciples, Mead avers, but a star nonetheless. Unlike many Lacanians, who as good disciples are prone to cite a Lacanian chapter and verse in every new turn of an argument, Žižek adverts to Marx and to philosophers—Kant, Hegel, Schelling, Heidegger—as much as to Lacan. He seldom quotes any actual texts of Lacan, and when he does point toward one it is usually a volume of Lacan's *séminaire* (begun, officially, in 1953), many of which, officially, remain untranslated (see comments on Miller, above). In this strategy of infrequent quotation and extensive glossing of Lacanian concepts, Žižek's work looks very much like the rereading of Freud by which Lacan ultimately displaced the Freudian to give us Lacanian theory. As Lacan's rereading of Freud was deeply rooted in Freud and extends Freudian textuality, so is Žižek's deeply rooted in Lacan and the textuality there as well. But as with Lacan vis à vis Freud, we must understand that, in his readings of Lacan, Žižek, perhaps inadvertently, creates a body of work seemingly beyond Lacan.

1

> I don't think that in Hegel one can simply oppose rationalism with a logic of contradiction and conflictuality. [...] On the contrary, Hegel's greatest idea was that contradiction and conflictuality are at their greatest in the conflictuality of reason itself.
> —Slavoj Žižek, *Conversations with Žižek*, 62

Because his subjects and citations range so widely, Žižek has been regarded as anything from a Marxist to a pragmatist.[3] To begin with, however, Žižek's work often looks more Hegelian than it does Lacanian. Of course, Žižek remains "Lacanian," as Lacan always remained "Freudian." Before there is ever any "going beyond Lacan," Žižek must be regarded as both a Hegelian and a Lacanian. We get a proper sense of the interaction of ideological influences in remarks he makes at the outset of *For They Know Not What They Do*. There he says, the "theoretical space of the present book is moulded by three centres of gravity: Hegelian dialectics, Lacanian psychoanalytic theory, and contemporary criticism of ideology." Then he does what, typically, he does: he contextualizes his commentary within other ideologies by which he has been influenced (Marxism) or against which he makes many of his distinctions (deconstruction), all the while connecting himself to Lacanian themes (the symptom, here). Adverting to one of Lacan's favorite textualizing schemas, he says: "These three circles form a Borromean knot: each of them connects the other two; the place that they all encircle, the 'symptom' in the midst, is of course the author's [...] enjoyment of what one depreciatingly calls 'popular culture': detective and horror movies, Hollywood melodramas." Then, in his most important claim (that is, important to me) he points out that the

> three theoretical circles are not, however, of the same weight: it is their middle term, the theory of Jacques Lacan, which is— as Marx would say—"the general illumination which bathes all the other colours and modifies their particularity," "the particular ether which determines the specific gravity of every being which has materialized within it." In other words, as the "deconstructivists" would put it, the very theoretical frame of the present book is enframed by the (Lacanian) part of its content. (2)

So, yes, he's Hegelian; yes, he appreciates Marxism and understands deconstruction. But, more important, he reminds readers that he is Lacanian, that his most important critical tool is Lacanian theory.

Not to be missed in Žižek's use of Lacan, however, are his roots in the very textuality underlying Lacanian theory. Throughout his career, Žižek has frequently employed textual schemas—especially the Greimasian logical square and versions of it. See for example *For They Know Not What They Do* (136, 195–96). But he has also happily used schemas of others to advance his own arguments. Regarding the Lacanian *objet a*, for instance, he uses one of Jacques-Alain Miller's in

Looking Awry (94). Better yet, in the interests of his own take on
Lacan, he has virtually specialized in explaining Lacan's schemas.
Perhaps the best example of use-cum-explanation occurs in the chapter
"*Che vuoi*," in *The Sublime Object of Ideology*, where Žižek provides
what in my view is the best elucidation ever of Lacan's notoriously
arcane graphs of desire (87–129). Readers of Žižek know that in his
twenty or so books he makes frequent—and enlightening—recourse to
schemas, but, as far as I know, always ones belonging to others—he
does not make up his own. Or, more accurately, though it is clear he
has them in mind, he does not display them on the page. No matter.

His roots in Lacanian textuality remain from any perspective. For
example, looked at generically, his dominant rhetorical strategies
employ, at a first level, a basic structuralist binary and, at a second
level of complexity, the logical square. In part, we might say, Lacan
makes perfectly good sense to Žižek because Lacan's methodology,
rooted (long before Structuralism) in binary oppositions and quaternary thinking, accords with Žižek's. When Žižek, as he habitually does,
opens an essay by resorting to any "commonplace" or "standard"
"view," "argument," "critique," or "understanding," he inevitably—
but typically only implicitly (it is "in mind," but "not on the page")—
invokes the logical square as well as Lacan's most basic, quaternary,
Schema L, rooted in that square. Identifying a "standard understanding," Žižek in effect starts with an Imaginary of some sort and then
generates his own arguments through relations determined by the
square, through, that is, contraries or contradictions or even complementaries that often produce associations with Lacan's Symbolic and
Real. Though beginning with strategies of the logical square, he does
not always follow them to the end. Often, frustratingly, as if he has lost
his rabbit, he truncates his expositions at the binary (contrary) stage,
somewhat more rarely pursuing thought through contradictory or complementary stages. That is, as Žižek frequently says, he may take a critique through a first approach or beyond, to a second approach or
even—but rarely—to a third approach, depending on his aims or needs.
Whether Žižek himself pursues all the steps made available in the
schema, the square, by allowing one to generate hypothetical positions
within a discourse, certainly allows Žižek, and any followers or disciples, to repeat a critical procedure. It works especially well, as writings
of a Marxist such as Fredric Jameson illustrate, as a matrix for raising
oppositional critiques.

If we find a link between Lacan and Žižek in their pervasive textuality, looking at them from another perspective we find a further link
between them in their shared reliance on Hegel. Somewhat notoriously,

Lacan found his Hegel in Alexander Kojève; Žižek, who earned a PhD in philosophy, admits to a project to return German idealism to a central place in postmodern thought. But in linking this triad of thinkers, Hegel, Lacan, and Žižek, it is probably not coincidental that the one who has historical priority, Hegel, made his most famous contribution to philosophy—the dialectic—in a procedure for analysis that is itself another expression of textuality. The dialectic is probably more central to Žižek than to Lacan. From the beginning of his career Žižek has worked in opposition, against received doxa—that is, Imaginary understandings, commonplace assumptions, standard interpretations. Thus his dialectical methodology and his ideological position work hand in hand. Ideologically, a basic oppositional stance is more important to Žižek than is the methodology, but in his generating those oppositional, contrary, idiosyncratic positions for which he is famous, the method, for which the Hegelian dialectic is the paradigm, is absolutely crucial for him. Indeed, it is sometimes difficult to separate content from method. For one thing, Hegel, as subject content, is a frequent object of Žižek's expositions. This is the case in the early *Sublime Object of Ideology* (1989) and *Tarrying with the Negative* (1993) as well as in the more recent *Ticklish Subject* (1999). In the latter, indeed, the chapter "The Hegelian Ticklish Subject" (70–123) gives him his title. For another thing, probably more important, Hegel provides Žižek with a method portable from subject to subject to subject. Hegel's dialectic or the triad of reflection (the double negation or "negation of the negation"), as it did for the philosopher himself, gives Žižek a mode for producing and structuring thought that almost automatically becomes oppositional. At any point in a book by Žižek we are likely to find him beginning with some standard doxa—those received, and therefore Imaginary, ideas about a given subject—any of which would represent a Hegelian abstract, separate, unreflected, unmediated thing. Then, we will find him—in a dialectical process relating that thing to others, in the process of "negative reason"—exposing contradictions in the standard doxa. Finally, we will find him exercising the Hegelian strategy of speculative logic, in his locating a positive reason in the unity of opposites found in their very opposition.

Though historically discredited now as really Hegel's terms, the stages of thesis (a positing, in other words), antithesis (negation of the positing), and synthesis (negation of the negation, a unity found in resolving contradictions) provide Žižek a critical procedure he repeats over and over. This process, which Sarah Kay discusses in her index of terms under "reflection," represents a "pattern of reversal and return [that] characterizes all his writing" (169). We find this triadic process/structure operating everywhere in Žižek. We may say the Žižekian paradigm for it appears in his earliest book in English, *The Sublime Object of Ideology*. There, on a macrolevel that Kay (34–38) discusses, he works across the triad of positing, external, and determinate reflection in detail (213–31). But easier to illustrate is a microlevel. For instance, he starts with the paradoxical notion that the only way to save democracy is to accept its "impossibility," the fact that at its heart is "an original 'trauma,' an impossible kernel which resists symbolization, totalization, symbolic integration." His book's thesis, he writes, "is that the most consistent model of such an acknowledgment of antagonism is offered by Hegelian dialectics." But the Hegel Žižek means is one he claims that standard doxa misrepresents (and in truth it does). Žižek's "understanding of Hegel inevitably runs counter to the accepted notion of 'absolute knowledge' as a monster of conceptual totality devouring every contingency; this commonplace of Hegel simply *shoots too fast*." Hegelianism neither necessarily fosters nor at all endorses totalitarianism. Rather, in the dialectic, it exposes the negativity in every ideology:

> far from being a story of its progressive overcoming, dialectics is for Hegel a systematic notation of the failure of all such attempts—"absolute knowledge" denotes a subjective position which finally accepts "contradiction" as an internal condition of every identity. In other words, Hegelian "reconciliation" is not a "panlogicist" sublation of all reality in the Concept but a final consent to the fact that the Concept itself is 'not-all' (to use this Lacanian term). (6)

Given Žižek's preoccupation with Hegelian concepts, Sarah Kay is quite right when—though "taken with" hardly expresses the power of Hegel's usefulness to Žižek—she suggests that "Žižek is much taken with the unceasing, restless movement of Hegel's dialectic and the implications this has for identity. No sooner does something approach identity with itself than it reverses into its opposite, a process Žižek repeatedly illustrates with the paradox that tautology is actually a form of contradiction" (26). The Hegelian notion of negation works similarly, for, as Žižek frequently reminds readers, holding to the positive in the negative—as is apparent in Žižek's analysis of Hegel—is perhaps the essence of the Hegelian dialectic itself.

2

[Žižek's] favorite mode of delivery is a kind of vaudevillian overstatement.
—Rebecca Mead, "The Marx Brother," 39

There are, of course, aspects of Žižek's dialectical rhetoric, a rhetoric of conflict or contradiction, that operate on a larger scale, beyond, that is, individual words or small clusters of words or clusters of "small" words or even sentences. We might call the one a "microrhetoric," the other, larger, a "macrorhetoric." In other words, the dialectical rhetoric operates both locally and globally and constitutes for Žižek an identifiable methodology. Thus, if Žižek's reinterpretation of Lacan goes beyond Lacan, as it threatens to do, its advance lies in this methodology more than in any content as such. While often we read Žižek for the sheer pleasure of his rhetoric, it is this method that drives Žižek's difference from Lacan. But as any longtime reader of Žižek understands, the method, apart from dialectic itself, seems rather *un*methodical and rather inimitable. Instead, because he appears to lose his rabbit a lot, the method seems quite subjective and associational— that is, he generates essays, which he folds into his books, by circling, associatively, around topics or themes or other preoccupations. As a putative methodology, then, it no doubt derives from what he tells Glyn Daly is his hatred of writing. He tells her that his "whole economy of writing is in fact based upon an obsessional ritual to avoid the actual act of writing. I never begin with the idea that I am going to write something. I always begin with one or two observations that lead on to other points—and so on" (*Conversations* 42). Clearly, there is an antimethod in his method. Although to describe it Žižek would perhaps prefer a metaphor from jazz, the technique he uses is somewhat like that of a standup comedian. He has said in fact, "I always perceived myself as the author of books [...with an] excessively and compulsively 'witty' texture" ("Preface" viii). Not surprisingly, then, in her profile of Žižek in *The New Yorker*, Rebecca Mead, touching on his use of paradox and his entertainingly comedic ways, points out that "his favored mode of delivery is a kind of vaudevillian overstatement, buttressed by the appearance of utter conviction" (39).

But, however much he disavows them, these very features are the ones that set him apart from other Lacanians and give his work such appeal. When Žižek performs at conferences and in speaking engagements, he is enormously entertaining because of the humor, the witty contradictions, and the utter conviction. We see it, for instance, when in fact he tells a joke and then explains its relevance to his reinterpretation of Lacan. In this respect, he models himself more on Freud than on Lacan. Lacan jokes, wittily, in puns and plays on words, but does not tell jokes. Freud does. Žižek often alludes to Freud and recasts ethnic jokes Freud used in *Jokes and Their Relation to the Unconscious* and elsewhere. On the absurdities of ethnic prejudice, Žižek says, "It is like the old sad joke: 'Jews and cyclists are at the root of all our problems! 'Why cyclists?' 'Why Jews?!'" (*Welcome to the Desert of the Real!* 56). Like Freud's, Žižek's jokes often hinge on a patent absurdity or, better, a paradox of the type "Since I wanted to mislead you, I told you the truth...[because I knew you would think I was lying]" (Žižek discusses this pattern in *Fragile Absolute* 80–81). If not precisely on paradox as such, Žižek's jokes and quips often rely on a form of absurdity Mead identifies as Marxian, as in Groucho not Karl. Mead recounts this story:

> In the week before Slovenia became an independent nation, Žižek contributed an essay to *Mladina* entitled "Hail Freedonia." In it, he adapted an old Marx Brothers joke— "You want a lawyer? Get a lawyer. You'll have more troubles, but at least you'll have a lawyer"—to the project of Slovenian nationalism: "You want to be independent? Be independent. You'll have more problems, but at least you'll be independent." (46)

Although in a preface to *The Žižek Reader* he disavows his notorious use of humor, humor nonetheless is a major reason Žižek appeals so strongly to so many readers. Indeed, the humor—the very readability of Žižek's texts despite the often complicated syntax of sentences— explains why we read Žižek rather than Jacques-Alain Miller. Moreover, and more important, not only has he a sense of humor, but also that humor, as in Freud, is always put to good ideological use. For instance, there is his allusion to American disavowals of responsibility for the mess in Iraq in the subtitle of *Iraq: The Borrowed Kettle* (2004): "The title refers to [...the kettle] in the joke evoked by Freud to illustrate the strange logic of dreams: (1) I never borrowed a kettle from you; (2) I returned it to you unbroken; (3) the kettle was already broken when I got it from you. Such an enumeration of inconsistent arguments, of course, confirms *per negationem* what it endeavours to deny—that I returned a broken kettle to you" (1). In this way, by often using comic narratives or exemplary illustrations, typically hinging on paradox or absurdity or ambiguity or mutual contradiction, Žižek communicates with immense energy and panache. Indeed, Žižek's writings sometimes smack of comic performances working through apparent free associations within a topical context. The comic says, "Take my wife..." Žižek says, "Take symptom...or subject or woman or phallus or fathers or ideology or the war in Iraq...."

But always, when he tells a joke, he makes entertaining and enlightening Lacanian points or points that inevitably produce witty

Hegelian contradictions. Calling his introduction to *For They Know Not What They Do* "Destiny of a Joke," he recounts two versions of the same joke. Each is a reversal of the other, but they occur under different historical circumstances, one before the fall of Communism, the other as it's falling. Each "explains" why Soviet Jews want to leave Russia. Before: "There are two reasons why. The first is that I'm afraid that the Communists will lose power in the Soviet Union, and the new forces will blame us Jews for the Communist Crimes." "But [. . .] this is pure nonsense, the power of the Communists will last for ever!" "Well, [. . .] that's my second reason." After: "There are two reasons why. The first is that I know that Communism in Russia will last for ever, nothing will really change here, and this prospect is unbearable for me." The other expostulates, again, that this is nonsense. "Communism is disintegrating all around! All those responsible for the Communist crimes will be severely punished!" The reply is the same: "That's my second reason!" (1). Either joke works because of the real reason, unspoken—antisemitism. Whatever happens, of course, the Jews will be blamed, and the Jew knows that.

In *The Puppet and the Dwarf* (2003), whose announced topic, ostensibly, lies in the subtitle *The Perverse Core of Christianity*, Žižek uses a very funny joke to make a variety of points that he inevitably connects to his argument about desire, mothers, fathers, and Christianity. "In an old Slovene joke," he begins,

> a young schoolboy has to write a short composition entitled "There is only one mother!," in which he is expected to illustrate, apropos of a specific experience, the love which links him to his mother; this is what he writes: "One day I came home from school earlier than usual, because the teacher was ill; I looked for my mother, and found her naked in bed with a man who was not my father. My mother shouted at me angrily: 'What are you staring at like an idiot? Why don't you run to the fridge and get us two cold beers?' I ran to the kitchen, opened the fridge, looked inside, and shouted back to the bedroom: 'There's only one, Mother!'" (24–25)

For Žižek, a joke is more than a joke. Thus, in his way, he begins, seemingly only associatively, to add on thematic points. Speaking, first, of the whole story, he asks, in one of those ubiquitous rhetorical questions, "Is this not a supreme case of interpretation which simply adds one diacritical sign that changes everything, as in the well-known parody of the first words of *Moby-Dick*: 'Call me, Ishmael!'" Then, perhaps because it is Freud who sets a precedent for using jokes in serious-minded psychoanalytic ways, Žižek sets the story against Freud's most famous literary exemplar. "The joke," Žižek adds, "stages a Hamlet-like confrontation of the son with the enigma of the mother's excessive desire." That done, he next takes the point of view of the mother, caught *in flagrante*, who, naturally, has a "deadlock" to resolve:

> in order to escape this deadlock, the mother, as it were takes refuge in (the desire for) an external partial object, the beer, destined to divert the son's attention from the obscene Thing of her being caught naked in bed with a man—the message of this demand is: "You see, even if I am in bed with a man, my desire is for something else that you can bring me, I am not excluding you by getting completely caught in the circle of passion with this man!"

But, as a Lacanian, Žižek can not rest with Freud. He must include a Lacanian reference as well. So, directly referring to one of Lacan's most significant essays, he turns the screw of interpretation yet once more: "The two beers (also) stand for the elementary signifying dyad, like Lacan's famous two restroom doors observed by two children from the train window in his 'Instance of the letter in the unconscious'" (25).

Having "heard" the mother, as it were, we next get to hear the son's reply: "from this perspective, the child's repartee is to be read as teaching the mother the elementary Lacanian lesson: 'Sorry, Mother, but there is only one signifier, for the man only, there is no binary signifier (for the woman), this signifier is *ur-verdrängt*, primordially repressed!' In short: you are caught naked, you are not covered by the signifier." Then, just to remind us that all these amusing twists and turns of perspective and commentary connect nonetheless to his announced religious topic, Žižek muses,

> And what if this is the fundamental message of monotheism— not the reduction of the Other to the One, but, on the contrary, the acceptance of the fact that the binary signifier is always-already missing? This imbalance between the One and its 'primordially repressed' counterpart is the radical difference, in contrast to the big cosmological couples (*yin* and *yang*, etc.) which emerge only within the horizon of the undifferentiated One (*tao*, etc.). (25)

Finally, and quite typically, by use of a rhetorical question, before this long, long paragraph of joke plus analysis comes to a close, Žižek slides to yet another aspect of popular consumer culture (colors of packets of artificial sweetener) to enhance his thematic point and, no doubt, our amusement as we think about the color we might choose. "And are not," he asks, "even attempts to introduce a balanced duality into the minor spheres of consumption, like the couple of small blue and red bags of artificial sweetener available in cafés everywhere, yet further desperate attempts to provide a symmetrical signifying couple for the sexual difference (blue 'masculine' bags versus red 'feminine' bags)?" (25–26). While the point here to an American reader might be clearer if the colors were blue ("It's a boy!") and pink ("It's a girl!"), there is a point, and it is certainly "Lacanian." "The point," he explains, "is not that sexual difference is the ultimate signified of all such couples, but that the proliferation of such couples, rather, displays an attempt to supplement the lack of the founding binary signifying couple that would stand directly for sexual difference" (26). Hmmm. Okay.

3

> So, true to his Hegelian and Lacanian roots, Žižek's discourse forces us to confront paradox *itself* as the primary rhetorical and theoretical form of the text and the socius.
> —Jeffrey Nealon, "The Cash Value of Paradox," 600

It is plain enough that Žižek is Lacanian, Hegelian, controversial, and a consummate rhetorician who uses humor and dialectics masterfully to produce rib-tickling entertainments and eye-popping paradoxes at virtually every moment in his discourse. But, really now, what sets him apart from every other run-of-the-mill Lacanian-Hegelian-stand-up-comedian-cultural critic? If there is another such as Žižek out there, the difference between them would be paradox itself. The "Thing" about Žižek, but the "Thing" that we are likely to miss, is that paradox is the Thing. It is the wheelbarrow. If I were Žižek, I would tell the hackneyed joke about the worker who is stealing from the factory. Every day the guard checks through the straw in the wheelbarrow to find what the worker is stealing. Nothing. Never anything. But the guard knows it has got to be something. Finally, he gives up and just asks the worker what it is. "It's wheelbarrows," he replies. In Žižek's work the thing he is getting away with—the wheelbarrow, the conveyance, the ground on which everything actually, but invisibly, rests—is paradox. He looks Hegelian or Lacanian or a Hegelian-Lacanian, but, really, he is a philosopher of paradox. Indeed, Žižek may be most of all like a Hegelian philosopher in that his method and content, as in the dialectic in Hegel, are virtually inseparable.

As a critical theorist, Žižek rewrites Lacan (to say nothing of
Hegel) within an implicit, perhaps even unconscious, premise that
everything—that is, everything important—can be reduced to paradox.
Or, put another way, the paradox in everything can be found, either by
invoking Hegel's dialectic or by invoking Lacanian principles. ForŽižek
the philosopher, it is not that paradox is the be-all and end-all but that
at the end of every be-all we find paradox—a philosophy, and of
course an attendant rhetoric, driven by paradox. When Lacan
"returns" to Freud, he does so by rewriting Freud around the motto
The unconscious is structured like a language. When Žižek "returns" to
Lacan, he does so by demonstrating that everything significantly
Lacanian is structured as a paradox. Paradoxically, we may say, even
when Žižek changes his views of a particular concept (the Real, for
example), his new views will nonetheless devolve to paradox. In Žižek,
there simply is no escaping it. But, then, there is no particular reason to
want to: this is what Žižek is all about. "For Žižek," Tony Myers says,
"the truth is always to be found in contradiction rather than the
smooth effacement of differences." Calling Žižek's "an *oxymoronic*
style of thought," Myers recognizes that contradictions "are not just
phrases." Rather, he says, "they are indicative of the whole approach
to thinking that Žižek calls dialectical and which he employs when
analysing everything from Hitchcock to European toilet designs" (17).
But while, certainly, paradox is an element of style (and, as Eagleton
and Gigante suggest, Žižek's style is important), Žižek's use of paradox
in no way reduces to style alone or to paradox taken as one trope
among many.

Or reduced to paradox as just a trope. On philosophical issues,
Vincent Deary, though apparently unaware himself that he is dealing in
paradox, makes more explicit the basis of Žižek's thought in the one
trope. Deary speaks of "three main keys" in Žižek's work. Each he calls
a trope, but they are, essentially, enabling premises for Žižek's thought
on such concepts as the Real, the 'Subject,' and the 'Act.' The primary
key, *the* "central Žižekian notion" opening up our "understanding [of]
his reworking of the Lacanian notion of the Real," Deary calls a "*trope
of a foreclosure.*" It is foreclosure that founds any "closed system of
meaning." For Deary, a second key is that for Žižek the *foreclosed* "of
any system is nothing but the inherent inconsistency of the system
(mis)perceived as" an external limit or obstacle. A third key addresses
Žižek's notion of the Act. "In a closed, deterministic universe," Deary
explains, freedom to act "is an illusion or a miracle—news from elsewhere." But there is a "loophole." Žižek argues that subjectivity itself is
that loophole, a gap in substance through which "an Act can emerge

that is literally unconditioned, not determined by the prevailing symbolic order or by its antecedents." In effect, the Act raises itself by its own bootstraps. It causes its own being. Thus, not part of the symbolic order from which it apparently comes, it "changes the symbolic order within which it occurs, without, however, appearing to break the chain of causality." It is, then, an Act's reciprocal relation to causality that is our third key. "The Act 'papers over' the gap of its occurrence [...] by positing its own presuppositions." That all these are essentially, though of course not merely, paradoxes becomes evident in Deary's own language when he speaks of that key regarding the Real: "Implicit here, then, is the *paradox* [my emphasis] that the Real is both the cause and the effect of the process of subjectivity/meaning formation." Moreover, that the only trope here is paradox lies in Deary's own paradoxical expression of what must be a truth of Žižek's thought: "The Subject, the Real, and the Act are essentially *identical*—an 'unbearable' excess which instigates/disrupts a reasonable order, all performing," Deary remarks, a "three-trope dance" that surely is, yet more paradoxically, a dance of the one trope, paradox. It is a dance performed, as it were, to the music of one hand clapping. Deary, of course, is not wrong here. It is just that he is, in effect, the guard searching through the straw in the wheelbarrow and fails to "see" the wheelbarrow itself, which *is* paradox.

Thus, we may extend Deary's list of "things carried" in paradox. Reading Žižek, one must finally understand that every concept he deems significantly Lacanian regarding sex, symptom, subject, woman, fathers, ideology, the unconscious—indeed, any topic Žižek considers— will exhibit paradoxical conditions of ambiguity, mutual contradiction, apparent impossibility.[4] From the start, as Lacan's Freud revolved around issues of language-cum-textuality, so Žižek's Lacan has revolved around textually and dialectically generated manifestations of paradox. In reading Žižek, then, it is imperative to recognize how any topic whatever devolves to revelation and exposition of paradox, for the structure of paradox governs not only content but also, as we have seen already, verbal and rhetorical strategies—a *style*—attending content. While Žižek often exposits paradoxes without ever using the overt verbal labeling, the easiest way to confirm the pervasiveness of paradox is simply to search for the word *paradox* and its variations. *Paradox*, *paradoxes*, *paradoxical*, and *paradoxically* appear, for instance, thirty times in the 60 pages of "The Symptom" in *The Sublime Object of Ideology* (1989) and over a hundred times in three hundred pages in *Tarrying with the Negative* (1993). In more recent books, Žižek does not abandon either 'paradox' (and its variations) or the phenomenon itself: my unscientific survey shows, for example, sixteen usages in the first 60 pages of *The Ticklish Subject* (1999), thirty-three in the 160 pages of *On Belief* (2001), and forty-six in the 170 pages of *The Puppet and the Dwarf* (2003). In *Looking Awry*, these words appear six times in just the last 4 pages of "The Real and Its Vicissitudes." To be sure, the first chapter of *Looking Awry* is about paradoxes, Zeno's and those of others, so naturally those words appear frequently—fifteen times in 18 pages. But as any habitual reader of Žižek knows, he discusses Zeno's paradox because his interest lies in the function of paradox either within Lacanian theory or in explanations of texts and concepts of others. In "The Paradoxes of the *Objet petit a*" (in *Looking Awry*), it is Lacanian theory. In *Tarrying with the Negative*, where those four words appear with astonishing frequency, and Žižek's subject is not paradox but "Kant, Hegel, and the Critique of Ideology," it is distinctly theories of others.

As Žižek inexorably exposits how virtually all of Lacan's basic concepts turn on the paradoxical, some, clearly, circulate around paradoxical constructions within Lacan. While there is no doubt that paradox has played a role in Lacanian theory, the question becomes whether Lacan's is a theory based on paradox. Regarding symptom only, Collette Soler has addressed the question and answered in the negative. Beyond Soler's view, mine is that any Lacan of paradox we find revealed in Žižek is a perspectival illusion generated by Žižek in his going beyond Lacan. In the first place, Lacan and Žižek simply do not use paradoxes for the same reasons. Lacan rarely uses those four magic words anyway, and he uses paradoxical constructions mainly for rhetorical and mnemonic effect. While any of the following is perhaps memorable, each is much more likely to confuse readers or audiences than to explain. Among those familiar, in some form, to Lacanians are these:

> The subject is an other.
> The gaze is a thing.
> The woman does not exist.
> The *objet petit a* is a thing that does not exist.
> The Phallus is a thing that does not exist.
> Lack is a surplus.
> Castration is a renunciation of renunciation.
> The Real is the impossible.
> Desire is the desire of the Other.
> The woman is a symptom.
> The woman is a symptom of man.
> Man exists only through woman as his symptom.
> There is no sexual relationship.

It would be fatuous to deny that Lacan loves paradoxical apothegms or sayings, but it is also very plain that when he uses those paradoxical or impossible or ambiguous constructions, he uses them within a rhetoric entirely different from Žižek's. Aiming for shock and awe, if not stunned confusion, Lacan's is simply not a rhetoric of paradox used for explanation. And, as Kay reminds us (173n5), do not even ask Jacques Derrida—and he is just one of many who complain similarly—about Lacan's rhetorical aim. It was, Derrida says, "constructed so as to check almost permanently any access to an isolable content, to an unequivocal, determinable meaning beyond writing" (420).

But Žižek's is aimed at explanation. Žižek's rhetoric of paradox both explains and increments Lacan's aims. This is to say, all significant construal or interpretation or explanation in Žižek inevitably takes a paradoxical turn. While many Lacanians "use" Lacan without ever mentioning paradox, Žižek would regard such an application as surpassingly weird. In *Tarrying with the Negative*, there is a wonderfully rich passage, invoking subjectivity, castration, desire, *jouissance*, the symbolic, and the Thing (as well as Žižek's touchstones—Kant, Hegel, Wagner), that will begin to illustrate the importance of paradox to any exposition Žižek makes. Where Lacan would say, "The subject is an other," Žižek would say, "The subject is a paradox." "Subjectivity," he writes, "involves a kind of loop, a vicious circle, an economical paradox which can be rendered in a multitude of ways, Hegel's, Wagner's, Lacan's." Taking them in reverse order, he says that for Lacan "castration means that the Thing-*jouissance* must be *lost in order to be regained* on the ladder of desire, i.e., the symbolic order *recovers its own constitutive debt*." Next, he says that for Wagner's *Parsifal* "the *wound is healed only by the spear that smote* you." Of the first who shall be last, he says that for Hegel "the immediate identity of the substance must be *lost in order to be regained* through the work of subjective mediation." Finally, he offers a summation that eventually brings in Kant, yet a fourth among his touchstone figures. To begin, he says, "What we call 'subject' is ultimately a name for this economic paradox or, more accurately, short-circuit, whereby the *conditions of possibility coincide with the conditions of impossibility* [Žižek's emphasis]. This double-bind, which constitutes the subject," he says, "was for the first time explicitly articulated by Kant: the I of transcendental apperception can be said to be 'self-conscious,' can experience itself as a free, spontaneous agent, *to the very extent to which it is inaccessible to itself* as the 'Thing which thinks'; the subject of practical reason *can act morally (out of duty) to the very extent to which any direct access to Supreme Good is barred* to him" (emphasis added). In a further, very nice, summing up, just in case we missed them, Žižek tells us, "The point of these paradoxes is that what we call 'subjectivization' (recognizing oneself in interpellation, assuming an imposed symbolic mandate) *is a kind of defense mechanism against an abyss, a gap, which 'is' the subject*" (171; emphasis added). Žižek, by someone and much to his professed regret, was once dubbed "the Giant of Ljubljana," and it may well have been because only a giant could take such huge strides in one paragraph from Kant to Hegel to Wagner to Lacan and get away with it.

For him the essence of Lacan—and Kant and Hegel and Marx and Wagner and Heidegger and any other serious thinker—is paradox. But in all of these it is only—or largely—Žižek himself who uncovers that essence. Since he is like a person with perfect pitch where paradox is concerned, he will find them regardless. Thus it is not really necessary for Lacan to provide Žižek with paradoxes as pump primers. Any grounding in paradox, in Lacan or in any other of these thinkers, thus belongs to Žižek. So, of course, because he considers himself predominantly a Lacanian, he thus frequently grounds analyses of others in Lacan. But we must always note the paradoxes. With Žižek, it is not "value-added." It is "paradox-added." First, look for the magic markers. In *Looking Awry*, for example, applying Lacan's dictum "There is no sexual relationship" to Wagner's *Ring* trilogy, Žižek writes: "And is not this extreme point at which radical ascetic renunciation *paradoxically* coincides with the most intense erotic fulfillment the very topic of Wagner's *Tristan*" (212; emphasis added). Or, again, of Lévi-Strauss's analysis of Wagner, and also invoking "lack is a surplus," he writes, "The domain of contracts, of giving and receiving something in return, is sustained by a *paradoxical* gesture that provides in its very capacity of withholding—a kind of generative lack, a withdrawal that opens up space, *a lack which acts as a surplus*" (217; emphasis added). As this latter passage suggests, it is Žižek's talent not only to "find" paradoxes in Lacan but also to "find" them in works to which he can apply Lacanian theory and even in the critics and scholars (such as, above, Lévi-Strauss) with whom he engages in debate.

Explaining (but inevitably expanding) Lacan, Žižek frequently teases out one paradox after another in Lacanian concepts. In *Tarrying with the Negative*, above, we just saw him explaining subjectivity. What about desire? Žižek addresses that concept at length in *The Sublime Object of Ideology*. In a chapter called "Che vuoi?" he offers, as I have said, the best explanation available of Lacan's notoriously daunting "Graphs of Desire." In an endnote in *Enjoy Your Symptom!* (1992), Žižek yet more concisely discusses aspects of desire in the larger context of Lacan's dictum "Desire is the desire of the other." In itself, Lacan's statement is not so much paradoxical as merely ambiguous. Its ambiguity lies in whether Lacan means the Other's desire or the subject's desire. Is the issue, that is, what the Other desires of/from me or is it the Other taken as the object of my desire? Is desire pointing from the other toward me, or is it pointing from me toward the other? These, let us say, become What does the Other want that is mine? versus What does the Other have that I want? In variations of that memorable line of the matron in *When Harry Met Sally*, on overhearing the feigned orgasmic moans of Meg Ryan, "I'll have what she's having" might become, from Ryan's perspective, She'll have what I'm having.

As in *The Sublime Object of Ideology*, in that note in *Enjoy Your Symptom!* Žižek focuses on "Che vuoi?" and such related topics as love, transference, and the role of the analyst. The early Lacan focused on the subjective genitive, what the Other desires, the late on the objective genitive, the Other as the object of desire. The question asked by the subject, says Žižek, "pertains to the very status of the subject of desire." It "is the famous '*Che vuoi?*'—what does the Other want of me, what does he see in me that causes his desire, which is that X, the object-treasure which makes me an object of the Other's desire?" Inevitably, for Žižek, this impasse or deadlock (How can you eat your cake and have it too?) devolves to a paradox that does permit you to have it both ways. In effect, it becomes, I'll have what she's having *because* she's already having what I'm having. In Žižek's words,

> The only way to get out of this impasse is to offer myself to the Other as the object of his desire: as Lacan puts it, in love, the subject "gives what he does not possess," *objet petit a*, the hidden treasure which is what is "in him more than himself." In this way, I simultaneously "return my love" to the Other, i.e., I determine my desire as the desire *for* the Other: I make him into the *object* of my desire in order to be able to avoid the [unknowable] abyss of *his* desire. (*Enjoy* 191n37)

When Žižek considers desire in Lacan's view of the analyst, paradox also ultimately emerges. It appears in the transference between patient and analyst. In the transference, explains Žižek, wherein "the analyst functions as the *sujet supposé savoir*, he is supposed to know the truth about the analysand's desire; yet he is simultaneously the object of the analysand's desire, the embodiment of *objet petit a*, possessing the mysterious *je ne sais quoi* which triggers transferential love." In Seminar 8, *Le transfert*, Lacan describes the paradoxical situation of the subject "supposed" (that is, presumed by someone else) to have knowledge. This subject "knows" only when it is unconscious: "at the very place where we are supposed to know [...], we are expected [...] to be nothing more and nothing else than the real presence, precisely insofar as this presence is *unconscious*" (*Le transfert* 315; qtd. Žižek, *Enjoy* 191n37; emphasis added). Žižek, in turn, exposits the paradox in his fashion: "The only way for us, analysts, to attain the mystery of the desire of the Other (analysand) is—temporarily, for the time of the transference—to occupy [...] the place of *objet petit a*, to incarnate the object-cause of his desire." Paradoxically, then, the truth of the subject appears in an illusion about itself: "the way to the *truth* about the Other's desire leads through the transferential *illusion* in which we incarnate the object of the Other's desire" (191n37).

In the chain of historical succession, we find in Žižek's rhetoric of paradox a link to Lacan's textuality. Lacan works his thought through various schematics (Schema L, Schema R, Borromean knots, the Graphs of Desire, and the like) that typically function either as binaries or like the so-called Greimasian logical square. Likewise, Žižek seems to work his thinking about matters through some sort of grid, certainly, at the lowest level, through a structuralist binary he would have learned when he studied French structuralism for his master's thesis (*Conversations* 28). Generating his particular mode of analysis, Žižek often appears to work from basic binary structures, a mutually contradictory doubling he stresses in rhetorical questions that inevitably yield paradoxes when he answers them, questions such as why are there always two fathers, why are there two mothers, why are there two views of the subject? As an example, a phenomenon of doubling dear to Žižek is how subjects "avoid the encounter with the real." There are, of course, two ways to avoid the Real. Both provide examples of Žižek's rhetoric of paradox and, by implication, a methodology of Žižekian, if not "late" Lacanian, analysis. Using an analogy of the analyst as detective, where either analyst or detective may be regarded as "subjects supposed to know," Žižek argues that we find one way to avoid the Real of desire in Sherlock Holmes. By solving a crime and "dissolv[ing] the impasse of [a] universalized, free-floating guilt by localizing it in a single subject and thus exculpating all others," the Holmesian detective thereby allows individuals to "desire without paying the price for it" (*Looking Awry* 59). By contrast, the other way—based on Žižek's reading of a hard-boiled detective, Philip Marlowe—localizes desire in figures of the femme fatale and permits the detective (as subject) to avoid it by rejecting her: "contrary to appearance, the *femme fatale* embodies a radical *ethical* attitude, that of 'not ceding one's desire,' of persisting in it to the very end when its true nature as the death drive is revealed. It is the [detective] who, by rejecting the femme fatale, breaks with this ethical stance" (63). The first paradox is that the two "ways" end up the same—the Holmesian criminal is simply the femme fatale, in whom is localized the universal guilt of being human. In another paradox, however, when subject becomes object, the femme fatale herself ends up representing for Žižek the very model of human subjectivity: "When she finally becomes an object *for herself also*, i.e., when she realizes that she is just a passive element in the interplay of libidinal forces, she 'subjectifies' herself." That is to say, "she *becomes* a 'subject'" (64; emphasis added). As subjects of our life stories, then, we are all, paradoxically, less like heroes than like criminals and femme fatales detectives must ferret out.

As these discussions indicate, when Žižek outlines paradoxes, he does not always stamp the label *paradox* or its variations on them. When we read Žižek, we must also look beyond the overt for the covert signs of paradox in his rhetoric. Besides overt labels, we find as well a metadiscursive rhetoric involving recurrent terms and strategies that attend—and, perforce, signal—expositions of the paradoxes themselves.[5] Although Žižek is amazingly gifted (that perfect pitch) at finding and outlining them, he will sneak them past readers if they are not paying attention. In the midst of them, we are easily dazzled by the intricate turns and twists of exposition. Thus, apart from "getting" paradoxes themselves, we need to become aware of those metadiscursive signs of them that, once we are aware, become quite evident, if indeed not obtrusive. Tracking the wily Paradox, we need to recognize its spoor. One hint that we're in its presence is Žižek's use of the words *deadlock* or *impasse* or *contradiction*. Like Fredric Jameson's "contradictions" avoided or resolved by the political unconscious, deadlocks and impasses and Žižek's contradictions may be escaped in ways almost invariably paradoxical. These words may also travel with sets of words going along with "the standard"—*doxa* or *ideology* or *attitude* or *commonplace* or *understanding*. In the thicket of these merely standard ways of thinking, we are very likely to discover Paradox. Often enough, "the standard blah-blah" conceals a Paradox exposed best through a "Lacanian answer." In "The Spectre of Ideology," for instance, Žižek says, "One of today's *commonplaces* is that so-called 'virtual' or 'cyber' sex presents a radical break with the past, since in it, actual sexual contact with a 'real other' is losing ground against masturbatory enjoyment, whose sole support is a virtual other," whether in phone-sex, pornography, or "computerized 'virtual sex.'"

The *Lacanian answer* to this is that first we have to expose the myth of "real sex" allegedly [occurring] "before" the arrival of virtual sex: Lacan's thesis that "there is no sexual relationship" means precisely that *the structure of the "real" sexual act (of the act with a flesh-and-blood partner) is already inherently phantasmic*—the "real" body of the other serves only as a support for our phantasmic projections. In other words, *"virtual sex"* in which a glove simulates the stimuli of what we see on the screen, and so on, *is not a monstrous distortion of real sex, it simply renders manifest its underlying phantasmic structure.* (2; emphasis added)

Likewise, elsewhere Žižek offers a "Lacanian answer" to troubling sociological questions of classism, racism, and ethnocentrism, questions of whether subjects can escape their "own ethnic, ideological universes." "Lacan's answer here," he says, "is paradoxical and deeply Hegelian. The mistake of this solipsistic view, that we can never be sure that we communicate with the other, is that we presuppose that we can communicate with ourselves." Then, in the guise of a yet further Lacanian answer, one dependent on Lacan's notion of the split subject, the subject *barré*, he heaps paradox on paradox. "Lacan's answer is that *we communicate with the others precisely because we cannot communicate with ourselves*, precisely because we are always split. The way we are split connects us with others; we look for the missing part in the other. The other fills our own gap." From paradoxes regarding self and other, Žižek extrapolates into a rhetorical question covering a paradox, a rule, a "Lacanian wager," regarding communication itself. When Lacan "answers the question of how communication is possible," he says, it "is the Lacanian wager: is not our culture, the way we structure the symbolic edifice of our culture, only an attempt to come to terms with some kind of traumatic impossibility?" ("Sublime Theorist" 89). As these examples attest (and, of course, they could be multiplied indefinitely), in Žižek's discourse, "It is paradox all the way down" (Nealon 600).

4

Lately, he has taken to writing a great deal about Christianity, his enthusiasm for which is matched only by his commitment to atheism.
—Rebecca Mead, "The Marx Brother," 39

Assuming now that there is a philosophy in Žižek, not just discussions of philosophy, we might ask whether there is change or evolution regarding that philosophy. Are there phases in Žižek? As with Lacan, do we have to worry about "which Žižek?" Ironically—or is it fittingly?—as Žižek delineates an early and late Lacan, so might one delineate an early and late (or "current") Žižek.[6] In the effect of retroaction defined by the act of the truth-event articulated in Žižek's preface to *The Žižek Reader* (dated 1 April 1998), Žižek's early period ranges from *The Sublime Object of Ideology* (1989) through *The Plague of Fantasies* (1997). The late period begins with his next book, *The Ticklish Subject* (1999), and thus also includes *The Fragile Absolute* (2000), *Did Somebody Say Totalitarianism?* (2001), *On Belief* (2001), *Welcome to the Desert of the Real* (2002), *The Puppet and the Dwarf* (2003), *Iraq: The Borrowed Kettle* (2004), and *Organs without Bodies* (2004) (and the hits keep coming). Regardless whether there is a Lacan of paradox, we now see there surely is a Žižek of paradox. But that Žižek, though he devotes much attention to German idealism, remains distinctly Lacanian in orientation. In this early stage, Žižek finds ways to make Lacan a universal cause, a theorist whose paradigms explain virtually everything under the sun. Indeed, I might add that to this point almost all of my exemplifications of Žižek's philosophy of paradox come from the early work.

In later Žižek, Lacanian theory of course remains just as important as a grounding, but in this Žižek there appears something different, some *objet petit a*, some *je ne sais quoi* that is more himself than himself. To illustrate that Thing, the *object petit a*, that is inside one and means more than oneself, he often uses as example a German product for children. Inside a hollow piece of candy, Kinder Chocolate, is a toy that is more the object cause of the child's desire than the candy itself. If I may be permitted the analogy, this thing inside the later Žižek that is more himself than himself is enigma or, at its furthest distance, mystery. Indeed, this thing, to give reality to a certain cliche, is a paradox wrapped in an enigma inside a mystery. That is, from *paradox* as his dominant term, Žižek of late seems to have shifted, at one level, to *enigma*, a term perhaps embodying paradox, but one less merely witty and formulaic, and, at another level, to *mystery*.[7] Moreover, the late Žižek, while retaining his philosophic, political, and politico-economic positions, now begins rather directly to make good his claim in that preface to the *Reader* to find a way beyond "the abstract messianic promise of some redemptive Otherness" (ix).

In the late Žižek, we find the beyond of paradox in enigma and mystery, especially ones found in Christianity. Go figure. In this Žižek, it is not so much that he gives up Lacan as that he finds a reciprocity between Lacanian theory and something in Christianity that, more even

than in the reciprocity between German idealism and Lacanianism, validates both ideologies for him.[8] If there is a criticism of the early Žižek
of paradox, it is that paradox, as a mode of analysis and a form of content, left him taking no apparent, fully articulated, position. As the
comic makes jokes, so Žižek, the Paradox Man, makes paradoxes. Who
cares about a position? In paradox, when one position is not subsumed
within dialectic, it simply cancels out the other. As Rebecca Mead puts
it in that *New Yorker* profile, though she seems inaccurate about followers, Žižek can attract no "Žižekian" graduate students because "he
contradicts himself all the time" (39). "Even to Žižek, it seemed,"
Mead suggests, in view of such grave issues as the war in Iraq, that
"pointing out paradoxes was an inadequate, if essential response" (47).
Given Žižek's background in Marxist theory and activist politics, it
surely must have become troubling that his very rhetorical-cum-philo-
sophical position, rooted in paradox, left him with no particular
grounds for ethical or political action. In Christianity, Žižek seems to
have found a way out of the simple contradictions or stalemates or
even resolutions of the merely paradoxical. As he once regarded his
Marxism as "humanist Marxism," it may well be that his Christianity
must be a "humanist Christianity." To be sure, he himself has pointed
out that it is an easy step from Marxism to Christianity. "For years,"
he writes in *The Ticklish Subject*, "the parallel between revolutionary
Marxism and Messianic Christianity was a common topic among liberal critics" (142). But in his next book, *The Fragile Absolute*, he calls
this "the old liberal slander" that Marxists typically reject, if for no
other reason than it connects Marxism and Christianity on the wrong
grounds. For Žižek, typically, a proper response is to take the offense
rather than remain defensive: "[I]nstead of [. . .] allowing the enemy to
define the terrain of the struggle, what one should do is to reverse the
strategy by *fully endorsing what one is accused of*: yes, there *is* a direct
lineage from Christianity to Marxism; yes, Christianity and Marxism
should fight on the same side of the barricade against the onslaught of
new spiritualisms." Why? Because "the authentic Christian legacy is
much too precious to be left to the fundamentalist freaks" (2).

If in anyone other than Hegel or Lacan, the new Žižek is rooted in
the work of Alain Badiou, a prolific author of books on many topics,
three of which topics—ethics, "the event," and Saint Paul—have much
affected Žižek's latest work. In a brief introduction to *The Fragile
Absolute*, Žižek indicates that his approach follows "Badiou's path-
breaking" (2) book of 1997, *Saint Paul: La fondation de l'universal-
isme*. Earlier, in *The Ticklish Subject*, in a chapter titled "The Politics
of Truth," Žižek addresses that notion of "truth-event" Badiou had

introduced in 1988 in *L'être et l'événement*. For Badiou, truth-events mark a radical—defining—break or separation between a time before and a time after. For example, in politics, the French Revolution and the October Revolution are truth-events, but so also, in art, is the "atonal revolution in music accomplished by the Second Viennese School" (*Ticklish* 167n3). On a smaller scale, in one's personal life, falling in love, in a break between a past and a future that defines a lover, is a sort of truth-event. We recognize a truth-event because it has a structure—a "naming," an ultimate goal, an "operator," and a subject or agent. The supreme example of a truth-event, Žižek suggests, belongs to Christianity. "The Event is Christ's incarnation and death; its ultimate Goal is the Last Judgment, the final Redemption; its 'operator' in the multiple of the historical situation is the Church; its 'subject' is the corpus of believers who intervene in their situation on behalf of the Truth-Event, searching in it for signs of God" (130).

As a political materialist and a post-Enlightenment subject, Žižek needs to reconcile his Christianity, humanist or otherwise, with Marxism and modern science. In the concept of the 'truth-event,' it becomes easy enough to forge links between Marxism and Christianity through Paul because, Žižek suggests, it is he whom Badiou names as "the one who articulated the Christian Truth-Event." Because of Paul's way of establishing the Church as an institution, Christ's resurrection is defined by Badiou as a "universal singular," that is, as "a singular event that interpellates individuals into subjects universally, irrespectively of their race, sex, social class," or "the conditions of the followers' fidelity to it." Through Badiou's Paul, Žižek can have both Marxism and Christianity. As for science, Badiou knows how hard it is in a time under its dominion to "accept the *fable* of the miracle of Resurrection as the form of the Truth-Event." In our time, the only acceptable truth-event, the only "intrusion of the traumatic Real that shatters the predominant symbolic texture," is one taking place "in a universe compatible with scientific knowledge," even if such an event not only occurs at the borders of science but questions as well its very presuppositions (142).

For Žižek, it is precisely because of the sort of scientific "facts" he himself has addressed as early as *Looking Awry* (43–47), in the work, for instance, of Stephen Hawking, that he *can* accept the "fable" of the truth-event of Christianity. Epistemologically, it seems to have come to pass that there is little difference between phenomena we might find not only in today's pop "religious obscurantism" but also in legitimate science. That is to say, the "absolute" in science becomes just as "fragile" as the one in religion. For Žižek, whether in science or religion, "universals" are founded on a Lacanian logic of the "nonall" and the exception that constitutes them. Universals, wherever they appear, are defined by the logic of the phallic signifier, and this logic must bring us back to the late Lacan, the Lacan of Seminar 20. As Jacques-Alain Miller taught Žižek, "There is no 'big Other' to guarantee the consistency of the symbolic space within which we dwell: there are only contingent, local and fragile points of stability" *(Fragile* 117). But, perhaps oddly, it is the very fragility of the absolute that seems to attract Žižek (see *Conversations* 69). It gives *The Fragile Absolute* titular focus and is used throughout that book as a thematic motif that fully validates Tony Myers's claim that Žižek's work is "profoundly poetic" (5). The Absolute, Žižek writes, "is thoroughly fragile and fleeting." It "appears to us in fleeting experiences—say, through the gentle smile of a beautiful woman, or even through the warm, caring smile of a person who may otherwise seem ugly and rude: in such miraculous but *extremely fragile* moments, another dimension transpires through our reality." Because such an Absolute is so fragile, "it slips all too easily through our fingers, and must be handled as carefully as a butterfly" *(Fragile* 128). Wow!

Equally fragile, and as powerful as the Absolute, is love. Žižek argues that love, as defined by both Saint Paul, in Corinthians, and Lacan, in *Encore*, is Christian charity. But the Christian charity that is love, says Žižek, "is rare and fragile," and is "something to be fought for and regained again and again" (118). Despite its fragility, love is yet powerful enough not only to unite reality and appearances but also to separate believers from all they once thought indispensable. Regarding reality and appearance, it is the mistrustful cynic, not the believer, who, paradoxically, becomes "the victim of the most radical self-deception" (127). For instance, the cynic recognizes neither the reality of "the appearance itself" nor how "fleeting, fragile and elusive it is" (128). By contrast, it is "the true believer [who not only] believes in appearances" but also recognizes "the magic dimension that 'shines through' an appearance." Moreover, because there is a grace in this ability to see through appearance, the believer "sees Goodness in the other where the other himself is not aware of it. Here appearance and reality are no longer opposed: precisely in trusting appearances, a loving person sees the other the way she/he effectively is, and loves her for her very foibles, not despite them." But just as critical to Christian life is the power given love or charity to separate—or "unplug"—from the ordinary. Indeed, it is love or Christian *agape* that for Žižek defines Christianity as a model of revolutionary ideology. As Paul explains *agape* as "the key intermediary term between faith and hope," so Žižek suggests "it is love itself that enjoins us to 'unplug' from the organic community into which we were born" (121).

Still more radically, Christian *agape* entails an unplugging that is the "condition" for the New Beginning of the Christian Gospel. To clean the sinner's slate, it entails "a terrifying *violence*" that must be connected to "the *death drive*"(127). As Žižek writes in that preface to *The Žižek Reader* marking his truth-event, "[T]here is no effective freedom without 'terror'—that is, without some form of the uncondi- tional pressure that threatens the very core of our being" (ix). Belonging not to Imaginary or Symbolic but to the Real, Christian *agape* is hard, unyielding, activist, revolutionary. In making the Christian choice to start anew, to make a break between an old life, self, community, the Christian must both engage in the hard work of love and separate—unplug—from the old community. "As every true Christian knows, love is the *work* of love—the hard and arduous work of repeated 'uncoupling' in which, again and again, we have to disen- gage ourselves from the inertia that constrains us to identify with the particular order we were born into" (*Fragile* 128–29). In choosing such a "work of compassionate love," moreover, we find ourselves as new subjects. Unfortunately, says Žižek, "it is *this* Christian heritage of 'uncoupling' that is threatened by today's 'fundamentalisms,' espe- cially when they proclaim themselves Christian" (129). Finally, being not merely some "inner contemplative stance," this Christian "*work of love*" is so revolutionary and unsettling it "necessarily" leads to the creation of an *alternative* community. Unlike Bakhtinian "carniva- lesque," which unplugs from established communally Symbolic rules and trespasses upon an existing order, "proper Christian" unplugging from community suspends no explicit laws in the Symbolic but "*their implicit spectral obscene supplement*" (129–30), the hidden double of Symbolic Law that reverses "the permissive 'You may!' into the pre- scriptive 'You must!'" (133), in which the tolerance of the oedipal father gives way to the imperative demands of Father himself split off from the primordial.

For Žižek, an important historical aspect of Christian unplugging connects to that "obscene spectral supplement," the hidden underside of Symbolic Law. This aspect lies in how it distinguishes Christianity, on the one hand, from pagan wisdom and, on the other, from a Judaism within which it developed. Regarding the former, "Christianity asserts as the highest act," Žižek insists, "precisely what pagan wisdom condemns as the source of Evil," that is, the very "gesture of *separa- tion*" itself, of "drawing" the line, "of clinging to an element that dis- turbs the balance of All." For Žižek, "The pagan criticism that the

Christian insight is not 'deep enough,' that it fails to grasp the primordial One-All, therefore misses the point." It is that "Christianity *is* the
miraculous Event that disturbs the balance of the One-All; it *is* the violent intrusion of Difference that precisely *throws the balanced circuit of
the universe off the rails*" (*Fragile* 121). As a truth-event, in Badiou's
terms, Christianity represents a radical, transformative break in the historical sequence from pagan or natural religion to Judaism to
Christianity. On the second transformation, then, the break between
Judaism and Christianity turns on how it relates to Symbolic Law.
Between Judaism and Christianity, and acting as a catalytic "vanishing
mediator," lies what Žižek calls "the vicious dialectic of Law and its
transgression," the cycle of guilt, transgression, and punishment,
explained by Saint Paul. While this cycle, this "invisible third term"
serving as mediator between the two, is a "spectre" haunting each,
Žižek suggests that "neither of the two religious positions actually
occupies its place." Rather, he suggests, "on the one hand, the Jews are
not yet there" because "they treat the Law as the written Real which
does not engage them in the vicious superego cycle of guilt; on the
other, as Saint Paul makes clear, the basic point of Christianity proper
is precisely to *break out* of the vicious superego cycle of the Law and its
transgression via Love" (145).

   Žižek follows up on many of these issues in *Did Somebody Say
Totalitarianism?* There, he argues that as the dialectic of Law and its
violation serves as the vanishing mediator between Judaism and
Christianity, so, ultimately, does Christ serve as a mediator "between
God and humanity: in order for humanity to be restored to God, the
mediator must sacrifice himself. In other words, as long as Christ is
there, there can be no Holy spirit, which *is* the figure of the reunifica-
tion of God and humanity." As mediator, here, Christ becomes a paradoxical figure of both "the condition of possibility *and* the condition of
impossibility between the two." That is to say, for Christ to bring
together the opposite poles, of Christ as God's Son and of Christ as
man's son, to reach the mediation's "conclusion," namely, a humanity
"fully united with God in the Holy Spirit," says Žižek, "the mediator
must erase himself from the picture." In Christ's erasure, the two poles
to be united become God and community. It is vitally important for
Žižek to make the point that Christ's intervention is not part of how
pagan religion celebrates a cycle of death and eternal return, an "eternal cycle of Divine incarnation and death, in which God repeatedly
appears and then withdraws into himself, in his Beyond." In Žižek's
argument, for the Christian Sacrifice to work, both poles of the opposition to be mediated—God and community—must be transformed.

Thus, adverting to Hegel, Žižek says that "what dies on the Cross is *not* the human incarnation of the transcendent God, but *the God of Beyond himself*. Through Christ's sacrifice, God himself is no longer beyond, but passes into the Holy Spirit (of the religious community)" (50–51). Accomplishing the authentic Christian transformation, "*both poles [are] radically changed*—that is to say, they [. . .] both undergo a transubstantiation in one and the same movement." Two changes thus occur. In one, passing into the Holy Spirit, God is transformed. In the second, passing into a "new spiritual *stage*," human community is also transformed (emphasis added). In a simultaneous moment of transubstantiation, God becomes Holy Ghost, and humanity assumes a new beginning. In sum, in that truth-event called "Crucifixion," Christ not only chooses to die, Žižek says, he *must* die, "not in order to enable direct communication between God and humanity, but because *there is no longer any transcendent God with whom to communicate*" (51).

It is in analysis of this moment that we find an index of difference between an early and a late or current Žižek. In *Enjoy Your Symptom!* (1992), early Žižek treats this same moment in Christianity in the chapter "Why Are There Always Two *Fathers*?" There, however, his analysis seems radically different from that of the late. For one thing, in a late book, *The Ticklish Subject* (1999), Žižek posits *three* fathers: the original two (the oedipal/good; the primordial/bad), plus a third, more "bad" than the primordial, one who, in becoming "*Father himself*"— "the obscene Father-*jouissance* prior to his murder and subsequent elevation into the agency of symbolic authority (Name-of-the-Father)"— thereby seems, as ultimate narcissistic evil, to replace, perhaps to share space with, the Maternal Thing (314). But whether the limit of fathers is two or three, there are always at least two.[9] More than once, early Žižek treats the two and in the treatment emphasizes paradoxical elements in the big Other. In the early *Enjoy Your Symptom!* he treats the two fathers in several venues—in Hitchcock, film noir, Greek Atè or Fate, *and* Christianity—but in none of these does either father move far toward anything redemptive. Suggesting, paradoxically, that "what expires on the cross is not an ephemeral, transitory incarnation of God but the God of Beyond himself, i.e., the notion of God *qua* inaccessible, transcendent, nonrevealed entity" (*Enjoy* 166), Žižek offers a very different, much less positive interpretation than that in his late work. The early Žižek explains that the deity perishing on the Cross is an "antique God," a "God [who] belongs to the Real." As in the later Žižek, Christianity, here, is left with a God who "ceases to be a transcendent entity who incarnates himself in a finite human figure." But the significance of this incarnation seems hardly to foreshadow the Good News

Gospel. Rather, this God "becomes a name for this very movement of incarnation/revelation: his existence is purely 'performative,' an effect of his own revelation in the Word" (167). Further, the paradoxical consequence here is that, with no external agency to define one's guilt, humanity is left not without guilt but with a guilt "redoubled." "The 'death of God,'" he says, becomes just a new name for a retreat that "makes our guilt absolute." Perhaps worse, it leaves us with an abyss called "modern-age subjectivity." When in *Enjoy Your Symptom!*, Žižek does offer a way out, it oddly, paradoxically, is offered not by Christ but by the femme fatale of film noir. Because, as Lacan claims, woman in the guise of the femme fatale functions as one of the Names of the Father, she offers to a subject at least a possibility of locating "himself again within the texture of symbolic fate" (169). But, in a context of two fathers or three, such a mere possibility seems a far cry from the Christian redemption outlined by late Žižek's analysis of Christ's sacrifice.

5

"Do you believe in God?" "No." "Stop dodging the issue! Give me a straight answer!"
—Žižek, *Welcome to the Desert of the Real*, 3

Although early Žižek totally immerses his rhetoric and mode of thinking in paradox, our late Žižek, when he addresses Christianity, suggests that for him paradox is not enough. Here, in the face of a need to combine ideology with political action, he seems confronted by concepts that exceed paradox's reach. Instead of 'paradox,' he now uses 'enigma' and 'mystery' to avoid deadlocks or impasses or contradictions. It seems, perhaps, that beyond mere cynical wit there is a different Žižek who expresses either, as in *The Fragile Absolute*, an almost puzzled awe before the enigmas of Christian sacrifice and its mysteries of love or, as in *Welcome to the Desert of the Real*, an angry despair that not the least modicum of Christian tolerance seems to operate in ostensibly Christian nations such as the United States (though not the United States alone). In *The Fragile Absolute*, he speaks of the enigma of love, its ultimate mystery. Explaining how Lacan's concept of 'love' (expressed in *Encore*) also overcomes the dialectic of Law and transgression, Žižek writes of how Saint Paul explains that, in love, "*I am also nothing* but, as it were, a Nothing humbly aware of itself, a Nothing paradoxically made rich through the very awareness of its lack" (146–47). Where he might once have made more of the paradoxical, now he stresses mystery: "Only a lacking, vulnerable being is capable of love: the ultimate mystery of love is therefore that incompleteness is in a way *higher than completion*" (147). Again, when Žižek adds that "perhaps the true achievement of Christianity is to elevate a loving (imperfect) Being to the place of God—that is, of ultimate perfection," where he might once have touted paradox, here he speaks once more of mystery, this one of the transcendence in Crucifixion. The "ultimate mystery," he says, is that "the Crucifixion, the death of the son of God, is a *happy* event—in it, the very structure of sacrifice, as it were, sublates itself, giving birth to a new subject," one "no longer rooted in a particular substance" and, in the Holy Spirit, "redeemed of all particular links" to a previous life (158).

Before we get too excited about Žižek's conversion, we must note that Christianity models—though not simply models—what occurs in psychoanalysis. Psychoanalysis is there first because the mystery of human subjectivity necessarily emerges prior to religion of any sort. If in Christianity the most awe-inspiring enigma or mystery for Žižek is that of the Otherness of God, it is nonetheless an enigma, however awesome, Žižek finds theorized in psychoanalysis. To be sure, its roots lie in Freud, in his "original insight" regarding "the traumatic external *encounter* of the Thing that embodies *jouissance*" (*Did Somebody* 55). Recognizing this trauma, which Freud identifies, and dismissing Jung's Gnostic answer (not much different, in Žižek's view, from that of pagan wisdom), Žižek nonetheless suggests that Christianity radically complicates matters regarding such trauma. He finds that a better response to analysis of description of the trauma lies in a "general theory of seduction" provided by Jean Laplanche in *Essays on Otherness*. According to Laplanche, Žižek says, the subject's "encounter" with the enigma of "unfathomable Otherness" harbors "the fundamental fact of the psychoanalytic experience" (*Did Somebody* 56). "The enigma leads back," Laplanche writes, "to the otherness of the other; and the otherness of the other is his response to his unconscious, that is to say, to his otherness to himself" (*Essays on Otherness*, 255; qtd. in *Did Somebody* 56). Turning the psychoanalyst's insight toward the mystery of God, Žižek suggests that we need to psychoanalyze God, to apply Laplanche's psychoanalytic premise to "the notion of *Dieu obscur*," the religious notion "of the elusive, impenetrable God." Must not such a God, he asks, "also be impenetrable to himself?" (*Did Somebody* 56). Must he not also "have a dark side, an Otherness in himself, something that is in himself more than himself?"

Returning to a preoccupation marking all the books of his late/current phase, Žižek suggests that this thesis might be one more way to explain "the shift from Judaism to Christianity: Judaism remains on the level of the enigma *of* God, while Christianity moves to the enigma *in* God Himself" (56–57). Here, Žižek connects revelation itself to the enigma in God. Christ offers revelation to humanity and God as well: "[I]t is precisely because God is also an enigma *in and for himself*, because he has an unfathomable Otherness in himself, that Christ had to emerge to reveal God not only to humanity, but *to God himself*." Moreover, and more important, "it is only *through Christ* that God fully actualizes *himself as God*" (emphasis added). This enigma, he suggests, is homologous to the Otherness to the self that psychoanalysis recognizes. The "truly radical Otherness," he argues, "is not the Otherness *in ourselves*, the 'stranger in our heart,' but *the Otherness of the Other itself to itself*" (emphasis added). To escape the bleakness of this condition—the very condition of the human—Žižek returns to love's enigma, its mystery. Only by recognizing, and accepting, the Other within oneself can love appear. "It is only within this move," moreover, that what Žižek calls "properly Christian love can emerge." As he found the notion of the traumatic Thing in Freud, so also does Žižek find in Lacan this theme of love of thy neighbor. "Lacan emphasized again and again," Žižek insists, that "love is always love for the Other in so far as he is lacking—we love the other *because* of his limitations." It is thus from Lacan, not religion, that Žižek draws his "radical conclusion": "[I]f God is to be love, he must be *imperfect*, inconsistent in himself; there has to be something 'in him more than himself'" (57).

If for Žižek the most awesome enigma is the mystery of Christian love and sacrifice, about Žižek it has to be the mystery of belief itself. Vigorously taking on the topic in *On Belief*, Žižek considers how it affects a range of venues, from cyberspace to politics to religion itself. Yet more succinctly than in *On Belief*, Žižek addresses the subject again in *Did Somebody Say Totalitarianism?* To begin with, of course, he must address what Lacan has to say on belief as such. Uncharacteristically, Lacan's position—"God is unconscious"—is clear and unambiguous. Naturally, for Žižek, such a claim becomes raw meat before a tiger. Žižek avers that Lacan means that "it is natural for the human being to succumb to the temptation of belief." In an age typically described as atheistic, secular, and scientific, one might presume that belief, in any traditional religious sense, must be totally alien. Yet it finds a place in late Lacan. There, Žižek says, belief connects to the impasse or deadlock of the Real. On the one hand, he says, "nobody can fully assume belief in the first person singular," for as soon as one says "*I* believe," the split constitutive of Lacanian subjectivity emerges. "On the other hand, however, no one really escapes belief." That, says Žižek, is "a feature that deserves to be emphasized especially today, in our allegedly godless times. That is to say: in our officially atheistic, hedonistic, post-traditional secular culture, where nobody is ready to confess his belief in public, the underlying structure of belief is all the more pervasive—*we all secretly believe*" (88; emphasis added). Do we necessarily assume that Žižek includes himself in that all, or is he the nonall, the Lacanian exception, the phallic signifier that proves the rule?

Addressing "the standard argument" that believers use to attack opponents, Žižek, as Lacan does, suggests that "the need to believe is consubstantial with human subjectivity." Whereas believers claim that "only those who believe can understand what it means to believe," Žižek argues that it is the "very predominance of belief" that undercuts such a premise. The position of the atheist, he says, "is not the zero-level which anyone can understand." Rather, "it means only the absence of (belief in) God," and no position, Žižek insists, "is more difficult to sustain." Nothing is more difficult than "to be a true material-ist." Indeed, Žižek says, even Sade and Stalinists were "believers." Of the philosophers, only Heidegger consistently took an atheistic posi-tion. Otherwise, Žižek says, only a psychoanalyst of a certain sort is likely to be a "true atheist." It takes a psychoanalyst who in fact "endorses the nonexistence of the big Other" to maintain the atheist's position, for that position must run counter to the structure of belief, the structure "of the fetishist split and disavowal." Says the believer, "I know that there is no big Other, but none the less . . . ," and Žižek fills in the ellipsis with, "I secretly believe in Him" (89). It is, indeed, this fetishist structure of belief—the role of Christ as the *objet petit a*, as a material object that protects the Christian against his split subjectiv-ity—that prompts Žižek to give *The Puppet and the Dwarf* as its subti-tle The Perverse Core of Christianity.

The break between early Žižek and late seems, ultimately, to focus precisely on the question of belief. But, as we would expect in a Lacanian and a dialectical materialist, the break is not so radical that Žižek gives up either materialism in philosophy or his epistemological roots in Lacanian psychoanalysis. The fact is, as he interprets belief, he is permitted to retain both Lacan and materialism. If in *On Belief* he concludes that, as the book's back cover expresses it, "we are all secretly believers," in *The Puppet and the Dwarf* he says that in our time what we typically experience as belief is "suspended" belief. It is a belief we can not admit publicly. Instead, it is kept as "a private obscene secret" (6). But in *Puppet* his thesis, he insists, goes well beyond such a relatively trivial, however interesting, claim. Rather, he says, "My claim here is not merely that I am a materialist through and through, and that the subversive kernel of Christianity is accessible also to a materialist approach; my thesis is much stronger: this kernel is accessible *only* to a materialist approach—and vice versa: to become a true dialectical materialist, one should go through the Christian experience." Though he never offers any explicit explanation of what "go through" might mean with regard to "the Christian experience," he does insist that "our task today is to resurrect the true Jesus from the mystifying Christian tradition of Jesus (as) Christ" (9).

To do that, he returns to Saint Paul. Reconfirming the influence of Badiou on late Žižek's thought, it is essentially Badiou's Paul to whom Žižek turns. Žižek admits that, for a leftist materialist, any "positive reference to Saint Paul [becomes] a very delicate issue" since Paul is now "the very symbol of the establishment of Christian orthodoxy" (9). But Žižek insists that Paul is crucial because he was not part of the early establishment. Rather, he was an outsider. "What enabled him to formulate the basic tenets of Christianity," Žižek says, "to elevate Christianity from a Jewish sect into a universal religion (religion of universality), was the very fact that he was not part of Christ's 'inner circle'" (10). The appeal of Paul, for Žižek, is that his approach to Christianity is not starry-eyed mysticism but is purely pragmatic and revolutionary. If Marx, let us say, is Christ, then Lenin is Paul. "Paul was a Leninist" is Žižek's astonished realization. To Paul, what matters, Žižek says, "is not Jesus as a historical figure." What matters is "only the fact that he died on the Cross and rose from the dead." Then, "after confirming Jesus' death and resurrection, Paul goes on to his true Leninist business, that of organizing the new party called the Christian community." For this Paul, Paul as a Leninist, "Revolution is already behind us, the old regime is out, freedom is here—*but* the hard work still lies ahead" (9).

It is in such a Paul that Žižek retains his leftist materialism. Moreover, he retains his claim to psychoanalysis as a mode of knowledge through Lacan's notion of the signifier and Laplanche's concept of the 'enigma.' From Lacan, it is the advent of the signifier in the life of the subject that gives Žižek his model for the traumatic break effected by belief—at least the conversion that grounds belief. In Seminar 4 (1956, *La relation d'objet*), Lacan, says Žižek, "proposed a short and clear definition of the Holy Spirit: 'The Holy Spirit is the entry of the signifier into the world. This is certainly what Freud brought us under the title of death drive'" (Lacan 48; qtd. in *Puppet* 9–10). Žižek suggests that, here, Lacan means to claim a parallel between Christianity's

Holy Spirit and the notion of the symbolic order found in Lacanian thought. For Žižek, the parallel grounds both the idea of traumatic break and Pauline activism. "What Lacan means, at this moment of his thought, is that the Holy Spirit stands for the symbolic order as that which cancels (or, rather, suspends) the entire domain of 'life'—lived experience, the libidinal flux, the wealth of emotions, or, to put it in Kant's terms, the 'pathological.'" As the trauma of entry into the symbolic order changes the subject, so also does the trauma of conversion. "When we locate ourselves within the Holy Spirit," Žižek says, "we are transubstantiated, we enter another life beyond the biological one." And this life, moreover, is precisely that grounded on Paul's activist role as outsider who founded "the basic tenets" of a religion based on the truth-event of the Crucifixion (10).

In this respect, Žižek suggests in *Did Somebody Say Totalitarianism?* Christ becomes *objet petit a*, a sort of "Kantian Negative Magnitude," a lack or void that functions because it is embodied in a particular object. Therein, Christianity retains its material basis, for it "offers Christ as a mortal-temporal individual, and insists that belief in the *temporal* Event of Incarnation is the only path to *eternal* truth and salvation" (151). Once more, in this argument, we see how "Christianity is a 'religion of Love'" as well as of conversion. In love, Žižek argues, "one privileges, focuses on, a finite temporal object which 'means more than anything else'" (151–52). In Christian conversion and the forgiveness of sins, "the same paradox is also at work." That is, "Conversion is a *temporal event* which changes *eternity itself*" (152). Through the mystery of Grace, conversion catapults the Christian into a new life. As Žižek puts it in *On Belief*, "Ultimately, the 'rebirth' of which Christianity speaks (when one joins the community of believers, one is born again) is the name for such a new Beginning." Moreover, in a distinction Žižek is at frequent pains to make, he says, "Against the pagan and/or Gnostic Wisdom which celebrates the (re)discovery of one's true Self—the return to it, the realization of its potentials or whatsoever—Christianity calls upon us to thoroughly reinvent ourselves" (148).

This reinvention is no less an enigma—or a mystery—than belief itself. In psychoanalysis, the call to conversion and rebirth comes through the enigmatic message from the Other. For Žižek, this intrusion breaks the "epistemological gridlock" between a simple material determinism (whether in Freud's seduction theory or in some determinism of a biological Real) and an evasive idealism found in the hermeneutics of cultural studies. Between the two, "Psychoanalysis points us towards a third way" (*Did Somebody* 58). Here, the traumatic message of the enigmatic signifier becomes what Žižek, in a term he uses frequently, calls a "vanishing mediator" (59). In that message is a "hard kernel" (58) that resists symbolization. But, Žižek says, "this kernel is not the immediate Real of instinctual or some other kind of causality, but the Real of an indigestible traumatic encounter, of an enigma that resists symbolization." Moreover, in this Real lies the "very condition" of freedom. When the Other's enigmatic message, "a signifier without signified" (58–59), captivates and "derails the subject's *automaton*," it thereby "opens up a gap which the subject is free to fill in with his (ultimately failed) endeavours to symbolize it." Thus, concludes Žižek, "Freedom is ultimately *nothing but* the space opened up by the traumatic encounter," a space now open to significations that the subject attempts to fill, albeit by "translations" always "contingent" and "inadequate" (58).

On the analogy Žižek sets up between conversion and the subject's receiving the traumatic irruption of the signifier, the deadening illusions of ordinary, "pathological," life are situated on the side of the mother's enigmatic desire (think: There's only one, Mother.), the "new" life after conversion on the side of the father's answer. Rather than a mere intrusion between the mother and the subject, between the mother's desire and the subject's *Che vuoi?*, "[W]hat does she really want, above and beyond *me*, since I am obviously not enough for her?" "father" is precisely the Lacanian answer, "the *symbolization* of the deadlock of the mother's desire" (60). In effect, therefore, in terms of Žižek's basic analogy, the answer, "Father," returns us to the ultimate mystery of belief, the very fragility of the Absolute. In *The Fragile Absolute*, Žižek says that when "we abandon the fantasmatic Otherness which makes life in constrained social reality bearable, we catch a glimpse of Another Space which can no longer be dismissed as a fantasmatic supplement to social reality" (159). In this "effect of the sublime at its purest," in this "momentary suspension of meaning which elevates the subject into another dimension" (158), in this very "dimension of Otherness," we surrender to that "magic moment when," "in all its fragility," "the *Absolute appears*" (159).

6

Life is not merely life. Life is always accompanied by a certain excess; something for which one can put at stake life itself.
— Slavoj Žižek, *Conversations with Žižek*, 107

Since the late 1990s, Žižek has begun to learn that superstardom brings its downside. For much of a decade after 1989's *Sublime Object of Ideology*, Žižek was simply the favorite pony for many who rode Lacan. But when it became plain that Žižek might be something more than a guide to Lacan and might be worthy of consideration as a theorist in his own right, critics began to contest his views. Early expositors of Žižek's rapidly growing *oeuvre* (such as Boynton, Eagleton, and Santner) were more fans than critics. As the fame grew, critics began to challenge Žižek on many fronts—aesthetic, linguistic, political, sociological, psychoanalytic. One of the earliest critics, Denise Gigante (1998), argues that Žižek "has no position" and is instead merely a "critical subject" in progress (153). "Žižek's effort to develop a critical argument," she suggests, "demonstrates the dialectic of critical self-creation" (156). Publication of *Contingency, Hegemony, Universality* (Butler et al.) in 2000, where Žižek debates Judith Butler and Ernesto Laclau, seems to have paved the way for several others to challenge him as well. In 2001, the journal *Paragraph* devoted an entire issue to Žižek, and in 2002 *JAC: Journal of Advanced Composition* devoted much of an issue to him after a controversial interview with Gary Olson and Lynn Worsham in a 2001 issue. The articles in *Paragraph* are largely positive. Edmond Wright extols Žižek for having used "Lacan's concept of the Real" to bring "psychoanalysis to bear on fields traditionally kept apart" (5). Jason Glynos argues that Žižek's Lacanian psychoanalytic joins very effectively with Marxian analysis to critique Global Capital and its deleterious effects on postmodern subjectivity. But several authors take Žižek to task for either being wrong on some subject (Flieger, on Žižek's take on cyberspace; Grigg, on Žižek's reading of Antigone's act) or for merely exercising no more than a personal fantasy in performing his ideological critiques. On this latter, Bran Nicol, somewhat like Gigante, suggests that Žižek's standard interpretive "mechanism" may simply be "the fundamental fantasy" at his core "supporting his very identity as a theorist." It is, Nicol says, "as if Žižek imagines he need give us just one more example of the traumatic encounter with the real and the dominance of the Big Other will be exposed and overthrown" (152–53).

Unwisely, but typically, Žižek compromised his credibility in that interview with Olson and Worsham when he again admitted (as three years previously in Boynton) that, quite cavalierly, he sometimes writes on films he has not seen. Although he found support in Peter McLaren—who, like Glynos, sees a Marxian Žižek—and Thomas Rickert, several critics jumped on Žižek for that interview. Largely disregarding a braggadocio clearly meant to shock American academics, these critics aimed at the rhetoric and views—aesthetic or epistemological, social or political or economic. On the rhetoric, Jeffrey Nealon

writes, "I wonder about the work done by a psychoanalytic emphasis
on paradox when it comes to engaging what Žižek identifies as the *real*
target of his intervention: economics" (601). On politics and aesthetics,
Robert Miklitsch (who had already taken Žižek's politics to task in
"Going through the Fantasy") suggests "that the sort of problems that
beset Žižek's politics also plague his theory of aesthetics and that part
of this problem, a very big part, is a direct result—as in his critique of
ideology—of his chronically negative, restrictive conception of fantasy"
("Passing" 606–07). On his Hegelianism, Robert Samuels, who also is
very perceptive, and rather acerbic, on Žižek's rhetorical mechanisms,
writes, "One of the main reasons for his theoretical blindness is that he
is locked into a modernist Hegelian conception of universality that
threatens to transform his entire corpus into a self-consuming rhetorical
machine" (331).

Apart from applications of Marxian political economy, Hegelian
dialectics, or Lacanian concepts to a relatively confined number of
topics, usually featuring either politics, psychoanalysis, or aspects of
popular culture, and apart from the wit, jokes, and aim to entertain,
many asked, what is Žižek *about?* Who does he want to be when he
grows up? Essentially, this is a question not of mere views but of beliefs
or convictions. Does Žižek have firm convictions on subjects, or does
he simply indulge himself in outrageous contradictions and play the
shell game of paradox? Sarah Kay argues that everything Žižek writes,
operating typically, as Edmond Wright suggests, from his fascination
with the Lacanian Real, devolves to a political agenda to change the
world. That may be true, but it is not always apparent to readers or
audiences to his public appearances. One answer to this question of
beliefs connects to one raised by Rebecca Mead, that is, whether Žižek
might attract disciples. If he attracts them, what is it about his work
that followers may hang on to? Is it the politics of a steely-eyed revolutionary, or, what he often appears to be, a highly skilled cultural critic
who has no concrete agenda apart from critique itself. Or, the better
question may be, is he trying to persuade to action or to understanding? Is he more like Lenin or more like Lacan? Lenin wanted to change
the world; Lacan, as far as I can tell, did not; Lacan wanted to add to
our fund of truth and knowledge. If Žižek were Hegel, would he be the
Hegel whose followers took up his philosophy or the Hegel whose followers took up his dialectical method? You want philosophy or
method? As Žižek might say, Yes, please. In his philosophy of paradox,
content and method are essentially the same (and the same may be said
of Hegel as well). It is clear to me that, contra Mead, Žižek has disciples (a quick online search of the MLA International Bibliography

attests to that), but his followers are cultural critics, not social revolutionaries. Many are as disturbed by recent trends in global politics and economics as Žižek himself, but they are not going to find in his work an articulated plan for structural change. Still, it is worthwhile to examine where he has come from and where, perhaps, he is headed.

It is quite plain that Žižek has staked his career on oppositional stances rather than a platform or methodology, whether Marxist, Hegelian, Lacanian, Hegelian-Marxist-Lacanian. Early in his career, his stance was largely what he called "Humanist Marxism" (*Conversations* 24), then, he says, he "passed to Heidegger" (25), going from there to French structuralist thought, before settling on Lacanian psychoanalysis by the late 1970s (28). While most of his books have been published in series that set themselves overtly in opposition to dominant political or economic ideologies, namely, western liberalism and global capitalism, the trajectory of stances taken in these series, at least as evidenced by their credos, moves progressively away from a specifically Marxist position (albeit of the "humanist" strain) to one more generically oppositional. His overt comments always suggest that he holds on to his socialist position, but more and more it seems to be modulated by idealist philosophy and Lacanian psychoanalysis. Early on, he published in a series called Phronesis devoted to leftist politics. His *Sublime Object of Ideology* (1989) appeared there, as well as the triply coauthored *Contingency, Hegemony, Universality* (2000), in which Žižek debated those titular topics with Judith Butler and Ernesto Laclau. Of Phronesis, series editors Laclau and Chantal Mouffe attest a desire for "reformulation of the socialist ideal." "Our objective is to establish a dialogue between [... various] theoretical developments and left-wing politics. We believe that an anti-essentialist theoretical stand is the sine qua non of a new vision for the Left conceived in terms of a radical and plural democracy" (*The Sublime Object of Ideology* ii).

In publishers' series under his own editorial control (there are, at last count, three of them), Žižek gradually modulates his oppositional stance toward, simply, opposition itself, a kind of ecumenical opposition that now embraces religion as much as philosophy and political economy. In the earliest series, Žižek turns his position just enough to link psychoanalysis as an equal to Marxist political economics. In this series, Wo Es War, Žižek has published, among others, Alenka Zupančič's *Ethics of the Real* and seven of his own: *The Metastases of Enjoyment* (1994), *The Indivisible Remainder* (1996), *The Plague of Fantasies* (1997), *The Ticklish Subject* (1999), *The Fragile Absolute* (2000), *Did Somebody Say Totalitarianism?* (2001), and *Iraq: The Borrowed Kettle* (2004). Taking his title for the series from Freud's

"Wo es war, soll ich werden," sometimes translated as "Where id was, so shall I be," Žižek translates it as "Where it was, I shall come into being." In his own oppositional analysis of subjectivity's dark side, Freud's id, Lacan, especially in "The Freudian Thing" and "The Agency [or "Instance"] of the Letter" (both in *Ecrits: A Selection*) had made much of Freud's saying. Žižek, in his editorial credo, appearing in *The Metastases of Enjoyment*, suggests how the series will reveal and examine the dark side, the id, or it or traumatic "thing," beneath contemporary global culture. He asks whether, today, within late capitalism, it remains possible to pursue "knowledge as liberation." "If 'it' today is the twin rule of pragmatic-relativist New Sophists and New Age obscurantists, what 'shall come into being' in its place?" His answer is a projected series of books using Marx and Lacan. "The premise of the series is that the explosive combination of Lacanian psychoanalysis and Marxist tradition detonates a dynamic freedom that enables us to question the very presuppositions of the circuit of Capital" (ii). In his newest series, Short Circuits, Žižek enunciates a credo that has become quite generically oppositional, one reflecting, perhaps, his emergent role as the oppositional critic of our time. In this one he has published his *Puppet and the Dwarf* (2003) and Zupančč's *Shortest Shadow: Nietzsche's Philosophy of the Two*. Short Circuits, he tells us in "Series Foreword," in *The Puppet and the Dwarf*, "intends to revive a practice of reading which confronts a classic text, author, or notion with its own hidden presuppositions, and thus reveals its disavowed truth. [...] After reading a book in this series, the reader should not simply have learned something new: the point is, rather, to make him or her aware of another—disturbing—side of something he or she knew all the time" (viii). In other words, nowadays, Žižek's interest lies in revealing "hidden presuppositions" and "disavowed" truths, whatever they might be or wherever they might lead. It is opposition itself that drives such analysis, not any revelation of specific ideological positions, Marxist, Lacanian, or otherwise.

One may argue that this position remains stylistic or perspectival. So, apart from a style or perspective or his status as a Hegelian-Marxist-Lacanian, what is there to consider adopting of Žižek's work? That Žižek has become a theorist apart from Lacan (and Hegel and Marx) is suggested, if not confirmed, in that he himself is now the subject of books and issues of journals. Perhaps more important, he now even has two readers devoted to his work, edited not by him but by others. The later of the two, *Interrogating the Real* (2005), edited by Rex Butler and Scott Stephens, brings together early writings, others associated with and preceding several of his major books, and still others focusing on the issue of ideology. But the earlier one seems to have been more important to Žižek's self reflection. It turns out that when Žižek was asked by the editors of *The Žižek Reader* to provide a preface for the book, writing it became a time for taking stock that seems to have become a turning point in his career. Žižek wrote the preface in April 1998, and *The Žižek Reader* appeared in 1999. In the preface, in another credo or manifesto of sorts, Žižek tells us what he is about. "So here I am today," he says. In the first place, he tells us what he is not: he is not a deconstructionist, a cognitive scientist, a Frankfurt school or Heideggerian phenomenologist, nor does he mean to be a new historicist or a New Age obscurantist—though he is often regarded as any or even all of these. Rather, though he clearly has not always made this plain, it is against these that he consciously opposes himself. In several categories of thought, he identifies precisely what he is against and what he is for. As we would predict, his own position is defined by its oppositions. In political economy, for instance, he defines his position in opposition to another commonplace, a view of Marxism that says "if one is to save its legacy, one has to renounce its crude 'economic essentialism,'" including such issues as class struggle, the proletariat, socialist revolution, and the like, "and maintain just the empty messianic emancipatory promise." In this view, "the new social order should not be 'ontologized,' but should remain an elusive democracy *à venir*." In other words, do not expect any actual social changes to be made real. Against this standard argument, Žižek contends that, "*mutatis mutandis*," there must be "a return to the centrality of the Marxist critique of political economy." Indeed, he believes that "the proliferation of the new forms of postmodern political agents" runs precisely counter to the standard position regarding capitalism, a "tacit acceptance" that "global capitalism" has become "the only game in town." Likewise, in politics, Žižek defines himself against the common view that "the Stalinist terror should teach us how idealism and cruelty are two sides of the same coin" and thus prompt us to abandon pursuit of "the ideal of a better society" because it leads to "extreme violence." For his part, advocating a version of the old omelette theory of social change (You can't make an omelette without breaking a few eggs), he contends that terror, though it must be a "good terror," and radical politics are necessarily wedded. We must persist, he says, despite "the horrible experience of the Stalinist terror," in "our search for a 'good terror' as the key ingredient of any truly radical politics." Indeed, he insists, "there is no effective freedom without 'terror'—that is, without some form of the unconditional pressure that threatens the very core of our being" (ix).

For one who has followed Žižek's career, his views on politics and political economy, however oppositional to commonplace arguments, are still perhaps rather predictable. The more these things change, the more they remain the same. But that makes what he "stands for" seem less predictable or, to some, even evident at all. In that *New Yorker* profile of him, Mead tells how audience members at one of his lectures keep asking him what he believes in, and she is prompted to suggest that he has no disciples because he has no clear-cut position. "Such a thing would be impossible," she says, "since one of the characteristics of Žižek's work is that he applies his critical methodology even to the results of his own critical inquiry, which is another way of saying that he contradicts himself all the time" (39). Žižek, in his conversations with Glyn Daly, indicates he is aware of the criticism. But rather than seeing the self-contradiction as a problem, he sees it as his very method, "a dialectical movement in [his] work" he likens to how Lacan keeps coming back to an example or a story and gnawing it for every last intellectual morsel (43). Žižek's self-contradictions emerge from a constant effort to squeeze some ultimate meaning from a joke, a cultural feature, or a Lacanian insight. He tells Daly that "some of my readers, I know, get annoyed, that some of my books may appear repetitive" (44). Though he tells Daly, "I believe in clear-cut positions," and says, "I think that the only way to be honest and to expose yourself to criticism is to state clearly and dogmatically where you are. You must take the risk and have a position," it is precisely for the absence of clear-cut positions that his critics fault him (45).

Indeed, that repetitiveness emanating from his dialectical self-critique often yields little but confusing differences. What is he saying today? So our determining what Žižek is about often means hitting a moving target. For instance, lately, he has begun to change his views on several Lacanian topoi, in particular the father (once "always" two, now three), the Real, *objet petit a*, and the death drive. Regarding one of these topics, in an author's preface to *Interrogating the Real*, Žižek avers that "my entire work circulates around [the] gap that separates the One from itself, for which the Lacanian designation is the Real" (10). On the Real, however, as Nicol shows, his views have gone far beyond any specific Lacanian enunciation. For Žižek, now, Lacan's triad of Real, Symbolic, Imaginary has produced a triad cubed, what amounts to a nine-box matrix producing an Imaginary Real, a Symbolic Real, and a Real Real, as well as an Imaginary Imaginary, a Symbolic Imaginary, and a Real Imaginary. Und so weiter. "The point is," he tells Daly, "that these three notions—real, imaginary, and symbolic—are intertwined in a radical sense; like a crystal structure in which the different elements are mapped onto and repeat themselves within each category" (69). This triadic triad may have become Žižek's basic, zero-level position, and I now suspect that apart from everything else that makes Žižek interesting and influential, this grid—expressing Žižek's debt to all those textual traces in Lacan—may become the most useful methodological tool in Žižek's kit.

Yes, Žižek does, as he claims, state positions dogmatically, but what is dogma at one moment, in one book, is dog meat in the next. Still, there is a core of belief, things "to die for," expressed in his work, and the ones that would seem most important to him these days, judging from the subjects of his books, pertain to philosophy, political economy, and, as previous discussion of Christianity indicates, religion. Naturally, his positions on these do not necessarily mesh, either each with the other or each one within itself. Given his Marxist education (it was only an education, for he tells Daly [31] that he was never exactly a Marxist and suffered four years of unemployment in the early 1970s for that failing), that he takes religion seriously at all might have seemed peculiar until recently. As to philosophy, since Žižek earned a PhD in that discipline and wrote a dissertation on Heidegger, it is not unexpected that he would write on philosophers and philosophical topics. What seems unpredictable, given his allegiance to Lacanian theory, is the view he takes. Here, too, he defines himself against a "commonplace," a contemporary view "that transcendental subjectivity is *passé*." According to this view, if we are to reassert "the notion of the subject," he says in the preface to *The Žižek Reader*, we must both "displace it" from "the standard Cartesian *cogito*" (viii) and regard "the new subject" as "divided, finite," as "a subject 'thrown' into a non-transparent, contingent life-world" (viii–ix). Although this all sounds essentially Heideggerian, it is against such a view, contends Žižek, that he stands. Instead, his "work relies on the full acceptance of the notion of modern subjectivity elaborated by the great German Idealists from Kant to Hegel." It is this tradition, he suggests, that provides an "unsurpassable horizon of our philosophical experience." Indeed, he claims, "the core of [his] entire work is the endeavour to use Lacan as a privileged intellectual tool to reactualize German Idealism." From that Lacanian perspective, he regards "the celebrated postmodern 'displacement' of subjectivity" as little more than an "unreadiness to come to terms with the truly traumatic core of the modern subject" (ix)—not that it is displaced but that it is founded on a void.

As on Christianity in particular, his position on religion in general is a sign of a break between one phase and another of his work. Religious themes have become extremely important since he composed that preface to the *Reader*. There, as always, he defines himself on religion against a commonplace view. This view holds that "if some form of religion is to survive, it has to abandon its direct ontological claims, and turn to the respect and veneration of a kind of vacuous Otherness *à la* Levinas" ("Preface" ix). There is not really a God, but let us nonetheless respect "Otherness." This is the sort of view, he suggests to Mead, that prompts people to react in horror whenever some religious shrine of an Other is attacked. "I was almost on the Taliban's side," he says, "when they were bombing the Bamian statues—everyone was so outraged but was also saying, 'Oh, but we don't really believe'" (40). Against such contradictions, Žižek contends that what is "theoretically and politically engaging in the religious legacy is not the abstract messianic promise of some redemptive Otherness, but, on the contrary, a religion in its properly dogmatic and institutional aspect" ("Preface" ix). In this regard, although he insists "I am an absolute materialist," he tells Daly, "I try to isolate a certain emancipatory kernel of religion." But that "kernel" ostensibly is political, not religious. His biblical touchstone is the story of Job, but it is a Job whose suffering demonstrates not Job's but God's failure, "the Father's impotence" (*Conversations* 162). In a typical paradox, though, it is this lesson of impotence that Žižek carries into global politics. Job's lesson, he says, is "the zero level of the critique of ideology" (161), the absolute initiating premise with which critique must begin, for Job teaches that a situation is not the result of fate or destiny, but is historically contingent and therefore can be changed. When "people are suffering" because a multinational company "restructures," we are not compelled to accept their suffering as "a temporary problem in the great scheme of things and that soon life will be better." Rather, rejecting the economist's God, the "invisible hand of the Market," we must take Job's position and reject "any necessity or fatalism" (162).

If it is Žižek's philosophy of paradox that sets him apart from—or beyond—Lacan, the big question now is whether beyond paradox there is a Žižek. Early Žižek or late, neither will resolve the problems in his work found by those critics who want a concrete political platform or a course of action, a critical methodology beyond a philosophy of paradox. What he brings to the game, always, is a stance oppositional to the status quo and a mode of analysis that, without proposing courses of action as such, locates its fault lines. In this respect, early Žižek is not really different from late, the difference perhaps simply subject matter. In early, he takes German idealism, literature and film, and aspects of popular culture as topical occasions within which he displays his adroit exploitation of paradoxes ostensibly rooted in Lacan. In late,

Žižek often trades German philosophy for Christianity and otherwise focuses more on international politics than on film, literature, or popular culture. But despite all the subtlety and apparent conviction with which Žižek analyzes a Christian thematics, our late Žižek still typically refuses to tell us how to fix the world (other than getting rid of capitalism) or to be pinned to any specific position more stable than paradox. There may be something more personal than paradox in enigma or mystery in late Žižek, but in fact they remain . . . paradoxes. We see this when he says, "If I were asked to provide a one-line description of where I stand, I would probably choose the paradoxical self-designation of a *Paulinian materialist*" ("Preface" ix). When he refers to a "legacy" in both dialectical materialism and Christianity, he means to endorse how each of these ideologies locates agendas for social change in concrete institutions. Nonetheless, when in *The Puppet and the Dwarf* he says that "to become a true dialectical materialist, one should go through the Christian experience" (6), we just do not know what going "through" may mean.

An unintended result of Jason Glynos's critique of Žižek's Marxian political economics is to suggest just how fundamentally paradoxical is Žižek's philosophy. Paradox, in effect, is a black hole with no exit: everything enters, and nothing returns. To conclude, Glynos suggests that Žižek's view of history is essentially that of Alexander Kojève "as applied to the field of subjectivity." Such a view is based on a premise of cuts or ruptures or mutations separating one historical moment from a succeeding one. Žižek's call for a subjectivity founded on drive, as opposed to the oedipal one based on desire that, in his view, fuels the subjectivity underlying capitalism itself, requires such a cut. "Žižek's anti-capitalism, then," writes Glynos, "amounts to nothing short of a call to another fundamental mutation in human subjectivity corresponding to the passage through fantasy and entailing an ethical stance that is adequate to the task" (100). An ethics of the drive—beyond desire, perhaps beyond Lacan—would simply do away with capitalism by removing the convective power of desire to fuel it. But for those—critics or followers alike—who want Žižek to represent concretely such a future, beyond Oedipus and capitalism both, the trap set by such a view of history and the subject is simple: no such representation is possible. "Thus, his aim is a purely negative one: he cannot offer up a concrete vision of what such a regime would look like, only what it would *not* look like." In effect, Žižek leaves us all waiting for the apocalypse. Whereas "the spontaneous formation of the Paris commune can be seen as a model for Marx's communism," says Glynos, there is no such model available yet for a future beyond desire and the postmodern subject for which Žižek calls. Instead, Glynos admits, in "our passage through the fundamental fantasy of capitalism," all we can do is "await the spontaneous invention of new models of socio-political arrangement" (101). But, like others of Žižek's critics, Glynos does finally suggest that someone, presumably Žižek most of all, needs to articulate, if not "an account of what will follow in concrete and predictive detail," at least "a precise, even if speculative, *theoretical* account of what the possible modalities of a subject of the drive might be at the *social* level." More than that, Žižek needs to address as well whether it is even possible to have "a *social* subject of the drive" (103). If there is one, it certainly is not Lacanian.

What Glynos implies is that Žižek leaves us with no more than this: "I don't know what it will be, but I'll know it when I see it." Boynton, in fact, writes that "as philosophy, Žižek's argument is breathtaking, but as social prescription, 'dream' may be an apt word" (69). Thus, if our sole interest in Žižek lies in political economy, then we are left not with a program but with a dream, an ineffable vision, one emanating lately from that admixture of Marx, Hegel, and Lacan. Oh, and Christ.[10] In his review of *Conversations with Žižek*, Vincent Deary, effectively renaming Žižek's Paulinian materialism, calls his ideology "a kind of transcendent materialism," and he sees in its very paradoxical fusions perhaps a new hope for philosophy if not for political reality. On the one hand, says Deary, "His vision is a compelling and, as befits this heir to German idealism, a romantic one. Human freedom and dignity are snatched from the teeth of materialist reductions, the virtues of courage and fidelity are asserted in the face of awful contingency." On the other, he concludes, "at the heart of this 'materialist' system lies something profoundly odd: an indescribable nothing that is simultaneously the subject's 'real core' and the ineffable beyond of the phenomenal world; a nothing that can never be described, only evoked by its predicates; the immaterial font of freedom."[11] In Deary's view, by his fusion of philosophy and "Judaeo-Christian mystical theology," "Žižek has put the Soul back into philosophy." Paradox, enigma, mystery: in the philosophy they give Žižek, they do not permit him a description of a new world order, but perhaps they will make him the beyond of Lacan.

Notes

Chapter 2. Which Lacan?

1. Whether Lacan intends to associate Antigone with desire or *jouissance* is in some dispute. My view ("The *Other* Desire"), different from Žižek's, is that even in *The Ethics* Lacan regards her as motivated by drive and thus *jouissance*—the "other" desire. Like Žižek, at least in his discussion of *The Ethics*, Frances L. Restuccia, in an exchange of letters with me through the Forum section of *PMLA* following the publication of my "Lacan and the New Lacanians," places Antigone on the side of desire. As Žižek also seems on occasions to suggest, Lacan was still in the process of making the shift from early to late theory even as he wrote of Antigone in *The Ethics*.

Chapter 3. *Invisible Man*: The Textual Unconscious and a Subject beyond History

1. Lacan discusses *aphanisis*, the fading or disappearance of the subject, in successive chapters—"The Subject and the Other: Alienation" (203–15) and "The Subject and the Other: Aphanisis" (216–29)—in *The Four Fundamental Concepts*. For more on the concept and a more extensive application of it, see my essay on the concept in Salinger's *Catcher in the Rye*.

2. These images are especially important to the young, because in the specular, presumably imitable icon, they suggest the possibility of psychical and physical wholeness. Such images, frequently, appear in the posters of athletes, rock stars, film actors, and the like that young people exhibit on the intimately symbolic space of their bedroom walls.

3. History is one of the most frequently discussed aspects of *Invisible Man*, but ordinarily the term refers to history as represented in one way or

another in the novel—to, in some sense, the novel as a historical novel. To get some idea just how significant is this feature in the novel, see, for example, Bone, Callahan, Finholt, Fischer, Foley (2), Henderson, Hull, Kostelanetz, Margolies, Moses, Reilly (2), Spillers, and Turner. Ellison himself has frequently commented on history in a variety of significations; see, for example, several essays in *Going to the Territory* and *Shadow and Act*, as well as "Society, Morality, and the Novel," "The Uses of History in Fiction," and the interview with him in John O'Brien, *Interviews with Black Writers*. Though not in Lacanian terms, on those novels by Styron, Bellow, and Updike, I give a sense of the philosophical thematics of history in several essays: see "This Unquiet Dust: The Problem of History in Styron's *The Confessions of Nat Turner*," "Consciousness Fills the Void: Herzog, History, and the Hero in the Modern World," and "The Novel as Lyric Elegy: The Mode of Updike's *The Centaur*." The quintessentially modernist *belles lettres* exploration of concepts of history is probably Henry Adams's *Education of Henry Adams*; on it, see my "Problem of Knowledge and *The Education of Henry Adams*." For an excellent discussion of the reflexiveness of book and reality in relation to history as well, see Gabriel Josipovici's *World and the Book*.

Chapter 4. *Méconnaissance*: "Saint" Flannery, Sexuality, and the Culture of Psychoanalysis

1. I need to address both psychoanalysis and fundamentalist Christianity within Williams's terms. Whereas psychoanalysis was a dominant ideology during O'Connor's lifetime, by the 1980s it was no longer. "In the years following World War II," writes Steven Marcus, "psychoanalysis was much closer to the centers of active, intellectual and cultural life in America than it appears to be now; psychoanalysis was a much more important, relevant, and momentous presence in the lives of those people who as groups constitute the intellectual and cultural professions in our society than it can claim to be at this moment" (256). The case is likewise for fundamentalist Christianity. While surely fundamentalist religion was in some sense dominant in the South throughout O'Connor's career, it was no longer dominant among intellectuals. Whereas during O'Connor's time, the split occurred between "mass" culture and "intellectual" culture, it occurs today between mass and media cultures. The case is oddly reversed for psychoanalysis today, where it probably has more purchase among media intellectuals than it has in the mass culture that embraced it in the 1920s, 1930s, and 1940s. Splits like these exhibit one problem cultural critics have discovered in using Williams's otherwise immensely useful terms.

2. According to Arthur F. Kinney (86), O'Connor owned and initialed "FOC" a copy of Freud's *Basic Writings of Sigmund Freud* as early as 1947, five years before publication of *Wise Blood*. She also owned Jung's *Modern Man in Search of a Soul*, but the copy in her personal library was a 1957

reprint of the 1933 edition. Since she mentioned the book by title to a correspondent as early as September 1955, one assumes she knew the 1933 edition perhaps even before completion of *Wise Blood*.

Chapter 5. The Forced Choice: *Le Père ou Pire* in Glaspell's "Jury of Her Peers"

1. As is well known, the story began as a one-act play titled *Trifles* Glaspell wrote for the Provincetown Players, then only recently formed by her and her husband, George Cram Cook, and eventually was made famous by the works of a young playwright named Eugene O'Neill. In the initial performance on 8 August 1916, Cook played a minor role as a neighboring farmer, and Glaspell herself played the role of one of the two lead characters, Mrs. Hale. It is through Hale's subjectivity that the story is largely represented. Play and story are very close; the latter generally (though not merely) transforms stage directions into narrative elements. Worth a study in itself, this transformation is vital to any reading of the story (see Mustazza's "Generic Translation"). Whereas an audience to a play might be forced to "read" signs in intonation and gesture, Glaspell must transform those same signs into actual language in the story's version. Critical to any Lacanian reading, this language makes themes overt that might well be masked in the dramatic version (see Worthen 53). Quite properly—as we see in, for example, Alkalay-Gut's "Jury" and "Murder," Ben-Zvi's "Murder," Fetterley, Hedges, Mael, Makowsky, and Smith—many have read most of those themes within feminist terms.

2. As a young woman, Glaspell worked as a journalist. At the age of twenty-four and for much of a year after December 1900, she covered for the *Des Moines Daily News* a sensational murder and the subsequent trial. The murdered man was an elderly farmer named John Hossack, killed by blows of an ax while he slept in his bed. Charged with the murder, his wife claimed to be asleep beside him and not to have known what went on. Eventually, Margaret Hossack was convicted of the crime, but she was ultimately freed on appeal, tried a second time, and later released when the jury hung on the decision and the state decided against a third trial. For a recent popular account of the Hossack murder, the trial, and its social implications, see also Bryan and Wolf's *Midnight Assassin*.

3. Melanie Klein and Julia Kristeva notwithstanding, psychoanalysis must assume that subjects valorizing the Imaginary and the hegemony of the ideal ego (Idealich) found in the (M)other are always regressive and potentially pathological. But since in his theory of the subject Lacan advances a structural description more than a developmental story, we must regard all stories that focus on a subject dominated by either the Imaginary or the Symbolic as merely moments in the subject's long history of desire, a desire that Lacan as well as Klein and Kristeva recognizes as founded on the mother, lying in the Imaginary,

and situated within narcissism. That is, in the history of any subject, the desire that drives him or her must inevitably be conditioned within social and economic contexts that will constitute desire in one way or another. Because these contexts may construct one "moment" (oedipal or narcissistic) as more imperative than another, subjects may—and do—change over time as they are affected by what Lacan calls the "dialectic of desire." Although perhaps too simplistic for analyzing any given complex situation, it is always for analysis a matter of Oedipus or Narcissus. But, even so, at any moment it is not necessarily always the one or the other.

4. In Lacan, the signifier of the Father—and variations Lacan calls the "Law," the "Law of the Father," the "Name of the Father," and, most redundantly, the "Law of the Name of the Father"—is the Phallus. There is no good way to avoid the much-deserved—not merely feminist—opprobrium directed toward the term. Not even the term *castration* draws as much hostility. One suspects that if Lacan had avoided use of *phallus* few feminists (or anyone else, for that matter) would much object to his theory. It is plain to any serious Lacanian that Lacan does not endorse the phallocentrism of patriarchal culture. He merely describes it, its effects upon subjects, and its role in psychoanalysis. Though clearly not a gender neutral term, the Phallus in Lacanian theory may "belong" to male or female, father or mother. Indeed, perhaps the most interesting discussions of the Phallus virtually always involve the phallic mother, not the phallic father. For some of these terms, Julia Kristeva offers a substitute that may be less offensive to those of us whose consciousnesses have been opened by feminist thought. Not at all negative like the phallic father, Kristeva's is "the father of individual prehistory." In Christianity, this father may also be identified with *agapé*. Could we rename the Phallus *agapé*? Probably not, but clearly the Phallus in Lacan is what Derrida objects to as a transcendental signifier. See Kristeva, *Revolution in Poetic Language* and *Powers of Horror*. On Kristeva, see Lechte 141. For further discussion, see also Parveen Adams, "Representation and Sexuality." On "Phallus," see also Evans, *An Introductory Dictionary of Lacanian Psychoanalysis*. For brief essays by several authors on a series of terms, including *phallic mother, phallogocentrism, phallus: definitions*, and *phallus: feminist implications*, see Wright, *Feminism and Psychoanalysis*.

5. Critiquing Žižek's take on the choices in the forced choice, Henry Krips distinguishes between one choice that is prudent, the other that is truly ethical. In these terms, Glaspell's two women split the difference and make a choice that seems prudently ethical, or is it ethically prudent?

Chapter 7. Hart's *Damage*, Lacanian Tragedy, and the Ethics of *Jouissance*

1. Whereas MacCannell focuses her main thesis on the dyad of brother and brother, she also suggests that the postoedipal family replacing the traditional

family of father, mother, and child is the dyad of brother and sister. But in what MacCannell calls "the primal scene of modernity," the brother discovers his castration in the sister and then both "suppresses his sister's specific desire [...] for equal access to identity" and seizes power by relegating her to "a general brotherhood" that, "because she is the [...] sole real basis of [his] identity," demotes her to "no special place" (26). Assuming the role of the "pseudo-oedipal father," the brother becomes just another tyrant and, in effacing the sister, repeats patriarchy's effacement of the mother. From a wide-ranging consideration of modern texts, MacCannell judges that it "is far less the father than the brother [whom] modern literature calls to account; less the mother than the sister who must be recognized and given her due as the real rather than the imaginary 'other' necessary to found male identity and group life" (39).

Chapter 8. Beyond Lacan: Slavoj Žižek, Things to Die for, and a Philosophy of Paradox

1. Apart from merely repeating ideas, themes, and subject matter, Žižek also simply recycles material. "Sometimes," Sarah Kay writes, "whole passages are repeated from one book to another. About 30 per cent of *The Abyss of Freedom* is lifted verbatim from *The Indivisible Remainder*, and there are extensive overlaps between *The Fragile Absolute* and *The Art of the Ridiculous Sublime*" (173n2).

2. Žižek is an astute, and effective, self-promoter, but the truth is he need provide little impetus to his burgeoning fame. A wonderfully articulate conversationalist whose speech seems little different in style or content from his writings, Žižek is often interviewed and willingly engages in dialogue with his critics. In *Diacritics*, for instance, he engages in a sharp exchange with Claudia Breger; her "Leader's Two Bodies" attacks Žižek's political stance, Žižek counters ("Response to Claudia Breger"), and Breger responds to the response ("The Rhetorics of Power"). Most famously, Žižek debates Judith Butler and Ernesto Laclau on the titular topics of *Contingency, Hegemony, Universality: Contemporary Dialogues on the Left*. See *Conversations with Žižek* (2004) for a series of interviews and exchanges between Glyn Daly and Žižek. As for Žižek as a subject of scholarly analysis, there are numerous articles (see, for instance, Dean; Daly, "Politics and the Impossible"; Eagleton; Gigante; Harpham; Johnston; Krips; Layton; Restuccia, "Impossible Love"; and Santner); there are as well at least four books devoted to him: Rex Butler's *Slavoj Žižek: Live Theory*, Kay's *Žižek: A Critical Introduction*, McLaren's *Slavoj Žižek's Naked Politics*, and Tony Myers's *Slavoj Žižek*. Several other books are known to be in the works. In addition, *Paragraph: A Journal of Modern Critical Theory* has devoted an issue (24.2, 2001) to "A Symposium on Slavoj Žižek: Faith and the Real."

3. McLaren, for instance, always assumes Žižek is essentially a Marxist, with Lacanian theory largely only an effective tool of social analysis. Gustavo

Guerra connects Žižek to William James and pragmatism. John Holbo calls him a "Leninist-Kierkegaardian." He's called "Hegelian" in the interview with Eric Dean Rasmussen. Often with tongue in cheek, Žižek uses a variety of terms—*cyber-communist* and *Paulinian materialist*, among them—for himself.

4. Jeffrey Nealon directly addresses paradox as more than rhetoric in Žižek. In "Ideology and Its Paradoxes," Daly uses it for analysis. In a form of rhetorical mimicry, many pick up some of Žižek's stylistic mannerisms, including use of paradox. In Žižek, the paradox of paradox is that it is so pervasive it becomes an environment of which we are often oblivious. Sarah Kay, for instance, offers a glossary of "Žižekian" terms as do the editors of *Interrogating the Real*, but neither one includes paradox as one of them. While Kay does not suppress the roots of Žižek's terminology in either Lacan or Hegel, in effect she does suppress paradox, no doubt only as a result of paradox's being the ground of Žižek's philosophy. Indeed, in the texts of Žižek Kay cites for her explanations, versions of the term *paradox* operate determinatively in most of them. In Žižek, as Nealon observes, paradox does all the work.

5. Several critics—Eagleton, Gigante, Harpham, Nicol, Samuels—have offered views of a "Žižekian" rhetoric. Nicol says that "typically Žižek will introduce an object of attention (a philosophical idea, a social event, a film), tell us how it is usually interpreted, then bring it all into focus with an expert adjustment of the lens until suddenly we are 'looking awry' at the object. Then he explains that in fact this is nothing other than a precise exemplification of this or that process in Lacan" (140). On a metadiscursive rhetoric in Žižek, one labeled a "mechanical program," Samuels argues that "the vast majority of his arguments follow the same four-part logical structure: he begins by paraphrasing the 'common' or 'standard' academic understanding of a certain problem; he then shows that our understanding of the original problem is wrong and that Lacanian theory or Hegelian dialectics can provide the true interpretation; he next turns to the realm of popular culture and/or everyday experience to provide proof for his interpretation; and he then returns to a combination of Hegelian philosophy and Lacanian theory to make a universalizing claim about the original problem. In fact, this final stage of his rhetorical strategy often presents a notion of universal negativity and meaninglessness, which acts to absorb all of the previous stages into a globalizing and self-negating argument" (335–36). With both asperity and irony, Samuels examines this program in detail. One surmises that if Žižek were to pay more attention to the politics and economics of the academic profession in America, Samuels would find more to endorse in that program.

6. So far as I am aware, other than Wright and Wright, faintly, in *The Žižek Reader*, only Harpham—and perhaps Johnston—notes anything like phases in Žižek's writings. Against his earlier claim of "very little development in his thinking," Harpham eventually concludes that Žižek, perhaps with *The Fragile Absolute* (2000), begins to stress a notion of the ethical act, an emphasis derived from Lacan, especially his analysis of Antigone in *The Four Fundamental Concepts of Psychoanalysis*.

7. As subsequent discussion shows, the later Žižek does not abandon either the word *paradox* (and its variations) or the phenomenon itself. The density of usages may drop a bit: my unscientific survey shows, for example, just sixteen usages in the first 60 pages of *The Ticklish Subject* (1999), thirty-three in the 160 pages of *On Belief* (2001), and forty-six in the 170 pages of *The Puppet and the Dwarf* (2003). But rhetorical dominance, not simple usage, of course, is the issue. Qualitatively, in the rhetoric, enigma and mystery dominate Žižek's thought after 1998.

8. Noting Žižek's recent interest in Christianity, Adrian Johnston seems on the verge of regarding it as a sign of a new phase in the career. Moriarty offers an excellent account of Žižek's linkage of metaphors from Christian theology to Žižek's "categories for the understanding of ideology" (137). Harpham connects Christianity in Žižek to his growing awareness, established in *Contingency, Hegemony, Universality*, of his own universalism. Santner is interested in Žižek's frequent treatment of antisemitism and the turn, seen as early as *Tarrying with the Negative*, that Christianity brings to that treatment: "Žižek's invocation of the Christian Sublime," Santner says, "suggests that the 'secret treasure' of the Jews does not yet represent the final secret of ethical feeling and imagination. It is only with what he calls the 'downward-synthesis' of the Christian incarnation, the grounding of dialectics in an abject 'piece of the real,' that this last and final secret is attained" (204). The secret is that whereas Jehovah is a God of beyond, separated from us by a gap we cannot cross, Christianity's God "is this gap itself" (*Tarrying* 51). Žižek's interest in theology—if not Christianity as such—is further expressed in two essays appearing in 2005: "Neighbors and Other Monsters: A Plea for Ethical Violence" (appearing in a book titled *The Neighbor: Three Inquiries in Political Theology*) and "The 'Thrilling Romance of Orthodoxy'" (appearing in *Theology and the Political: The New Debate*).

9. In some ways, the most obvious sign of an ideological shift in Žižek is that moment in *The Ticklish Subject* when he takes up the Lacanian notion of a third father. For an analysis of those three Lacanian fathers, see Jagodzinski's "Recuperating the Flaccid Phallus."

10. A typical complaint among Žižek's critics is that he relies on the wrong authorities. Attacking Žižek's Lacanian unconscious, Layton argues he would do better to rely on relational theories, for in her view they provide better social critique since they rely more on contingency than on universality. Questioning the general acceptance of art and literature as symptoms of culture, Dean argues that Žižek conflates issues of politics and ethics in cultural study and fails vis à vis Althusser. Devolving, ultimately, to linguistic issues, Harpham, troubled by Žižek's reliance on Saussure through Lacan, argues that by seeming to deny the possibility of a knowledge outside the symbolic order, Žižek fails vis à vis Chomsky. (Incidentally, Berger connects him to the matter of "the linguistic turn" of modernism and postmodernism, suggesting in passing that Žižek's valorization of the Real actually belongs to a counterlinguistic turn indicative of a pervasive desire to escape or transcend language.) But in

arguing that Žižek ought to take authorities other than Marx or Hegel or Lacan, they may as well suggest he be someone else. As Dean would like him to be Althusser, and Harpham, Chomsky, there are Benjamin (for Chisholm), Derrida (Daly), Klein (Layton), Trilling (Holbo), Saul Alinsky (Krips), Kristeva (Restuccia's "Impossible"), Kristeva and Judith Butler (Nonnekes), Butler (Butler), Laclau (Laclau). For better or worse, Žižek is, simply, Žižek.

11. In *The Parallax View* (2006), Žižek's most recent major book (so far as I am aware), the 'core' of which Deary speaks becomes for Žižek the "gap"—the parallax gap—between the two perspectives found in the paradox of the parallax view. In this book, advertised as addressing the conceptual framework structuring his work, Žižek examines three modes of parallax, those found in politics, ontology, and in the epistemology of modern science. Described by Žižek in a publisher's blurb as his magnum opus (thus displacing 1999's *The Ticklish Subject),* the book may well initiate a turn to a third phase of his thought beyond that initiated by *Ticklish.* But if so, this phase does not yet appear to generate a philosophy of parallax beyond that of paradox. Rather, if anything, it suggests that paradox and parallax belong to the same conceptual domain. Indeed, they seem aspects of the same phenomenon, for Žižek's examination of modes of parallax exposits through those three modalities the theoretical "space" opening up within paradox itself. I think, therefore, that the book represents a shift in focus but not a radical shift in the mode of thought and rhetoric marking Žižek's philosophy to date. So . . . paradox or parallax? Yes, please.

Works Cited

Adams, Parveen. "Of Female Bondage." *Between Feminism and Psychoanalysis*. New York: Routledge, 1989. 247–65.

———. "Representation and Sexuality." *The Woman in Question*. Ed. Parveen Adams and Elizabeth Cowie. London: Verso, 1990. 233–52.

Alkalay-Gut, Karen. "Jury of Her Peers: The Importance of Trifles." *Studies in Short Fiction* 21 (1984): 1–9.

———. "Murder and Marriage: Another Look at *Trifles*." Ben-Zvi, *Susan Glaspell* 71–81.

Asals, Frederick. "The Double in Flannery O'Connor's Stories." *Flannery O'Connor Bulletin* 9 (1980): 49–86.

Barthes, Roland. "The Death of the Author." *Image, Music, Text* 142–48.

———. "From Work to Text." *Image, Music, Text* 155–64.

———. *Image, Music, Text*. Trans. Stephen Heath. New York: Hill and Wang, 1977.

———. "Theory of the Text." Trans. Ian McLeod. *Untying the Text: A Post-Structuralist Reader*. Ed. Robert Young. Boston: Routledge and Kegan Paul, 1981. 31–47.

Bellemin-Noel, Jean. *Vers l'inconscient du texte*. Paris: Presses Universitaires de France, 1979.

Ben-Zvi, Linda. "*Murder*, She Wrote: The Genesis of Susan Glaspell's *Trifles*." *Susan Glaspell* 19–48.

———, ed. *Susan Glaspell: Essays on Her Theater and Fiction*. Ann Arbor: U of Michigan P, 1995.

Berger, James. "Falling Towers and Postmodern Wild Children: Oliver Sacks, Don DeLillo, and Turns against Language." *PMLA* 120 (2005): 341–61.

Bloom, Alexander. *Prodigal Sons: The New York Intellectuals and Their World.* New York: Oxford UP, 1986.

Bone, Robert. "Ralph Ellison and the Uses of the Imagination." *Tri-Quarterly* 6 (1966): 39–54.

Bordwell, David. *Making Meaning: Inference and Rhetoric in the Interpretation of Cinema.* Cambridge: Harvard UP, 1989.

Boynton, Robert S. "Enjoy Your Žižek." 1998. *Quick Studies: The Best of Lingua Franca.* Ed. Alexander Star. New York: Farrar, Straus, and Giroux, 2002. 55–70.

Braunstein, Néstor A. "Deciphering Jouissance." Trans. Françoise Massardier-Kenney et al. *Studies in Psychoanalytic Theory* 4.2 (1995): 69–95.

———. "Desire and Jouissance in the Teachings of Lacan." Rabaté 10–15.

Breger, Claudia. "The Leader's Two Bodies: Slavoj Žižek's Postmodern Political Theology." *Diacritics* 31.1 (2001): 73–90.

———. "The Rhetorics of Power: Response to Slavoj Žižek." *Diacritics* 31.1 (2001): 105–08.

Bruccoli, Matthew J. "Headnote." Fitzgerald, *The Short Stories of F. Scott Fitzgerald* 217.

Bryan, Patricia L., and Thomas Wolf. *Midnight Assassin: A Murder in America's Heartland.* Chapel Hill: Algonquin, 2005.

Burhans, Clinton S., Jr. "'Magnificently Attune to Life': The Value of 'Winter Dreams.'" *Studies in Short Fiction* 6 (1969): 401–12.

Burke, Virginia M. "The Veil and the Vision." *Black American Literature Forum* 11.3 (1977): 91–94.

Butler, Judith. *Bodies That Matter: On the Discursive Limits of "Sex."* New York: Routledge, 1993.

———. *Gender Trouble: Feminism and the Subversion of Identity.* New York: Routledge, 1990.

Butler, Judith, Ernesto Laclau, and Slavoj Žižek. *Contingency, Hegemony, Universality: Contemporary Dialogues on the Left.* New York: Verso, 2000.

Butler, Rex. *Slavoj Žižek: Live Theory.* New York: Continuum, 2005.

Callahan, John F. "Chaos, Complexity and Possibility: The Historical Frequencies of Ralph Waldo Ellison." *Black American Literature Forum* 11.4 (1977): 130–38.

Chisholm, Dianne. "Žižek's Exemplary Culture." *JPCS: Journal for the Psychoanalysis of Culture and Society* 6.2 (2001): 242–52.

Copjec, Joan. *Read My Desire: Lacan against the Historicists.* Cambridge: Massachusetts Institute of Technology P, 1994.

Cowie, Elizabeth. "Film Noir and Women." *Shades of Noir: A Reader.* Ed. Joan Copjec. London: Verso, 1993. 121–65.

Crews, Frederick. "The Critics Bear It Away." *The Critics Bear It Away: American Fiction and the Academy.* New York: Random House, 1992. 143-67.

Culler, Jonathan. "Textual Self-Consciousness and the Textual Unconscious." *Style* 18 (1984): 369–76.

Daly, Glyn. "Ideology and Its Paradoxes: Dimensions of Fantasy and Enjoyment." *Journal of Political Ideologies* 4 (1999): 219–38.

———. "Politics and the Impossible: Beyond Psychoanalysis and Deconstruction." *Theory, Culture, and Society* 16.4 (1999): 75–98.

Davis, Robert Con. "Poe, Lacan, and Narrative Repression." *Lacan and Narration: The Psychoanalytic Difference in Narrative Theory.* Ed. Davis. Baltimore: Johns Hopkins UP, 1983. 983-1005.

Dean, Tim. "Art as Symptom: Žižek and the Ethics of Psychoanalytic Criticism." *Diacritics* 32.2 (2002): 21–41.

Deary, Vincent. "News from Elsewhere." *London Times Literary Supplement.* July 16, 2004: 25.

Derrida, Jacques. *Of Grammatology.* 1967. Trans. Gayatri Chakravorty Spivak. Baltimore: Johns Hopkins UP, 1976.

———. *The Post Card: From Socrates to Freud and Beyond.* 1980. Trans. Alan Bass. Chicago: U of Chicago P, 1993.

———. "The Purveyor of Truth." Trans. W. Domingo et al. *Yale French Studies* 52 (1975): 31–113.

Downing, Crystal. "Unheimliche Heights: The (En)Gendering of Brontë Sources." *Texas Studies in Literature and Language* 40 (1998): 347–69.

DuBois, W. E. B. *Souls of Black Folk.* 1903. New York: Fawcett, 1961.

Ducrot, Oswald, and Tzvetan Todorov. *Encyclopedic Dictionary of the Sciences of Language.* 1972. Trans. Catherine Porter. Baltimore: Johns Hopkins UP, 1979.

Eagleton, Terry. "Enjoy!" *Paragraph* 24 (2001): 40–52.

Ellison, Ralph. *Going to the Territory.* New York: Random House, 1986.

———. *Invisible Man*. 1952. New York: Vintage International, 1995.

———. "Ralph Ellison." *Interviews with Black Writers*. Ed. John O'Brien. New York: Liveright, 1973. 63–77.

———. *Shadow and Act*. 1964. New York: New American Library, 1966.

———. "Society, Morality, and the Novel." *The Living Novel*. Ed. Granville Hicks. New York: Macmillan, 1957.

———. "The Uses of History in Fiction." *Southern Literary Journal* 1.2 (1969): 57–90.

Evans, Dylan. "Borromean Knots." *Introductory Dictionary* 18–20.

———. *An Introductory Dictionary of Lacanian Psychoanalysis*. New York: Routledge, 1996.

Fetterley, Judith. "Reading about Reading: 'A Jury of Her Peers,' 'The Murders in the Rue Morgue,' and 'The Yellow Wallpaper.'" *Gender and Reading: Essays on Readers, Texts, and Contexts*. Ed. Elizabeth A. Flynn and Patrocinio P. Schweickart. Baltimore: Johns Hopkins UP, 1986. 147–64.

Finholt, Richard. "Ellison's Chattering Monkey Blues." *American Visionary Fiction: Mad Metaphysics and Salvation Psychology*. Port Washington: Kennikat, 1978. 98–111.

Fink, Bruce. *A Clinical Introduction to Lacanian Psychoanalysis: Theory and Technique*. Cambridge: Harvard UP, 1997.

———. *The Lacanian Subject: Between Language and Jouissance*. Princeton: Princeton UP, 1995.

Fischer, Russell G. "*Invisible Man* as History." *CLA Journal* 20 (1974): 338–67.

Fitzgerald, F. Scott. *The Short Stories of F. Scott Fitzgerald*. Ed. Matthew J. Bruccoli. New York. Scribner's, 1989.

———. "Winter Dreams." *The Short Stories of F. Scott Fitzgerald* 217–36.

Flieger, Jerry Aline. "Has Oedipus Signed Off (or Struck Out)? Žižek, Lacan and the Field of Cyberspace." *Paragraph* 53–77.

———. "Trial and Error: The Case of the Textual Unconscious." *Diacritics* 11 (1981): 56–67.

Foley, Barbara. "From *U.S.A.* to *Ragtime*: Notes on the Forms of Historical Consciousness in Modern Fiction." *American Literature* 50 (1978): 85–105.

———. "History, Fiction, and the Ground Between: The Uses of the Documentary Mode in Black Literature." *PMLA* 95 (1980): 389–403.

Freud, Sigmund. *The Standard Edition of the Complete Psychological Works of Sigmund Freud.* 24 vols. Trans. James Strachey. London: Hogarth, 1954–1972.

Friedman, Susan Stanford. "Weavings: Intertextuality and the (Re)Birth of the Author." *Influence and Intertextuality in Literary History.* Ed. Jay Clayton and Eric Rothstein. Madison: U of Wisconsin P, 1991. 146–80.

Gigante, Denise. "Toward a Notion of Critical Self-Creation: Slavoj Žižek and the 'Vortex of Madness.'" *New Literary History* 29 (1998): 153–68.

Gilbert, Susan M., and Susan Gubar. *The Madwoman in the Attic: The Woman Writer and the Nineteenth-Century Literary Imagination.* New Haven: Yale UP, 1979.

Gilligan, Carol. *In a Different Voice: Psychological Theory and Women's Development.* Cambridge: Harvard UP, 1982.

Glaspell, Susan. "A Jury of Her Peers." *Lifted Masks and Other Works: Susan Glaspell.* Ed. Eric S. Rabkin. Ann Arbor: U of Michigan P, 1993. 279–306.

Glynos, Jason. "'There Is No Other of the Other': Symptoms of a Decline in Symbolic Faith, or, Žižek's Anti-Capitalism." *Paragraph* 78–110.

Golan, Ruth, et al., eds. *Almanac of Psychoanalysis.* Tel Aviv: Groupe Israelienne de l'Ecole Europeene, 1998.

Grigg, Russell. "Absolute Freedom and Major Structural Change." *Paragraph* 111–24.

Grosz, Elizabeth. *Jacques Lacan: A Feminist Introduction.* New York: Routledge, 1990.

———. "Kristeva, Julia." *Feminism and Psychoanalysis: A Critical Dictionary.* Ed. Elizabeth Wright. Cambridge: Blackwell, 1992. 194-200.

Guerra, Gustavo. "Thinking Aslant: Žižek and Pragmatism." *JPCS: Journal for the Psychoanalysis of Culture and Society* 6.1 (2001): 21–28.

Hallgren, Sherri. "'The Law Is the Law—and a Bad Stove Is a Bad Stove': Subversive Justice and Layers of Collusion in 'A Jury of Her Peers.'" *Violence, Silence, and Anger: Women's Writing as Transgression.* Ed. Deidre Lashgari. Charlottesville: UP of Virginia, 1995. 203–18.

Harari, Roberto. *How James Joyce Made His Name: A Reading of the Final Lacan.* Trans. Luke Thurston. New York: Other P, 2002.

———. "The *Sinthome*: Turbulence and Dissipation." Thurston, *Re-Inventing the Symptom* 45–57.

Harpham, Geoffrey Galt. "Doing the Impossible: Slavoj Žižek and the End of Knowledge." *Critical Inquiry* 29 (2003): 453–85.

Hart, Josephine. *Damage*. 1991. London: Vintage, 1996.

Hedges, Elaine. "Small Things Reconsidered: Susan Glaspell's 'A Jury of Her Peers.'" *Women's Studies* 12.1 (1986): 89–110.

Henderson, Harry E., *Versions of the Past: The Historical Imagination in American Fiction*. New York: Oxford UP, 1974.

Hertz, Neil. *The End of the Line: Essays on Psychoanalysis and the Sublime*. New York: Columbia UP, 1985.

Hoens, Dominiek, and Ed Pluth. "The *Sinthome*: A New Way of Writing an Old Problem?" Thurston, *Re-Inventing the Symptom* 1–18.

Holbo, John. "On Žižek and Trilling." *Philosophy and Literature* 28 (2004): 430–40.

Hull, Gloria T. "Notes on a Marxist Interpretation of Black American Literature." *Black American Literature Forum* 12.4 (1978): 148–53.

Jagodzinski, Jan. "Recuperating the Flaccid Phallus: The Hysteria of Post-Oedipal Masculine Representation and the Return of the Anal Father." *JPCS: Journal for the Psychoanalysis of Culture and Society* 6.1 (2001): 29–39.

Jakobson, Roman. "Two Aspects of Language and Two Types of Aphasia." Roman Jakobson and Morris Halle. *Fundamentals of Language*. The Hague: Mouton, 1956. 53–82.

Jameson, Fredric. "The Ideology of the Text." *The Ideologies of Theory, Essays 1971–1986*. Vol. 1. Minneapolis: U of Minnesota P, 1988. 17–71.

———. *The Political Unconscious: Narrative as a Socially Symbolic Act*. Ithaca: Cornell UP, 1981.

———. *Postmodernism, or, The Cultural Logic of Late Capitalism*. Durham: Duke UP, 1991.

———. "The Vanishing Mediator; or Max Weber as Storyteller." *The Ideologies of Theory, Essays 1971–1986*. Vol. 2. Minneapolis: U of Minnesota P, 1988. 3–34.

Johnston, Adrian. "The Cynic's Fetish: Slavoj Žižek and the Dynamics of Belief." *JPCS: Journal for the Psychoanalysis of Culture and Society* 9.3 (2004): 259–83.

Josipovici, Gabriel. *The World and the Book: A Study of Modern Fiction*. London: Macmillan, 1971.

Jung, Carl G. *The Portable Jung*. Ed. with an introduction by Joseph Campbell; trans. R. F. C. Hull. New York: Viking, 1971.

Kay, Sarah. *Žižek: A Critical Introduction.* Cambridge: Polity, 2003.

Kehl, D. G. "Flannery O'Connor's 'Fourth Dimension': The Role of Sexuality in Her Fiction." *Mississippi Quarterly* 48 (1995): 255–76.

Kinney, Arthur F. *Flannery O'Connor's Library: Resources of Being.* Athens: U of Georgia P, 1985.

Klug, M. A. "Flannery O'Connor and the Manichean Spirit of Modernism." *Southern Humanities Review* 17 (1983): 303–14.

Kostelanetz, Richard. "The Politics of Ellison's Booker: *Invisible Man* as Symbolic History." *Chicago Review* 19.2 (1967): 5–26.

Krauss, Rosalind E. *The Optical Unconscious.* Cambridge: Massachusetts Institute of Technology P, 1993.

Kreyling, Michael. "Introduction." *New Essays on* Wise Blood. Ed. Kreyling. New York: Cambridge UP, 1995. 1–24.

Krips, Henry. "Couching Politics: Žižek's Rules for Radicals." *JPCS: Journal for the Psychoanalysis of Culture and Society* 9.1 (2004): 126–41.

Kristeva, Julia. "L'Abjet de l'amour." *Tel Quel* 91 (1982): 17–32.

_____. "Approaching Abjection." *Powers of Horror* 1–31.

_____. "The Bounded Text." 1969. *Desire in Language* 36–63.

_____. *Desire in Language: A Semiotic Approach to Literature and Art.* Ed. Leon S. Roudiez. Trans. Thomas Gora et al. New York: Columbia UP, 1980.

_____. *Powers of Horror: An Essay on Abjection.* 1980. Trans. Leon Roudiez. New York: Columbia UP, 1982.

_____. *Revolution in Poetic Language.* Trans. Margaret Waller. New York: Columbia UP, 1984.

Kuehl, John. *F. Scott Fitzgerald: A Study of the Short Fiction.* Boston: Twayne, 1991.

Lacan, Jacques. "The Agency of the Letter in the Unconscious or Reason since Freud." *Écrits: A Selection,* 146–75.

_____. "Desire and the Interpretation of Desire in *Hamlet*." Trans. James Hulbert. *Yale French Studies* 55–56 (1977): 11–52.

_____. *Écrits.* Paris: Seuil, 1966.

_____. *Écrits: A Selection.* Trans. Alan Sheridan. New York: Norton, 1977.

_____. *Encore. On Feminine Sexuality: The Limits of Love and Knowledge. Book XX 1972–1973.* The Seminar of Jacques Lacan. Ed. Jacques-Alain Miller. Trans. Bruce Fink. New York: Norton, 1998.

_____. *The Ethics of Psychoanalysis. Book VII 1959–1960.* The Seminar of Jacques Lacan. Ed. Jacques-Alain Miller. Trans. Dennis Porter. New York: Norton, 1992.

_____. *Feminine Sexuality: Jacques Lacan and the* École Freudienne. Ed. Juliet Mitchell and Jacqueline Rose. Trans. Rose. New York: Norton, 1983.

_____. *The Four Fundamental Concepts of Psychoanalysis. Book XI 1964.* The Seminar of Jacques Lacan. Ed. Jacques-Alain Miller. Trans. Alan Sheridan. New York: Norton, 1978.

_____. *Freud's Papers on Technique. Book I 1953–1954.* The Seminar of Jacques Lacan. Ed. Jacques-Alain Miller. Trans. John Forrester. New York: Norton, 1988.

_____. "Kant *avec* Sade." *Écrits* 765–90.

_____. "A Lacanian Psychosis: Interview by Jacques Lacan." Ed. Jacques-Alain Miller. Ed. and trans. Schneiderman, *Returning to Freud* 19–41.

_____. "The Neurotic's Individual Myth." Trans. Martha Noel Evans. *Psychoanalytic Quarterly* 48 (1979): 405–25.

_____. "Preface by Jacques Lacan." Lemaire, *Jacques Lacan* vii–xv.

_____. *The Psychoses. Book III 1955–1956.* The Seminar of Jacques Lacan. Ed. Jacques-Alain Miller. Trans. Russell Grigg. New York: Norton, 1994.

_____. *Le séminaire, livre IV: La relation d'objet, 1956–1957.* Ed. Jacques-Alain Miller. Paris: Editions du Seuil, 1994.

_____. *Le séminaire, livre VIII: Le transfert, 1960–61.* Ed. Jacques-Alain Miller. Paris: Seuil, 1991.

_____. "The Seminar on 'The Purloined Letter.'" Trans. Jeffrey Mehlman. *Yale French Studies* 48 (1972): 39–72.

_____. "The Signification of the Phallus." *Écrits: A Selection* 281–91.

Lanser, Susan. "Toward a Feminist Narratology." *Feminisms: An Anthology of Feminist Literary Criticism.* Ed. Robyn R. Warhol and Diane Price Herndl. New Brunswick: Rutgers UP, 1991. 610–29.

Layton, Lynne. "A Fork in the Royal Road: On 'Defining' the Unconscious and Its Stakes for Social Theory." *JPCS: Journal for the Psychoanalysis of Culture and Society* 9.1 (2004): 33–51.

Lechte, John. *Fifty Key Contemporary Thinkers: From Structuralism to Postmodernity*. New York: Routledge, 1994.

LeClair, Thomas. "Flannery's O'Connor's *Wise Blood*: The Oedipal Theme." *Mississippi Quarterly* 29 (1976): 197–205.

Lemaire, Anika. *Jacques Lacan*. 1970. Trans. David Macey. Boston: Routledge and Kegan Paul, 1977.

Lynch, William F. "Theology and the Imagination." *Thought* 29 [112] (1954): 61–86.

MacCannell, Juliet Flower. *The Regime of the Brother: After the Patriarchy*. New York: Routledge, 1991.

———. "The Unconscious." Wright, Elizabeth, *Feminism and Psychoanalysis* 440–44.

Macey, David. "The Final State." *Lacan in Contexts*. New York: Verso, 1988: 1–25.

Mael, Phyllis. "*Trifles*: The Path to Sisterhood." *Literature/Film Quarterly* 17.4 (1989): 281–84.

Makowsky, Veronica. *Susan Glaspell's Century of American Women: A Critical Interpretation of Her Work*. New York: Oxford UP, 1993.

Malle, Louis, dir. *Damage*. New Line, 1993.

Marcus, Steven. 1984. *Freud and the Culture of Psychoanalysis: Studies in the Transition from Victorian Humanism to Modernity*. New York: Norton, 1987.

Margolies, Edward. "History as Blues: Ralph Ellison's *Invisible Man*." *Native Sons: A Critical Study of Twentieth-Century Negro American Authors*. Philadelphia: Lippincott, 1968. 127–48.

Mazlish, Bruce. *The Riddle of History*. New York: Harper and Row, 1966.

McCullagh, James C. "Symbolism and the Religious Aesthetic: Flannery O'Connor's *Wise Blood*." *Flannery O'Connor Bulletin* 2 (1973): 43–58.

McGann, Jerome. *Radiant Textuality: Literature after the World Wide Web*. New York: Palgrave, 2002.

McLaren, Peter. *Slavoj Žižek's Naked Politics*. Lanham: Rowman and Littlefield, 2003.

———. "Slavoj Žižek's Naked Politics: Opting for the Impossible, a Secondary Elaboration." *JAC: A Journal of Composition Theory* 21.3 (2001): 613–47.

Mead, Rebecca. "The Marx Brother." *The New Yorker* 5 May 2003: 38–47.

Mellard, James M. "Consciousness Fills the Void: Herzog, History, and the Hero in the Modern World." *Modern Fiction Studies* 25 (1979): 75–91.

———. "The Disappearing Subject: A Lacanian Reading of *The Catcher in the Rye*." *Essays on J. D. Salinger*. Ed. Joel Salzberg. Boston: Hall, 1989. 197–214.

———. Forum. Reply. *PMLA* 114 (1999): 104–05.

———. "Framed in the Gaze: Haze, *Wise Blood*, and Lacanian Reading." *New Essays on* Wise Blood. Ed. Michael Kreyling. New York: Cambridge UP, 1995. 51–69.

———. "Inventing Lacanian Psychoanalysis: Linguistics and Tropology in 'The Agency of the Letter.'" *Poetics Today* 19 (1998): 499–530.

———. "Lacan and the New Lacanians: Josephine Hart's *Damage*, Lacanian Tragedy, and the Ethics of *Jouissance*." *PMLA* 113 (1998): 395–407.

———. The Novel as Lyric Elegy: The Mode of Updike's *The Centaur*." *Texas Studies in Literature and Language* 21 (1979): 112–27.

———. "The *Other* Desire: Good, Beauty, Death, and the Thing in Lacan's *Antigone*." *Clinical Studies* 3.1 (1997): 11–30.

———. "The Problem of Knowledge and *The Education of Henry Adams*." *South Central Review* 3.2 (1986): 55–68.

———. "This *Unquiet* Dust: The Problem of History in Styron's *The Confessions of Nat Turner*." *Mississippi Quarterly* 36 (1983): 525–43.

———. "Triangulating the Freudian Field: Freud, Lacan, and Contemporary American Fiction." *Germany and German Thought in American Literature and Cultural Criticism*. Ed. Peter Freese. Essen: Verlag Die Blaue Eule, 1990. 369–88.

Michelman, Stephen. "Sociology before Linguistics: Lacan's Debt to Durkheim." *Disseminating Lacan*. Ed. David Pettigrew and François Raffoul. Albany: State U of New York P, 1996. 123–50.

Miklitsch, Robert. "'Going through the Fantasy': Screening Slavoj Žižek." *South Atlantic Quarterly* 97 (1998): 477–507.

———. "Passing on Popular Culture: 'Art for Lacan's Sake.'" *JAC: A Journal of Composition Theory* 21 (2001): 605–13.

Miller, Jacques-Alain. "To Interpret the Cause: From Freud to Lacan." *Newsletter of the Freudian Field* 3.1–2 (1989): 30–50.

———. "An Introduction to Seminars I and II: Lacan's Orientation prior to 1953 (I)." *Reading Seminars I and II: Lacan's Return to Freud.*

Ed. Richard Feldstein et al. Albany: State U of New York P: 1996. 3–14.

———. "Introductory Talk at Sainte-Anne Hospital." *Reading Seminar XI: Lacan's Four Fundamental Concepts of Psychoanalysis.* The Paris Seminars in English. Ed. Richard Feldstein, Bruce Fink, and Maire Jaanus. Albany: State U of New York P, 1995. 233–41.

———. "Lacan's Later Teaching." Trans. Barbara P. Fulks. *Lacanian Ink* 21 (2003): 4–41.

———. "Teachings of the Case Presentation." Ed. and trans. Schneiderman, *Returning to Freud* 42–52.

———, and Eric Laurent. "The Other Who Does Not Exist and His Ethical Committees." Trans. Michele Julien et al. Golan et al 15–35.

Miller, James E., Jr. *F. Scott Fitzgerald: His Art and His Technique.* New York: New York UP, 1967.

Mizener, Arthur. *The Far Side of Paradise: A Biography of F. Scott Fitzgerald.* 2nd ed. Boston: Houghton Mifflin, 1965.

Møller, Lis. *The Freudian Reading: Analytical and Fictional Constructions.* Philadelphia: U of Pennsylvania P, 1991.

Moriarty, Michael. "Žižek, Religion, and Ideology." *Paragraph* 125–37.

Morrison, Toni. *Beloved.* New York: Knopf, 1987.

Moses, Wilson J. "*Invisible Man* and the American Way of Intellectual History." Parr and Savery 58–64.

Mowitt, John. *Text: The Genealogy of an Antidisciplinary Object.* Durham: Duke UP, 1992.

Mustazza, Leonard. "Gender and Justice in Susan Glaspell's 'A Jury of Her Peers.'" *Law and Semiotics.* Vol. 2. Ed. Roberta Kevelson. New York: Plenum, 1988. 271–76.

———. "Generic Translation and Thematic Shift in Susan Glaspell's 'Trifles' and 'A Jury of Her Peers.'" *Studies in Short Fiction* 26 (1989): 489–96.

Myers, Tony. *Slavoj Žižek.* New York: Routledge, 2003.

Nealon, Jeffrey T. "The Cash Value of Paradox: Žižek's Rhetoric." *JAC: A Journal of Composition Theory* 21 (2001): 599–605.

Neighbors, Jim. "Plunging (Outside of) History: Naming and Self-Possession in *Invisible Man.*" *African American Review* 36 (2002): 227–42.

Nicol, Bran. "As If: Traversing the Fantasy in Žižek." *Paragraph* 140–55.

Nobus, Dany. "Illiterature." Thurston, *Re-Inventing the Symptom* 45–58.

Nonnekes, Paul. "Love and Christianity: A Critique of Žižek." *JPCS: Journal for the Psychoanalysis of Culture and Society* 6.2 (2001): 253–61.

O'Connor, Flannery. *The Habit of Being: The Letters of Flannery O'Connor.* Ed. Sally Fitzgerald. New York: Farrar, Straus, and Giroux, 1979.

———. *The Violent Bear It Away.* New York: Farrar, Straus, and Giroux, 1960.

———. *Wise Blood.* 1952. 2nd. ed. New York: Farrar, Straus, and Giroux, 1962.

Olson, Gary A., and Lynn Worsham. "Slavoj Žižek: Philosopher, Cultural Critic, and Cyber-Communist." Interview. *JAC: A Journal of Composition Theory* 21 (2001): 251–86.

Paragraph. Special Issue. "A Symposium on Slavoj Žižek: Faith and the Real." Ed. Elizabeth Wright and Edmond Wright. 24.2 (2001).

Parr, Susan Resneck, and Pancho Savery, ed. *Approaches to Teaching Ellison's Invisible Man.* New York: Modern Language Association, 1989.

Petry, Alice Hall. *Fitzgerald's Craft of Short Fiction: The Collected Stories 1920–1935.* Ann Arbor: UMI Research P, 1989.

Pickering, James H., ed. *Fiction 100: An Anthology of Short Stories.* 9th ed. Englewood Cliffs: Prentice-Hall, 2000.

Piper, Henry Dan. *F. Scott Fitzgerald: A Critical Portrait.* New York: Holt Rinehart Winston, 1965.

Rabaté, Jean-Michel, ed. *The Cambridge Companion to Lacan.* Cambridge: Cambridge UP, 2003.

Rasmussen, Eric Dean. "The Last Hegelian: An Interview with Slavoj Žižek." *Minnesota Review* 61–62 (2004): 79–93.

Reilly, John M. "Discovering an Art of the Self in History: A Principle of Afro-American Life." Parr and Savery 37–42.

———. "The Reconstruction of Genre as Entry into Conscious History." *Black American Literature Forum* 13.1 (1979): 3–6.

Restuccia, Frances L. Forum. Letter. *PMLA* 114 (1999): 103–04.

———. "Impossible Love in *Breaking the Waves*: Mystifying Hysteria." *Literature and Psychology* 47 (2001): 34–53.

Rickard, John S. *Joyce's Book of Memory: The Mnemotechnics of* Ulysses. Durham: Duke UP, 1999.

Rickert, Thomas. "Enjoying Theory: Žižek, Critique, Accountability." *JAC: A Journal of Composition Theory* 22 (2002): 627–40.

Ricoeur, Paul. *Freud and Philosophy: An Essay on Interpretation.* Trans. Denis Savage. New Haven: Yale UP, 1970.

Riffaterre, Michael. "The Intertextual Unconscious." 1987. *The Trial(s) of Psychoanalysis.* Ed. Françoise Meltzer. Chicago: U of Chicago P, 1988. 211–25.

Rorty, Richard. "Nineteenth-Century Idealism and Twentieth-Century Textualism." *The Consequences of Pragmatism.* Minneapolis: U of Minnesota P, 1982: 139–59.

Rose, Jacqueline. "Introduction—II." Lacan, *Feminine Sexuality* 27–57.

———. "Julia Kristeva—Take Two." *Sexuality in the Field of Vision.* London: Verso, 1986. 141–64.

Roudinesco, Elisabeth. *Jacques Lacan.* Trans. Barbara Bray. New York: Columbia UP, 1997.

Said, Edward. *The World, The Text, and the Critic.* Cambridge: Harvard UP, 1983.

Salecl, Renata. "Interview: Renata Salecl and Slavoj Žižek: Interviewed by Andrew Long and Tara McGann." *Journal for the Psychoanalysis of Culture and Society* 2.2 (1997): 147–51.

Samuels, Robert. "Slavoj Žižek's Rhetorical Matrix: The Symptomatic Enjoyment of Postmodern Academic Writing." *JAC: A Journal of Composition Theory* 22 (2002): 327–54.

Santner, Eric. "Freud, Žižek, and the Joys of Monotheism." *American Imago* 54.2 (1997): 197–207.

Satterfield, Ben. "*Wise Blood*, Artistic Anemia, and the Hemorrhaging of O'Connor Criticism." *Studies in American Fiction* 17 (1989): 33–50.

Schneiderman, Stuart. *Returning to Freud: Clinical Psychoanalysis in the School of Lacan.* New Haven: Yale UP, 1980.

Sheridan, Alan. "Translator's Note." Lacan, *Écrits: A Selection* vii–xii.

Sklar, Robert. *F. Scott Fitzgerald: The Last Laocoön.* New York: Oxford UP, 1967.

Smith, Beverly A. "Women's Work—*Trifles*? The Skill and Insights of Playwright Susan Glaspell." *International Journal of Women's Studies* 5.2 (1982): 172–84.

Smith, Valerie. "The Meaning of Narration in *Invisible Man*." *New Essays on* Invisible Man. Ed. Robert O'Meally. New York: Cambridge UP, 1988. 25–53.

Soler, Collette. "The Paradoxes of the Symptom in Psychoanalysis." Rabaté 86–101.

Spillers, Hortense. "Ellison's 'Usable Past': Toward a Theory of Myth." *Interpretations* 9 (1977): 53–69.

Steele, R. S. "A Critical Hermeneutics for Psychology: Beyond Positivism to an Exploration of Textual Unconscious." *Entering the Circle: Hermeneutic Investigation in Psychology.* Ed. M. J. Packer and R. B. Addison. Albany: State U of New York P, 1989. 223–37.

Sulloway, Frank J. *Freud: Biologist of the Mind.* New York: Basic, 1979.

Tate, Claudia. *Psychoanalysis and Black Novels: Desire and the Protocols of Race.* New York: Oxford UP, 1998.

Tate, J. O. "The Essential Essex." *Flannery O'Connor Bulletin* 12 (1983): 47–59.

Thurston, Luke, ed. *Re-Inventing the Symptom: Essays on the Final Lacan.* New York: Other P, 2002.

———. "*Sinthome.*" Evans, *Introductory Dictionary* 188–90.

Torok, Maria, and Nicolas Abraham. *The Wolf Man's Magic Word: A Cryptonomy.* Minneapolis: U of Minnesota P, 1986.

Trimmer, Joseph. "The Grandfather's Riddle in Ralph Ellison's *Invisible Man.*" *Black American Literature Forum* 12.2 (1978): 46–50.

Turner, Darwin T. "Black Fiction: History and Myth." *Studies in American Fiction* 5.1 (1977): 109–26.

White, Hayden V. *The Content of the Form: Narrative Discourse and Historical Representation.* Baltimore: Johns Hopkins UP, 1987.

———. *Figural Realism: Studies in the Mimesis Effect.* Baltimore: Johns Hopkins UP, 1999.

———. *Metahistory: The Historical Imagination in Nineteenth-Century Europe.* Baltimore: Johns Hopkins UP, 1973.

———. *Tropics of Discourse: Essays in Cultural Criticism.* Baltimore: Johns Hopkins UP, 1978.

Williams, Raymond. "Base and Superstructure in Marxist Cultural Theory." *Problems in Materialism and Culture.* London: Verso, 1980. 31–49.

Worthen, W. B. *Modern Drama and the Rhetoric of Theater.* Berkeley: U of California P, 1992.

Wright, Edmond. "Introduction: Faith and the Real." *Paragraph* 5–22.

Wright, Elizabeth, ed. *Feminism and Psychoanalysis: A Critical Dictionary.* Cambridge: Blackwell, 1992.

Žižek, Slavoj. *The Abyss of Freedom/Ages of the World.* Ann Arbor: U of Michigan P, 1997.

———. *Did Somebody Say Totalitarianism? Five Interventions in the (Mis)use of a Notion.* New York: Verso, 2001.

———. *Enjoy Your Symptom! Jacques Lacan in Hollywood and Out.* New York: Routledge, 1992.

———. *For They Know Not What They Do: Enjoyment as a Political Factor.* New York: Verso, 1991.

———. *The Fragile Absolute: Or, Why Is the Christian Legacy Worth Fighting For?* New York: Verso, 2000.

———. *Interrogating the Real.* Ed. Rex Butler and Scott Stephens. New York: Continuum, 2005.

———. "Interview: Renata Salecl and Slavoj Žižek: Interviewed by Andrew Long and Tara McGann." *Journal for the Psychoanalysis of Culture and Society* 2.2 (1997): 147–51.

———. *Iraq: The Borrowed Kettle.* New York: Verso, 2004.

———. "Is There a Cause of the Subject?" *Supposing the Subject.* Ed. Joan Copjec. New York: Verso, 1994. 84–105.

———. *Looking Awry: An Introduction to Jacques Lacan through Popular Culture.* Cambridge: Massachusetts Institute of Technology P, 1991.

———. *Metastases of Enjoyment: Six Essays on Woman and Causality.* New York: Verso, 1994.

———. "Neighbors and Other Monsters: A Plea for Ethical Violence." *The Neighbor: Three Inquiries in Political Theology.* Slavoj Žižek, Eric L. Santner, and Kenneth Reinhard. Chicago: U of Chicago P, 2005. 134–90.

———. *On Belief.* New York: Verso, 2001.

———. *Organs without Bodies: Deleuze and Consequences.* New York: Routledge, 2004.

———. *The Parallax View.* Cambridge: Massachusetts Institute of Technology P, 2006.

———. "Passing from 'False' to 'True' Universality: A Reply to Robert Samuels." *JAC: A Journal of Composition Theory* 22 (2002): 623–27.

———. "Preface: Burning the Bridges." *Žižek Reader* vii–x.

———. *The Puppet and the Dwarf: The Perverse Core of Christianity.* Cambridge: Massachusetts Institute of Technology P, 2003.

———. "The Real and Its Vicissitudes." *Looking Awry* 21–47.

———. "Re-visioning 'Lacanian' Social Criticism: The Law and Its Obscene Double." *Journal for the Psychoanalysis of Culture and Society* 1.1 (1996): 15–25.

———. "Response to Claudia Breger." *Diacritics* 31.1 (2001): 91–104.

———. "The Spectre of Ideology." *Mapping Ideology.* Ed. Slavoj Žižek. New York: Verso, 1994. 1–33.

———. *The Sublime Object of Ideology.* London: Verso, 1989.

———. "The Sublime Theorist of Slovenia: Peter Canning Interviews Slavoj Žižek." *Artforum* (March 1993): 84–89.

———. *Tarrying with the Negative: Kant, Hegel, and the Critique of Ideology.* Durham: Duke UP, 1993.

———. "There Is No Sexual Relationship." *Gaze and Voice as Love Objects.* Ed. Renata Salecl and Slavoj Žižek. Durham: Duke UP, 1996. 208–49.

———. "The 'Thrilling Romance of Orthodoxy.'" *Theology and the Political: The New Debate.* Ed. Creston Davis, John Milbank, and Slavoj Žižek. Durham: Duke UP, 2005. 52–71.

———. *The Ticklish Subject: The Absent Centre of Political Ontology.* New York: Verso, 1999.

———. "The Truth Arises from Misrecognition." *Lacan and the Subject of Language.* Ed. Ellie Ragland-Sullivan and Mark Bracher. New York: Routledge, 1991. 188–212.

———. *Welcome to the Desert of the Real! Five Essays on September 11 and Related Dates.* New York: Verso, 2002.

———. "Why Are There Always Two *Fathers*?" *Enjoy Your Symptom!* 149–93.

———. *The Žižek Reader.* Ed. Elizabeth Wright and Edmond Wright. Oxford: Blackwell, 1999.

———, and Glyn Daly. *Conversations with Žižek.* Cambridge: Polity, 2004.

Zupančič, Alenka. *Ethics of the Real: Kant, Lacan.* New York: Verso, 2000.

Index

www.ingramcontent.com/pod-product-compliance
Lightning Source LLC
Chambersburg PA
CBHW030643270326
41929CB00007B/186